SUBSTANCE ABUSE
SOURCEBOOK

Health Reference Series

Volume Fourteen

SUBSTANCE ABUSE SOURCEBOOK

Basic Health-Related Information about the Abuse of Legal and Illegal Substances such as Alcohol, Tobacco, Prescription Drugs, Marijuana, Cocaine, and Heroin; and Including Facts about Substance Abuse Prevention Strategies, Intervention Methods, Treatment and Recovery Programs, and a Section Addressing the Special Problems Related to Substance Abuse During Pregnancy

Edited by
Karen Bellenir

Omnigraphics, Inc.

Penobscot Building / Detroit, MI 48226

BIBLIOGRAPHIC NOTE

This volume contains numbered publications issued by the National Institutes of Health (NIH): 93-3057, 93-3507, 93-3521, 94-3478, 94-3818; the Substance Abuse and Mental Health Services Administration (SMA) 93-1998, 93-2011, 93-2045, 94-2060; and the Alcohol, Drug Abuse, and Mental Health Administration (ADM) 90-1657, 91-1572, 91-1806, 91-1810, 92-1557, 92-1912, 92-1916; unnumbered publications produced by the Drug and Crime Data Center and Clearinghouse, the U.S. Drug Enforcement Administration, the Office of National Drug Control Policy, the Center for Substance Abuse Prevention, the U.S. Department of Education, and the American Council for Drug Education, along with selected articles from the *FDA Consumer*, the U.S. Department of Education's *The Challenge*, the National Institute on Alcohol Abuse and Alcoholism's *Alcohol Alerts*, and the National Institute on Drug Abuse's *Capsules*. In addition, this volume contains excerpts from "The Definition of Alcoholism," © 1992 *Journal of the American Medical Association*, and "Drug Misuse Among the Elderly: A Covert Problem © 1989 *Health Values*. All copyrighted material is reprinted with permission. Document numbers where applicable and specific source citations are provided on the first page of each chapter.

Edited by Karen Bellenir

Peter D. Dresser, Managing Editor, *Health Reference Series*

Omnigraphics, Inc.

Matthew P. Barbour, *Production Manager*
Laurie Lanzen Harris, *Vice President, Editorial*
Peter E. Ruffner, *Vice President, Administration*
James A. Sellgren, *Vice President, Operations and Finance*
Jane J. Steele, *Vice President, Research*

Frederick G. Ruffner, Jr., *Publisher*

Copyright © 1996, Omnigraphics, Inc.

Library of Congress Cataloging-in-Publication Data

```
Substance abuse sourcebook : basic health-related information about
   the abuse of legal and illegal substances such as alcohol, tobacco,
   prescription drugs, marijuana, cocaine, and heroin ; and including
   facts about substance abuse prevention strategies, intervention
   methods, treatment and recovery programs, and a section addressing
   the special problems related to substance abuse during pregnancy /
   edited by Karen Bellenir.
       p.    cm. -- (Health reference series)
   Includes bibliographical references and index.
   ISBN 0-7808-0038-9 (library bdg. : alk. paper)
   1. Substance abuse.    I. Bellenir, Karen.    II. Series.
RC564.S8372   1996
616.86--dc20                                                  96-9511
                                                                 CIP
```

Printed in the United States

Contents

v

Part III: Other Licit and Illicit Substances of Abuse

Part IV: Special Problems Related to Substance Abuse During Pregnancy

Part V: Prevention

Part VI: Intervention, Treatment, and Recovery

Preface

About This Book

This book focuses on the health effects of substance abuse. The term *substance* covers a wide range of legally available and illicit drugs. The term *abuse* is used to describe the use of drugs—and the participation in drug-related activities—in a way that produces negative consequences. The impact specific drugs have on individual users varies considerably. As a result, the line between "use" and "abuse" is not always clearly drawn.

The documents selected for inclusion in this volume were chosen to aid the lay person in understanding how various substances of abuse affect the human body, how addictions develop, and how to help an afflicted person find his or her way to recovery. The individual substances discussed in detail were chosen to represent those most commonly abused in today's society.

How to Use this Book

This book is divided into parts and chapters. Parts focus on broad areas of interest. Chapters are devoted to single topics within a part.

Part I: General and Statistical Information about Substance Abuse provides background information. It describes how drugs affect the human brain as well as their impact on families. Historical and statistical data help place the nation's current struggle with drugs in context. To help readers identify specific substances, a chapter defining common street terms is also included.

Part II: Alcohol offers information about the most commonly used drug in the United States. Individual chapters address topics such as the definition of alcoholism, hereditary factors, how alcohol affects different populations, and the health consequences of alcohol abuse on the various organs of the human body.

Part III: Other Licit and Illicit Substances of Abuse gives information about other types of legally available drugs—including tobacco, inhalants, and prescription drugs—along with information about illicit substances such as marijuana, cocaine, heroin, lysergic acid diethylamide (LSD), and phencyclidine (PCP).

Part IV: Special Problems Related to Substance Abuse During Pregnancy addresses the effects of substance abuse on fetal development.

Part V: Prevention includes information on helping people, especially children, make the appropriate decisions to avoid the problem of substance abuse.

Part VI: Intervention, Treatment, and Recovery provides information for people whose lives have already been touched by substance abuse. Topics include how to get help, how to help someone close to you get help, various types of treatment and aftercare programs, and a list of mutual help groups.

Acknowledgements

The special contributions of two individuals—Margaret Mary Missar and Bruce the Scanman—cannot be overlooked. Margaret Mary dug through mountains of documents to find information for this book, and Bruce the Scanman provided technical assistance and day-to-day support. Their help is gratefully acknowledged.

Note from the Editor

This book is part of Omnigraphics' *Health Reference Series*. The series provides basic information about a broad range of medical concerns. It is not intended to serve as a tool for diagnosing illness, in prescribing treatments, or as a substitute for the physician/patient relationship. All persons concerned about medical symptoms or the possibility of disease are encouraged to seek professional care from an appropriate health care provider.

Part One

General and
Statistical Information about
Substance Abuse

Chapter 1

Drugs and the Brain

Introduction

We live in a world that sometimes seems saturated with drugs. If you have a headache, you take a pill. If you have a runny nose, you take another kind of pill. You cannot sleep too well? Well, there's a pill for that, too. Do you want to lose some weight, or simply relax? You can take pills for these things. Everywhere we turn, on the television and in the newspapers and magazines, we see advertisements that urge us to take some kind of drug for the myriad of problems, serious and superficial, which ail all of us.

So it should not be too surprising that in addition to using legal drugs, people turn to illegal drugs, or they abuse legal ones, to try to solve their problems. People may be bored or anxious, or feel hopeless, and they turn to drugs to escape. Alcohol, tobacco, marijuana, cocaine, heroin, PCP, and a slew of other compounds do indeed change our moods and alter our perceptions. While some people are able to use some drugs in moderation, others cannot. They lose control of their drug-taking behavior and become addicted. Because drug abuse and addiction have become problems of significant consequence, it is important to understand why people abuse drugs and how drugs exert their addictive effects.

To begin with, we should bear in mind that drug abuse and drug addiction are entirely different phenomenon. Drug abuse is a voluntary activity, but drug addiction is a compulsion. A drug abuser can

NIH Pub. No. 93-3057.

3

choose whether or not to use a drug. People who are addicted, by contrast, have for all intents and purposes lost their free will to decide whether or not to use drugs. They feel they have no more choice about using drugs than they do about eating or breathing.

How can certain drugs produce such overpowering effects? The key lies in how these drugs affect the brain and some of its networks of nerve cells. To understand how drugs influence the brain, we need to examine some of the constituents of the brain and how they work.

The Brain and Its Nerve Cells

The brain can be divided into several large regions, each responsible for some of the activities vital for living. The brain's lowest portion, called the brain stem, controls basic functions such as heart rate, breathing, eating, and sleeping. When one of these basic needs must be fulfilled, the brain stem structures can direct the rest of the brain and body to work toward that end. While these structures may be simple, they can exert powerful effects on our behavior.

Above the brain stem and encompassing two-thirds of the human brain mass are the two hemispheres of the cerebral cortex. It is the cortex, the convoluted outer covering of nerve cells and fibers, that is the most recent part of the brain to evolve, developing completely only in mammals. Because they have a cortex, all mammals have more complex behavioral repertoires than creatures with simpler brains, like birds and reptiles. But, it is the large size and increased complexity of the human cerebral cortex that makes us different even from other mammals.

Though the cells throughout the entire extent of the cerebral cortex are remarkably similar, the cortex can be divided into dozens of specific areas, each with a highly specialized function. It is like a collection of small computers, each working on a different aspect of a large problem. Much of the cerebral cortex is devoted to our senses—enabling us to see, hear, smell, taste, and touch. Other areas give us the ability to generate complex movements; still other regions allow us to speak and understand words, and different regions altogether allow us to think, plan, and imagine.

On top of the brain stem and buried under the cortex, there is another set of more primitive brain structures called the limbic system. These limbic system structures are crucial for connecting the cortex, which deals mainly with the outside world, with our emotions and motivations, which reflect our internal environment and survival

4

needs. These connections allow us to experience a wide range of feelings and to influence these feelings with our perceptions and actions. They also enable us to use our impressive cognitive abilities to help us do the things we need to do to survive. Two large limbic structures, called the hippocampus and the amygdala, are also critical for memory. Sensory information flows from the cortex to these primitive brain regions, which take into account what is going on inside the brain and body and then instruct the cortex to store what is important.

One of the reasons that drugs of abuse can exert such powerful control over our behavior is that they act directly on the more primitive brain stem and limbic structures, which can override the cortex in controlling our behavior. In effect, they eliminate the most human part of our brain from its role in controlling our behavior.

Surprisingly, the feeling of pleasure turns out to be one of the most important emotions for our survival. In fact, the feeling of pleasure is so important that there is a circuit of specialized nerve cells devoted to producing and regulating it. One important set of nerve cells, which uses a special chemical messenger, a neurotransmitter called dopamine, sits at the top of the brain stem. These dopamine-containing neurons relay messages about pleasure through their nerve fibers to nerve cells in a limbic structure called the nucleus accumbens. Still other fibers reach to a related part of the frontal region of the cerebral cortex. So, the pleasure circuit spans the survival-oriented brain stem, the emotional limbic system, and the complex information processor, the cerebral cortex.

The reason that pleasure, which scientists call reward, is a powerful biological force for our survival is that pleasure reinforces any behavior that elicits it. If you do something pleasurable, the brain is wired so that you tend to do that again. That is why a rat or monkey so readily learns to press a lever for food. The animal does it because it is reinforcing—pressing the lever gets food and eating food turns on the pleasure center, an action that helps ensure that the animal will do again what got him that food in the first place. And all of this happens unconsciously. We do not have to think about it or pay attention. It is an automatic brain function.

Thus, life's sustaining activities, such as eating a good meal or engaging in sex, activate this pleasure circuit. By doing so, they teach us to do these things again and again. But, certain substances, including all the drugs people abuse, also can potently activate the brain's pleasure circuit. Unfortunately the more a person uses these

5

drugs to get feelings of pleasure, the more the person learns to repeat the drug-taking behavior and the more the brain learns to depend on drugs to evoke pleasure.

So, that is the key reason why people repeatedly abuse drugs; drugs make them feel good by directly turning on the pleasure circuit. It also is a reason why drug addiction is so difficult to treat: addicts find that only drugs can give them pleasure. Drug addiction is a biologically based disease that alters the way the pleasure center, as well as other parts of the brain, function. By directly turning on our pleasure circuits, many addictive drugs make our brains behave as if these compounds were as important for survival as food, sex, and all the other natural rewards that also turn on the pleasure circuits. Thus, drugs pervert to a destructive end a strong emotion that helps to activate one of the brain's most powerful learning mechanisms.

This is a general description of how drugs influence our behavior by working on one important brain center. To really understand how drugs produce their effects, however, we need to understand how nerve cells interact with the molecules that make up drugs.

To do this, we need to examine the fine structure of nerve cells, the communications network of the brain. Each nerve cell, or neuron, contains three important parts. The central cell body directs all the activities of the neuron. Messages from other nerve cells are relayed directly to the cell body through a set of branches called dendrites. Having examined the information relayed to it by its dendrites, the cell body then can send messages out to its neighbors through a cablelike fiber called an axon. But the axon does not make direct contact with the dendrites of other neurons. A tiny gap separates the terminal of the axon, sending the message from the dendrites of the cell with which it seeks to communicate. This gap is called a synapse.

The message is sent across the synaptic gap between the two nerve cells by a chemical called a neurotransmitter. The little packets of the neurotransmitter are released at the end of the axon and diffuse across the gap to bind to special molecules, called receptors, that sit on the surface of the dendrites of the adjacent nerve cell.

When the neurotransmitter couples to a receptor, it is like a key fitting into a lock that starts the process information flow in that neuron. First, this coupling allows the receptor molecules to link with other molecules that extend through the cell membrane to the inside of the cell. This is how the neurotransmitter that can only affect a receptor molecule sitting on the outside edge of the cell can change the way the cell behaves. Once the receptor activates these other molecules, its mission is complete. The neurotransmitter then is either destroyed or sucked back into the nerve cell that released it. This whole process is called chemical neurotransmission.

Almost all drugs that change the way the brain works do so by tinkering with chemical neurotransmission. Some drugs, like heroin, mimic the effects of a natural neurotransmitter. Others, like LSD, block receptors and thereby prevent neuronal messages from getting through. Still others, like cocaine, interfere with the process by which neurotransmitters are sucked up by the neurons that release them. Others, like caffeine and PCP, exert their effects by interfering with the way messages proceed from the surface receptors into the cell interior.

When drugs interfere with the delicate mechanisms through which nerve cells transmit, receive, and process the information critical for daily living, we lose some of our ability to control our own lives. The continued use of these drugs can actually change the way the brain works. This is the biological basis of addiction.

Observations of people and experiments with animals have taught us that addiction begins when a drug is inappropriately and repeatedly used to stimulate the nerve cells of the pleasure circuit of the brain. Rats hooked up to a drug pump will repeatedly press the lever for doses of illicit drugs that activate dopamine-containing nerve cells in the ventral tegmental area or the neurons that these cells end on in the nucleus accumbens and the frontal cortex. In fact, there is a remarkable similarity between the drugs humans like to abuse and the ones that laboratory monkeys will self-administer. Given the opportunity, both monkeys and humans will use cocaine, amphetamines, heroin, alcohol, phenobarbital, nicotine, and virtually every opiate drug. Hallucinogens seem to be the only class of drugs that are preferred only by people.

Animal experiments have taught us that cocaine turns on the pleasure circuit by allowing dopamine to accumulate in the synapses where it is released. Because the amount of dopamine is allowed to build up, strong feelings of pleasure, even euphoria, are elicited. Heroin turns on the pleasure circuit by directly activating opiate receptors on other neurons in this circuit. Even drugs like marijuana, which animals do not like to self-administer, can make it easier for other drugs or natural pleasures to turn on the pleasure circuit. This may be why people compulsively use even a relatively weak addictive drug like marijuana.

7

So, people abuse drugs and animals self administer them because drugs turn on the pleasure center. They do this by altering the normal process of chemical neurotransmission. But, in order to understand why different people use different drugs and how repeated drug use can lead to addiction, it is useful to understand the specific effects of different classes of drugs and the particular brain areas they target.

Opiates

This drug class—which includes opium, codeine, morphine, and heroin—comes from the white, milky liquid exuded by the poppy flower. Opium, codeine, and morphine can be extracted directly from the fluid, while heroin is produced by chemically joining two molecules of morphine. Heroin injected into a vein reaches the brain in a mere seven or eight seconds and, because of its chemical structure, penetrates into the brain even faster than morphine, which is probably why most addicts in the United States choose heroin. Once heroin reaches the brain, it quickly binds to the opiate receptors that are found in many brain regions. Activation of the opiate receptors in the pleasure circuit causes intense euphoria, called a rush. This rush lasts only briefly, but is followed by a couple of hours of a relaxed, contented state.

By binding to opiate receptors in other parts of the brain and body, opiates also can stop diarrhea (an important medical use), depress breathing, and cause nausea and vomiting. People who try heroin for the first time often get nauseous or vomit, and some decide they will never use the drug again. But many get past this side effect.

Much more serious is heroin's ability, in large doses, to make breathing shallow or even stop altogether. It does this by binding to opiate receptors that are found on the neurons that control breathing. Activation of these opiate receptors by heroin actually causes the neurons to slow down or stop working altogether. Thousands of people have died because they stopped breathing after a heroin overdose. A number of years ago, however, scientists developed drugs that can block heroin from attaching to opiate receptors. These medications are called opiate antagonists. If someone who has overdosed on heroin is treated with one of these drugs in time, the heroin effects can be completely reversed.

In addition to their many other effects, opiates are the most potent painkillers available. Yet many people who have had surgery or are suffering from advanced cancer receive inadequate pain relief because they, their families, or their doctors worry they will become addicted to opiates. But the truth is, this rarely happens. Many studies have shown that pain patients can be treated effectively with strong opiates and either maintain indefinitely or, when their pain is gone, withdraw from the drug with little problem.

One reason that opiates have so many effects is because opiate receptors are widely distributed throughout the brain and body. The brain also produces its own opiatelike neurotransmitters, called endorphins, that act just like but more weakly than morphine. Neurons that produce endorphins and neurons that contain opiate receptors are involved in many brain and body functions. The nucleus accumbens contains a large population of opiate receptors, which may be how opiates turn on the pleasure circuit, but regions of the brain involved in emotions and memory—the hippocampus—as well as the cerebral cortex also contain many receptors for opiates.

Cocaine

Cocaine comes from the leaves of the coca plant, which grows in the mountains of South America. One of the most highly addictive forms of cocaine is crack, a chemically altered form of cocaine that can be smoked. When a person smokes this drug, it enters the brain in seconds and produces a rush of euphoria and feelings of power and self-confidence.

Cocaine, like other stimulants, increases alertness, makes one feel more energetic, and suppresses hunger. In fact, a similar kind of stimulant, the amphetamines, for years were prescribed as appetite suppressants for dieters. One kind of amphetamine, methamphetamine, is now making its way back into illegal use in a smokeable form called ice. This, too, is a highly addictive drug.

Repeated exposure to stimulants can make a person feel anxious, hyperactive, and irritable. People can become psychotic, in a way that resembles paranoid schizophrenia, from taking too high a dose of these drugs. For many years, scientists have studied an animal model of psychosis induced by amphetamines to better understand the symptoms of schizophrenia. Finally, a cocaine or amphetamine overdose can cause tremors and lethal brain seizures.

By tracing the path of radioactive cocaine in the brain of human volunteers, researchers have tracked the drug's activity. For a period of up to about six minutes, when feelings of euphoria are most intense, cocaine can be found in the frontal cortex regions. After that time, the drug begins to dwindle in that area and is concentrated in another region densely packed with dopamine receptors and axons from dopamine-containing nerve cells.

Because cocaine acts to prevent reabsorption of the neurotransmitter dopamine after its (release from nerve cells, cocaine addicts often have higher than normal levels of dopamine in their synapses. This may explain an important finding: the brains of chronic cocaine abusers appear to contain fewer dopamine receptors than normal brains. The excess dopamine causes the neurons that have dopamine receptors to decrease the number of dopamine receptors they make. This phenomenon is called down regulation and may explain the craving for cocaine that occurs during withdrawal from cocaine addiction.

When cocaine is no longer taken and dopamine levels return to their normal, lower concentration, the smaller number of dopamine receptors available for the neurotransmitter to bind to is insufficient to fully activate nerve cells. Because these nerve cells can no longer do their job the end result may be such common withdrawal symptoms as depression and a craving for the drug. The depression may reflect the brain's response to the lower level of dopamine action, and the craving is its way of telling the addict to get the dopamine level back up by taking cocaine. This is not unlike the way that hunger motivates us to eat.

Marijuana and Hallucinogens

Unlike opiates and stimulants, marijuana and hallucinogens (including LSD and mescaline) alter our perception of reality. These drugs distort the way our senses work and our sense of time, space, and self. In people who are particularly sensitive to them, hallucinogens can produce intense anxiety and even precipitate a psychotic episode.

It is not yet clear exactly how these effects are produced, but radioactive tracing shows that THC, the active ingredient in marijuana, binds to receptors that recognize it. There are many THC receptors in parts of the brain that coordinate movement. This may explain why animals given large doses of marijuana collapse and cannot move.

The hippocampus, a structure involved with the storage of memory, also contains many THC receptors. This may explain why people intoxicated with marijuana have poor short-term memory. Scientists already have shown that chronic administration of THC to rats actually can damage the hippocampus. They are trying to find out if this damage may lead to permanent memory impairment.

PCP

This drug has a variety of actions—it is a hallucinogen, a stimulant, and an anesthetic all in one. PCP blocks the way some receptors communicate their message to the inside of the cell and it also blocks certain kinds of receptors. It can produce euphoria, alleviate pain, and lead to disorganized thinking. Depending on the person, PCP can cause drowsiness or aggressiveness, passivity or hostility. A major concern about the drug is the unpredictability of its effects from one time to the next and from one person to the next.

Depressants

Alcohol may be the most familiar depressant, but this class of drugs also includes tranquilizers, like valium, and sleeping pills, like phenobarbital. A major action of all of these drugs is to reduce anxiety. They may, however, first produce a brief period of excitement or euphoria before they produce calmness, sedation, and sleep.

In higher doses, these compounds can produce anesthesia and relax muscles, and some may serve as antiseizure medications. In fact, valium and phenobarbital are excellent antiepileptic medicines, but most people find them too sedating for regular use.

People who get drunk may feel alert at first, but then they start to feel depressed and lose their coordination. Most of us have seen the unpleasant and potentially dangerous behavior of drunks. An overdose of alcohol or other depressants can produce stupor and death. Another important effect of these drugs is to impair judgment. People who are drunk often think they are functioning well. This may help to explain why 23,000 people are killed by drunk drivers every year.

Designer Drugs

So-called "street or basement chemists" have designed a slew of compounds that differ only slightly from the chemical structure of illegal drugs. Until a few years ago when the laws were changed, these compounds were technically legal, but still had the addictive effects of their chemical cousins. For example, people have modified the stimulant methamphetamine, developing a compound called MDMA, commonly known on the street as ecstasy. It has a combination of stimulant and hallucinogenic properties, and animal studies have shown that it causes a severe, possibly permanent, loss of serotonin-containing nerve fibers of the cortex. The Drug Enforcement Administration has declared MDMA illegal.

In general, depending on the origin of the designer drug and how the source drug was modified, the new compound may have widely different properties ranging from stimulant to opiate to hallucinogenic.

Drugs and the Fetus

Many babies are now being born addicted to cocaine, PCP, or heroin. Normal development of the fetus is a highly complex and intricately timed process that is easily disrupted by drugs. The effects of drugs on the fetus can be absolutely devastating; there is no safe way for a pregnant woman to take drugs.

To understand the effect of drugs on fetal development, consider the opiate receptors in the cortex of the adult and newborn monkey. An adult has three distinct, localized bands of opiate receptors while an infant has only one fairly uniform band.

Newborns actually have many more of these receptors than needed. In the normal course of development in animals, the extra receptors are gradually eliminated because no endorphin-containing nerve fibers contact them. Because the receptors are never activated, they are eliminated. But if a mother has taken opiates during her pregnancy, the fetus' opiate receptors all receive constant activation. As a consequence, the receptors do not disappear as they normally would after birth and the normal functioning and continued development of the brain can be disrupted.

Addicted babies are irritable, sensitive, and unusually hard to handle. They have developmental abnormalities as if their brains are trying to get back on track, attempting to develop properly even though they have been thrown off track by drugs. Because normal development is an exquisitely timed process that builds one event upon another, it is not surprising that drugs can disrupt it so easily.

Steps to Addiction

No matter what kind of drug a person is using, nobody begins taking drugs thinking he or she will become addicted. The person says,

"I can handle it. I'll just take this a few times and then I'll stop." The fact is, many people can do this. They can experiment with drugs and then stop. But many others cannot. And while we cannot predict who will and who will not get in trouble with drugs, we do know some of the steps along the path to addiction. Knowing the signposts along this route may help people recognize when they have gotten or are about to get into trouble.

Drugs make most people feel good; this is why they want to take drugs more than once or twice. In scientific terms, drug use is a "rewarding behavior" because the high or pleasure it induces tends to reinforce the drug-taking activity. For some people, this reinforcing experience, this learning about the pleasures of drug use, may lead from experimentation to more regular, social use of a drug. Many people start to use drugs at parties and with friends. Some people stay at this second level of use for many, many years and never get into trouble. There are, for example, many social drinkers who have never had a problem controlling their level of alcohol consumption.

But for other people, drug use does get out of hand. These people learn to take drugs for emotional support: one person had a tough day, another's boss yelled at her, still another has not done his homework and knows he will be in big trouble at school. People get bored, lonely, or just do not like their world very much. Taking drugs to try to solve problems like these helps set the stage for addiction.

At first a person might say, "Well I didn't do my homework tonight. I feel really guilty, so I'm going to get stoned, forget about it, and go to bed." Then it progresses—snorting cocaine in the stockroom, having a few drinks at lunch, or sneaking a drink or smoking dope in the bathroom to deal with stress. If this continues, physiological changes will begin to take place. Friends may even notice: "You know, he can drink anyone under the table. The guy has a hollow leg." What is happening is that the person has become tolerant to alcohol. If it used to take one or two drinks for that person to get high, after a period of drinking it takes three or four drinks, then five or six. Similarly, the dose needed to get high from marijuana, heroin, or crack also escalates. So the drug user is not only taking drugs more frequently, that person is exposing his or her body to higher doses.

Then, as regular drug use continues, a second related kind of change begins. The body of a habitual drug user begins to need the drug to work normally. The person cannot function without it; when the drug is not available, the person experiences symptoms of withdrawal. Deprived of the drug, the individual may feel anxious, generally lousy, or sick. Using the drug again alleviates these symptoms.

Until a person goes into withdrawal, there may be little, if any, evidence that the user is physically dependent on a drug.

Most importantly, avoiding withdrawal is a powerful force motivating people to keep using drugs. The user now has entered a new stage in his or her relationship with drugs. The user not only needs drugs to produce pleasure, but the person must have them to avoid the pain and discomfort of withdrawal.

But physical dependence is not addiction. For example, people who take opiates to relieve chronic pain can become physically dependent on their painkilling medication. They would experience withdrawal if they suddenly stopped taking their narcotic. But the drug is not the focus of their existence. Indeed, they use their narcotic medication to live a normal life. Addicts, by contrast, have no life without their drugs. This may be why virtually all pain patients have no trouble giving up their opiates if their pain is relieved, while addicts tend to relapse into drug use after they have been withdrawn and put in treatment for their addiction.

Addiction, then, is more than drug tolerance and physical dependence, though these may be necessary preconditions. Our experience with pain patients has taught us that the defining conditions for addiction also include psychological dependence on the drug. The addicts perceive themselves as chained to the drug and their behavior becomes characterized by compulsive drug-seeking and drug-taking behavior. The focus of life is obtaining drugs, taking drugs, getting high, and then getting more drugs. Everything else—family, friends, job—falls by the wayside. The addict may get fired because he or she cannot function while high; an addict's family may throw the person out because the individual has stolen their money to support a drug habit. And at the same time that the addict now needs the drug not only for pleasure, but also to avoid the sick feeling associated with withdrawal. Thus, the addict's ability to choose whether or not to use a drug has been severely compromised because only drugs bring pleasure, the solution to most of life's problems has become drug use, and doing without drugs brings the anxiety and sickness of withdrawal.

Animal studies indicate that the destructive behavior associated with addiction is not unique to humans and thus confirms its biological basis. Rats given free access to cocaine will eventually kill themselves taking it, foregoing even food and drink. They just keep taking cocaine until they die. Some humans stop or seek help before their habit kills them, but others cannot. And to make it worse, intravenous drug users run the risk of infecting themselves, their spouses, and their unborn children with AIDS. This fatal disease of the immune system is increasing most rapidly among intravenous drug users, including prostitutes who shoot up and then spread the disease among their customers.

Treatment

Addicts have a tremendous ability for self-delusion. Some believe and will tell others, "I can stop any time I want. I can handle it." These people are actively denying that their drug problem even exists. But eventually, such people end up in the emergency room with an overdose, they get busted for selling or buying drugs, or they might end up on the street rejected by friends and family. Many have to hit some kind of bottom that finally prompts them to seek treatment.

One of the first things to understand about treatment for drug addiction is that it is not a cure. There is no cure for addiction in the way that an ear infection or strep throat can be cured. Drug addiction is a chronic disease that has the potential for relapse. Successful treatment of drug addiction means that the addict significantly reduced use of the drug to which he or she is addicted and that the individual has learned new behaviors that avoid drug use and other self-destructive activities.

From this perspective, drug addiction can be considered much like hypertension, atherosclerosis, or adult diabetes. There also are chronic diseases that are typically caused by voluntary activities, such as poor diet, poor stress management, and lack of exercise. These diseases cannot really be cured, but they can be controlled through appropriate changes in lifestyle and perhaps with the aid of some medications. Those who treat alcoholics have long recognized the chronic relapsing nature of alcohol addiction; even if an alcoholic has not taken a drink for years, that person is still referred to as "recovering," not "recovered." That is because they know that the potential for relapse always exists and that staying sober requires continuing effort. It is a life-long process. The same is true for any drug addict. The long-term goal in drug addiction treatment is to teach the addict how to live without drugs.

The first goal of any treatment program, however, must be to stop the use of illicit drugs. In order for any treatment program to work, a person's basic brain biochemistry has to be stabilized and allowed to return to normal so that both the problems that led to drug use in the first place as well as the problems caused by addiction can be addressed. The cessation of drug use often reduces the criminal or antisocial behaviors—including stealing, chronic lying, or the sharing of needles—associated with the drug habit. Often addicts must be taught new skills and habits to replace the destructive behaviors related to addiction.

There are essentially two different approaches that are now used to reach these goals. The first begins with detoxification, the process of removing the addictive substances from the addict's brain and body. This can be done slowly or quickly and often means undergoing withdrawal, though it is possible that the most extreme symptoms can be medically treated. After this process, a drug-free treatment can begin that emphasizes psychotherapy or counseling and group therapy sessions as ways to teach people to solve their problems without resorting to drugs. Many addicts also may have an underlying mental illness that must be treated before effective drug abuse treatment can begin. For otherwise healthy people with a stable family and a job, drug abuse treatments might be successfully undertaken on an outpatient basis.

For people without these social supports, or for those who have been deeply involved in criminal and antisocial activity, residing in a specially designed drug-free community for a year or two may be necessary. These communities typically feature strict controls over behavior with rewards for appropriate behavior and punishments for failure to comply with the rules. Such communities not only protect the recovering addict from drugs and the environmental cues that often led to drug use in the past, but they also surround the addict with other people who are undergoing the same recovery process and who can act as role models and lend moral and psychological support.

Skills development, especially for the many adolescent addicts who never learned the social skills necessary to go to school or hold a job, is also critical for continued recovery. Many people have to learn new ways to cope with old problems. They may need remedial education to hold down a job or attend school; fear or shame about poor reading ability or other inadequate skills may have facilitated the turn to drugs in the first place. Without new skills to deal with the world, relapse into drug use becomes almost inevitable. Drug-free treatments aim to obliterate the old habits associated with drug use and replace those with new coping skills that are essential for a drug-free life.

The alternative to drug-free treatment is medication therapy. Currently, there are only two medications—methadone and naltrexone, that can be used for this type of therapy, and they are both useful only for opiate addicts. It is crucial to note, however, that medications by themselves are not effective treatments for addiction. They must be used as part of a comprehensive treatment program that includes many of the therapeutic activities described above.

Methadone, the best-known maintenance agent, replaces the heroin that addicts are taking. Like heroin, methadone is an opiate agonist, stimulating opiate receptors in the brain. But unlike heroin, which must be injected into a vein four to six times each day to avoid withdrawal, methadone can be taken by mouth and lasts for 24 hours. Instead of repeatedly disrupting brain chemistry, like those repeated shots of heroin do, it stabilizes the brain so an addict can participate in a recovery program. Given in a proper dose, methadone prevents withdrawal and blocks the effects of heroin if the addict should "shoot up" after taking the dose of methadone. It also helps to break the habit of repeatedly injecting drugs and it gets people off needles so their chance of contracting or spreading AIDS goes way down.

Methadone does not produce the intense euphoria associated with heroin and many people have been successfully maintained on methadone for years. These people are able to hold jobs, interact positively with their families, and contribute productively to society. There is little question that when it is properly used, methadone is an effective treatment for some heroin addicts.

Naltrexone is an opiate antagonist; it prevents heroin and other opiates from activating opiate receptors. A person taking naltrexone cannot get high from shooting up heroin. The problem with naltrexone is that most addicts do not want to take it and now it is used only by highly motivated addicts.

A new addition to some drug treatment programs is deconditioning procedures. Even months after they have stopped using drugs, people with a long history of drug use feel strong urges to use drugs again when they encounter places or situations in which they have used drugs in the past. They have been conditioned to expect to use drugs in those situations just like Pavlov's dogs were conditioned to salivate whenever they received food. Although initially only the food caused salivation, after the food and bell are presented together often enough, the brain learns that the bell means food and the bell itself causes the animal to salivate. This powerful learning mechanism, called Pavlovian conditioning, takes place without us being aware of it and is very difficult to overcome. Deconditioning techniques were developed in animal experiments and now are being applied directly in some treatment programs.

Whether or not a person receives drug-free or maintenance treatment or there is deconditioning, a key component of successful recovery is some form of aftercare that usually includes regular attendance at group meetings with other recovering addicts. These groups, which are largely patterned after Alcoholics Anonymous, supply the support many people need to maintain their drug-free state. One reason they are productive is because addicts can effectively break through the psychological barriers of other addicts. They can best point out the lies that people tell themselves to rationalize their drug behavior, and they can offer poignant support because they are going through the same process of recovery. But whatever form of therapy or aftercare program an addict may use, it is important to understand that treatment can work.

Drugs, Genetics and Biology

Many people use drugs for years without getting addicted, while others report they felt like an addict the first time they smoked crack. Such observations beg the question: Is there a genetic component to drug addiction? Are some people simply born more vulnerable than others to the effects of drugs? Researchers have found evidence that at least some alcoholics are genetically predisposed to alcoholism. We do not know if people have a genetic predisposition to become addicted to other drugs, but some addicts report that they do not use drugs to get high, but rather to feel normal. It may be they have an inborn chemical imbalance in brain chemistry that is corrected by drugs. Such people would have genetic predispositions to become addicted.

Other suggestive evidence has come from animal studies; rats can be bred to either work for cocaine or avoid it, to be dramatically affected by opiates or have smaller than normal responses to the compounds. These different responses are due to the genetic makeup of the individual strains of animals.

But whether or not some people are genetically vulnerable to drug addiction, it seems clear that biology predisposes us to drug use. Drugs alter the way the brain works by acting directly on our nerve cells. Long-term drug use can lead to long-term changes in brain chemistry. We do not know yet whether these changes are permanent. Most alcoholics and other recovering addicts know that even one drink or snort of cocaine can lead to an uncontrollable binge of drug use. This suggests that addiction has caused permanent changes in the way the brain responds to drugs.

Because of all we have learned about how drugs affect the brain, scientists now are able to create new medications that may prevent the drugs from getting a foothold in the brain or that can reverse their effects. Currently, investigators at the National Institute on Drug Abuse and other research institutions are working hard to develop medications that may be used to treat addiction. A drug that can block cocaine's ability to stimulate nerve cells is an important priority. Other drugs that can block the drug hunger or craving, which is such a common cause of relapse, also are being sought.

Because of what we have learned from studying both animals and people, it is now clear that addiction is a biologically based disorder of the brain that, like hypertension or diabetes, can be treated with medical and behavioral techniques. As our understanding of the addictive process and its consequences grows, we will continue to create new prevention and treatment techniques to improve our ability to deal with the devastation of addiction.

Chapter 2

Drug Abuse: A Family Affair

How Do Alcohol and Other Drug Problems Affect The Family?

As a drug or alcohol user becomes increasingly disabled by chemical dependency, family members often begin to carry an extra load to keep the family functioning. But unlike the teamwork that exists in a healthy family, responsibilities in a user's family are unfairly distributed. As a result, the family members bearing the burden begin to feel resentful, angry and frustrated. To make matters worse, instead of confronting the user about his or her behavior, they often withhold their feelings to avoid arguments and uncomfortable scenes.

Family Secrets

Family members remember when the alcohol or drug user didn't have a problem. They convince themselves that, in time, the user will return to "normal" and no one will ever know. More often than not, those on the outside already know that a problem exists. The family's efforts to keep it secret are really a form of denial. They become enablers who make it possible for that person to continue using drugs and alcohol.

Information in this chapter was provided by the Drug Enforcement Administration and produced by the American Council for Drug Education.

What Kinds of Alcohol and Other Drug Problems Do Families Have?

Children

Most of us recognize that a child's alcohol or drug use places enormous strain on a family. Parents become emotionally exhausted by the problems (at home, at school and sometimes with the police and court systems) created by the child's destructive behavior. Many feel betrayed by the alcohol- and drug-using child and their hurt, anger, and embarrassment come out in a variety of ways, including physical ailments, depression and irritability.

Children with alcohol and other drug problems also take up a lot of time. Normal family activities and relationships suffer, including the amount of attention given to other children in the household. Parents frequently blame one another for the user's behavior and the marriage sometimes suffers. In some cases, parents spend large sums of money on legal or medical fees, or in making restitution for stolen or destroyed items. These expenses often deprive others in the household and create an additional strain on family life.

Alcohol and other drug use among children in a household can be "contagious." If one child uses, the others are likely to use as well. Parents not only have to deal with the identified user, but must be on the alert for troubling symptoms among their other youngsters.

Adults

Children, however, are not the only possible alcohol and drug users in a family. A mother or father can also suffer from chemical dependency—a situation that creates many serious problems for every member of the household.

Families with a parent who is a drug or alcohol abuser are often:

- socially isolated;
- less interested in the children;
- socially disorganized, with few rules, rituals, or traditions to govern and shape family life; and
- exhibiting high levels of family stress, including spousal abuse, child abuse, fighting and depression.

Men

Cocaine, especially crack cocaine, is a serious problem for many husbands and fathers. Because the drug provides a sense of increased energy and well-being during the early stages of use, many men believe it helps them perform better in their jobs. Later, as the user's need for cocaine becomes more important than anything else, financial problems often develop as the user spends salary and family savings on the drug. Severe family problems soon follow; in many cases, there is permanent separation from the wife and children.

When a husband is an alcohol or drug abuser, the wife frequently becomes a "codependent" personality. She takes on the role of caretaker or protector by covering up or denying the problem, as well as by caring for the husband when he is high, intoxicated or hung over. She depends on this role to give her a sense of identity and some meaning in her life. As a result, she will often interfere with her husband's efforts to stop drinking or using drugs, whether consciously or unconsciously, and will even find opportunities to provoke her husband to drink or use drugs.

Women

Although a smaller percentage of women than men abuse drugs and alcohol, chemical dependency is still a problem. Studies show that chemical abuse and dependency is the second most commonly reported mental health disorder for women between the ages of 18 and 24. Experts also estimate that one out of four persons diagnosed as having drug or alcohol problems is a woman.

Changing social values appear to have influenced women's alcohol- and drug-using behavior. Many women now use abusable substances in much the same way that men do. However, young women are more likely to smoke or use stimulants regularly to control their appetites and lose weight.

Even though more women are using and developing problems with drugs and alcohol, society still tends to protect them from exposure and from suffering the same consequences experienced by men. The criminal justice system, for example, tends to be more lenient with women, and workplace supervisors are less likely to spot the signs of substance abuse among female employees. Within the home, both husbands and children may deny the mother's problem for years. This is unfortunate for all concerned because when women finally receive treatment for chemical dependency, they do very well. Providing help early avoids many problems and may protect the family from the spillover effects of this disease.

Drugs and Pregnancy

If a pregnant woman uses drugs or alcohol, she is placing both herself and her baby at risk. Any substance the mother consumes passes directly through the placenta to the developing fetus. The baby may be born with low birthweight or risk the serious problems of a small head or other physical abnormalities, respiratory diseases and severe mental retardation. Later, these children may have problems learning in school and getting along with other children.

Older Adults in the Household

Elderly relatives also may have problems with alcohol or drugs. Experts believe that older adults consume about 25 percent of the prescription and 10 percent of the over-the-counter (OTC) drugs sold in the United States. Many seniors take an average of eight different medications per day.

As the body ages, it distributes, stores and eliminates drugs differently. Drugs may have stronger effects or last longer than they did when the patient was younger. The sheer number of medications taken means that dangerous interactions among drugs are more likely to occur. Studies have shown that one-quarter to one-half of elderly patients take their medications incorrectly. Some drugs, for example, will not work properly if patients take them without food or while using antacids. When drugs are combined with alcohol, serious medical problems may result.

In addition to problems created by the misuse of prescription and OTC drugs, some older adults develop problems with alcohol. This often happens after retirement, job loss or the death of a spouse. As with any other member of a household, negative changes in an elderly person's personality and behavior makes life more difficult for everyone in the family.

What Can Family Members Do?

If this discussion of families troubled by drug and alcohol use is familiar to you, it is important to:

* Admit that a problem may exist.

* Understand that the drug or alcohol user may be suffering from a chronic and progressive illness which usually gets worse unless something is done to stop it.

* Call the local Al-Anon, Alateen, Narcotics Anonymous or Adult Children of Alcoholics group in your community for information and support.

* Seek professional help from local service agencies or through your company's employee assistance program or medical division, if one is available. This may include help for other family members as well as the alcohol- or drug-using member.

For More Information and Assistance

American Council for Drug Education
204 Monroe Street, Suite 110
Rockville, MD 20850
(800) 488-DRUG (3784)
(301) 294-0600

Al-Anon Family Group Headquarters, Inc.
P.O. Box 182
Madison Square Station
New York, NY 10159-0182
(800) 356-9996
(212) 633-1771

Narcotics Anonymous
World Service Office
P.O. Box 9999
Van Nuys, CA 91409
(818) 780-3951

National Association for Children of Alcoholics
31706 Coast Highway, Suite 201
South Laguna, CA 92677

National Council on Alcoholism & Drug Dependency
12 West 21st Street
New York, NY 10010
(800) 622-2255
(212) 206-6770

National Clearinghouse for Alcohol and Drug Information
Box 2345
Rockville, MD 20852
(800) 729-6686
(301) 468-2345

Chapter 3

Historical Overview of Drug Abuse in the United States

Alcohol

Alcoholic beverages have been a part of the Nation's past since the landing of the Pilgrims. According to *Alcohol and Public Policy: Beyond the Shadow of Prohibition*, a publication commissioned by NIAAA [National Institute on Alcohol Abuse and Alcoholism] and prepared by the National Academy of Sciences, the colonists brought with them from Europe a high regard for alcoholic beverages, which were considered an important part of their diet. Drinking was pervasive because alcohol was regarded primarily as a healthy substance with preventive and curative powers, not as an intoxicant. Alcohol was also believed to be conducive to social as well as personal health. It played an essential role in rituals of conviviality and collective activity, such as barn raisings. While drunkenness was condemned and punished, it was viewed only as an abuse of a God-given gift.

The first temperance movement began in the early 1800s in response to dramatic increases in production and consumption of alcoholic beverages, which also coincided with rapid demographic changes. Agitation against ardent spirits and the public disorder they spawned gradually increased during the 1820s. In addition, inspired by the writings of Benjamin Rush, the concept that alcohol was addicting, and that this addiction was capable of corrupting the mind and the

---

Excerpted from *Prevention Primer*, DHHS Pub. No. (SMA)94-2060; subheads added.

body, took hold. The American Society of Temperance, created in 1826 by clergymen, spread the anti-drinking gospel. By 1835, out of a total population of 13 million citizens, 1.5 million had taken the pledge to refrain from distilled spirits. The first wave of the temperance movement (1825 to 1855) resulted in dramatic reductions in the consumption of distilled spirits, although beer drinking increased sharply after 1850.

The second wave of the temperance movement occurred in the late 1800s with the emergence of the Women's Christian Temperance Movement, which, unlike the first wave, embraced the concept of prohibition. It was marked both by the recruitment of women into the movement and the mobilization of crusades to close down saloons. The movement set out to remove the destructive substance, and the industries that promoted its use, from the country. The movement held that while some drinkers may escape problems of alcohol use, even moderate drinkers flirted with danger.

The culmination of this second wave was the passage of the 18th Amendment and the Volstead Act, which took effect in 1920. While Prohibition was successful in reducing per capita consumption and some problems related to drinking, its social turmoil resulted in its repeal in 1933.

Since the repeal of Prohibition, the dominant view of alcohol problems has been that alcoholism is the principal problem. With its focus on treatment, the rise of the alcoholism movement depoliticized alcohol problems as the object of attention, as the alcoholic was considered a deviant from the predominant styles of life of either abstinence or "normal" drinking. The alcoholism movement is based on the belief that chronic or addictive drinking is limited to a few, highly susceptible individuals suffering from the disease of alcoholism. The disease concept of alcoholism focuses on individual vulnerability, be it genetic, biochemical, psychological, or social/cultural in nature. Under this view if the collective problems of each alcoholic are solved, it follows that society's alcohol problem will be solved.

Nevertheless, the pre-Prohibition view of alcohol as a special commodity has persisted in American society and is an accepted legacy of alcohol control policies. Following Repeal, all States restricted the sale of alcoholic beverages in one way or another in order to prevent or reduce certain alcohol problems. In general, however, alcohol control policies disappeared from the public agenda as both the alcoholism movement and the alcoholic beverage industry embraced the view, "the fault is in the man and not in the bottle."

This view of alcoholism problems has also been the dominant force in contemporary alcohol problem prevention. Until recently the principal prevention strategies focused on education and early treatment. Within this view education is intended to inform society about the disease and to teach people about the early warning signs so that they can initiate treatment as soon as possible. Efforts focus on "high risk" populations and attempt to correct a suspect process or flaw in the individual, such as low self esteem or lack of social skills. The belief is that the success of education and treatment efforts in solving each alcoholic's problem will solve society's alcohol problem as well.

Contemporary alcohol problem prevention began in the 1970s as new information on the nature, magnitude, and incidence of alcohol problems raised public awareness that alcohol can be problematic when used by any drinker, depending upon the situation. There was a renewed emphasis on the diverse consequences of alcohol use—particularly trauma associated with drinking and driving, fires, and violence, as well as long term health consequences.

Other Drugs of Abuse

The history of nonmedical drug use, and the development of policies in response to drug use, also extends back to the early settlement of the country. Like alcohol, the classification of certain drugs as legal, or illegal, has changed over time. These changes sometimes had racial and class overtones. According to Mosher and Yanagisako, for example, Prohibition was in part a response to the drinking practices of European immigrants, who became the new lower class. Cocaine and opium were legal during the 19th century, and were favored drugs among the middle and upper classes. Cocaine became illegal after it became associated with African Americans following Reconstruction. Opium was first restricted in California in 1875 when it became associated with Chinese immigrant workers. Marijuana was legal until the 1930s when it became associated with Mexicans. LSD, legal in the 1950s, became illegal in 1967 when it became associated with the counterculture.

By the end of the 19th century concern had grown over the indiscriminate use of these drugs, especially the addicting patent medicines. Cocaine, opium, and morphine were common ingredients in various potions sold over the counter. Until 1903, cocaine was an ingredient of Coca-Cola®. Heroin, which was isolated in 1868, was hailed as a nonaddicting treatment for morphine addiction and alcoholism.

States began to enact control and prescription laws and, in 1906, Congress passed the Pure Food and Drug Act. It was designed to control opiate addiction by requiring labels on the amount of drugs contained in products, including opium, morphine, and heroin. It also required accurate labeling of products containing alcohol, marijuana, and cocaine.

The Harrison Act (1914) imposed a system of taxes on opium and coca products with registration and record-keeping requirements in an effort to control their sale or distribution. However, it did not prohibit the legal supply of certain drugs, especially opiates.

Current drug laws are rooted in the 1970 Controlled Substances Act. Under this measure drugs are classified according to their medical use, their potential for abuse, and their likelihood of producing dependence. The Act contains provisions for adding drugs to the schedule, and rescheduling drugs. It also establishes maximum penalties for the criminal manufacture or distribution of scheduled drugs.

Substance Abuse Prevention Issues Gain Prominence

Increases in per capita alcohol consumption as well as increased use of illegal drugs during the 1960s raised public concern regarding alcohol and other drug problems. Prevention issues gained prominence on the national level with the creation of the National Institute on Alcohol Abuse and Alcoholism (NIAAA) in 1971 and the National Institute on Drug Abuse (NIDA) in 1974. In addition to mandates for research and the management of national programs for treatment, both Institutes included prevention components.

To further prevention initiatives at the Federal level, the Anti-Drug Abuse Act of 1986 created the U.S. Office for Substance Abuse Prevention (OSAP), which consolidated alcohol and other drug prevention activities under the Alcohol, Drug Abuse, and Mental Health Administration (ADAMHA). The ADAMHA block grant mandate called for States to set aside 21 percent of the alcohol and drug funds for prevention. In a 1992 reorganization, OSAP was changed to the Center for Substance Abuse Prevention (CSAP), part of the new SAMHSA, retaining its major program areas, while the research institutes of NIAAA and NIDA transferred to NIH [National Institutes of Health].

The Office of National Drug Control Policy (ONDCP) was established by the Anti-Drug Abuse Act of 1988. Its primary objective was to develop a drug control policy that included roles for the public and private sector to "restore order and security to American neighborhoods, to dismantle drug trafficking organizations, to help people break the habit of drug use, and to prevent those who have never used illegal drugs from starting." In early 1992 underage alcohol use was included among the drugs to be addressed by ONDCP.

While Federal, State, and local governments play a substantial role in promoting prevention agendas, much of the activity takes place at grass roots community levels. In addition to funding from CSAP's "Community Partnerships" grant program, groups receive support from private sources, such as The Robert Wood Johnson "Fighting Back" program.

While alcohol and other drug problems continue to plague the Nation at intolerably high levels, progress is being made. National surveys document a decline in illicit drug use and a leveling off of alcohol consumption. And indicators of problem levels, such as alcohol-involved traffic crashes, show significant declines.

References

A Promising Future: Alcohol and Other Drug Problem Prevention Services Improvement. CSAP Prevention Monograph 10 (1992) BK191.

National Household Survey on Drug Abuse: Main Findings 1990 (1991) BKD67.

Mosher, J.F. and Yanagisako, K.L. *"Public Health, Not Social Warfare: A Public Health Approach to Illegal Drug Policy," Journal of Public Health Policy* 12(3) 278-322, 1991.

Chapter 4

Current Drug Use in America

Illicit drug use continues to be one of the Nation's most serious problems. Although considerable progress has been made in reducing the number of casual drug users, much remains to be done to reduce the number of chronic, hardcore drug users. Compared with the casual drug user, the chronic, hardcore drug user consumes substantially more drugs and is responsible for the preponderance of crime and other negative social consequences.

Today, there is increasing evidence of two disturbing trends. First, rates of illicit drug use are rising among the Nation's youth and second, rates of heroin use are increasing, particularly because existing drug users are adding heroin to the list of drugs they consume. In addition, there are new users of heroin, many of them youth. The increase of drug use among youth threatens previous progress made against casual drug use and ultimately could lead to an upsurge in the number of chronic, hardcore drug users and the problems they create. This chapter discusses these trends and the evidence that supports them.

Casual Drug Use

According to the 1993 National Household Survey on Drug Abuse (NHSDA), more than 77 million people reported that they had used

Excerpted from *National Drug Control Strategy*, Office of National Drug Control Policy, The White House, February 1995. A copy of the entire report may be purchased from the U.S. Government Printing Office, Superintendent of Documents, Mail Stop: SSOP, Washington, DC 20402-9328.

illicit drugs at some time during their lives. Almost 70 million of these people reported using marijuana, 23 million had tried cocaine, 4 million had tried crack cocaine, 18 million had tried hallucinogens, and more than 2 million had tried heroin. Figure 4.1 shows that in 1993, 37.2 percent of the civilian noninstitutionalized population ages 12 and older reported illicit drug use in their lifetimes. Almost 11.8 percent reported using illicit drugs within the past year, and 5.6 percent reported using illicit drugs within the past month.[1]

Marijuana was the most frequently used illicit drug, with 33.7 percent of the civilian noninstitutionalized population reporting its use some time during their lives. Nine percent reported marijuana use within the past year, and 4.3 percent reported use within the past month. Marijuana use is considered problematic because it long has been considered a gateway drug. Like alcohol and tobacco, marijuana use can lead to the use of stronger drugs such as cocaine and heroin.[2] Furthermore, the National Institute on Drug Abuse reports that marijuana use interferes with short-term memory, learning, and motor skills performance. There also is the evidence that regular marijuana smoking harms the pulmonary function.

Cocaine was the next most frequently used illicit drug, with 11.3 percent of the civilian noninstitutionalized population reporting its use within their lifetimes. Past-year use of cocaine was 2.2 percent, and past-month use was 0.6 percent. It is important to note that the actual use of these drugs by the total U.S. population is probably higher, both because survey respondents underreport drug use and because chronic, hardcore drug users probably are not well represented in drug prevalence surveys.[3] The Office of National Drug Control Policy's (ONDCP's) most recent *Pulse Check*[4] for the quarter ending December 1994 reports cocaine use and availability have stabilized in most areas of the country. However, cocaine, especially crack-cocaine, continues to be in high demand throughout the country, and in some areas, cocaine use is reported to be on the rise.

Figure 4.2 shows that since 1985, past-month use of illicit drugs has declined significantly. The total number of individuals from the NHSDA reporting current illicit drug use declined from 22.3 million users in 1985 to 11.7 million users in 1993. A decline in marijuana use that began after 1979 accounts for most of this success. The total number of current marijuana users has declined from 22.5 million users in 1979 to 9 million users in 1993. During that same period, current cocaine use declined from 4.2 million to 1.3 million. Although this long-term trend is encouraging, the results from the 1993 NHSDA

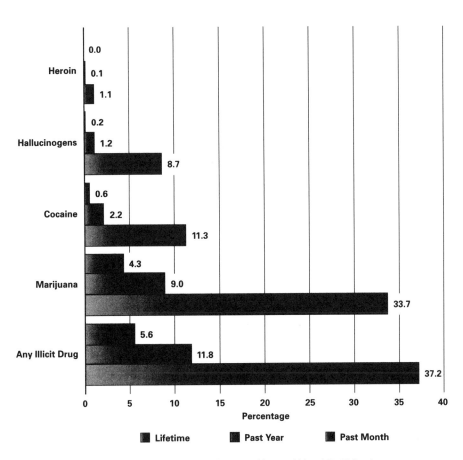

Figure 4.1. Percentages of Individuals in Households Reporting Lifetime, Past Year, and Past Month Use of Illicit Drugs, 1993.

Source: National Household Survey on Drug Abuse, Substance Abuse and Mental Health Services Administration, 1993

35

suggest that the general decline may have ended. No significant changes in illicit drug use, up or down, were reported in 1993, compared with 1992. The net effect is that current drug use appears to have stabilized in the general population during 1993. However, as mentioned in this chapter's outset, illicit drug use by adolescents is increasing.

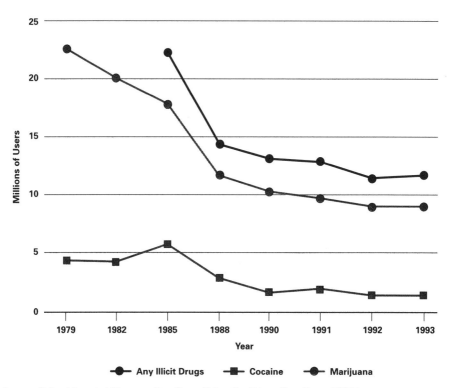

Source: National Household Survey on Drug Abuse, National Institute on Drug Abuse, 1979-91, Substance Abuse and Mental Health Services Administration, 1992-93

Figure 4.2. *Past Month Use of Any Illicit Drugs, Marijuana/Hashish, and Cocaine, 1979-93.*

Hardcore Drug Use

Currently, national surveys such as the NHSDA are limited in their ability to accurately estimate the number of chronic, hardcore users of illicit drugs.[5] In an effort to gain needed knowledge about this population, ONDCP has initiated a major 2-year research project, the Hardcore User Survey Pilot Study. This project will test the efficacy of a new methodology to derive estimates of the number of hardcore drug users, using an application of mathematical models that represent the processes by which people who use drugs make contact with various elements of the criminal justice, drug treatment, and health care systems. The study is being conducted in Cook County, Illinois, and the results of the test phase should be available by the fall of 1995.

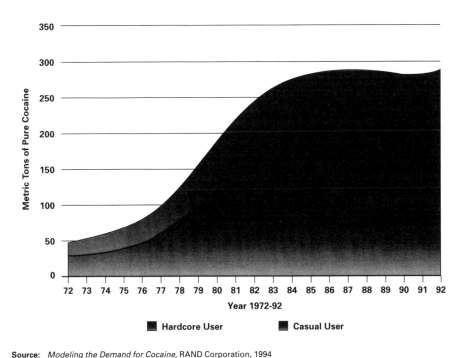

Source: *Modeling the Demand for Cocaine*, RAND Corporation, 1994

Figure 4.3. *Annual U.S. Consumption of Cocaine by Type of User, 1972-92.*

37

Until the results of the Hardcore User Survey Pilot Study are available, ONDCP is estimating the size of this drug user population by using a statistical estimation technique using data drawn from several sources.[6] The results indicated by this method suggest that the numbers of hardcore drug users of cocaine and heroin have remained relatively unchanged since 1988, and the total population of chronic, hardcore drug users was 2.7 million in 1993—with about 2.1 million people using primarily cocaine and 600,000 using primarily heroin.

Chronic, hardcore drug users continue to be responsible for the bulk of illicit drug consumption in America today. Figure 4.3 illustrates the disproportionate amount of drugs they consume. For example, chronic users—only 20 percent of the drug-using population—consume about two-thirds of the total amount of cocaine in this country. The large amount of cocaine consumed by a minority of users makes one thing clear: The goal of reducing the overall rates of illicit drug use in this country cannot be achieved without targeting the chronic, hardcore-drug-using population with intensified programmatic efforts.

Emerging Drug Use Trends

As mentioned at the beginning of this chapter, two alarming trends are emerging. Of greatest concern are the trend indicating the increase in adolescent drug use and the changes in young people's attitudes about the dangers of illicit drug use and the acceptability of such use. Use of marijuana shows the most increase, and while other illicit drugs do not yet appear to be following the same track, marijuana often is a gateway to other drugs, such as cocaine and heroin, both of which are readily available on the streets of the Nation's cities.

Adolescent Drug Use

Antidrug messages are losing their potency among the Nation's youth. Drug use surveys report that adolescents may be increasing their use of illicit drugs, particularly marijuana and hallucinogens. Figures 4.4 through 4.7 show drug use trends among the adolescent population. The data are from the 1994 Monitoring the Future (MTF) study, which provides information on drug use trends and patterns by students in the 8th, 10th, and 12th grades. The 1991 MTF study found evidence that attitudes against regular use of marijuana were weakening among youth.[7] This attitude change was followed by an increase in reported drug use in the 1992 MTF study, a trend that is

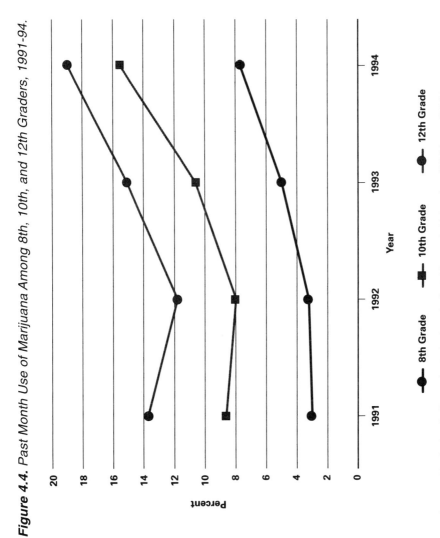

Figure 4.4. Past Month Use of Marijuana Among 8th, 10th, and 12th Graders, 1991-94.

Source: Monitoring the Future Study, Institute for Social Research, University of Michigan, 1991-94

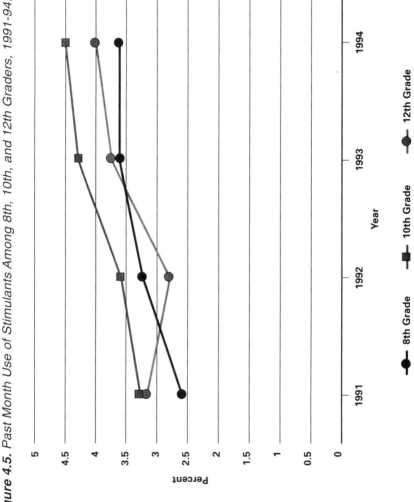

Figure 4.5. Past Month Use of Stimulants Among 8th, 10th, and 12th Graders, 1991-94.

Source: Monitoring the Future Study, Institute for Social Research, University of Michigan, 1991-94

40

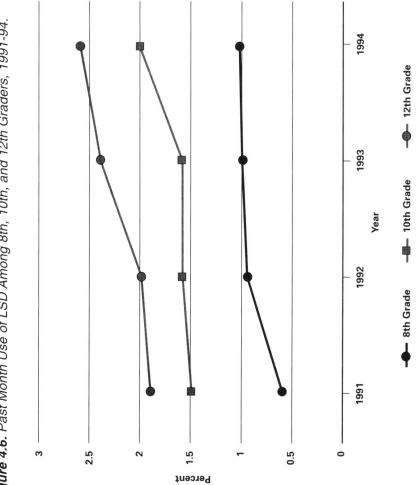

Figure 4.6. *Past Month Use of LSD Among 8th, 10th, and 12th Graders, 1991-94.*

Source: Monitoring the Future Study, Institute for Social Research, University of Michigan, 1991-94

41

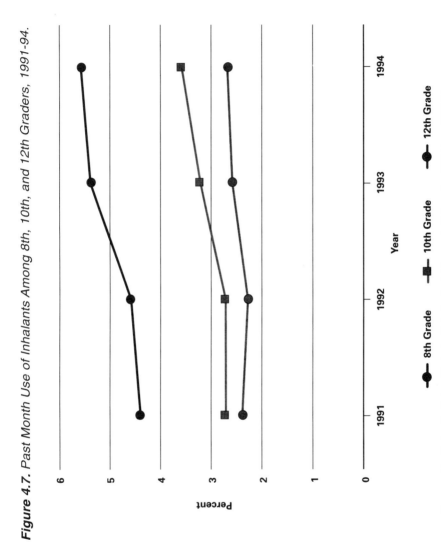

Figure 4.7. Past Month Use of Inhalants Among 8th, 10th, and 12th Graders, 1991-94.

Source: Monitoring the Future Study, Institute for Social Research, University of Michigan, 1991-94 continuing into the present. For the second year in a row, past-month use of marijuana as well as of other drugs such as stimulants, hallucinogens, and inhalants continued to increase among this particular population.[8] The 1994 MTF study reported that lifetime, annual, and 30-day prevalence of drug use increased between 1993 and 1994 for 8th, 10th, and 12th grade students. Findings concerning drug use include the following:

- Lifetime, annual, 30-day, and daily use of marijuana increased significantly for 8th, 10th, and 12th grade students between 1993 and 1994.

- Annual use of LSD (lysergic acid diethylamide) increased significantly for 10th grade students between 1993 and 1994.

- Lifetime, annual, and 30-day use of cocaine powder increased significantly for 8th grade students between 1993 and 1994. Cocaine powder use also increased significantly for 10th graders for reported lifetime and annual use. Crack-cocaine showed a similar pattern, except for the 10th grade students, who reported significant increases in annual use only.

- The prevalence of other drug use (e.g., stimulants and inhalants) increased between 1993 and 1994. However, these increases were not statistically significant.

The 1994 MTF study also reported a further deterioration in attitudes about and perceptions of risks associated with drug use. Trends in perceived harmfulness of drugs—defined by the percentage of students saying there was "great risk" associated with drug use—showed declines in many areas. Findings concerning attitudes about the harmfulness of drug use include the following:

- Eighth and 10th grade students reported statistically significant declines in marijuana's perceived harmfulness.

- Eighth and 10th grade students reported statistically significant declines in LSD's perceived harmfulness.

- Eighth grade students reported statistically significant declines in the perceived harmfulness of cocaine powder and crack-cocaine use. Twelfth grade students perceived cocaine use to be more harmful, but the increase was not statistically significant.

Trends in disapproval of drug use, as defined by students saying they "disapprove" or "strongly disapprove" of people who use drugs, also showed deterioration; these findings include the following:

- Eighth, 10th, and 12th grade students reported significant declines in disapproval rates for students who use marijuana.

- Tenth and 12th grade students reported significant declines in disapproval rates for those students who use LSD once or twice.

- Eighth and 10th grade students reported significant declines in disapproval rates for students who use crack-cocaine or cocaine powder.

The 1993 NHSDA confirmed the decreases in disapproval rates for those within the 12 to 17 age bracket. The national Parent Resource Institute for Drug Education (PRIDE) survey, another survey of students, also reported a similar trend in its review of drug use within selected school systems for the school years 1992-93 and 1993-94.[9]

Upsurges in illicit drug use among adolescents are linked to their use of alcohol and tobacco. The Center on Addiction and Substance Abuse at Columbia University performed a study that found evidence to suggest a consistent statistical relationship between adolescents smoking tobacco cigarettes and drinking alcohol and their subsequent smoking of marijuana, and between adolescent use of cigarettes, alcohol, and marijuana and their subsequent use of illicit drugs such as cocaine and heroin.[10] The study includes the following findings:

- Eighty-nine percent of those who tried cocaine had first used alcohol, tobacco, or marijuana.

- Ninety percent of youth (ages 12 to 17) and adults who used marijuana had first smoked cigarettes or drank alcohol.

- Youth who used the gateway drugs (alcohol, tobacco, and marijuana) were 266 times more likely to use cocaine than were youth who had never used a gateway drug.

Unless the increased marijuana use by the Nation's youth is reversed, it is likely that new, younger users will progress into more severe and debilitating drug use. ONDCP's *Pulse Check*, a quarterly research report on trends in drug abuse as observed by drug ethnographers, epidemiologists, treatment providers, and police, has noted the beginnings of this process.

Heroin Consumption

The increased availability of heroin has the potential to attract new users who have forgotten or ignored the messages about heroin's addictive properties. As long as heroin continues to be inexpensive, abundant, and highly potent, there is a threat of increasing rates of heroin use, or even another heroin epidemic.[11]

The strongest sign of an epidemic is the entry of a large number of new users (new initiates) into illicit drug use. There is no systematic evidence that this is the case with heroin, even though ONDCP's *Pulse Check* is reporting an increasing number of new initiates into heroin use in some areas. New users are of particular concern, because they tend to instigate drug use among their friends and peers. New users, especially those in their first year of use, are more likely to get others to use drugs because they have not begun to suffer the health and legal consequences of their drug use. Long-term users, especially chronic, hardcore drug users, are the least likely to initiate new users into illicit drug use.[12]

There are clear indications that heroin consumption is increasing, especially among existing heroin users (i.e., the amount consumed per user is going up). This trend is normal among older, long-term heroin users and can explain some consumption rate increases. However, heroin use also is on the rise among drug users whose prime drug of abuse is not heroin. The heroin-cocaine link is especially strong for long-term cocaine users, particularly long-term crack-cocaine users. These users often move into combined use with heroin because they find that it softens the impact of the "crash" that often follows a crack-cocaine binge. Furthermore, evidence suggests that heroin snorting has become more commonplace in those areas of the country in which high-purity heroin is readily available, primarily in the northeastern United States.

The *Pulse Check* has been the most useful source of information about current heroin use trends. It has reported that heroin use nationwide is still low but is increasing. Heroin use is generally higher in most areas of the Northeast and Midwest then in portions of the

South and West. The majority of heroin users are reported to be in their 30s or older, and they inject the drug. Also, an increasing number of adolescents and young adults now are beginning to use heroin, and some are shifting from inhaling to injecting the drug. Heroin dealers are trying to encourage this trend by packaging heroin for those who inject and for those who inhale in different ways. In some areas, heroin dealers have begun tempting new users by first offering the drug processed for smoking rather than injecting. Throughout the country, treatment providers are reporting an increase in persons seeking treatment for heroin, with most new clients being males older than 30 years of age who inject the drug.

The observations of the *Pulse Check* are supported by another ONDCP report, *Tracking the Incidence of Heroin Use*, which found evidence of increased heroin use among the same populations.[13] ONDCP will monitor the heroin situation closely to ensure that it appropriately responds to any signs that the situation is worsening.[14]

Emerging Drug Use Trends

The *Pulse Check* has reported that the use of other illicit drugs also is on the rise in certain areas of the country. Hallucinogens are increasingly popular in some cities, including Atlanta and New York. In other cities—including San Francisco, Denver, and Los Angeles—there are reports that amphetamine use, especially in combination with other drugs, is becoming a significant problem. In Florida and Texas, teenagers and college students are reported to be using ephedrine, a chemical precursor of amphetamine and a component of over-the-counter cold medications. It is often taken as a substitute for amphetamines, and its use could presage an increase in amphetamine use. Nearly all illicit drug users continue to combine alcohol with other drugs. The most recent *Pulse Check* found that nationwide, hallucinogens and amphetamines are now the most common among emerging drugs.

Endnotes

1. For a long-term perspective of trends in drug use, see Harrison, L., and Kopstein, A. "A Twenty-Plus Year Perspective on Adolescent Drug Use." Paper presented at the Annual Meeting of the American Society of Criminology, November 9-12, 1994, Miami, FL.

2. Califano, J. *Cigarette, Alcohol, Marijuana: Gateways to Illicit Drug Use*. Columbia University Center on Addiction and Substance Abuse. New York: October 1994.

3. *Drug Use Measurement: Strengths, Limitations, and Recommendations for Improvements*. United States General Accounting Office, Report to the Chairman, Committee on Government Operations, House of Representatives, June 1993. (GAO/PEMD-93-18).

4. ONDCP's *Pulse Check* is a quarterly report that summarizes and reports on the observations of street ethnographers, police officials, and treatment providers. It provides the only source of current, subjective information on drug use and availability. This information is in contrast with the comparatively out-of-date, objective profiles provided by drug surveys. *Pulse Check* data are intended to complement, not substitute for, traditional data sources. The value of *Pulse Check* lies in its timeliness. Information for the end of a particular quarter is available for use by policymakers within 30 days.

5. Existing prevalence surveys tend to produce unreliable estimates for this user population of chronic, hardcore drug user. For many reasons, chronic, hardcore drug users are difficult to locate and contact for interviews. Even if they are located and interviewed, a large portion of hardcore drug users often are involved in significant criminal activity and are prone to denial as a defensive technique, so they tend to downplay all of their negative behaviors, including drug use.

6. For a discussion of the methodology used to estimate the number of hardcore users of cocaine and heroin, see the report by Abt Associates, Inc., *What America's Users Spend on Illegal Drugs, 1981-1991*, prepared under contract to ONDCP, July 1993.

7. The 1991 MTF survey reported that the percentage of students disapproving of regular marijuana use declined from the previous year, reversing a 13-year trend.

8. The *Pulse Check* also reports marijuana use is on the rise, particularly among teenagers and persons in their early twenties. Use is reported to be on the rise everywhere in the country.

47

Most users are young, but marijuana also is being used by older heroin and cocaine users. Individuals seeking treatment generally consider marijuana to be a secondary drug to alcohol and other drugs. However, users seeking treatment in many areas of the country have begun to indicate that they have problems with marijuana on its own.

9. Each school year, PRIDE, a private national drug prevention organization based in Atlanta, GA, interviews more than 200,000 junior high and high school students about the use and availability of drugs and alcohol. Although the data are not nationally representative, the information collected by PRIDE provides much insight into drug use patterns and trends among the Nation's youth.

10. Califano, J. *Cigarette, Alcohol, Marijuana: Gateways to Illicit Drug Use*. Columbia University Center on Addiction and Substance Abuse. New York: October 1994.

11. In general, national prevalence surveys are of little value in exposing the nature and extent of heroin use in the United States. The 1993 NHSDA reported a decline in the number of past-month users, but the decline was not judged to be statistically significant.

12. For more discussion about the conditions for a heroin epidemic, see BOTEC Analysis Corp.'s "Heroin Situation Assessment," a report prepared for the Office of National Drug Control Policy, January 1992.

13. Hunt, D., and Rhodes, W. *Tracking the Incidence of Heroin Use*. Abt Associates, Inc., 1993.

14. ONDCP is reviewing the heroin situation and developing a new heroin strategy. For more discussion, refer to the ONDCP's *National Drug Control Strategy*, Chapter VIII, "Action Plan for Strengthening Interdiction and International Efforts."

Chapter 5

Drug Use and Its Consequences

The heavy toll drug use exacts on the United States is most easily measured by the criminal and medical costs imposed on and paid for by the Nation's taxpaying citizens. One estimate places the total cost of drug use at $67 billion.[1] Almost 70 percent of this is attributable to the costs of crimes; the remainder reflects medical and death-related costs. Research has shown that drug users, especially those who are most severely addicted, are responsible for many of these crimes. Furthermore, the expense of building new jails and prisons adds to this estimate because the bulk of the incarcerated population growth stems from drug law violations. A large percentage of the increase in drug-related homicides, especially among youth, is also related to drug use and drug trafficking. Any reasonable strategy aimed at reducing the crime, violence, and health consequences related to drug use must include steps to address the full range of problems associated with chronic, hardcore drug use.

Drugs, Crime, and Violence

Nowhere are the consequences of illicit drug use and drug trafficking more visible than in the magnitude and pattern of drug-related violence. Nationally, the number of drug-related murders has risen

Excerpted from *National Drug Control Strategy*, Office of National Drug Control Policy, The White House, February 1995. A copy of the entire report may be purchased from the U.S. Government Printing Office, Superintendent of Documents, Mail Stop: SSOP, Washington, DC 20402-9328.

steadily since the mid-1980s, peaking at 7.4 percent of all murders in 1989 (see Figure 5.1). Since then the rate has declined to 5.2 percent of all murders, but this level of drug-related violence still is unacceptable.

	1986	1987	1988	1989	1990	1991	1992	1993
Total murders	19,257	17,963	17,971	18,954	20,273	21,676	22,540	24,526
Murder related to narcotic drugs laws	751	880	1,006	1,403	1,358	1,344	1,285	1,287
Percent of all murders	3.9	4.9	5.6	7.4	6.7	6.2	5.7	5.2

Source: Bureau of Justice Statistics. Drug and Crime Facts, 1993-1994.

Figure 5.1. Drug-Related Murders: United States, 1986-93.

More troubling is the change in the age-specific pattern for murders during this period. A recent study on youth, violence, and the illicit drug industry identified two major changes that have occurred between 1985 and 1992.[2] Age-specific statistics indicate the following:

• The number of homicides committed by youth ages 18 and younger has more than doubled, while there has been no growth in homicide rates by adults ages 24 and older.

• The number of homicides committed by juveniles involving guns has more than doubled, while there has been no change in the number of homicides committed by juveniles not involving guns.

The study speculates that these changes may relate to the nature of illegal drug markets, the predatory practices of drug dealers, and the inability of the juvenile justice system to adequately deal with violent juvenile offenders. The study notes with particular concern the practice of drug dealers actively recruiting juveniles and arming them with guns because they are not subject to the same criminal penalties as older individuals. This practice in large part is responsible for today's high levels of drug-related violence among juveniles.

50

Drug Use and Its Consequences

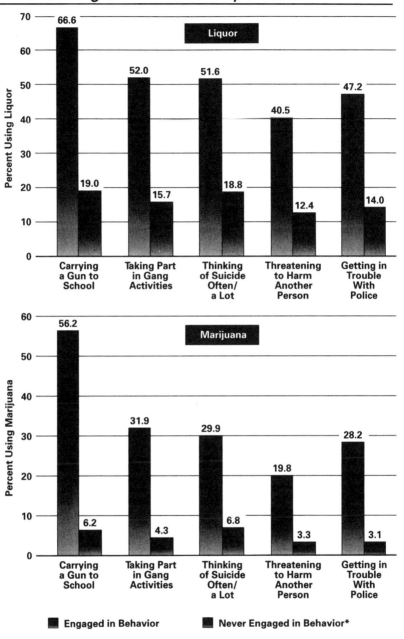

Engaged in Behavior **Never Engaged in Behavior***

* For "Thinking of Suicide Often/A Lot," the responses are never, seldom, and some.

Source: 1993-94 PRIDE USA Survey

Figure 5.2. *Use of Liquor and Marijuana Among 6th-8th Graders According to Engagement in Violent Behavior, 1993-94.*

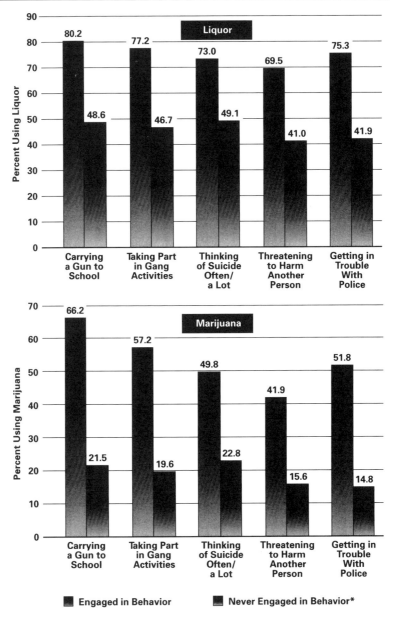

* For "Thinking of Suicide Often/A Lot," the responses are never, seldom, and some.

Source: 1993-94 PRIDE USA Survey

Figure 5.3. Use of Liquor and Marijuana Among 9th-12th Graders According to Engagement in Violent Behavior, 1993-94.

The Parent Resource Institute for Drug Education (PRIDE) has investigated the correlation between violent behavior and the use of various drugs. The most recent PRIDE survey demonstrated strong supporting evidence for a link between drug use and violent crime among the Nation's youth (see Figures 5.2 and 5.3).[3] The survey reported that students who bring guns to school, participate in gang activities, threaten a teacher or another student at school, contemplate suicide, or are in trouble with the police, are more likely to use drugs than are students who do not engage in these behaviors. In addition, the study found the following:

- A relationship exists between cocaine use and violence. Of the students surveyed, 4.3 percent of those in junior high school and 7.4 percent of those in high school reported that they carried guns to school. Of those in high school who reported having carried guns to school, 31 percent used cocaine; of those who never carried guns to school, only 2 percent used cocaine. The same relationship was found among junior high school students: 27 percent of those who had carried guns to school reported using cocaine, whereas less than 1 percent of those who never carried guns to school reported using cocaine.

- An ever stronger relationship exists between marijuana use and violence. For high school students, 66 percent of those who had carried guns to school used marijuana. For junior high school students, 56 percent of those who had carried guns to school used marijuana.

- Marijuana and cocaine use and gang activity also were highly related. Fourteen percent of high school students and 15 percent of junior high school students claimed to have participated in some type of gang activity. Nineteen percent of those in gangs reported cocaine use, compared with 2 percent of those who were not in gangs.

Drugs, drug use, and crime are inextricably linked, and progress in reducing drug use will have a direct and positive impact on reducing criminal activity. Drug users often commit criminal offenses such as theft and prostitution to support an existing drug habit. There also is a certain amount of violence associated with the drug market, both violence from the effects of the drugs, such as cocaine-induced psychosis, and violence between rural distributors competing for market advantage. Of those incarcerated for violent offenses in Federal and State prisons in 1991, 55 percent of Federal inmates and 57 percent of State inmates reported regular use of an illicit drug at some point in the past. One-quarter of inmates in prison for violent offenses committed the offenses while under the influence of drugs. Many of these inmates reported committing crimes to obtain money for drugs.[4]

The National Institute of Justice's (NIJ's) Drug Use Forecasting (DUF) program also has demonstrated the strength of the drug-crime relationship.[5] The DUF program assesses drug use among those arrested and charged with crimes by taking urine specimens from a sample of arrested individuals and testing the specimens for the presence of 10 drugs. In 1993 the 23 DUF sites around the Nation reported that more than 50 percent of arrestees tested positive for an illicit substance.[6] Among the sites, positive tests for cocaine ranged from 19 to 66 percent in males and from 19 to 70 percent in females. Tests showed that heroin and opiate use ranged from 1 to 28 percent for males and from 3 to 23 percent for females. Not surprisingly, the DUF sites that experienced the highest rates of drug prevalence are located in cities with high crime rates.

An independent study by the National Institute on Drug Abuse (NIDA) also presents data on the extent of illegal activity among drug users.[7] Figure 5.4 indicates a high incidence of criminal activity among drug users who are not in treatment. Approximately one-half of the respondents in the study reported legal sources of income, but one-half also reported illegal sources. Of those reporting legal income, 38 percent reported receiving support from family and friends, 46 percent reported some work-related income, and 47 percent reported that they derived income from public assistance. Of those reporting illegal sources of income, 42 percent reported drug-related income, 30 percent reported income from property crime, and 23 percent reported income from prostitution.

The following study findings indicate the key role drug use plays in the total number of accidental deaths due to driving under the influence of alcohol and other drugs each year:

- From January 1988 through July 1989, 18.2 percent of the 643 New York City drivers who died within 48 hours of being involved in an automobile accident tested positive for cocaine.[8]

- Almost 60 percent of reckless-driving arrestees in Memphis, Tennessee, who were not under the influence of alcohol tested positive for illicit drugs—33 percent for marijuana, 13 percent

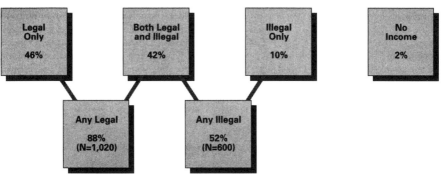

LEGAL SOURCES:

(of those with any legal income)

Public assistance	47%
Paid job, salary, self-employment	46%
Family, friends	38%
Social Security, disability	13%
Unemployment	2%

ILLEGAL SOURCES:

(of those with any illegal income)

Drug-related *(Median amount of drug-related income, $450)*	42%
Property crimes *(Median amount of property crime income, $450)*	30%
Commercial sex *(Median amount of commercial sex income, $300)*	42%
Violent crimes	2%

MEDIAN INCOME AMOUNTS (past month)

Total Sample:

Median legal income	$320
Median illegal income	$35
Median total income	$630

Of Those Reporting Illegal Income:

Median legal income	$280
Median illegal income	$448
Median total income	$900

[1] All percentages are adjusted for missing responses due to recall or refusal.

[2] "Paid job, salary, self-employment" may include hustling or day work paid in cash; not all of this income is likely to be legal.

[3] Due to skewed distributions for income amounts, median legal and illegal income do not add to median total income.

Figure 5.4. *Income Amounts,[1,2,3] Past 30 Days (N=1,154).*

for cocaine, and 12 percent for both drugs. Of those who were intoxicated, 85 percent also tested positive for marijuana and cocaine.[9]

To reduce the rate of criminal activity associated with chronic, hardcore drug use, the Nation must address the problems of the chronic, hardcore user. The fastest and most cost-effective way to accomplish this objective is to force more chronic, hardcore drug users into treatment.[10]

Drug Arrests

The Federal Bureau of Investigation reported an estimated 1,126,300 total arrests for drug law violations in the United States in 1993. These offenders are straining the criminal justice system and in some instances taking up prison space that is needed to incarcerate violent offenders. Figure 5.5 shows that this is below the peak level of arrests of 1,361,700 in 1989; however, it should be noted that arrests in 1993 represent the second highest level on record. Arrests for drug offenses accounted for 8 percent of all arrests nationwide.

	1988	1989	1990	1991	1992	1993
Total arrests	13,812,300	14,340,900	14,195,100	14,211,900	14,075,100	14,036,300
Drug-related arrests	1,155,200	1,361,700	1,089,500	1,010,000	1,066,400	1,126,300
Percent of all arrests	8.4	9.5	7.7	7.1	7.6	8.0

Source: National Uniform Crime Reporting Program, Federal Bureau of Investigation, 1988-93.

Figure 5.5. Drug-Related Arrests: United States, 1988-93.

The growth in the number of persons arrested for drug law violations is the principal reason for the growth in the prison population. In turn, the increase in the number of persons arrested for drug law violations reflects increasingly stringent drug laws, and in particular, the enforcement of mandatory minimum sentences. According to the Department of Justice, Bureau of Justice Statistics (BJS), in 1994 the Nation's Federal and State prison population exceeded 1 million for the first time in history.[11] At the end of June 1994, State prisons held 919,143 inmates, and Federal prisons held 93,708 inmates.

Drugs and Health

The health costs of drug use are growing quickly, especially as an increasing number of chronic, hardcore drug users seek medical attention for health problems relating to their long-term drug use. Nowhere is this growth in health costs more clearly visible than in the Nation's hospitals. For example, 466,900 drug-related hospital emergency room (ER) episodes were reported to the Drug Abuse Warning Network (DAWN)[12] in 1993. The rate of drug-related ER episodes per 100,000 of the total U.S. population increased 22 percent, from 167 in 1990 to 204 in 1993. Nearly one-half of all episodes involved the use of two or more drugs. The increase in cocaine-related ER episodes is the principal reason for increased total drug-related ER episodes from 1985 through 1993 (except for 1990). The percentage of drug-related ER episodes caused by cocaine use increased from 1 percent in 1978 to 26 percent in 1993. During the same period, heroin-related ER episodes increased from 4 to 13 percent of total drug-related ER episodes.

A drug-related hospital ER episode represents a valuable opportunity for referring drug abusers to appropriate treatment programs. Unfortunately, the present lack of drug treatment capacity prevents inpatient hospital services from helping drug users in their care and making referrals to treatment facilities. ERs across the Nation are burdened with these types of medical cases. This issue is discussed in more detail later in this chapter.

Figure 5.6 shows that in 1993 the most frequently cited reason for a drug-related ER visit was "overdose," accounting for 53 percent of all drug-related ER episodes. "Unexpected reaction" and "chronic effects" were the next most frequently cited reasons. Figure 5.7 shows recent trends in heroin and cocaine ER episodes. Heroin-related episodes have been increasing steadily since the early 1980s, and they reached their highest level in 1993. DAWN study findings for heroin-related ER episodes include the following:

- In 1993, 41 percent of heroin-related episodes occurred among individuals between the ages of 34 and 44. Heroin episodes have more than doubled for this age group since 1988.

Figure 5.6. Reason for Emergency Room Contact, 1993.

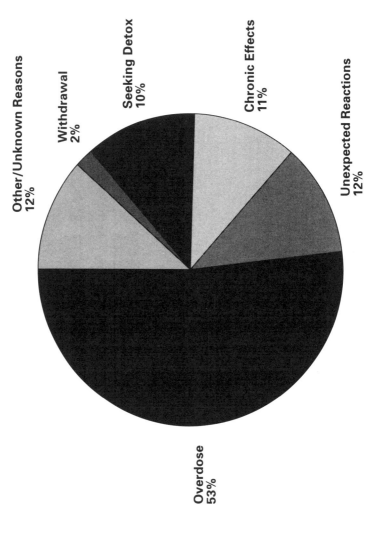

Other/Unknown Reasons
12%

Withdrawal
2%

Seeking Detox
10%

Chronic Effects
11%

Unexpected Reactions
12%

Overdose
53%

Source: Drug Abuse Warning Network, Substance Abuse and Mental Health Services Administration, 1993

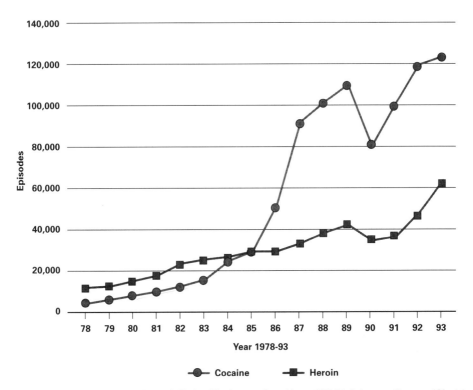

Figure 5.7. Heroin and Cocaine Hospital Emergency Room Episodes, 1978-93.

- An analysis of the heroin data[13] suggests that the record number of cases of heroin-related ER episodes could be the result of the cumulative adverse health effects of prolonged heroin use. The analysis also suggests that heroin-related episodes will continue to increase as long as chronic, hardcore heroin use continues unabated.

DAWN reports that the strong upward trend in cocaine-related ER episodes has stabilized, but the episodes remain at record levels. For example, an estimated 123,300 cocaine-related episodes were reported in 1993. DAWN reports the following findings:

- In 1993, 43 percent of cocaine-related episodes occurred among individuals between the ages of 26 and 34.

- "Seeking detoxification" was the most commonly cited reason for an emergency department visit by cocaine users, followed by "unexpected reaction" and "chronic effects."

- Since 1990 the number of cocaine-related ER episodes for those older than 35 years has more than doubled. As is the case for heroin, it appears that prolonged cocaine use has an adverse effect on the health of its users.

The number of marijuana-related ER episodes has increased rapidly in recent years. Total episodes rose from 20,000 in 1990 to 29,200 in 1993—a 46 percent increase. Marijuana was likely to be mentioned in combination with other drugs, particularly alcohol and cocaine. In 1993 alcohol and cocaine were mentioned in 50 percent of marijuana-related episodes; only 20 percent of marijuana episodes involved marijuana alone.

A strong linkage exists between certain diseases and illicit intravenous (IV) drug use; this type of drug use and the behaviors related to it harm users mostly by exposing them to HIV (Human Immuno-deficiency Virus), hepatitis, and other diseases. However, chronic, hardcore drug users also exhibit high-risk sexual behaviors that are associated with transmission of certain diseases. A recent study that compared crack-cocaine users with nonusers found that users' high-risk sexual practices accounted for their having higher rates of HIV infection.[14] According to the Centers for Disease Control and Prevention (CDC), almost one-third of AIDS (Acquired Immune Deficiency

Syndrome) cases were associated with IV drug users. The CDC also reports that almost 60 percent of children under age 13 with AIDS contracted the disease from mothers who were IV drug users or who were the sex partners of IV drug users.

Targeting Chronic, Hardcore Drug Use

Chronic, hardcore drug use is clearly related to the high levels of crime, health problems, and violence in cities, towns, and neighborhoods across the Nation. This *Strategy's* immediate priority, therefore, is to target the problems created by this population of drug users. The following evidence supports this prioritization:

- Chronic, hardcore drug users account for two-thirds of the total amount of cocaine consumed in the United States, even though they comprise only 20 percent of all cocaine users. Therefore, it is the chronic, hardcore drug users who keep the major drug traffickers in business.

- Chronic, hardcore drug use causes severe and long-term health consequences. A Department of Health and Human Services (HHS) study of the record number of heroin medical emergencies in 1993 suggests that prolonged heroin use produces cumulative adverse health effects.

- When a user is going through periods of heavy or addictive drug use, the frequency and severity of his or her criminal activity rises dramatically. Drug-related criminal activity is one of the main reasons for the substantial growth of U.S. prison and jail populations.

The Case for Treating Hardcore Drug Users

When effectively administered, drug treatment can reduce the consequences of illicit drug use. It has been proven that when drug-dependent individuals receive appropriate treatment, they decrease their drug use, decrease their criminal activity, increase their employment, improve their social and interpersonal functioning, and improve their physical health.

Reducing health care costs created by illicit drug use requires a comprehensive response. First, drug prevention efforts must increase their focus on populations who are at risk for drug use. Making individuals aware of the health consequences of illicit drug use may ultimately prevent the onset or continuation of chronic, hardcore drug use and related health-threatening behaviors. Second, the chronic, hardcore drug users, who are suffering the health consequences of prolonged drug use, must be provided access to effective treatment for their addiction and related health problems.

Numerous studies confirm the fact that treatment of chronic, hardcore addicts, both within the correctional setting and in community-based programs, is the most cost-effective response and the course of action that makes the most practical sense.

The most compelling demonstration of the cost-effectiveness of treatment is from a recent California study assessing drug and alcoholism treatment effectiveness.[15] This study found that in 1992 alone, the cost of treating approximately 150,000 drug users in California was $209 million. Approximately $1.5 billion was saved while these individuals were in treatment and in the first year after their treatment. Most of these savings were in the form of reductions in drug-related crime (a two-thirds decline in the level of criminal activity among these drug users was observed from pretreatment to posttreatment).

Even if incarcerating drug addicts on a long-term basis were feasible or affordable for States and localities, such a measure would not address the addict's drug habit and its destructive consequences. Drug treatment must be available for chronic, hardcore users, whether they are inside or outside the criminal justice system, to ensure that progress is made in reducing the negative health and crime consequences of drug use.

The Nation must utilize every opportunity to get chronic, hardcore drug users into treatment. Locking up drug users and drug addicts does not go far enough to protect communities from the problems created by drug use. The Nation must recognize that, eventually, most of these users will be released back to the communities from which they came, and unless they have received treatment for their problems, many will continue to prey on others to support their drug habit or to continue drug-dealing activities. Clearly, drug treatment is vital to protecting Americans from the serious and violent consequences of illicit drug use.

Addressing the Shortage of Drug Treatment Capacity

The United States currently lacks adequate treatment capacity to treat all those individuals who need drug treatment. According to HHS estimates, more than 1 million people who need some type of drug treatment are unable to access programs. Closing the treatment gap is a national priority, and the Administration continues to press for more treatment capacity, especially within the criminal justice system.

As the success of managed care has shown, treatment capacity can be allocated more efficiently. For example, managed care in Massachusetts has demonstrated that more efficient use of resources increases access to treatment and reduces costs. Programs in Minnesota similarly have shown that by managing care, costs can be contained, and resources can be applied more effectively.

HHS estimates that more than 3.8 million users of illicit drugs exhibit behavioral problems or physical manifestations resulting from their illicit drug use. For some users with less acute problems, testing and monitoring are enough to reduce or eliminate their drug use. Others are able to end drug use on their own with the support of family and friends. However, some chronic, hardcore users need more intensive treatment. HHS estimates that 2.4 million of the more than 3.8 million users need some type of drug treatment program. As the next section shows, the current treatment system lacks the capacity to treat this number of users.

Treatment Capacity Outside the Criminal Justice System

HHS estimates that in 1994 the drug treatment system had the capacity to provide specialized drug treatment services to about 1.4 million individuals. Therefore, out of the 2.4 million drug users who could benefit from specialty drug treatment, about 1 million (or 40 percent) could not access such treatment at any time during the year.

According to the 1992 National Drug and Alcohol Treatment Utilization Survey (NDATUS), an estimated 945,000 clients were involved in specialty drug abuse treatment as of September 30, 1992.[16] Outpatient services accounted for 87 percent of all client services. Most outpatient clients were enrolled in drug-free programs or programs not utilizing pharmacological interventions such as methadone (74 percent). Some, however, did receive methadone (14 percent). Twelve percent of clients were in 24-hour treatment—11 percent in rehabilitation and 1 percent in detoxification. The 1992 NDATUS also revealed the following:

- Although the number of providers and clients reporting to NDATUS has increased substantially since 1980, the broad characteristics of treatment services and clients in treatment have stayed relatively the same.

- Of those in treatment, 60 percent were white, 22 percent were African American, and 15 percent were Hispanic. The racial and ethnic composition of clients changed very little between 1980 and 1992.

- The ratio of males to females in treatment was more than 2 to 1.

The Federal Government also provides treatment for military personnel and veterans. In 1993 the Department of Veterans Affairs provided substance abuse treatment for almost 160,000 patients in 327 programs. Of these programs, 196 specialized, inpatient programs served 54,195 drug users, while the 131 outpatient programs served 105,800 drug users.

Treatment Capacity Inside the Criminal Justice System

The most recent DUF data indicate that the criminal justice system offers an opportunity to identify those individuals who need treatment and to match their specific needs with appropriate drug treatment programs. On any given day, more than 4 million people are under the care or custody of a correctional agency, either on probation, on parole, in jail, or in Federal or State prisons.

The criminal justice system can intervene to affect an individual's drug use through a variety of means. In some cases, drug testing is adequate to deter continued drug use, especially when it is a condition of probation or parole. For those in jail or prison, drug treatment programs may involve individual counseling, group counseling, or support group participation. [Treatment for this population is discussed in detail in Chapter V of the Office of National Drug Control Policy's *National Drug Control Strategy*.]

A 1991 BJS survey reported that of those inmates sentenced for violent offenses, 55 percent of Federal inmates and 57 percent of State inmates reported using drugs regularly, and 43 percent of Federal inmates and 46 percent of State inmates reported using drugs in the month prior to their offense.[17] Twenty-five percent of Federal inmates and 28 percent of State inmates reported that they were under the influence of drugs while committing the offense for which they were incarcerated. Many of these inmates were receiving treatment while in prison. At the time of the survey, about 43 percent of Federal inmates and 48 percent of State inmates who had used drugs in the month prior to their offenses had been enrolled in prison treatment programs at some point during their incarcerations. More than 20 percent in each population had completed treatment programs since admission to prison.

Enrolling more drug users in treatment programs is one of the surest ways to counter the severe, negative effects on the U.S. economy, health care system, and quality of life that result from illicit drug use. More than 1 million chronic, hardcore users are caught in the gap in available treatment services; many of the available programs rely on modalities of treatment that do not address these users' problems. If this treatment shortfall remains unaddressed, the economic, health care, and social problems created by chronic, hardcore users will become even more expensive and complex in the years to come.

Endnotes

1. *Substance Abuse: The Nation's Number One Health Problem, Key Indicators for Policy*. Institute for Health Policy. Brandeis University. 1993.

2. Blumstein, A. *Youth, Violence, and the Illicit Drug Industry*. H. John Heinz II School of Public Policy and Management, Working Paper Series. July 1994.

3. *PRIDE Questionnaire Report, 1992-93 National Summary— USA, Grades 6 to 12*. PRIDE, Inc. August 3, 1994.

4. Harlowe, C.W. Comparing Federal and State Inmates, 1991. U.S. Department of Justice, Office of Justice Programs, Bureau of Justice Statistics. NCJ-145864. Tables 13-15. September 1994.

5. DUF data clearly are useful for exposing the link between drug use and other criminal activities. Beyond this, DUF data also reveal much about the extent of drug use in the United

States. The data show steady levels of cocaine use and increasing levels of marijuana use—trends confirmed by other data sources.

6. *Drug Use Forecasting 1993 Annual Report on Adult Arrestees: Drugs and Crime in America's Cities and Drug Use Forecasting 1993 Annual Report on Juvenile Arrestees/Detainees: Drugs and Crime in America's Cities.* Washington, DC: National Institute of Justice, Office of Justice Programs. According to the 1993 DUF Reports, there were increased rates of marijuana use, largely unchanged rates of cocaine and opiate use, and slightly increased rates of multiple drug use among male arrestees. Cocaine remains the principal drug of use among male arrestees. Young males were less likely to test positive for cocaine than older males. Among females, the data show a slight decline in the prevalence of cocaine, largely unchanged rates of marijuana and opiate use, and a slight increase in multiple drug use.

7. Needle, R., and Mills, A. *Drug Procurement Practices of the Out-of-Treatment Chronic Drug Abuser.* U.S. Department of Health and Human Services, National Institute on Drug Abuse. National Institutes of Health Publication No. 94-3820. 1994.

8. *Drugs, Crime, and The Criminal Justice System: A National Report from the Bureau of Justice Statistics.* U.S. Department of Justice, Office of Justice Programs, Bureau of Justice Statistics. NCJ-133652. December 1992. p. 13.

9. "Testing Reckless Drivers for Cocaine and Marijuana." Abstract, *New England Journal of Medicine.*

10. NIJ and the Office of National Drug Control Policy (ONDCP) plan to work closely to pursue a research agenda focusing on issues of drug procurement and drug use. The DUF program offers tremendous possibilities as a research platform. NIJ and ONDCP will work closely to develop assessment and interview strategies that capitalize on the opportunity DUF presents to interview approximately 30,000 arrestees within hours of their apprehension in jails throughout major U.S. cities.

11. *State and Federal Prison Population Tops One Million.* Department of Justice, BJS Advance Release. October 27, 1994.

12. *Estimates from the Drug Abuse Warning Network, Advance Report No. 8.* U.S. Department of Health and Human Services, Substance Abuse and Mental Health Services Administration, Office of Applied Studies. October 1994.

13. Based on analysis conducted by the Substance Abuse and Mental Health Service Administration, Office of Applied Studies.

14. See Edlin, B., Irwin, K., et. al. "Intersecting Epidemics—Crack Cocaine Use and HIV Infection Among Inner-City Young Adults." *New England Journal of Medicine.* November 1994, pp. 1422-1427.

15. Evaluating Recovery Services: *The California Drug and Alcohol Treatment Assessment (CALDATA).* July 1994.

16. Overview of the National Drug and Alcoholism Treatment Utilization Survey (NDATUS): 1992 and 1980-1992. Advance Report Number 9. U.S. Department of Health and Human Services, Substance Abuse and Mental Health Services Administration. January 1995. This survey classifies drug users into three groups: alcohol only, drug only, and both. The survey provides a snapshot of treatment providers and clients on September 30, 1992.

17. Harlow, C.W. *Comparing Federal and State Inmates, 1991.* U.S. Department of Justice, Office of Justice Programs, BJS. NCJ-145864. Table 15. September 1994.

Chapter 6

Street Terms: Drugs and the Drug Trade

A single term or similar terms may refer to various drugs or have different meanings, reflecting geographic and demographic variations in slang. All known meanings and spellings are included. No attempt was made to determine which usage is most frequent or widespread. Different definitions for a single term are separated by semi-colons (;). The use of commas (,) and the connective "and" indicates that the term refers to the use of the specified drugs in combination.

For source information, please contact the ONDCP Drugs & Crime Clearinghouse at 1-800-666-3332.

A

A—LSD; amphetamine
AD—PCP
Abe—$5 worth of drugs
Abe's cabe—$5 bill
Abolic—veterinary steroid
Acapulco gold—marijuana from S.W. Mexico
Acapulco red—marijuana
Ace—marijuana; PCP
Acid—LSD

Acid head—LSD user
Adam—MDMA
African black—marijuana
African bush—marijuana
African woodbine—marijuana cigarette
Agonies—withdrawal symptoms
Ah-pen-yen—opium
Aimies—amphetamine; amyl nitrite
AIP—heroin from Afghanistan, Iran, and Pakistan

Information in this chapter was provided by the Office of National Drug Control Policy, Drugs and Crime Clearinghouse Fact Sheet NCJ-151622 dated March 1995.

Air blast—inhalant
Airhead—marijuana user
Airplane—marijuana
Alice B. Toklas—marijuana brownie
All lit up—under the influence of drugs
All star—user of multiple drugs
All-American drug—cocaine
Alpha-ET—alpha-ethyltyptamine
Ames—amyl nitrite
Amidone—methadone
Amoeba—PCP
Amp—amphetamine
Amp joint—marijuana cigarette laced with some form of narcotic
Amped-out—fatigue after using amphetamines
Amping—accelerated heartbeat
AMT—dimethyltryptamine
Amys—amylnitrate
Anadrol—oral steroid
Anatrofin—injectable steroid
Anavar—oral steroid
Angel—PCP
Angel dust—PCP
Angel hair—PCP
Angel mist—PCP
Angel poke—PCP
Angie—cocaine
Angola—marijuana
Animal—LSD
Animal tranq—PCP
Animal tranquilizer—PCP
Antifreeze—heroin
Apache—fentanyl
Apple jacks—crack
Aries—heroin
Aroma of men—isobutyl nitrite
Artillery—equipment for injecting drugs
Ashes—marijuana
Atom bomb—marijuana and heroin
Atshitshi—marijuana
Aunt Hazel—heroin
Aunt Mary—marijuana
Aunt Nora—cocaine
Aunti—opium
Aunti Emma—opium
Aurora borealis—PCP

B

B—amount of marijuana to fill a matchbox
B-40—cigar laced with marijuana and dipped in malt liquor
B.J.'s—crack
Babe—drug used for detoxification
Baby—marijuana
Baby bhang—marijuana
Baby habit—occasional use of drugs
Babysit—guide someone through first drug experience
Baby T—crack
Backbreakers—LSD and strychnine
Back door—residue left in a pipe
Backjack—injecting opium
Back to back—smoking crack after injecting heroin or heroin used after smoking crack
Backtrack—allow blood to flow back into a needle during injection
Backup—prepare vein for injection
Backwards—depressant
Bad bundle—inferior quality heroin
Bad—crack
Bad go—bad reaction to a drug
Bad seed—peyote; heroin; marijuana
Bag—container for drugs
Bag bride—crack-smoking prostitute
Bag man—person who transports money
Bagging—using inhalant
Bale—marijuana
Ball—crack
Balling—vaginally implanted cocaine
Balloon—heroin supplier
Ballot—heroin
Bam—depressant; amphetamine
Bambalacha—marijuana
Bambs—depressant
Bang—to inject a drug; inhalant
Bank bandit pills—depressant
Bar—marijuana
Barb—depressant
Barbies—depressant
Barbs—cocaine
Barrels—LSD

Base—cocaine; crack
Baseball—crack
Base crazies—searching on hands and knees for crack
Base head—person who bases
Bash—marijuana
Basuco—cocaine; coca paste residue sprinkled on marijuana or regular cigarette
Bathtub speed—methcathinone
Batt—IV needle
Battery acid—LSD
Batu—smokable methamphetamine
Bazooka—cocaine; crack
Bazulco—cocaine
Beam me up Scottie—crack dipped in PCP
Beamer—crack user
Beans—amphetamine; depressant; mescaline
Beast—LSD
Beat artist—person selling bogus drugs
Beat vials—vials containing sham crack to cheat buyers
Beautiful boulders—crack
Bebe—crack
Bedbugs—fellow addicts
Beemers—crack
Behind the scale—to weigh and sell cocaine
Beiging—chemicals altering cocaine to make it appear a higher purity
Belladonna—PCP
Belt—effects of drugs
Belushi—cocaine and heroin
Belyando spruce—marijuana
Bender—drug party
Bennie—amphetamine
Benz—amphetamine
Bernice—cocaine
Bernie—cocaine
Bernie's flakes—cocaine
Bernie's gold dust—cocaine
Bhang—marijuana, Indian term
Big bag—heroin
Big bloke—cocaine
Big C—cocaine

Big 8—1/8 kilogram of crack
Big D—LSD
Big H—heroin
Big Harry—heroin
Big flake—cocaine
Big man—drug supplier
Big O—opium
Big rush—cocaine
Bill Blass—crack
Billie hoke—cocaine
Bindle—small packet of drug powder; heroin
Bing—enough of a drug for one injection
Bingers—crack addicts
Bingo—to inject a drug
Bings—crack
Birdie powder—heroin; cocaine
Biscuit—50 rocks of crack
Bite one's lips—to smoke marijuana
Biz—bag or portion of drugs
Black—opium; marijuana
Black acid—LSD; LSD and PCP
Black and white—amphetamine
Black bart—marijuana
Black beauties—depressant; amphetamine
Black birds—amphetamine
Black bombers—amphetamine
Black ganga—marijuana resin
Black gold—high potency marijuana
Black gungi—marijuana from India
Black gunion—marijuana
Black hash—opium and hashish
Black mo/black moat—highly potent marijuana
Black mollies—amphetamine
Black mote—marijuana mixed with honey
Black pearl—heroin
Black pill—opium pill
Black rock—crack
Black Russian—hashish mixed with opium
Black star—LSD
Black stuff—heroin
Black sunshine—LSD
Black tabs—LSD

71

Black tar—heroin
Black whack—PCP
Blacks—amphetamine
Blanco—heroin
Blanket—marijuana cigarette
Blanks—low quality drugs
Blast—to smoke marijuana; to smoke crack
Blast a joint—to smoke marijuana
Blast a roach—to smoke marijuana
Blast a stick—to smoke marijuana
Blasted—under the influence of drugs
Blizzard—white cloud in a pipe used to smoke cocaine
Block—marijuana
Block busters—depressant
Blonde—marijuana
Blotter—LSD; cocaine
Blotter acid—LSD
Blotter cube—LSD
Blow—cocaine; to inhale cocaine; to smoke marijuana
Blow a fix/blow a shot/blow the vein—injection misses the vein and is wasted in the skin
Blow a stick—to smoke marijuana
Blow blue—to inhale cocaine
Blowcaine—crack diluted with cocaine
Blow coke—to inhale cocaine
Blow one's roof—to smoke marijuana
Blow smoke—to inhale cocaine
Blowing smoke—marijuana
Blowout—crack
Blow up—crack cut with lidocaine to increase size, weight, and street value
Blue—depressant; crack
Blue acid—LSD
Blue angels—depressant
Blue barrels—LSD
Blue birds—depressant
Blue boy—amphetamine
Blue bullets—depressant
Blue caps—mescaline
Blue chairs—LSD
Blue cheers—LSD
Blue de hue—marijuana from Vietnam
Blue devil—depressant

Blue dolls—depressant
Blue heaven—LSD
Blue heavens—depressant
Blue madman—PCP
Blue microdot—LSD
Blue mist—LSD
Blue moons—LSD
Blue sage—marijuana
Blue sky blond—high potency marijuana from Columbia
Blue tips—depressant
Blue vials—LSD
Blunt—marijuana inside a cigar; marijuana and cocaine inside a cigar
Bo-bo—marijuana
Boat—PCP
Bobo—crack
Bobo bush—marijuana
Body packer—person who ingests crack or cocaine to transport it
Body stuffer—person who ingests crack vials to avoid prosecution
Bogart a joint—salivate on a marijuana cigarette; refuse to share
Bohd—marijuana; PCP
Bolasterone—injectable steroid
Bolivian marching powder—cocaine
Bolo—crack
Bolt—isobutyl nitrite
Bomb—crack; heroin; large marijuana cigarette; high potency heroin
Bomb squad—crack-selling crew
Bomber—marijuana cigarette
Bombido—injectable amphetamine; heroin; depressant
Bombita—amphetamine; heroin; depressant
Bombs away—heroin
Bone—marijuana; $50 piece of crack
Bonecrusher—crack
Bones—crack
Bong—pipe used to smoke marijuana
Bonita—heroin
Boo—marijuana
Boom—marijuana
Boomers—psilocybin/psilocin
Boost—to inject a drug; to steal
Boost and shoot—steal to support a habit

Booster—to inhale cocaine
Boot—to inject a drug
Boot the gong—to smoke marijuana
Booted—under the influence of drugs
Boppers—amyl nitrite
Botray—crack
Bottles—crack vials; amphetamine
Boubou—crack
Boulder—crack; $20 worth of crack
Boulya—crack
Bouncing powder—cocaine
Boxed—in jail
Boy—heroin
Bozo—heroin
Brain damage—heroin
Brain ticklers—amphetamine
Breakdowns—$40 crack rock sold for $20
Break night—staying up all night until day break
Brewery—place where drugs are made
Brick—1 kilogram of marijuana; crack
Brick gum—heroin
Bridge up or bring up—ready a vein for injection
Britton—peyote
Broccoli—marijuana
Broker—go-between in a drug deal
Brown—heroin; marijuana
Brown bombers—LSD
Brown crystal—heroin
Brown dots—LSD
Brown rhine—heroin
Brown sugar—heroin
Brownies—amphetamine
Browns—amphetamine
Bubble gum—cocaine; crack
Buck—shoot someone in the head
Bud—marijuana
Buda—a high-grade marijuana joint filled with crack
Buffer—crack smoker; a woman who exchanges oral sex for crack
Bugged—annoyed; to be covered with sores and abscesses from repeated use of unsterile needles
Bull—narcotics agent or police officer
Bullet—isobutyl nitrite
Bullet bolt—inhalant

Bullia capital—crack
Bullion—crack
Bullyon—marijuana
Bumblebees—amphetamine
Bummer trip—unsettling and threatening experience from PCP intoxication
Bump—crack; fake crack; boost a high; hit of ketamine ($20)
Bundle—heroin
Bunk—fake cocaine
Burese—cocaine
Burn one—to smoke marijuana
Burn the main line—to inject a drug
Burned—purchase fake drugs
Burned out—collapse of veins from repeated injections; permanent impairment from drug abuse
Burnese—cocaine
Burnie—marijuana
Burnout—heavy abuser of drugs
Bush—cocaine; marijuana
Businessman's LSD—dimethyltryptamine
Businessman's trip—dimethyltryptamine
Businessman's special—dimethyltryptamine
Busted—arrested
Busters—depressant
Busy bee—PCP
Butt naked—PCP
Butter—marijuana; crack
Butter flower—marijuana
Buttons—mescaline
Butu—heroin
Buzz—under the influence of drugs
Buzz bomb—nitrous oxide

C

C—cocaine
C joint—place where cocaine is sold
C & M—cocaine and morphine
C-dust—cocaine
C-game—cocaine
Caballo—heroin
Cabello—cocaine

73

Caca—heroin
Cactus—mescaline
Cactus buttons—mescaline
Cactus head—mescaline
Cad/Cadillac—1 ounce
Cadillac—PCP
Cadillac express—methcathinone
Cakes—round discs of crack
Caine—cocaine; crack
California cornflakes—cocaine
California sunshine—LSD
Cam trip—high potency marijuana
Cambodian red/Cam red—marijuana
 from Cambodia
Came—cocaine
Can—marijuana; 1 ounce
Canadian black—marijuana
Canamo—marijuana
Canappa—marijuana
Cancelled stick—marijuana cigarette
Candy—cocaine; crack; depressant;
 amphetamine
Candy C—cocaine
Cannabinol—PCP
Cannabis tea—marijuana
Cap—crack; LSD
Caps—crack
Cap up—transfer bulk form drugs to
 capsules
Capital H—heroin
Caps—heroin; psilocybin/psilocin
Carburetor—crack stem attachment
Carga—heroin
Carmabis—marijuana
Carne—heroin
Carnie—cocaine
Carpet patrol—crack smokers search-
 ing the floor for crack
Carrie—cocaine
Carrie Nation—cocaine
Cartucho—package of marijuana ciga-
 rettes
Cartwheels—amphetamine
Casper the ghost—crack
Cat—methcathinone
Cat valium—ketamine
Catnip—marijuana cigarette
Caviar—crack

Cavite all star—marijuana
Cecil—cocaine
Chalk—methamphetamine; amphet-
 amine
Chalked up—under the influence of
 cocaine
Chalking—chemically altering the
 color of cocaine so it looks white
Chandoo/chandu—opium
Channel—vein into which a drug is
 injected
Channel swimmer—one who injects
 heroin
Charas—marijuana from India
Charge—marijuana
Charged up—under the influence of
 drugs
Charley—heroin
Charlie—cocaine
Chase—to smoke cocaine; to smoke
 marijuana
Chaser—compulsive crack user
Chasing the dragon—crack and heroin
Chasing the tiger—to smoke heroin
Cheap basing—crack
Check—personal supply of drugs
Cheeba—marijuana
Cheeo—marijuana
Chemical—crack
Chewies—crack
Chiba chiba—high potency marijuana
 from Columbia
Chicago black—marijuana, term from
 Chicago
Chicago green—marijuana
Chicken powder—amphetamine
Chicken scratch—searching on hands
 and knees for crack
Chicle—heroin
Chief—LSD; mescaline
Chieva—heroin
China cat—high potency heroin
China girl—fentanyl
China town—fentanyl
China White—fentanyl
Chinese molasses—opium
Chinese rod—heroin
Chinese tobacco—opium

Chip—heroin
Chipper—occasional Hispanic user
Chipping—using drugs occasionally
Chippy—cocaine
Chira—marijuana
Chocolate—opium; amphetamine
Chocolate chips—LSD
Chocolate ecstasy—crack made brown by adding chocolate milk powder during production
Cholly—cocaine
Chorals—depressant
Christina—amphetamine
Christmas rolls—depressant
Christmas tree—marijuana; depressant; amphetamine
Chronic—marijuana; marijuana mixed with crack
Chucks—hunger following withdrawal from heroin
Churus—marijuana
Cid—LSD
Cigarette paper—packet of heroin
Cigarrode cristal—PCP
Citrol—high potency marijuana, from Nepal
CJ—PCP
Clarity—MDMA
Clear up—stop drug use
Clicker—crack and PCP
Cliffhanger—PCP
Climax—crack; isobutyl nitrite; heroin
Climb—marijuana cigarette
Clips—rows of vials heat-sealed together
Clocking paper—profits from selling drugs
Closet baser—user of crack who prefers anonymity
Cloud—crack
Cloud nine—crack
Cluck—crack smoker
Co-pilot—amphetamine
Coasting—under the influence of drugs
Coasts to coasts—amphetamine
Coca—cocaine
Cocaine blues—depression after extended cocaine use

Cochornis—marijuana
Cocktail—cigarette laced with cocaine or crack; partially smoked marijuana cigarette inserted in regular cigarette
Cocoa puff—to smoke cocaine and marijuana
Coconut—cocaine
Coco rocks—dark brown crack made by adding chocolate pudding during production
Coco snow—benzocaine used as cutting agent for crack
Cod—large amount of money
Coffee—LSD
Coke—cocaine; crack
Coke bar—bar whore cocaine is openly used
Cola—cocaine
Cold turkey—sudden withdrawal from drugs
Coli—marijuana
Coliflor tostao—marijuana
Colorado cocktail—marijuana
Columbian—marijuana
Columbo—PCP
Columbus black—marijuana
Comeback—benzocaine and mannitol used to adulterate cocaine for conversion to crack
Come home—end a "trip" from LSD
Conductor—LSD
Connect—purchase drugs; supplier of illegal drugs
Contact lens—LSD
Cook—mix heroin with water; heating heroin to prepare it for injection
Cook down—process in which users liquify heroin in order to inhale it
Cooker—to inject a drug
Cookies—crack
Coolie—cigarette laced with cocaine
Cooler—cigarette laced with a drug
Cop—obtain drugs
Copping zones—specific areas where buyers can purchase drugs
Coral—depressant
Coriander seeds—cash
Cork the air—to inhale cocaine

Corrinne—cocaine
Cosa—marijuana
Cotics—heroin
Cotton—currency
Cotton brothers—cocaine, heroin and morphine
Courage pills—heroin; depressant
Course note—bill larger than $2
Cozmo's—PCP
Crack—cocaine
Crack attack—craving for crack
Crack back—crack and marijuana
Crack cooler—crack soaked in wine cooler
Cracker jacks—crack smokers
Crackers—LSD
Crack gallery—place where crack is bought and sold
Crack spot—area where people can purchase crack
Crank—methamphetamine; amphetamine; methcathinone
Cranking up—to inject a drug
Crap/crop—low quality heroin
Crash—sleep off effects of drugs
Crazy coke—PCP
Crazy Eddie—PCP
Crazy weed—marijuana
Credit card—crack stem
Crib—crack
Crimmie—cigarette laced with crack
Crink—methamphetamine
Cripple—marijuana cigarette
Cris—methamphetamine
Cristy—smokable methamphetamine
Crisscross—amphetamine
Cristina—methamphetamine
Croak—crack and methamphetamine
Cross tops—amphetamine
Crossroads—amphetamine
Crown crap—heroin
Crumbs—tiny pieces of crack
Crunch & Munch—crack
Cruz—opium from Veracruz, Mexico
Crying weed—marijuana
Crypto—methamphetamine
Crystal—methamphetamine; PCP; amphetamine; cocaine

Crystal joint—PCP
Crystal meth—methamphetamine
Crystal T—PCP
Crystal tea—LSD
Cube—1 ounce; LSD
Cubes—marijuana tablets
Culican—high potency marijuana from Mexico
Cupcakes—LSD
Cura—heroin
Cushion—vein into which a drug is injected
Cut—adulterate drugs
Cut-deck—heroin mixed with powdered milk
Cycline—PCP
Cyclones—PCP

D

D—LSD; PCP
Dabble—use drugs occasionally
Dagga—marijuana
Dama blanca—cocaine
Dance fever—fentanyl
Dawamesk—marijuana
Dead on arrival—heroin
Decadence—MDMA
Deca-duabolin—injectable steroid
Deck—1 to 15 grams of heroin, also known as a bag; packet of drugs
Deeda—LSD
Delatestryl—injectable steroid
Demo—crack stem; crack is a sample-size quantity
Demolish—crack
Dep-testosterone—injectable steroid
DET—dimethyltryptamine
Detroit pink—PCP
Deuce—$2 worth of drugs; heroin
Devil's dandruff—crack
Devil's dick—crack pipe
Devil's dust—PCP
Devilsmoke—crack
Dew—marijuana
Dews—$10 worth of drugs
Dexies—amphetamine
Diambista—marijuana

Dianabol—veterinary steroid
Diet pills—amphetamine
Dihydrolone—injectable steroid
Dimba—marijuana from West Africa
Dime—crack; $10 worth of crack
Dime bag—$10 worth of drugs
Dime's worth—amount of heroin to cause death
Ding—marijuana
Dinkie dow—marijuana
Dip—crack
Dipper—PCP
Dipping out—crack runners taking a portion of crack from vials
Dirt—heroin
Dirt grass—inferior quality marijuana
Dirty basing—crack
Disco biscuits—depressant
Disease—drug of choice
Ditch—marijuana
Ditch weed—marijuana inferior quality, Mexican
Djamba—marijuana
DMT—Dimethyltryptamine
Do a joint—to smoke marijuana
Do a line—to inhale cocaine
Do it Jack—PCP
DOA—PCP; crack
Doctor—MDMA
Dog—good friend
Dog food—heroin
Dogie—heroin
Dollar—$100 worth of drugs
Dolls—depressant
Domes—LSD
Domestic—locally grown marijuana
Domex—PCP and MDMA
Dominoes—amphetamine
Don jem—marijuana
Dona Juana—marijuana
Dona Juanita—marijuana
Doobie/dubbe/duby—marijuana
Doogie/doojee/dugie—heroin
Dooley—heroin
Dope—heroin; marijuana; any other drug
Dope fiend—crack addict
Dope smoke—to smoke marijuana

Dopium—opium
Doradilla—marijuana
Dots—LSD
Doub—$20 rock of crack
Double bubble—cocaine
Double cross—amphetamine
Double dome LSD
Double rock—crack diluted with procaine
Double trouble—depressant
Double ups—a $20 rock that can be broken into two $20 rocks
Double yoke—crack
Dove—$35 piece of crack
Dover's powder—opium
Downer—depressant
Downie—depressant
Draf weed—marijuana
Drag weed—marijuana
Draw up—to inject a drug
Dream—cocaine
Dream gum—opium
Dream stick—opium
Dreamer—morphine
Dreams—opium
Dreck—heroin
Drink—PCP
Dropper—to inject a drug
Drowsy high—depressant
Dry high—marijuana
Duct—cocaine
'Due—residue of oils trapped in a pipe after smoking base
Duji—heroin
Dummy dust—PCP
Durabolin—injectable steroid
Durog—marijuana
Duros—marijuana
Dust—heroin; cocaine; PCP; marijuana mixed with various chemicals
Dust joint—PCP
Dust of angels—PCP
Dusted parsley—PCP
Dusting—adding PCP, heroin, or another drug to marijuana
Dymethzine—injectable steroid
Dynamite—heroin and cocaine
Dyno—heroin

Dyno-pure—heroin

E

Earth—marijuana cigarette
Easing powder—opium
Eastside player—crack
Easy score—obtaining drugs easily
Eating—taking a drug orally
Ecstasy—MDMA
Egg—crack
Eight ball—1/8 ounce of drugs
Eightball—crack and heroin
Eighth—heroin
El diablito—marijuana, cocaine, heroin and PCP
El diablo—marijuana, cocaine and heroin
Electric Kool Aid—LSD
Elephant—PCP
Elephant tranquilizer—PCP
Embalming fluid—PCP
Emergency gun—instrument used to inject other than syringe
Emsel—morphine
Endo—marijuana
Energizer—PCP
Enoltestovis—injectable steroid
Ephedrone—methcathinone
Equipose—veterinary steroid
Erth—PCP
Esra—marijuana
Essence—MDMA
Estuffa—heroin
ET—alpha-ethyltyptamine
Eve—MDEA
Explorers club—group of LSD users
Eye opener—crack; amphetamine

F

Factory—place where drugs are packaged, diluted, or manufactured
Fake STP—PCP
Fall—arrested
Fallbrook redhair—marijuana, term from Fallbrook, CA
Famous dimes—crack

Fantasia—dimethyltryptamine
Fat bags—crack
Fatty—marijuana cigarette
Feed bag—container for marijuana
Ferry dust—heroin
Fi-do-nie—opium
Fields—LSD
Fiend—someone who smokes marijuana alone
Fifteen cents—$15 worth of drugs
Fifty-one—crack
Finajet/finaject—veterinary steroid
Fine stuff—marijuana
Finger—marijuana cigarette
Fir—marijuana
Fire—to inject a drug; crack and methamphetamine
Fire it up—to smoke marijuana
First line—morphine
Fish scales—crack
Five cent bag—$5 worth of drugs
Five C note—$500 bill
Five dollar bag—$50 worth of drugs
Fives—amphetamine
Fix—to inject a drug
Fizzies—methadone
Flag—appearance of blood in the vein
Flake—cocaine
Flakes—PCP
Flame cooking—smoking cocaine base by putting the pipe over a stove flame
Flamethrowers—cigarette laced with cocaine and heroin
Flash—LSD
Flat blues—LSD
Flat chunks—crack cut with benzocaine
Flea powder—low purity heroin
Florida snow—cocaine
Flower—marijuana
Flower tops—marijuana
Fly Mexican airlines—to smoke marijuana
Flying—under the influence of drugs
Following that cloud—searching for drugs
Foo foo stuff—heroin; cocaine
Foo-foo dust—cocaine

Foolish powder—heroin; cocaine
Footballs—amphetamine
45 Minute Psychosis—Dimethyltryptamine
Forwards—amphetamine
Fraho/frajo—marijuana
Freebase—smoking cocaine; crack
Freeze—cocaine; renege on a drug deal
French blue—amphetamine
French fries—crack
Fresh—PCP
Friend—fentanyl
Fries—crack
Frios—marijuana laced with PCP
Frisco special—cocaine, heroin and LSD
Frisco speedball—cocaine, heroin and LSD
Friskie powder—cocaine
Fry—crack
Fry daddy—crack and marijuana; cigarette laced with crack
Fu—marijuana
Fuel—marijuana mixed with insecticides; PCP
Fuete—hypodermic needle
Fuma D'Angola—marijuana Portuguese term

G

G—$1000 or 1 gram of drugs; term for an unfamiliar male
G.B.—depressant
GHB—gamma hydroxy butyrate
G-rock—one gram of rock cocaine
G-shot—small dose of drugs used to hold off withdrawal symptoms until full dose can be taken
Gaffel—fake cocaine
Gaffus—hypodermic needle
Gage/gauge—marijuana
Gagers—methcathinone
Gaggers—methcathinone
Galloping horse—heroin
Gamot—heroin
Gange—marijuana

Gangster—marijuana
Gangster pills—depressant
Ganja—marijuana from Jamaica
Gank—fake crack
Garbage—inferior quality drugs
Garbage heads—users who buy crack from street dealers instead of cooking it themselves
Garbage rock—crack
Gash—marijuana
Gasper—marijuana cigarette
Gasper stick—marijuana cigarette
Gato—heroin
Gauge butt—marijuana
Gee—opium
Geek—crack and marijuana
Geekers—crack user
Geeze—to inhale cocaine
Geezer—to inject a drug
Geezin a bit of dee gee—injecting a drug
George smack—heroin
Get a gage up—to smoke marijuana
Get a gift—obtain drugs
Get down—to inject a drug
Get high—to smoke marijuana
Get lifted—under the influence of drugs
Get off—to inject a drug; get "high"
Get the wind—to smoke marijuana
Get through—obtain drugs
Ghana—marijuana
Ghost—LSD
Ghost busting—smoking cocaine; searching for white particles in the belief that they are crack
Gick monster—crack smoker
Gift-of-the-sun—cocaine
Giggle smoke—marijuana
Gimmick—drug injection equipment
Gimmie—crack and marijuana
Gin—cocaine
Girl—cocaine; crack; heroin
Girlfriend—cocaine
Give wings—inject someone or teach someone to inject heroin
Glacines—heroin
Glad stuff—cocaine

Glading—using inhalant
Glass—hypodermic needle; amphetamine
Glass gun—hypodermic needle
Glo—crack
Gluey—person who sniffs glue
Go-fast—methcathinone
Go into a sewer—to inject a drug
Go loco—to smoke marijuana
Go on a sleigh ride—to inhale cocaine
God's drug—morphine
God's flesh—psilocybin/psilocin
God's medicine—opium
Gold—marijuana; crack
Gold dust—cocaine
Gold star—marijuana
Golden Dragon—LSD
Golden girl—heroin
Golden leaf—very high quality marijuana
Golf ball—crack
Golf balls—depressant
Golpe—heroin
Goma—opium; black tar heroin
Gondola—opium
Gong—marijuana; opium
Goob—methcathinone
Good—PCP
Good and plenty—heroin
Good butt—marijuana cigarette
Good giggles—marijuana
Good go—proper amount of drugs for the money paid
Good H—heroin
Good lick—good drugs
Goodfellas—fentanyl
Goof butt—marijuana cigarette
Goofball—cocaine and heroin; depressant
Goofers—depressant
Goofy's—LSD
Goon—PCP
Goon dust—PCP
Gopher—person paid to pickup drugs
Goric—opium
Gorilla biscuits—PCP
Gorilla pills—depressant
Gorilla tab—PCP

Got it going on—fast sale of drugs
Graduate—completely stop using drugs or progress to stronger drugs
Gram—hashish
Grape parfait—LSD
Grass—marijuana
Grass brownies—marijuana
Grata—marijuana
Gravel—crack
Gravy—to inject a drug; heroin
Grease—currency
Great bear—fentanyl
Great tobacco—opium
Green—inferior quality marijuana; PCP; ketamine
Green double domes—LSD
Green dragons—depressant
Green frog—depressant
Green goddess—marijuana
Green gold—cocaine
Green goods—paper currency
Green leaves—PCP
Green single domes—LSD
Green tea—PCP
Green wedge—LSD
Greens/green stuff—paper currency
Greeter—marijuana
Greta—marijuana
Grey shields—LSD
Griefo—marijuana
Griff—marijuana
Griffa—marijuana
Griffo—marijuana
Grit—crack
Groceries—crack
Ground control—guide or caretaker during a hallucinogenic experience
Gum—opium
Guma—opium
Gun—to inject a drug; needle
Gungun—marijuana
Gutter—vein into which a drug is injected
Gutter junkie—addict who relies on others to obtain drugs
Gyve—marijuana cigarette

H

H—heroin
H & C—heroin and cocaine
H Caps—heroin
Hache—heroin
Hail—crack
Hairy—heroin
Half—1/2 ounce
Half-a-C—$50 bill
Half a football field—50 rocks of crack
Half G—$500
Half load—15 bags (decks) of heroin
Half moon—peyote
Half piece—1/2 ounce of heroin or cocaine
Half track—crack
Hamburger helper—crack
Hand-to-hand—direct delivery and payment
Hand-to-hand man—transient dealers who carry small amounts of crack
Hanhich—marijuana
Hanyak—smokable methamphetamine
Happy cigarette—marijuana cigarette
Happy dust—cocaine
Happy powder—cocaine
Happy trails—cocaine
Hard candy—heroin
Hard line—crack
Hard rock—crack
Hard stuff—opium; heroin
Hardware—isobutyl nitrite
Harry—heroin
Hats—LSD
Has—marijuana
Have a dust—cocaine
Haven dust—cocaine
Hawaiin—very high potency marijuana
Hawaiian sunshine—LSD
Hawk—LSD
Hay—marijuana
Hay butt—marijuana cigarette
Haze—LSD
Hazel—heroin
HCP—PCP

Head drugs—amphetamine
Headlights—LSD
Heart-on—inhalant
Hearts—amphetamine
Heaven & Hell—PCP
Heaven dust—heroin; cocaine
Heavenly blue—LSD
Heeled—having plenty of money
Helen—heroin
Hell dust—heroin
He-man—fentanyl
Hemp—marijuana
Henpicking—searching on hands and knees for crack
Henry—heroin
Henry VIII—cocaine
Her—cocaine
Herb—marijuana
Herb and Al—marijuana and alcohol
Herba—marijuana
Herms—PCP
Hem—heroin
Hero of the underworld—heroin
Heroina—heroin
Herone—heroin
Hessle—heroin
Highbeams—the wide eyes of a person on crack
Hikori—peyote
Hikuli—peyote
Him—heroin
Hinkley—PCP
Hippie crack—inhalant
Hironpon—smokable methamphetamine
Hit—crack; marijuana cigarette; to smoke marijuana
Hit house—house where users go to shoot up and leave the owner drugs as payment
Hit the hay—to smoke marijuana
Hit the main line—to inject a drug
Hit the needle—to inject a drug
Hit the pit—to inject a drug
Hitch up the reindeers—to inhale cocaine
Hitter—little pipes designed for only one hit

81

Hitting up—injecting drugs
Hocus—opium; marijuana
Hog—PCP
Holding—possessing drugs
Hombre—heroin
Hombrecitos—psilocybin
Homegrown—marijuana
Honey—currency
Honey blunts—Marijuana cigars sealed with honey
Honey oil—ketamine; inhalant
Honeymoon—early stages of drug use before addiction or dependency develops
Hong-yen—heroin in pill form
Hooch—marijuana
Hooked—addicted
Hooter—cocaine; marijuana
Hop/hops—opium
Hopped up—under the influence of drugs
Horn—to inhale cocaine; crack pipe
Horning—heroin; to inhale cocaine
Horse—heroin
Horse heads—amphetamine
Horse tracks—PCP
Horse tranquilizer—PCP
Hot dope—heroin
Hot heroin—poisoned to give to a police informant
Hot ice—smokable methamphetamine
Hot load/hot shot—lethal injection of an opiate
Hot stick—marijuana cigarette
Hotcakes—crack
House fee—money paid to enter a crackhouse
House piece—crack given to the owner of a crackhouse or apartment where crack users congregate
How do you like me now?—crack
Hows—morphine
HRN—heroin
Hubba, I am back—crack
Hubba pigeon—crack user looking for rocks on a floor after a police raid
Hubbas—crack, term from Northern CA

Huff—inhalant
Huffer—inhalant abuser
Hulling—using others to get drugs
Hunter—cocaine
Hustle—attempt to obtain drug customers
Hyatari—peyote
Hype—heroin addict; an addict
Hype stick—hypodermic needle

I

I am back—crack
Ice—cocaine; methamphetamine; smokable methamphetamine; PCP; MDMA
Ice cream habit—occasional use of drugs
Ice cube—crack
Icing—cocaine
Idiot pills—depressant
In—connected with drug suppliers
Inbetweens—depressant; amphetamine
Inca message—cocaine
Indian boy—marijuana
Indian hay—marijuana from India
Indica—species of cannabis, found in hot climate, grows 3.5 to 4 feet
Indo—marijuana, term from Northern CA
Indonesian bud—marijuana; opium
Instant zen—LSD
Interplanetary mission—travel from one crackhouse to another in search of crack
Isda—heroin
Issues—crack

J

J—marijuana cigarette
Jab/job—to inject a drug
Jack—steal someone else's drugs
Jackpot—fentanyl
Jack-Up—to inject a drug
Jag—keep a high going
Jam—amphetamine; cocaine

Jam cecil—amphetamine
Jane—marijuana
Jay smoke—marijuana
Jay—marijuana cigarette
Jee gee—heroin
Jefferson airplane—used match cut in half to hold a partially smoked marijuana cigarette
Jellies—depressant
Jelly—cocaine
Jelly baby—amphetamine
Jelly bean—amphetamine; depressant
Jelly beans—crack
Jet—ketamine
Jet fuel—PCP
Jim Jones—marijuana laced with cocaine and PCP
Jive—heroin; marijuana; drugs
Jive doo jee—heroin
Jive stick—marijuana
Johnson—crack
Joint—marijuana cigarette
Jojee—heroin
Jolly bean—amphetamine
Jolly green—marijuana
Jolly pop—casual user of heroin
Jolt—to inject a drug; strong reaction to drugs
Jones—heroin
Jonesing—need for drugs
Joy flakes—heroin
Joy juice—depressant
Joy plant—opium
Joy pop—to inject a drug
Joy popping—occasional use of drugs
Joy powder—heroin; cocaine
Joy smoke—marijuana
Joy stick—marijuana cigarette
Juju—marijuana cigarette
Juan Valdez—marijuana
Juanita—marijuana
Juggle—sell drugs to another addict to support a habit
Juggler—teen-aged street dealer
Jugs—amphetamine
Juice—steroids; PCP
Juice joint—marijuana cigarette sprinkled with crack

Jum—sealed plastic bag containing crack
Jumbos—large vials of crack sold on the streets
Junk—cocaine; heroin
Junkie—addict

K

K—PCP
Kabayo—heroin
Kabuki—crack pipe made from a plastic rum bottle and a rubber sparkplug cover
Kali—marijuana
Kaksonjae—smokable methamphetamine
Kangaroo—crack
Kaps—PCP
Karachi—heroin
Kaya—marijuana
Kentucky blue—marijuana
KGB (killer green bud)—marijuana
K-blast—PCP
K-hole—periods of ketamine-induced confusion
Kibbles & Bits—small crumbs of crack
Kick—getting off a drug habit; inhalant
Kick stick—marijuana cigarette
Kiddie dope—prescription drugs
Kiff—marijuana
Killer—marijuana; PCP
Killer joints—PCP
Killer weed (1980s)—marijuana and PCP
Killer weed (1960s)—marijuana
Kilo—2.2 pounds
Kilter—marijuana
Kind—marijuana
King ivory—fentanyl
King Kong pills—depressant
King's habit—cocaine
Kit—equipment used to inject drugs
KJ—PCP
Kleenex—MDMA
Klingons—crack addicts
Kokomo—crack

Kools—PCP
Kryptonite—crack
Krystal—PCP
Krystal joint—PCP
Kumba—marijuana
KW—PCP

L

L—LSD
L.A.—long-acting amphetamine
L.A. glass—smokable methamphet-
amine
L.A. ice—smokable methamphetamine
L.L.—marijuana
Lace—cocaine and marijuana
Lady—cocaine
Lady caine—cocaine
Lady snow—cocaine
Lakbay diva—marijuana
Lamborghini—crack pipe made from
plastic rum bottle and a rubber
sparkplug cover
Las mujercitas—psilocybin
Lason sa daga—LSD
Laugh and scratch—to inject a drug
Laughing gas—nitrous oxide
Laughing grass—marijuana
Laughing weed—marijuana
Lay back—depressant
Lay-out—equipment for taking drugs
LBJ—LSD; PCP; heroin
Leaf—marijuana; cocaine
Leaky bolla—PCP
Leaky leak—PCP
Leapers—amphetamine
Leaping—under the influence of drugs
Legal speed—over the counter asthma
drug; trade name MiniThin
Lemon 714—PCP
Lemonade—heroin; poor quality drugs
Lens—LSD
Lenos—PCP
Lethal weapon—PCP
Lettuce—money
Lib (Librium)—depressant
Lid—1 ounce of marijuana
Lid proppers—amphetamine

Light stuff—marijuana
Lightning—amphetamine
Lima—marijuana
Lime acid—LSD
Line—cocaine
Lipton Tea—inferior quality drugs
Lit up—under the influence of drugs
Little bomb—amphetamine; heroin;
depressant
Little ones—PCP
Little smoke—marijuana; psilocybin/
psilocin
Live ones—PCP
Llesca—marijuana
Load—25 bags of heroin
Loaded—high
Loaf—marijuana
Lobo—marijuana
Locker room—isobutyl nitrite
Locoweed—marijuana
Log—PCP; marijuana cigarette
Logor—LSD
Loused—covered by sores and ab-
scesses from repeated use of unster-
ile needles
Love—crack
Love affair—cocaine
Love boat—marijuana dipped in form-
aldehyde; PCP
Love drug—MDMA; depressant
Love pearls—alpha-ethyltyptamine
Love pills—alpha-ethyltyptamine
Love trip—MDMA and mescaline
Love weed—marijuana
Lovelies—marijuana laced with PCP
Lovely—PCP
LSD—lysergic acid diethylamide
Lubage—marijuana
Lucy in the sky with diamonds—LSD
Ludes—depressant
Luding out—depressant
Luds—depressant

M

M—marijuana; morphine
M.J.—marijuana
M.O.—marijuana

M.S.—morphine
M.U.—marijuana
M&M—depressant
Machinery—marijuana
Macon—marijuana
Mad dog—PCP
Madman—PCP
Magic—PCP
Magic dust—PCP
Magic mushroom—psilocybin/psilocin
Magic smoke—marijuana
Main line—to inject a drug
Mainliner—person who injects into the vein
Make up—need to find more drugs
Mama coca—cocaine
Manhattan silver—marijuana
Marathons—amphetamine
Mari—marijuana cigarette
Marshmallow reds—depressant
Mary—marijuana
Mary and Johnny—marijuana
Mary Ann—marijuana
Mary Jane—marijuana
Mary Jonas—marijuana
Mary Warner—marijuana
Mary Weaver—marijuana
Maserati—crack pipe made from a plastic rum bottle and a rubber sparkplug cover
Matchbox—1/4 ounce of marijuana or 6 marijuana cigarettes
Matsakow—heroin
Maui wauie—marijuana from Hawaii
Max—gamma hydroxy butyrate dissolved in water and mixed with amphetamines
Maxibolin—oral steroid
Mayo—cocaine; heroin
MDM—MDMA
MDMA—methylenedioxymethamphetamine
Mean green—PCP
Meg—marijuana
Megg—marijuana cigarette
Meggie—marijuana
Mellow yellow—LSD
Merchandise—drugs
Merk—cocaine

Mesc—mescaline
Mescal—mescaline
Mese—mescaline
Messorole—marijuana
Meth—methamphetamine
Meth head—regular user of methamphetamine
Meth monster—person who has a violent reaction to methamphetamine
Methatriol—injectable steroid
Methyltestosterone—oral steroid
Mexican brown—heroin; marijuana
Mexican horse—heroin
Mexican mud—heroin
Mexican mushroom—psilocybin/psilocin
Mexican red—marijuana
Mexican reds—depressant
Mezc—mescaline
Mickey Finn—depressant
Mickey's—depressant
Microdot—LSD
Midnight oil—opium
Mighty Quinn—LSD
Mighty Joe Young—depressant
Mighty mezz—marijuana cigarette
Mind detergent—LSD
Minibennie—amphetamine
Mint leaf—PCP
Mint weed—PCP
Mira—opium
Miss—to inject a drug
Miss Emma—morphine
Missile basing—crack liquid and PCP
Mission—trip out of the crackhouse to obtain crack
Mist—PCP; crack smoke
Mister blue—morphine
Modams—marijuana
Mohasky—marijuana
Mojo—cocaine; heroin
Monkey—drug dependency; cigarette made from cocaine paste and tobacco
Monkey dust—PCP
Monkey tranquilizer—PCP
Monos—cigarette made from cocaine paste and tobacco
Monte—marijuana from South America

Mooca/moocah—marijuana
Moon—mescaline
Moonrock—crack and heroin
Mooster—marijuana
Moota/mutah—marijuana
Mooters—marijuana cigarette
Mootie—marijuana
Mootos—marijuana
Mor a grifa—marijuana
More—PCP
Morf—morphine
Morning wake-up—first blast of crack from the pipe
Morotgara—heroin
Mortal combat—high potency heroin
Mosquitos—cocaine
Mota/moto—marijuana
Mother—marijuana
Mother's little helper—depressant
Mouth worker—one who takes drugs orally
Movie star drug—cocaine
Mow the grass—to smoke marijuana
Mud—opium; heroin
Muggie—marijuana
Mujer—cocaine
Mule—carrier of drugs
Murder one—heroin and cocaine
Murder 8—fentanyl
Mushrooms—psilocybin/psilocin
Musk—psilocybin/psilocin
Mutha—marijuana
Muzzle—heroin

N

Nail—marijuana cigarette
Nailed—arrested
Nanoo—heroin
Nebbies—depressant
Nemmies—depressant
New acid—PCP
New magic—PCP
New Jack Swing—heroin and morphine
Nexus—2C-B
Nice and easy—heroin
Nickel bag—$5 worth of drugs; heroin

Nickel deck—heroin
Nickel note—$5 bill
Nickelonians—crack addicts
Niebla—PCP
Nimbies—depressant
Nix—stranger among the group
Nod—effects of heroin
Noise—heroin
Nontoucher—crack user who doesn't want affection during or after smoking crack
Nose—heroin
Nose candy—cocaine
Nose drops—liquified heroin
Nose stuff—cocaine
Nose powder—cocaine
Nubs—peyote
Nugget—amphetamine
Nuggets—crack
Number—marijuana cigarette
Number 3—cocaine; heroin
Number 4—heroin
Number 8—heroin

O

O—opium
O.J.—marijuana
O.P.—opium
O.P.P.—PCP
Octane—PCP laced with gasoline
Ogoy—heroin
Oil—heroin; PCP
Old Steve—heroin
On a mission—searching for crack
On a trip—under the influence of drugs
On ice—in jail
On the bricks—walking the streets
On the nod—under the influence of narcotics or depressant
One and one—to inhale cocaine
One on one house—where cocaine and heroin can be purchased
One box tissue—one ounce of crack
One-fifty-one—crack
One way—LSD
Ope—opium

Optical illusions—LSD
Orange barrels—LSD
Orange crystal—PCP
Orange cubes—LSD
Orange haze—LSD
Orange micro—LSD
Orange wedges—LSD
Oranges—amphetamine
Outerlimits—crack and LSD
Owsley—LSD
Owsley's acid—LSD
Oz—inhalant
Ozone—PCP

P

P—peyote; PCP
PCP—phencyclidine
PCPA—PCP
P.R. (Panama Red)—marijuana
P-dope—20-30% pure heroin
P-funk—heroin; crack and PCP
Pack—heroin; marijuana
Pack of rocks—marijuana cigarette
Pakalolo—marijuana
Pakistani black—marijuana
Panama cut—marijuana
Panama gold—marijuana
Panama red—marijuana
Panatella—large marijuana cigarette
Pancakes and syrup—combination of glutethimide and codeine cough syrup
Pane—LSD
Pangonadalot—heroin
Panic—drugs not available
Paper acid—LSD
Paper bag—container for drugs
Paper blunts—marijuana within a paper casing
Paper boy—heroin peddler
Parabolin—veterinary steroid
Parachute—crack and PCP smoked; heroin
Paradise—cocaine
Paradise white—cocaine
Parlay—crack
Parsley—marijuana; PCP

Paste—crack
Pat—marijuana
Patico—crack (Spanish)
Paz—PCP
Peace—LSD; PCP
Peace pill—PCP
Peace tablets—LSD
Peace weed—PCP
Peaches—amphetamine
Peanut—depressant
Peanut butter—PCP mixed with peanut butter
Pearl—cocaine
Pearls—amyl nitrite
Pearly gates—LSD
Pebbles—crack
Peddlar—drug supplier
Peep—PCP
Pee Wee—crack; $5 worth of crack
Peg—heroin
Pellets—LSD
Pen yan—opium
Pep pills—amphetamine
Pepsi habit—occasional use of drugs
Perfect High—heroin
Perico—cocaine
Perp—fake crack made of candle wax and baking soda Peth—depressant
Peruvian—cocaine
Peruvian flake—cocaine
Peruvian lady—cocaine
Peter Pan—PCP
Peyote—mescaline
Phennies—depressant
Phenos—depressant
Pianoing—using the fingers to find lost crack
Piece—1 ounce; cocaine; crack
Piedras—crack (Spanish)
Pig killer—PCP
Piles—crack
Pimp—cocaine
Pimp your pipe—lending or renting your crack pipe
Pin—marijuana
Pin gon—opium
Pin yen—opium
Ping-in-wing—to inject a drug

Pink blotters—LSD
Pink hearts—amphetamine
Pink ladies—depressant
Pink panther—LSD
Pink robots—LSD
Pink wedge—LSD
Pink witches—LSD
Pipe—crack pipe; marijuana pipe; vein into which a drug is injected; mix drugs with other substances
Pipero—crack user
Pit—PCP
Pixies—amphetamine
Plant—hiding place for drugs
Pocket rocket—marijuana
Pod—marijuana
Poison—heroin; fentanyl
Poke—marijuana
Polvo—heroin; PCP
Polvo blanco—cocaine
Polvo de angel—PCP
Polvo do estrellas—PCP
Pony—crack
Poor man's pot—inhalant
Pop—to inhale cocaine
Poppers—isobutyl nitrite; amyl nitrite
Poppy—heroin
Pot—marijuana
Potato—LSD
Potato chips—crack cut with benzocaine
Potten bush—marijuana
Powder—heroin; amphetamine
Powder diamonds—cocaine
Power puller—rubber piece attached to crack stem
Pox—Opium
Predator—heroin
Prescription—marijuana cigarette
Press—cocaine; crack
Pretendica—marijuana
Pretendo—marijuana
Primo—crack; marijuana mixed with crack
Primobolan—injectable and oral steroid
Primos—cigarettes laced with cocaine and heroin

Proviron—oral steroid
Pseudocaine—phenylpropanolamine, an adulterant for cutting crack
Puff the dragon—to smoke marijuana
Puffer—crack smoker
Puffy—PCP
Pulborn—heroin
Pullers—crack users who pull at parts of their bodies excessively
Pumping—selling crack
Pure—heroin
Pure love—LSD
Purple—ketamine
Purple barrels—LSD
Purple haze—LSD
Purple hearts—LSD; amphetamine; depressant
Purple flats—LSD
Purple ozoline—LSD
Purple rain—PCP
Push—sell drugs
Push shorts—to cheat or sell short amounts
Pusher—one who sells drugs; metal hanger or umbrella rod used to scrape residue in crack stems

Q

Q—depressant
Quad—depressant
Quarter—1/4 ounce or $25 worth of drugs
Quarter bag—$25 worth of drugs
Quarter moon—hashish
Quarter piece—1/4 ounce
Quartz—smokable methamphetamine
Quas—depressant
Queen Ann's lace—marijuana
Quicksilver—isobutyl nitrite
Quill—methamphetamine; heroin; cocaine
Quinolone—injectable steroid

R

R2—Rophynol; see "roofies"
Racehorse charlie—cocaine; heroin

Ragweed—inferior quality marijuana; heroin

Railroad weed—marijuana

Rainbows—depressant

Rainy day woman—marijuana

Rambo—heroin

Rane—cocaine; heroin

Rangood—marijuana grown wild

Rap—criminally charged; to talk with someone

Raspberry—female who trades sex for crack or money to buy crack

Rasta weed—marijuana

Raw—crack

Rave—party designed to enhance a hallucinogenic experience through music and behavior

Razed—under the influence of drugs

Ready rock—cocaine; crack; heroin

Recompress—change the shape of cocaine flakes to resemble "rock"

Recycle—LSD

Red—under the influence of drugs

Red and blue—depressant

Red bullets—depressant

Red caps—crack

Red cross—marijuana

Red chicken—heroin

Red devil—depressant; PCP

Red dirt—marijuana

Reds—depressant

Red eagle—heroin

Red phosphorus—smokable speed

Reefer—marijuana

Regular P—crack

Reindeer dust—heroin

Rhine—heroin

Rhythm—amphetamine

Riding the wave—under the influence of drugs

Rig—equipment used to inject drugs

Righteous bush—marijuana

Ringer—good hit of crack

Rippers—amphetamine

Roach—butt of marijuana cigarette

Roach clip—holds partially smoked marijuana cigarette

Road dope—amphetamine

Roca—crack (Spanish)

Roche—Rophynol (see "roofies")

Rock attack—crack

Rock house—place where crack is sold and smoked

Rock(s)—cocaine; crack

Rocket caps—dome shaped caps on crack vials

Rocket fuel—PCP

Rockets—marijuana cigarette

Rockette—female who uses crack

Rocks of hell—crack

Rock star—female who trades sex for crack or money to buy crack

Rocky III—crack

Roid rage—aggressive behavior caused by excessive steroid use

Roller—to inject a drug

Rollers—police

Rolling—MDMA

Roofies—Rophynol; a sedative; causes users to appear drunk

Rooster—crack

Root—marijuana

Rope—marijuana

Roples—Rophynol, (see "roofies")

Rosa—amphetamine

Rose marie—marijuana

Roses—amphetamine

Rox—crack

Roxanne—cocaine; crack

Royal blues—LSD

Roz—crack

Ruderalis—species of cannabis, found in Russia, grows 1 to 2.5 feet

Ruffles—Rophynol; (see "roofies")

Runners—people who sell drugs for others

Running—MDMA

Rush—isobutyl nitrite

Rush snappers—isobutyl nitrite

Russian sickles—LSD

S

Sack—heroin

Sacrament—LSD

Sacred mushroom—psilocybin

Salt—heroin
Salt and pepper—marijuana
Sam—federal narcotics agent
Sancocho—to steal (Spanish)
Sandoz—LSD
Sandwich—two layers of cocaine with a layer of heroin in the middle
Santa Marta—marijuana
Sasfras—marijuana
Satan's secret—inhalant
Satch—papers, letter, cards, clothing, etc., saturated with drug solution (used to smuggle drugs into prisons or hospitals)
Satch cotton—fabric used to filter a solution of narcotics before injection
Sativa—species of cannabis, found in cool, damp climate, grows up to 18 feet
Scaffle—PCP
Scag—heroin
Scat—heroin
Scate—heroin
Schmeck—cocaine
Schoolboy—cocaine; codeine
Schoolcraft—crack
Scissors—marijuana
Score—purchase drugs
Scorpion—cocaine
Scott—heroin
Scottie—cocaine
Scotty—cocaine; crack; the high from crack
Scramble—crack
Scratch—money
Scruples—crack
Scuffle—PCP
Seccy—depressant
Seeds—marijuana
Seggy—depressant
Sen—marijuana
Seni—peyote
Serial speedballing—sequencing cocaine, cough syrup, and heroin over a 1-2 day period
Sernyl—PCP
Serpico 21—cocaine
Server—crack dealer

Sess—marijuana
Set—place where drugs are sold
Sevenup—cocaine; crack
Sewer—vein into which a drug is injected
Sezz—marijuana
Shabu—ice
Shake—marijuana
Shaker/baker/water—materials needed to freebase cocaine; shaker bottle, baking soda, water
Sharps—needles
She—cocaine
Sheet rocking—crack and LSD
Sheets—PCP
Shermans—PCP
Sherms—PCP; crack
Shmeck/schmeek—heroin
Shoot/shoot up—to inject a drug
Shoot the breeze—nitrous oxide
Shooting gallery—place where drugs are used
Shot—to inject a drug
Shot down—under the influence of drugs
Shrooms—psilocybin/psilocin
Siddi—marijuana
Sightball—crack
Silly Putty—psilocybin/psilocin
Simple Simon—psilocybin/psilocin
Sinse—marijuana
Sinsemilla—potent variety marijuana
Sixty-two—2 1/2 ounces of crack
Skee—opium
Skeegers/skeezers—crack-smoking prostitute
Sketching—coming down from a speed induced high
Skid—heroin
Skied—under the influence of drugs
Skin popping—injecting drugs under the skin
Skunk—marijuana
Skuffle—PCP
Slab—crack
Slam—to inject a drug
Slanging—selling drugs
Sleeper—heroin; depressant

Sleet—crack
Slick superspeed—methcathinone
Slime—heroin
Smack—heroin
Smears—LSD
Smoke—heroin and crack; crack; marijuana
Smoke Canada—marijuana
Smoke-out—under the influence of drugs
Smoking—PCP
Smoking gun—heroin and cocaine
Snap—amphetamine
Snappers—isobutyl nitrite
Sniff—to inhale cocaine; inhalant; methcathinone
Snop—marijuana
Snort—to inhale cocaine; use inhalant
Snorts—PCP
Snot—residue produced from smoking amphetamine
Snot balls—rubber cement rolled into balls and burned
Snow—cocaine; heroin; amphetamine
Snowball—cocaine and heroin
Snow bird—cocaine
Snowcones—cocaine
Snow pallets—amphetamine
Snow seals—cocaine and amphetamine
Snow soke—crack
Snow white—cocaine
Society high—cocaine
Soda—injectable cocaine used in Hispanic communities
Softballs—depressant
Soles—hashish
Soma—PCP
Sopers—depressant
Space base—crack dipped in PCP; hollowed out cigar refilled with PCP and crack
Space cadet—crack dipped in PCP
Space dust—crack dipped in PCP
Space ship—glass pipe used to smoke crack
Spark it up—to smoke marijuana
Sparkle plenty—amphetamine

Sparklers—amphetamine
Special "K"—ketamine
Special la coke—ketamine
Speed—methamphetamine; amphetamine; crack
Speed boat—marijuana, PCP, crack
Speed freak—habitual user of methamphetamine
Speed for lovers—MDMA
Speedball—heroin and cocaine; amphetamine
Spider blue—heroin
Spike—to inject a drug; needle
Splash—amphetamine
Spliff—marijuana cigarette
Splim—marijuana
Split—half and half or to leave
Splivins—amphetamine
Spoon—1/16 ounce of heroin; paraphernalia used to prepare heroin for injection
Spores—PCP
Sporting—to inhale cocaine
Spray—inhalant
Sprung—person just starting to use drugs
Square mackerel—marijuana, term from Florida
Square time Bob—crack
Squirrel—smoking cocaine, marijuana and PCP: LSD
Stack—marijuana
Stacking—taking steroids without a prescription
Star—methcathinone
Stardust—cocaine; PCP
Star-spangled powder—cocaine
Stash—place to hide drugs
Stash areas—drug storage and distribution areas
Stat—methcathinone
Steerer—person who directs customers to spots for buying crack
Stem—cylinder used to smoke crack
Stems—marijuana
Step on—dilute drugs
Stick—marijuana; PCP
Stink weed—marijuana

Stoned—under the influence of drugs
Stones—crack
Stoppers—depressant
STP—PCP
Straw—marijuana cigarette
Strawberries—depressant
Strawberry—female who trades sex for crack or money to buy crack
Strawberry fields—LSD
Strung out—heavily addicted to drugs
Stuff—heroin
Stumbler—depressant
Sugar—cocaine; LSD; heroin
Sugar block—crack
Sugar cubes—LSD
Sugar lumps—LSD
Sugar weed—marijuana
Sunshine—LSD
Super—PCP
Super acid—ketamine
Super C—ketamine
Super Grass—PCP
Supergrass—marijuana
Super ice—smokable methamphetamine
Super joint—PCP
Super kools—PCP
Super weed—PCP
Surfer—PCP
Sweet dreams—heroin
Sweet Jesus—heroin
Sweet Lucy—marijuana
Sweet Morpheus—morphine
Sweet stuff—heroin; cocaine
Sweets—amphetamine
Swell up—crack
Synthetic cocaine—PCP
Synthetic THT—PCP

T

T—cocaine; marijuana
TT 1—PCP
TT 2—PCP
TT 3—PCP
T-buzz—PCP
TAC—PCP
T.N.T.—heroin; fentanyl

Tabs—LSD
Tail lights—LSD
Taima—marijuana
Taking a cruise—PCP
Takkouri—marijuana
Tango & Cash—fentanyl
Tar—opium; heroin
Tardust—cocaine
Taste—heroin; small sample of drugs
Taxing—price paid to enter a crackhouse; charging more per vial depending on race of customer or if not a regular customer
Tea—marijuana; PCP
Tea party—to smoke marijuana
Teardrops—dosage units of crack packaged in the cut-off corners of plastic bags
Tecate—heroin
Tecatos—Hispanic heroin addicts
Teeth—cocaine; crack
Tension—crack
Tex-mex—marijuana
Texas pot—marijuana
Texas tea—marijuana
Thai sticks—bundles of marijuana soaked in hashish oil; marijuana buds bound on short sections of bamboo
THC—tetrahydrocannabinol
The beast—heroin
The C—methcathinone
The devil—crack
The witch—heroin
Therobolin—injectable steroid
Thing—heroin; cocaine; main drug interest at the moment
Thirst monsters—heavy crack smokers
Thirteen—marijuana
Thoroughbred—drug dealer who sells pure narcotics
Thrust—isobutyl nitrite
Thrusters—amphetamine
Thumb—marijuana
Tic—PCP in powder form
Tic tac—PCP
Ticket—LSD
Tie—to inject a drug
Tin—container for marijuana

Tish—PCP
Titch—PCP
Tissue—crack
Toilet water—inhalant
Toke—to inhale cocaine; to smoke marijuana
Toke up—to smoke marijuana
Toncho—octane booster which is inhaled
Tooles—depressant
Tools—equipment used for injecting drugs
Toot—cocaine; to inhale cocaine
Tooties—depressant
Tootsie roll—heroin
Top gun—crack
Topi—mescaline
Tops—peyote
Torch—marijuana
Torch cooking—smoking cocaine base by using a propane or butane torch as a source of flame
Torch up—to smoke marijuana
Torpedo—crack and marijuana
Toss up—female who trades sex for crack or money to buy crack
Totally spent—MDMA hangover
Toucher—user of crack who wants affection before, during, or after smoking crack
Tout—person who introduces buyers to sellers
Toxy—opium
Toys—opium
TR-6s—amphetamine
Track—to inject a drug
Tracks—row of needle marks on a person
Tragic magic—crack dipped in PCP
Trails—LSD induced perception that moving objects leave multiple images or traits behind them
Trank—PCP
Tranq—depressant
Trap—hiding place for drugs
Trays—bunches of vials
Travel agent—LSD supplier
Trip—LSD; alpha-ethyltyptamine

Troop—crack
Trophobolene—injectable steroid
Truck drivers—amphetamine
Tuie—depressant
Turbo—crack and marijuana
Turf—place where drugs are sold
Turkey—cocaine; amphetamine
Turnabout—amphetamine
Turned on—introduced to drugs; under the influence
Tutti-frutti—flavored cocaine developed by a Brazilian gang
Tweak mission—on a mission to find crack
Tweaker—crack user looking for rocks on the floor after a police raid
Tweaking—drug-induced paranoia; peaking on speed
Tweek—methamphetamine-like substance
Tweeker—methcathinone
Twenty—$20 rock of crack
Twenty-five—LSD
Twist—marijuana cigarette
Twistum—marijuana cigarette
Two for nine—two $5 vials or bags of crack for $9

U

Ultimate—crack
Uncle—Federal agents
Uncle Milty—depressant
Unkie—morphine
Up against the stem—addicted to smoking marijuana
Uppers—amphetamine
Uppies—amphetamine
Ups and downs—depressant
Utopiates—hallucinogens
Uzi—crack; crack pipe

V

V—the depressant Valium
Viper's weed—marijuana
Vodka acid—LSD

W

Wac—PCP on marijuana
Wack—PCP
Wacky weed—marijuana
Wake ups—amphetamine
Wasted—under the influence of drugs; murdered
Water—methamphetamine; PCP
Wave—crack
Wedding bells—LSD
Wedge—LSD
Weed—marijuana
Weed tea—marijuana
Weightless—high on crack
Wheat—marijuana
When-shee—opium
Whippets—nitrous oxide
White—amphetamine
White ball—crack
White boy—heroin
White cloud—crack smoke
White cross—methamphetamine; amphetamine
White dust—LSD
White ghost—crack
White girl—cocaine; heroin
White-haired lady—marijuana
White horizon—PCP
White horse—cocaine
White junk—heroin
White lady—cocaine; heroin
White lightning—LSD
White mosquito—cocaine
White nurse—heroin
White Owsley's—LSD
White powder—cocaine; PCP
White stuff—heroin
White sugar—crack
White tornado—crack
Whiteout—isobutyl nitrate
Whites—amphetamine
Whiz bang—cocaine and heroin
Wild cat—methcathinone and cocaine
Window glass—LSD
Window pane—LSD
Wings—heroin; cocaine
Winstrol—oral steroid
Winstrol V—veterinary steroid
Witch—heroin; cocaine
Witch hazel—heroin
Wobble weed—PCP
Wolf—PCP
Wollie—rocks of crack rolled into a marijuana cigarette
Wonder star—methcathinone
Woolah—a hollowed out cigar refilled with marijuana and crack
Woolas—cigarette laced with cocaine; marijuana cigarette sprinkled with crack
Woolies—marijuana and crack or PCP
Wooly blunts—Marijuana and crack or PCP
Working—selling crack
Working half—crack rock weighing half gram or more
Works—equipment for injecting drugs
Worm—PCP
Wecking crew—crack

X

X—marijuana; MDMA; amphetamine
X-ing—MDMA
XTC—MDMA

Y

Yahoo/yeaho—crack
Yale—crack
Yeh—marijuana
Yellow—LSD; depressant
Yellow bam—methamphetamine
Yellow bullets—depressant
Yellow dimples—LSD
Yellow fever—PCP
Yellow jackets—depressant
Yellow submarine—marijuana
Yellow sunshine—LSD
Yen pop—marijuana
Yen Shee Suey—opium wine
Yen sleep—restless, drowsy state after LSD use
Yerba—marijuana
Yerba mala—PCP and marijuana

Yesca—marijuana
Yesco—marijuana
Yeyo—cocaine, Spanish term
Yimyom—crack

Z

Z—1 ounce of heroin
Zacatecas purple—marijuana from Mexico
Zambi—marijuana
Zen—LSD

Zero—opium
Zig Zag man—LSD; marijuana; marijuana rolling papers
Zip—cocaine
Zol—marijuana cigarette
Zombie—PCP; heavy user of drugs
Zombie weed—PCP
Zooie—holds butt of marijuana cigarette
Zoom—PCP; marijuana laced with PCP
Zoomers—individuals who sell fake crack and then flee

Part Two

Alcohol

Chapter 7

The Definition of Alcoholism

To establish a more precise use of the term *alcoholism*, a 23-member multi-disciplinary committee of the National Council on Alcoholism and Drug Dependence and the American Society of Addiction Medicine conducted a 2-year study of the definition of alcoholism in the light of current concepts. The goals of the committee were to create by consensus a revised definition that is (1) scientifically valid, (2) clinically useful, and (3) understandable by the general public.

The Revised Definition of Alcoholism

Alcoholism is a primary, chronic disease with genetic, psychosocial, and environmental factors influencing its development and manifestations. The disease is often progressive and fatal. It is characterized by impaired control over drinking, preoccupation with the drug alcohol, use of alcohol despite adverse consequences, and distortions in thinking, most notably denial. Each of these symptoms may be continuous or periodic.

"Primary" refers to the nature of alcoholism as a disease entity in addition to and separate from other pathophysiologic states that may

---

This chapter contains excerpts from "The Definition of Alcoholism," by Robert M. Morse, MD and Daniel K. Flavin, MD for the Joint Committee of the National Council on Alcoholism and Drug Dependence and the American Society of Addiction Mecidine to Study the Definition and Criteria for the Diagnosis of Alcoholism, *JAMA*, August 26, 1992—Vol 268, No. 8 pp 1012-1014, used by permission; and excerpts from "Tips for Teens about Alcohol," produced by the Center for Substance Abuse Prevention.

be associated with it. It suggests that as an addiction, alcoholism is not a symptom of an underlying disease state.

"Disease" means an involuntary disability. Use of the term involuntary in defining disease is descriptive of this state as a discrete entity that is not deliberately pursued. It does not suggest passivity in the recovery process. Similarly, use of this term does not imply the abrogation of responsibility in the legal sense. Disease represents the sum of the abnormal phenomena displayed by the group of individuals. These phenomena are associated with a specified common set of characteristics by which certain individuals differ from the norm and which places them at a disadvantage.

"Often progressive and fatal" means that the disease persists over time and that physical, emotional, and social changes are often cumulative and may progress as drinking continues. Alcoholism causes premature death through overdose; through organic complications involving the brain, liver, heart, and other organs; and by contributing to suicide, homicide, motor vehicle accidents, and other traumatic events.

"Impaired control" means the inability to consistently limit on drinking occasions the duration of the drinking episode, the quantity of alcohol consumed, and/or the behavioral consequences.

"Preoccupation" used in association with "alcohol use" indicates excessive, focused attention given to the drug alcohol and to its effects or its use (or both). The relative value the person assigns to alcohol often leads to energy being diverted from important life concerns.

"Adverse consequences" are alcohol-related problems, "disabilities," or impairments in such areas as physical health (eg, alcohol withdrawal syndromes, liver disease, gastritis, anemia, and neurologic disorders), psychologic functioning (eg, cognition and changes in mood and behavior), interpersonal functioning (eg, marital problems, child abuse, and troubled social relationships), occupational functioning (eg, scholastic or job problems), and legal, financial, or spiritual problems. Although the alcohol dependence syndrome may theoretically occur in the absence of adverse consequences, we believe that the latter are evident in virtually all clinical cases.

"Denial" is used in the definition not only in the psychoanalytic sense of a single psychologic defense mechanism disavowing the significance of events but more broadly to include a range of psychologic maneuvers that decrease awareness of the fact that alcohol use is the cause of a person's problems rather than a solution to those problems.

100

Denial becomes an integral part of the disease and is nearly always a major obstacle to recovery. Denial in alcoholism is a complex phenomenon determined by multiple psychologic and physiologic mechanisms. These include the pharmacologic effects of alcohol on memory, the influence of euphoric recall on perception and insight, the role of suppression and repression as psychologic defense mechanisms, and the impact of social and cultural enabling behavior.

How Do I Know If I Have a Drinking Problem?

Chances are if you're even asking the question, you have a drinking problem. But here are some other factors:

- inability to control your drinking—it seems that regardless of what you decide beforehand, you frequently wind up drunk.

- using alcohol to escape your problems.

- changing from your usual reserved character into the "life of the party."

- a change in personality—does drinking turn you from Dr. Jekyll to Mr. Hyde?

- a high tolerance level—you can drink just about everybody under the table.

- blackouts—sometimes you don't remember what happened when you were drinking.

- problems at work or in school as a result of drinking.

- concern shown by your family and friends about your drinking.

If you have a drinking problem, or if you suspect you have a drinking problem, there are many others out there like you, and there is help available. Talk to [someone you trust—such as a school counselor, a friend, or a parent—and contact one of the mutual-help organizations listed in Chapter 60].

If You Suspect a Friend Has a Drinking Problem

- don't be judgmental or preachy—remember, alcoholism is a disease.

- be willing to listen.

- voice your concern about your friend's drinking—but don't ever do it when your friend is under the influence!

- offer your help—go to an AA meeting with your friend or offer to get him/her educational materials.

- be encouraging and positive if your friend takes some initiative.

Chapter 8

The Genetics of Alcoholism

The idea that alcoholism runs in families is an ancient one. In recent decades, science has advanced this idea from the status of folk-observation to systematic investigation. In the 1970s, studies documented that alcoholism does run in families. But does alcoholism run in families because a child learns to become an alcoholic from parents and the home environment, or because a child inherits genes that create an underlying predisposition for alcoholism? Or both? The studies did not resolve these questions.

Why do we do genetic research? The discovery of a specific genetic effect on the development of alcoholism would be beneficial for at least three reasons. First, it would lead to the identification of some people at risk, who could act to avoid developing alcohol-related problems. Second, it may help us to understand the role of environmental factors that are critical in the development of alcoholism. Third, it may lead to better treatments, based on new understandings of the physiological mechanisms of alcoholism.

Although investigations of the inheritance of a *vulnerability to alcoholism* are discussed here, a separate and distinct issue, not addressed here, is the possibility that a *vulnerability to organ damage* by alcohol is under some genetic control.

Researchers investigate possible genetic components of alcoholism by studying populations and families as well as genetic, biochemical,

National Institute on Alcohol Abuse and Alcoholism (NIAAA), *Alcohol Alert*, No. 18, PH328, October 1992 and *Alcohol Alert Supplement*, No 18, PH328S, October 1992.

and neurobehavioral markers and characteristics. Two major methods of investigating the inheritance of alcoholism are studies of twins and of adoptees. Twin studies compare the incidence of alcoholism in identical twins with the incidence of alcoholism in fraternal twins. If there is a genetic component in the risk for alcoholism, then identical twins, who have identical genes, would be expected to exhibit similar histories of developing alcoholism (or not developing alcoholism). Fraternal twins, who are genetically different individuals born at the same time, would be more likely to differ in their tendencies to develop alcoholism. In general, researchers using the twin method have found these expectations to be true.

For example, Pickens and co-workers studied 169 same-sex pairs of twins, both males and females, at least one of which had sought treatment for alcoholism. The researchers found greater concordance of alcohol dependence in identical twins than in fraternal twins. They also found greater concordance of alcohol abuse (defined by *DSM-III— Diagnostic and Statistical Manual of Mental Disorders, Third Edition*, of the American Psychiatric Association) in identical male twins but not in identical female twins. Other twin studies have produced more detailed information; for example, Partanen and co-workers, in studying 902 male Finnish twins, found that less severe drinking patterns were less heritable, and more severe drinking patterns were more heritable.

Among the difficulties in designing twin studies is accounting for unequal environmental conditions. Early studies assumed that the environments of two fraternal twins were as similar to each other as were the environments of two identical twins. Later studies showed that the environments of identical twins are more alike than are the environments of fraternal twins, and recent twin studies have taken this difference into account. The results of twin studies are useful and have suggested the possibility of a genetic component in inheritance; however, because focuses of the studies have varied, the results are difficult to interpret.

Adoption studies may employ a number of techniques. One is to compare the histories of children of alcoholics who are adopted by nonalcoholics and grow up in a nondrinking environment with the histories of children of nonalcoholics similarly raised in a nondrinking environment. If genetic factors play a role, then the adopted children of alcoholics should preferentially develop alcoholism as adults.

Problems in designing and interpreting adoption studies result from, among other things, the lack of detailed data on parents who give up children for adoption, and environmental biases (as in the predominance of a certain type of adopting family).

In a pioneering study of adopted Danish children, Goodwin and co-workers found some evidence for the expected trends. Cloninger and co-workers subsequently performed a series of much larger studies of adoptees, which also revealed these trends.

Cloninger and co-workers hypothesized that so-called type II alcoholics—characterized as having an early onset of drinking problems, usually being male, and displaying personality disorders such as antisocial behavior—had a more heritable form of alcoholism. However, other researchers have argued that the scenario of inheritance is more complex, and what is inherited is a mix of personality traits, such as those related to antisocial behavior, rather than alcoholism itself. Genes might play a direct role in the development of alcoholism, as in affecting the body's metabolism of alcohol; or they might play a less direct role, influencing a person's temperament or personality in such a way that the person becomes vulnerable to alcoholism.

Different models for the way in which alcoholism runs in families have been suggested by a limited number of family studies. Interpretation of these studies has been complicated by the likelihood that alcoholism is a heterogeneous condition, that is, a collection of different conditions that look similar, but whose mechanisms and modes of inheritance may differ. Additional studies are needed to sort out the mechanisms of transmission.

Population and family studies such as those cited above attempt to establish the presence of a broad genetic influence on alcoholism. To investigate specific genes, researchers have employed genetic marker studies. If specific human genes are related to alcoholism, then genes lying close to them on the same chromosome—and the traits they determine—may be inherited at the same time that the risk of alcoholism is inherited. This phenomenon is called linkage. An assortment of genes hypothesized to be linked to alcoholism has been examined, but none has passed a rigorous test for linkage.

Still being studied is a marker referred to as the dopamine D_2 receptor, which Blum and co-workers found to be present more often in alcoholics than in nonalcoholics. In animal studies, the dopamine D_2 receptor had been associated with brain functions relating to reward, reinforcement, and motivation. However, a number of researchers have been unable to duplicate the results of Blum's study. Some researchers believe dopamine D_2 might modulate the severity of alcoholism, rather than serve as a primary cause. The dopamine D_2 association continues to be interesting, but it does not seem to be transmitted in families in such a way that it is responsible for alcoholism; its role, if any, has yet to be determined.

To search the human genome for specific genes related to alcoholism, researchers employ two experimental techniques. The first, the candidate gene approach, involves hypothesizing that particular genes are related to the physiology of alcoholism and then individually testing these genes for linkage. The second approach, scanning of the human genome, involves characterizing, piece by piece, the entire length of DNA and finding genes that relate to alcoholism, without proposing candidate genes.

Additionally, researchers use animal models to study the genetics of alcoholism. These models have several advantages over human subjects. Using animals, researchers can study larger numbers and more generations of subjects, can arrange informative matings, can better manipulate the environment, and can make measurements that would not be possible on humans. The main limitation of using animals to study alcoholism is that there is no animal model of alcoholism that encompasses the whole spectrum of alcoholic behaviors in humans.

Researchers nevertheless have studied alcohol-related behaviors in animals that are believed to resemble aspects of human alcoholism. These include consumption of and preference for alcohol, sedation induced by alcohol, locomotor activation by alcohol (thought by some investigators to model the euphoric effects of alcohol in humans), motor discoordination and hypothermia induced by alcohol, withdrawal from alcohol, and tolerance to various effects of alcohol. Researchers have succeeded in breeding lines of rodents with high or low measures of most of these traits; this success demonstrates that the traits are substantially genetically determined in rodents.

Researchers, using animals, have yet to identify a single gene responsible for any alcohol-related behavior. They have established that all of the above-mentioned traits are determined by multiple genes, and that the individual traits are, for the most part, determined independently of each other. One useful distinction revealed by studies using animals is that genes determining the tendency to become tolerant to certain effects of alcohol are different from genes determining the severity of withdrawal symptoms (even though in a clinical setting these reactions are often seen together). Using the powerful genetic methods available in animals, investigators are beginning to map genes responsible for some of the animals' alcohol-related behaviors. The recent development of a scheme that makes it possible to predict the location on the human genome of a similar gene mapped in a mouse will provide an additional source of candidate genes for linkage studies in humans. This approach also will help to distinguish those animal behaviors now under study that will be most valuable for understanding human alcohol-related behavior.

NIAAA's Genetic Research

Substantial evidence indicates that genetic factors play a significant role in the development of at least some forms of alcoholism. The National Institute on Alcohol Abuse and Alcoholism (NIAAA) both conducts and sponsors research to answer such questions as, What are the genetic risk factors for vulnerability to alcoholism? How does heredity interact with the environment in the development of alcoholism? What markers may enable us to recognize an individual at high risk for problem drinking?

Family (Pedigree) Studies

In the fall of 1989, NIAAA initiated a Cooperative Agreement on Genetics of Alcoholism (COGA), involving seven research institutions throughout the Nation. This multi-disciplinary, collaborative study will attempt to determine how vulnerability to alcoholism is transmitted through families. Pedigrees of large families will be collected in an effort to map genes predisposing to the development of alcoholism. Traits that are cotransmitted with alcoholism will be identified. These traits can then be used as markers to identify people at increased risk for alcoholism. Markers may include measurements of brain electrical activity, or behavioral, neurological, or psychological characteristics. The study will ultimately attempt to pinpoint the actual chromosomal locations of genes that influence the susceptibility to alcoholism. Several hundred families with multiple alcoholic members will be examined. A repository of DNA samples from alcoholics and family members, along with associated data files, are expected to become a national resource to be shared with the research community.

A wide range of additional NIAAA-supported research is using twin and family studies to explore various specific aspects of alcoholism. An example is a study pertaining to the genetic and environmental risk factors for adolescent drinking. Researchers will interview adolescent twins and their parents to assess alcohol consumption and alcohol-related problems, as well as behavioral and psychiatric risk factors such as other drug use and depression. Subjects will be selected from families with a history of parental problem drinking, as well as from families without such history. Genetic analysis will be used to test hypotheses concerning the developmental pathways by which genetic risk for alcoholism, as well as environmental risk factors, operate; to identify factors that moderate these developmental pathways; and to explore the interaction of genetic and environmental risk factors in these pathways.

An ongoing pedigree-based study attempts to determine the molecular genetic basis of susceptibility to subtypes of alcoholism. Genetic analysis has provided preliminary evidence for the major effect of a single gene in the families of so-called type II alcoholics, who have early onset, several alcoholic relatives, and antisocial personality traits.

It has been suggested that certain anomalies of brain function may be markers of a vulnerability to alcoholism. For example, an alteration of an electrical brain wave known as P300 has been found in young boys who have never used alcohol, but who are at risk for alcoholism because their fathers are alcoholic. One study is comparing P300 and other measures of brain function in different subgroups of abstinent alcoholics classified according to specific clinical factors and family history. These studies should provide data for identifying markers associated with alcoholism.

NIAAA scientists have completed a study on another genetic variant of brain electrical activity known as low voltage alpha (LVA). In a population study, the LVA trait was found to be at least four times more common in alcoholics and in persons with anxiety disorder than in the general population. A genetic transmission and linkage study is underway to identify genes for LVA.

Genetics and Alcohol Metabolism

It has been suggested that genetic differences in the enzymes responsible for alcohol metabolism and elimination may account for a substantial part of individual differences in alcohol consumption and its consequences. There are various subtypes of the two major alcohol-metabolizing enzymes. NIAAA-sponsored research is underway to clone the genes that code for these enzyme subtypes so that they can be compared. Researchers at NIAAA have already cloned a subtype of the enzyme alcohol dehydrogenase and have mapped it to a specific chromosomal location in both mouse and humans.

One project has examined some of the genetic antecedents of protection from alcoholism in certain populations of Asians. A single-gene mutation in these populations renders inactive an enzyme involved in alcohol metabolism, resulting in an unpleasant facial flushing reaction following alcohol ingestion. This study will continue to explore the interrelationships among enzyme activity, the flushing response, and family history of alcoholism in different populations of interest.

Studies on Women

Traditionally, most alcohol-related studies on humans have used mostly male subjects, despite the possibility of sex-related differences in both vulnerability to alcoholism and alcohol-related health effects. An NIAAA-funded project is currently applying statistical and genetic methods to study 1,033 same-sex female twins in Virginia and their surviving parents to quantify the role of genetic and environmental factors in the origins of alcohol dependence in women.

Another study is assessing the transmission of alcoholism within families of alcoholic women to determine if the mode of transmission suggests the involvement of multiple genes or one major gene, and to attempt to quantify the lifetime risk of developing alcoholism among children of alcoholic mothers.

The Genetics of Alcohol's Health Effects

Approximately 10 percent of detoxified alcoholics are severely impaired as a result of alcohol-associated chronic organic brain disorders. It is hypothesized that an aberrant form of the enzyme transketolase may be a risk factor for alcoholic brain damage. Two NIAAA-funded projects study the gene that determines the structure of the enzyme transketolase. Results will be used in family studies to evaluate the association between forms of transketolase and alcoholic organic brain disease.

Additional studies sponsored by NIAAA include an investigation of the genetics of differential susceptibility to alcohol-induced liver disease, and the influence of genetic differences on susceptibility to alcohol-related birth defects.

Animal Studies on Susceptibility

It has been suggested that there may be a link between alcohol's reinforcing capabilities and its ability to cause increased motor activity in laboratory animals (activation). Whether this link exists, and, if it does, the mechanism that may account for it are being studied.

Laboratory studies using physical activity levels in mice as a measure of motor activity have shown clear genetic influences on this effect. Studies are using genetically defined mouse strains to identify any relationships between alcohol's activating effect, its anxiety-reducing effects, and its potential aggression-stimulating properties, relationships important for the evaluation of some of the current theories of alcoholism subtypes. Genetic experiments on mice will attempt to map individual genes contributing to these effects.

Animal Studies on Neurochemistry

Alcohol affects the function of the brain receptor for the inhibitory neurotransmitter GABA, and this altered function is thought to be involved in alcohol withdrawal symptoms. Some researchers believe that the GABA receptor is also involved in baseline sensitivity of the nervous system to alcohol, although the mechanism of this involvement is unclear. In ground-breaking research, NIAAA-supported investigators have shown that one target for the action of alcohol on the GABA receptor is one of the roughly 16 different proteins that compose that receptor. Using mice, these investigators hope to determine how a mutation in the gene encoding this protein might affect the response to alcohol.

Mapping Genes in Diseases That Have Complex Genetic Origins

An important step in the analysis of a putative alcoholism-related gene (or any gene under study) is its mapping. Mapping is the process of determining the position of a gene on a chromosome relative to other genes on that chromosome. Most alcohol-metabolizing enzymes are encoded by single genes or families of related genes. But alcohol-related behavior (such as sensitivity, tolerance, dependence, or withdrawal) is more complex. People differ quantitatively in such behavioral traits, rather than in an all-or-none fashion; differences in such traits are correspondingly determined by more than one gene, each responsible for only part of the observed variation. These genes are known collectively as quantitative trait loci (QTL), and their effects are additive.

Recent advances in mapping methodology have made it possible for the first time to map individual QTLs, even when they are responsible for as little as 5 percent of the observed variation. The ability to map QTLs is an important breakthrough in the field of alcohol genetics. It has already revolutionized the way researchers approach genetic studies on alcohol-related behavior in animals; studies are becoming more specific, concentrating on identifying and locating individual genes. Mapping of these genes paves the way for their eventual isolation and characterization, which will lead to great strides in our understanding of how alcohol affects behavior.

One NIAAA-funded project is characterizing two widely used strains of laboratory mice on an extensive battery of alcohol-related traits, applying QTL analysis to the data. Another study involves Long-Sleep (LS) and Short-Sleep (SS) lines of mice, so called because of their differential sensitivity to the anesthetizing action of alcohol. It is estimated that seven genes are responsible for this differential sensitivity. Investigators will map these genes, and will then isolate and clone the genes responsible for differential sensitivity to the effects of alcohol on the nervous system.

Perhaps most importantly, QTL analysis will provide a critical way of validating many of the animal genetic models used in alcohol research. A reservation that has been expressed about animal genetic research is that we do not know how the comparatively simple behaviors observed in animals relate to the exceedingly complex behavioral spectrum of human alcoholism. Isolation of mouse QTLs that determine differences in alcohol-related behaviors will enable researchers to search for equivalent genes in humans. Having identified these genes, it will be possible to test whether alcoholics actually differ from nonalcoholics at any of these genes. This research will not only provide a new set of genes that may be involved in the development of human alcoholism, but will also enable researchers to decide more objectively which alcohol-related animal behaviors will be most informative about alcoholism.

The coming decade will be a period of unprecedented progress in genetics. Results of research on the genetics of alcoholism will enable the identification of persons at high risk for alcoholism, and will support the development of more effective treatment and prevention strategies.

A Commentary by NIAAA Director Enoch Gordis, M.D.

Progress has been made in understanding genetic vulnerability to alcoholism. We know, for instance, that more than one gene is likely to be responsible for this vulnerability. We now must determine what these genes are and whether they are specific for alcohol or define something more general, such as differences in temperament or personality that increase an individual's vulnerability to alcoholism. We must also determine how genes and the environment interact to influence vulnerability to alcoholism. Based on our current understanding, it is probable that environmental influences will be at least as important, and possibly more important, than genetic influences. Success in uncovering the genes involved in a vulnerability to alcoholism will help us to recognize the potential for alcoholism in high-risk individuals, to intervene at an early stage, and to develop new treatments for alcohol-related problems. This is a productive area of research that will continue to yield important answers to the basic questions of what causes alcoholism and how we can prevent and treat it.

Chapter 9

Alcohol and Minorities

Do blacks, Hispanics, American Indians, and Asians and Pacific Islanders in the United States drink more or less than whites drink? Do they have more alcohol-related medical problems? Do they receive treatment in proportion to their problems? In 1990, 68.3 percent of whites, 64.5 percent of Hispanics, and 55.6 percent of blacks used alcohol. Although these percentages appear similar, different patterns of use and abuse and varying prevalence of alcohol-related problems underlie the numbers. This *Alcohol Alert* considers why some minorities have more medical problems than others and whether minorities receive adequate treatment and prevention services. It examines genetic and environmental factors that may put minorities at risk for or protect them from alcohol problems. It also reviews research on screening to identify those at risk for alcoholism or alcohol abuse.

Medical Consequences and Alcohol-Related Trauma

Given major underreporting of alcohol-related diagnoses, minimum estimates from one survey of non-Federal, short-stay hospitals in 1991 found 54.5 patient discharges for alcohol-related diagnoses for every 10,000 people in the United States over age 15. The rate for whites was 48.2 per 10,000; however, the rate for blacks was 102.9 per 10,000 population. Because it is not known whether the rates of

National Institute on Alcohol Abuse and Alcoholism (NIAAA), *Alcohol Alert*, No. 23, PH347, January 1994.

underreporting are equal among ethnic groups, it is difficult to interpret the meaning of such reported differences.

A study of alcohol-related mortality in California showed that blacks and Hispanics had higher rates of mortality from alcoholic cirrhosis than did whites or Asian-Americans. Nationwide, death rates attributed to alcohol dependence syndrome also were highest for blacks, although a higher percentage of blacks than whites abstain from using alcohol. The high rates of medical problems seen in blacks thus occur among a smaller percentage of the black population when compared with whites.

The California study suggests that for many alcohol-related causes of death such as alcohol dependence syndrome and alcoholic hepatitis, Hispanics had either similar or lower mortality rates compared with whites. However, the mortality rate among Hispanics from alcohol-related motor vehicle crashes was 9.16 per 100,000, significantly higher than the rates for whites (8.15) or blacks (8.02).

The group identified as "Asian/Other" in the California study had lower rates of alcohol-related mortality than any other group for most causes of death. Their mortality rate from motor vehicle crashes, for example, was 5.39 per 100,000. Asians tend to have lower rates of drinking and alcohol abuse than whites.

Although highly variable among tribes, alcohol abuse is a factor in five leading causes of death for American Indians, including motor vehicle crashes, alcoholism, cirrhosis, suicide, and homicide. Mortality rates for crashes and alcoholism are 5.5 and 3.8 times higher, respectively, among American Indians than among the general population. Among tribes with high rates of alcoholism, reports estimate that 75 percent of all accidents, the leading cause of death among American Indians, are alcohol related.

Fetal Alcohol Syndrome (FAS)

The prevalence of FAS among select groups of Navajo, Pueblo, and Southwestern Plains Indians has been studied. Among two populations of Southwestern Plains Indians ages newborn to 14 years, 10.7 of every 1,000 children were born with FAS. This was compared with 2.2 per 1,000 for Pueblo Indians and 1.6 for Navajo. Overall rates for FAS in the United States range from 1 to 3 per 1,000. Cultural influences, patterns of alcohol consumption, nutrition, and differing rates of alcohol metabolism or other innate physiological differences may account for the varying FAS rates among Indian communities.

The incidence of FAS among blacks appears to be about seven times higher than among whites, although more blacks than whites abstain from drinking. The reasons for this difference in FAS rates are not yet known. Paradoxically, one study has found that black women believe drinking is acceptable in fewer social situations than do white women. Ten percent of black compared with 23 percent of white women surveyed said that drinking more than one or two drinks at a bar with friends is acceptable. This attitudinal difference could help to explain why fewer black women are frequent, high-quantity drinkers than are white women. Nevertheless, FAS seems to be more prevalent among blacks than among whites.

Genetic Influences

Certain minority groups may possess genetic traits that either predispose them to or protect them from becoming alcoholic. Few such traits have so far been discovered. However, the flushing reaction, found in the highest concentrations among people of Asian ancestry, is one example.

Flushing has been linked to variants of genes for enzymes involved in alcohol metabolism. It involves a reddening of the face and neck due to increased blood flow to those areas and can be accompanied by headaches, nausea, and other symptoms. Flushing can occur when even small amounts of alcohol are consumed.

Japanese-Americans living in Los Angeles have been studied. Among those with quick flushing responses (flushing occurs after one drink or less), fewer consumed alcohol than did those with no or with slow flushing responses (flushing occurs after two or more drinks). In another group of Japanese-American students in Los Angeles, flushing was far less correlated with abstention from alcohol than it was in the first group. Thus, although flushing appears to deter alcohol use, people with the trait may nevertheless consume alcohol.

Another genetic difference between ethnic groups occurs among other enzymes involved in metabolizing alcohol in the liver. Variations have been observed between the structures and activity levels of the enzymes prevalent among Asians, blacks, and whites. One enzyme found in Japanese, for example, has been associated with faster elimination of alcohol from the body when compared with whites. Interesting leads relating these varying rates of alcohol metabolism among minorities to medical complications of alcoholism, such as liver disease, are now being followed.

115

Influence of Acculturation

Acculturation has a dramatic effect on drinking patterns among immigrants to the United States and successive generations. Comparisons of drinking among immigrant and second and third generation Mexican-American women reveal that drinking rates of successive generations approach those of the general population of American women. Seventy-five percent of Mexican immigrant women in one study abstained from alcohol; only 38 percent of third generation Mexican-American women abstained. This rate is close to the 36-percent abstention rate for women in the general U.S. population. Rates of alcohol-related problems also may be affected by acculturation. A study has found that Hispanic women who are at least second generation Americans have higher rates of social and personal problems than either foreign born or first generation Hispanic women. Studies of Asian-Americans have suggested that their drinking rates conform to those of the U.S. population as acculturation occurs.

Identification and Treatment

Do screening instruments for alcohol-related problems, validated in primarily white populations, accurately detect alcohol problems among minorities? One study evaluated the Self-Administered Alcoholism Screening Test (SAAST), translated into Spanish, in Mexico City and the original English version in Rochester, MN. The Spanish translation identified alcoholics and nonalcoholics at rates comparable to those of the English version. The study found that the questions that best predicted alcoholism were the same in both versions. This study suggests that translations or other revisions of screening tools may be just as accurate as the original instruments, but more studies are needed before firm conclusions can be drawn.

It is not known whether all treatment programs are effective for members of minority groups. Among minority patients who enter treatment programs for the general population, success rates are equal to those of whites in the same programs. Also, despite the existence of programs designed to treat specific minority groups, no evidence exists that either supports or denies their ability to produce improved outcomes.

Do minorities have the same access to alcoholism treatment as do whites? Access to treatment for minorities has not been assessed widely, but several factors have been studied. There is evidence that not everyone in these groups who needs treatment receives it. For example, Hispanics and blacks are less likely to have health insurance and more likely to be below the poverty level than whites, factors that may decrease their access to treatment.

No studies focus on access to alcoholism treatment for the U.S. Hispanic population as a whole. Some culturally sensitive programs exist for Hispanics and are often aimed at specific cultures within this group, such as Puerto Ricans. These programs have not been evaluated.

Prevention

Prevention efforts that work among the general population have been shown to be effective among some minorities. However, it is unclear whether interventions designed for specific minorities also would be beneficial. For example, programs incorporating peer counseling, enhancing adolescents' coping skills, and alcohol education appear to be effective among American Indians. One study has demonstrated that specific populations of American Indian adolescents who completed such a program used less alcohol when compared with their peers 6 months after completion of the program. A second study showed that American Indian participants in another program decreased their own use of alcohol when evaluated 12 months after the program's completion.

The effectiveness of warning labels on alcoholic beverage containers has been evaluated in a group of black women. A study showed that 6 months after the label was mandated by law, pregnant black women who were light drinkers slightly reduced their drinking during pregnancy, whereas black women who were heavier drinkers did not change their drinking habits.

A Commentary by NIAAA Director Enoch Gordis, M.D.

The increasing number of studies of alcohol problems among minorities has produced both important findings and new questions to answer. Higher abstention rates among African-Americans coexist with higher cirrhosis mortality. Native American groups vary greatly in their drinking practices, but the specific contributions of social, cultural, and genetic influences to these variations are not yet known. We need to understand why acculturation seems to increase drinking among successive generations of Hispanics and diminishes the

117

"protective" effect of the flushing reaction among succeeding generations of Asian-Americans. Finally, we need to know more about disparities in access to treatment and prevention among minority groups and whether culturally relevant treatment approaches improve treatment outcome.

Chapter 10

Alcohol and Women

Much of our knowledge of alcoholism has been gathered from studies conducted with a predominance of male subjects. Recent studies involving more female subjects reveal that drinking differs between men and women.

Studies in the general population indicate that fewer women than men drink. It is estimated that of the 15.1 million alcohol-abusing or alcohol-dependent individuals in the United States, approximately 4.6 million (nearly one-third) are women. On the whole, women who drink consume less alcohol and have fewer alcohol-related problems and dependence symptoms than men, yet among the heaviest drinkers, women equal or surpass men in the number of problems that result from their drinking.

Drinking behavior differs with the age, life role, and marital status of women. In general, a woman's drinking resembles that of her husband, siblings, or close friends. Whereas younger women (aged 18-34) report higher rates of drinking-related problems than do older women, the incidence of alcohol dependence is greater among middle-aged women (aged 35-49).

Contrary to popular belief, women who have multiple roles (e.g., married women who work outside the home) may have lower rates of alcohol problems than women who do not have multiple roles. In fact, role deprivation (e.g., loss of role as wife, mother, or worker) may increase a woman's risk for abusing alcohol. Women who have never

National Institute on Alcohol Abuse and Alcoholism (NIAAA), *Alcohol Alert*, No. 10, PH290, October 1990.

married or who are divorced or separated are more likely to drink heavily and experience alcohol-related problems than women who are married or widowed. Unmarried women living with a partner are more likely still to engage in heavy drinking and to develop drinking problems.

Heath and colleagues studied drinking behavior among a select sample of female twins to identify possible environmental factors that may modulate drinking behavior. They reported that, among women, marital status appears to modify the effects of genetic factors that influence drinking habits. Marriage or a marriage-like relationship lessens the effect of an inherited liability for drinking.

Several researchers have explored whether drinking patterns and alcohol-related problems vary among women of different racial or ethnic groups. Black women (46 percent) are more likely to abstain from alcohol than white women (34 percent). Further, although it is commonly assumed that a larger proportion of black women drink heavily, researchers have disproved this assumption: Equal proportions of black and white women drink heavily. Black women report fewer alcohol-related personal and social problems than white women, yet a greater proportion of black women experience alcohol-related health problems.

Data from self-report surveys suggest that Hispanic women are infrequent drinkers or abstainers, but this may change as they enter new social and work arenas. Gilbert found that reports of abstention are greater among Hispanic women who have immigrated to the United States; reports of moderate or heavy drinking are greater among younger, American-born Hispanic women.

The interval between onset of drinking-related problems and entry into treatment appears to be shorter for women than for men. Moreover, studies of women alcoholics in treatment suggest that they often experience greater physiological impairment earlier in their drinking careers, despite having consumed less alcohol than men. These findings suggest that the development of consequences associated with heavy drinking may be accelerated or "telescoped" in women.

In addition to these many psychosocial and epidemiological differences, the sexes also experience different physiological effects of alcohol. Women become intoxicated after drinking smaller quantities of alcohol than are needed to produce intoxication in men. Three possible mechanisms may explain this response.

First, women have lower total body water content than men of comparable size. After alcohol is consumed, it diffuses uniformly into all body water, both inside and outside cells. Because of their smaller quantity of body water, women achieve higher concentrations of alcohol in their blood than men after drinking equivalent amounts of alcohol. More simply, blood alcohol concentration in women may be likened to the result of dropping the same quantity of alcohol into a smaller pail of water.

Second, diminished activity of alcohol dehydrogenase (the primary enzyme involved in the metabolism of alcohol) in the stomach also may contribute to the gender-related differences in blood alcohol concentrations and a woman's heightened vulnerability to the physiological consequences of drinking. Julkunen and colleagues demonstrated in rats that a substantial amount of alcohol is metabolized by gastric alcohol dehydrogenase in the stomach before it enters the systemic circulation. This "first-pass metabolism" of alcohol decreases the availability of alcohol to the system. Frezza and colleagues reported that, because of diminished activity of gastric alcohol dehydrogenase, first-pass metabolism was decreased in women compared with men and was virtually nonexistent in alcoholic women.

Third, fluctuations in gonadal hormone levels during the menstrual cycle may affect the rate of alcohol metabolism, making a woman more susceptible to elevated blood alcohol concentrations at different points in the cycle. Research findings to date, however, have been inconsistent.

Chronic alcohol abuse exacts a greater physical toll on women than on men. Female alcoholics have death rates 50 to 100 percent higher than those of male alcoholics. Further, a greater percentage of female alcoholics die from suicides, alcohol-related accidents, circulatory disorders, and cirrhosis of the liver.

Increasing evidence suggests that the detrimental effects of alcohol on the liver are more severe for women than for men. Women develop alcoholic liver disease, particularly alcoholic cirrhosis and hepatitis, after a comparatively shorter period of heavy drinking and at a lower level of daily drinking than men. Proportionately more alcoholic women die from cirrhosis than do alcoholic men.

The exact mechanisms that underlie women's heightened vulnerability to alcohol-induced liver damage are unclear. Differences in body weight and fluid content between men and women may be contributing factors. In addition, Johnson and Williams suggested that the combined effect of estrogens and alcohol may augment liver damage. Finally, alcoholic women may be more susceptible to liver damage because of the diminished activity of gastric alcohol dehydrogenase in first-pass metabolism.

Drinking also may be associated with an increased risk for breast cancer. After reviewing epidemiological data on alcohol consumption and the incidence of breast cancer, Longnecker and colleagues reported that risk increases when a woman consumes 1 ounce or more of absolute alcohol daily. Increased risk appears to be related directly to the effects of alcohol. Moreover, risk for breast cancer and lower levels of alcohol consumption are weakly associated. Data from other studies, however, do not concur with these findings, suggesting that more research is needed to explore the relationship between drinking and breast cancer.

Menstrual disorders (e.g., painful menstruation, heavy flow, premenstrual discomfort, and irregular or absent cycles) have been associated with chronic heavy drinking. These disorders can have adverse effects on fertility. Further, continued drinking may lead to early menopause.

Animal studies have provided data that replicate the findings of studies in humans to determine the effects of chronic alcohol consumption on female reproductive function. Studies in rodents and monkeys demonstrated that prolonged alcohol exposure disrupts estrus regularity and increases the incidence of ovulatory failure.

Researchers have begun to examine whether women and men require distinct treatment approaches. It has been suggested that women alcoholics may encounter different conditions that facilitate or discourage their entry into treatment.

Women represent 25.4 percent of alcoholism clients in traditional treatment centers in the United States. Although it appears that they comprise a small proportion of the treatment population (25 percent women compared with 75 percent men), the proportion of female alcoholics to male alcoholics in treatment is similar to the proportion of all female alcoholics to male alcoholics (30 percent women to 70 percent men). In addition, women drinkers pursue avenues other than traditional alcoholism programs, such as psychiatric services or personal physicians, for treatment.

Women alcoholics may encounter motivators and barriers to seeking treatment that differ from those encountered by men. Women are more likely to seek treatment because of family problems, and they often are encouraged by parents or children to pursue therapy. Men usually are encouraged to pursue therapy by their wives. Fewer women than men reach treatment through the criminal justice system or through employee assistance programs. Lack of child care is one of the most frequently reported barriers to treatment for alcoholic women.

Sokolow and colleagues attempted to compare treatment outcome between men and women and reported that, among those who completed treatment, abstinence was slightly higher among women than among men. Women had a higher abstinence rate if treated in a medically oriented alcoholism facility, whereas the abstinence rate was higher for men treated in a peer group-oriented facility. Treatment outcome was better for women treated in a facility with a smaller proportion of female clients and better for men in a facility with a larger proportion of female clients. This study provided preliminary data on gender-specific treatment outcome; however, the trials were not controlled. Although the question of whether women should have separate treatment opportunities is an important one, the supporting evidence still has not been found.

A Commentary by NIAAA Director Enoch Gordis, M.D.

The extent of women's participation in alcoholism treatment appears to equal roughly the prevalence of alcohol-related problems among women. Even so, some women may face barriers that limit access to treatment. Limited financial resources may be one barrier. For example, many women do not have access to the employer-paid alcoholism treatment provided by larger industries, where men tend to predominate in the work force. Child-care concerns and the fear that an identified alcohol problem will cause the loss of dependent children also may create barriers to treatment. With regard to treatment, many questions remain to be answered by research, including whether specialized treatment in a women-only program is more effective than treatment in a mixed-gender setting.

Previous concerns about a lack of women as research subjects in alcohol studies are beginning to be addressed. However, there have been recent charges that alcohol research on women is discriminatory. Research on fetal alcohol and drug effects and the fear of discriminatory actions, such as imprisoning pregnant women solely because of their addiction, is central to this controversy. The issue of fetal effects and how to prevent and treat them will not go away simply because discriminatory policies have been suggested. The challenge for alcohol research will be how both sexes can benefit from the fruits of science.

Chapter 11

Estimating the Economic Cost of Alcohol Abuse

Alcohol abuse and its related problems cost society many billions of dollars each year. Estimates of the economic costs of alcohol abuse attempt to assess in monetary terms the damage that results from the misuse of alcohol. These costs include expenditures on alcohol-related problems and opportunities that are lost because of alcohol. This *Alcohol Alert* addresses issues pertaining to estimates of the costs of alcohol abuse, focusing on the types of costs considered and on the various problems associated with their estimation.

While many difficulties in cost estimation are common to cost-of-illness studies in other health fields, two problems are particularly relevant to the case of alcohol abuse. First, researchers attempt to identify costs that are caused by, and not merely associated with, alcohol abuse, yet it is often hard to establish causation. Second, many costs resulting from alcohol abuse cannot be measured directly. This is especially true of costs that involve placing a dollar value on lost productivity. Researchers use mathematical and statistical methods to estimate such costs, yet recognize that this is imprecise. Moreover, costs of pain and suffering of both people who abuse alcohol and people affected by them cannot be estimated in any reliable way, and are therefore not considered in most cost studies. These difficulties underscore the fact that although the economic cost of alcohol abuse can be estimated, it cannot be measured precisely. Nevertheless, estimates

National Institute on Alcohol Abuse and Alcoholism (NIAAA), *Alcohol Alert*, No. 11, PH293, January 1991.

of the cost give us an idea of the dimensions of the problem, and the breakdown of costs suggests to us which categories are most costly.

In the most recent cost study, Rice and co-workers estimated that the cost to society of alcohol abuse was $70.3 billion in 1985; a previous study by Harwood and colleagues estimated that the cost for 1980 was $89 billion. By adjusting cost estimates for the effects of inflation and the growth of the population over time, Rice projected that the total cost of alcohol abuse in 1988 was $85.9 billion, and Harwood projected that the cost in 1983 was $116 billion.

The differences among the estimates produced by these and earlier studies largely are the result of changes in methodology and sources of data. Because of these key changes, one cannot conclude firmly that the differences in the estimates reflect changes in actual costs. Although an improvement over earlier efforts, the Rice study underestimates some costs, such as the high costs of injury related to alcohol abuse. The differences among the results of the studies underscore the lack of precision that might be expected in such a large and complex estimation.

To estimate costs of illness, researchers have developed standard categories of costs. Most of the costs of alcohol abuse result from the adverse effects of alcohol consumption on health. The principal categories of health-related costs of alcohol abuse are (1) expenditures on medical treatment (a large proportion of which is for the many medical consequences of alcohol consumption; the remainder is for treatment of alcohol abuse and dependence themselves), (2) the lost productivity that results from workers' abuse of alcohol, and (3) the losses to society from premature deaths that are due to alcohol problems. The first category of costs is that of treating the medical consequences of alcohol abuse and treating alcohol abuse and dependence themselves. To estimate these costs, Rice and colleagues developed a new procedure. They estimated treatment costs in short-stay hospitals using hospital discharge records, and estimated costs incurred in other settings using a variety of procedures. Rice and co-workers calculated a cost of $6.3 billion for treatment of the medical consequences of alcohol abuse and treatment of alcohol dependence in all settings in 1985, and in addition, nearly $500 million for support costs, such as the costs of training medical staffs. In the prior study, Harwood and co-workers estimated that in 1980, such treatment costs were more than $9 billion, and support costs were nearly $1 billion.

Rice and colleagues estimated treatment costs in short-stay hospitals using the average cost per patient—about $460 per day in 1985—and applied this average daily cost to the approximately 5 million days of care for discharges for alcohol dependence, alcohol abuse, and a set of medical disorders linked to alcohol use. This yielded a cost of $2.3 billion for 1985.

Added to this was an assessment of the additional costs of treating other medical conditions when they are accompanied by a secondary diagnosis indicating alcohol involvement. Rice and colleagues assessed, for such cases, the costs for extra days of care beyond the average hospital stay when alcohol is not involved in the diagnosis. Finally, the researchers added the costs of treatment in a variety of other settings, including alcohol treatment facilities, nursing homes, Veterans Administration hospitals, military hospitals, Indian Health Service facilities, and physicians' offices.

This new approach may underestimate treatment costs because alcohol involvement often is undiagnosed or unreported in hospital discharge records, and because medical conditions that researchers use as indicators of alcohol abuse in an individual (e.g., alcoholic cirrhosis of the liver) represent only a portion of those conditions that might be caused by alcohol abuse. An example of relevant information often not reflected in hospital discharge records is the role of alcohol in the occurrence of many injuries.

The second category of health-related costs includes losses in productivity by workers who abuse alcohol. These costs are difficult to measure, in part because of the lack of records on goods and services that are not produced. To approximate the value of goods and services that are lost because of alcohol abuse, economists use a substitute measure—the reductions in income suffered by workers who abuse alcohol. This technique is subject to various problems, however, including the possible lack of representativeness in data, and difficulties in specifying the complex causal linkages between alcohol abuse and impaired productivity. Further, some productivity losses, such as declines in product quality and disruption of workplace processes by absences, cannot be captured using the lost-income approach. Rice and co-workers estimated that the costs of reduced productivity because of alcohol abuse were more than $27 billion in 1985, and Harwood estimated that they were $54 billion in 1980.

The third category of health-related costs is the loss to society because of premature deaths due to alcohol abuse. It is controversial to assign a monetary value to human life, yet such an accounting is an essential part of any cost-of-illness estimate. One technique is to approximate the loss associated with a premature death as the value of future earnings lost. This "human capital" approach is standard in cost-of-illness studies, including the studies by Rice and Harwood.

Critics of this approach contend that it understates the value of human life, especially for women and retired people. Using the "human capital" approach, Rice estimated that the costs of premature deaths due to alcohol abuse were $24 billion in 1985, and Harwood estimated that they were $14.5 billion in 1980.

There is a special cost of alcohol abuse that is considered separately from the costs already mentioned here. This is the cost of fetal alcohol syndrome. Costs associated with this disease include the costs of residential care, neonatal care, and treatment for hearing loss, mental impairment, and anatomical abnormalities. Rice and co-workers estimated that the costs of fetal alcohol syndrome were $1.6 billion in 1985. In addition to the health-related costs of alcohol abuse are costs involving the criminal justice system, social welfare administration, property losses from alcohol-related motor vehicle crashes and fires, and lost productivity of the victims of alcohol-related crime and individuals imprisoned as a consequence of alcohol-related crime. Rice and co-workers estimated these costs to be $10.5 billion for 1985.

A Commentary by NIAAA Director Enoch Gordis, M.D.

Measuring the economic cost of an illness is one way to assess the overall impact of that illness on society. Although there are problems in estimating such costs, the fact that two major studies of the cost of alcohol abuse and alcoholism, using different methodologies, arrived at similar results, confirms the enormous magnitude of the damage done to society by alcohol-related problems.

I wish to emphasize that the costs of treating alcoholism are only a minority of total alcohol-related health costs; medical consequences of alcohol use—trauma, cirrhosis, pancreatitis, and so forth—account for the majority. Perhaps if patients at risk for alcohol-related problems were identified before repeated traumas or health problems occur, these costs might be reduced. Although some progress has been made to improve early identification and referral of alcohol abusers by physicians and other health care personnel, we still have not reached the point where attention to a patient's alcohol use pattern is a routine part of medical care.

Finally, a caveat. Studies of the economic cost of illness do not provide guidance as to what remedies are likely to be effective or what the costs of possible remedies might be. Therefore, although they provide important information on the magnitude of an illness. These studies, alone, should not be used as the basis for public policy decisions.

Chapter 12

Moderate Drinking

Moderate drinking is difficult to define because it means different things to different people. The term is often confused with "social drinking," which refers to drinking patterns that are accepted by the society in which they occur. However, social drinking is not necessarily free of problems. Moderate drinking may be defined as drinking that does not generally cause problems, either for the drinker or for society. Since there are clearly both benefits and risks associated with lower levels of drinking, this *Alcohol Alert* will explore potentially positive and adverse effects of "moderate" drinking.

It would be useful if the above definition of moderate drinking were bolstered by numerical estimates of "safe" drinking limits. However, the usefulness of quantitative definitions of moderate drinking is compromised by the likelihood that a given dose of alcohol may affect different people differently. Adding further complexity, the pattern of drinking is also an important determinant of alcohol-related consequences. Thus, while epidemiologic data are often collected in terms of the "average number of drinks per week," one drink taken each day may have different consequences than seven drinks taken on a Saturday night.

Despite the complexity, numerical definitions of moderate drinking do exist. For example, guidelines put forth jointly by the U.S. Department of Agriculture and the U.S. Department of Health and Human Services define moderate drinking as no more than one drink

National Institute on Alcohol Abuse and Alcoholism (NIAAA), *Alcohol Alert*, No. 16, PH315, April 1992.

a day for most women, and no more than two drinks a day for most men. A standard drink is generally considered to be 12 ounces of beer, 5 ounces of wine, or 1.5 ounces of 80-proof distilled spirits. Each of these drinks contains roughly the same amount of absolute alcohol—approximately 0.5 ounce or 12 grams.

These guidelines exclude the following persons, who should not consume alcoholic beverages: women who are pregnant or trying to conceive; people who plan to drive or engage in other activities that require attention or skill; people taking medication, including over-the-counter medications; recovering alcoholics; and persons under the age of 21. Although not specifically addressed by the guidelines, alcohol use also is contraindicated for people with certain medical conditions such as peptic ulcer.

The existence of separate guidelines for men and women reflects research findings that women become more intoxicated than men at an equivalent dose of alcohol. This results, in part, from the significant difference in activity of an enzyme in stomach tissue of males and females that breaks down alcohol before it reaches the bloodstream. The enzyme is four times more active in males than in females. Moreover, women have proportionately more fat and less body water than men. Because alcohol is more soluble in water than in fat, a given dose becomes more highly concentrated in a female's body water than in a male's.

Since the proportion of body fat increases with age, Dufour and colleagues recommend a limit of one drink per day for the elderly.

Benefits of Moderate Drinking

Psychological Benefits of Moderate Drinking

A review of the literature suggests that lower levels of alcohol consumption can reduce stress; promote conviviality and pleasant and carefree feelings; and decrease tension, anxiety, and self-consciousness. In the elderly, moderate drinking has been reported to stimulate appetite, promote regular bowel function, and improve mood.

Cardiovascular Benefits of Moderate Drinking

There is a considerable body of evidence that lower levels of drinking decrease the risk of death from coronary artery disease (CAD).

This effect has been demonstrated in a broad range of older epidemiologic studies. More recently, Boffetta and Garfinkel found that white American men who reported in 1959 that they consumed an average of fewer than three drinks per day were less likely to die during the next 12 years than men who reported abstinence. This finding was due primarily to a reduction in CAD. In a similar study using a wide range of ethnic groups, De Labry and colleagues found that rates of overall mortality were lowest for men who consumed fewer than three drinks per day over a 12-year period.

Similar results have been obtained with female subjects. Stampfer and colleagues analyzed data on middle-aged women and determined that consumption of approximately one drink per day decreases the risks of coronary heart disease. Razay and colleagues, using a random population sample, found consumption of up to two drinks per day to be associated with lower levels of cardiovascular risk factors in women. In postmenopausal women, the apparent protective effect of alcohol may be explained in part by an alcohol-induced increase in estrogen levels.

Various researchers have suggested that moderate drinking is not protective against CAD, arguing that higher mortality among abstainers results from including among them people who have stopped drinking because of ill health. Higher mortality among these "sick quitters" would explain the comparative longevity of moderate drinkers. However, studies investigating the "sick quitter" effect do not support that conclusion; including "sick quitters" in the abstinent category cannot completely explain the apparent protective effect of moderate drinking against CAD.

Risks of Moderate Drinking

There are risks that might offset the benefits of moderate drinking. Research shows that adverse consequences may occur at relatively low levels of consumption.

Stroke

A review of epidemiologic evidence concludes that moderate alcohol consumption increases the potential risk of strokes caused by bleeding, although it decreases the risk of strokes caused by blocked blood vessels.

Motor Vehicle Crashes

While there is some evidence to suggest that low blood alcohol concentrations (BACs) bear little relationship to road crashes, impairment of driving-related skills by alcohol has been found to begin at 0.05 percent BAC or lower, with rapidly progressing deterioration as the BAC rises. A man weighing 140 pounds might attain a BAC of 0.05 percent after two drinks.

Interactions with Medications

Alcohol may interact harmfully with more than 100 medications, including some sold over the counter. The effects of alcohol are especially augmented by medications that depress the function of the central nervous system, such as sedatives, sleeping pills, anticonvulsants, antidepressants, antianxiety drugs, and certain painkillers. There is a consequent increased danger of driving an automobile after even moderate drinking if such medications are taken. In advanced heart failure, alcohol may not only worsen the disease, but also interfere with the function of medications to treat the disease.

Cancer

Although most evidence suggests an increased risk for certain cancers only among the heaviest drinkers, moderate drinking may be weakly related to female breast cancer. In one study, breast cancer was approximately 50 percent more likely to develop in women who consumed three to nine drinks per week than in women who drank fewer than three drinks per week. Although evidence concerning large bowel cancer is conflicting, one study suggests the possibility of a weak relation to consumption of one or more drinks per day.

Birth Defects

Several ongoing studies are exploring the fetal risks associated with low levels of alcohol consumption. In one study, children whose mothers reported consuming an average of two to three drinks per day during pregnancy were smaller in weight, length, and head circumference and had an increased number of minor physical anomalies when examined at intervals through the age of 3. In addition, mothers' self-reported consumption of as few as two drinks per day during pregnancy was found to be related to a decrease in IQ scores of 7-year-old children.

The question of whether moderate drinking is a risk factor for the fetus is not altogether settled, because mothers' self-reports of alcohol consumption may be underestimates. However, animal research provides additional evidence for adverse fetal effects from low levels of drinking. Nervous system abnormalities occurred in monkeys whose mothers were exposed weekly to low doses of alcohol. An effect occurred at a maternal BAC as low as 0.024 percent. A 120-pound woman might attain this BAC after one drink. Similarly, low prenatal alcohol doses produced biochemical and physiological changes in rat brains.

Shift to Heavier Drinking

Recovering alcoholics, as well as people whose families have alcohol problems, may not be able to maintain moderate drinking habits. Once a person progresses from moderate to heavier drinking, the risks of social problems (for example, drinking and driving, violence, trauma) and medical problems (for example, liver disease, pancreatitis, brain damage, reproductive failure, cancer) increase greatly.

A Commentary by NIAAA Director Enoch Gordis, M.D.

As noted in this *Alcohol Alert*, drinking at "moderate levels" (up to two drinks a day for men and one drink a day for women) has both benefits and risks. Therefore, it should not be surprising that there are questions about what advice to give to individuals about using alcohol.

Research aimed at more clearly defining the circumstances that increase risk and the categories of individuals who are at risk for alcohol-related problems will help individuals and the professionals who advise them to make more informed decisions concerning alcohol use. Better understanding of the biological mechanisms involved in the cardioprotective aspects of moderate alcohol use also could lead researchers to find alternate ways to provide the same protection.

Current advice to individuals should acknowledge that there are tradeoffs involved in each decision about drinking: reducing risk of developing coronary artery disease, for example, may be offset by risk of developing another alcohol-related health condition. In general, if an individual is drinking "moderately" and does not fit into one of the special risk categories discussed in the *Alcohol Alert*, there is no reason to recommend anything different. Similarly, individuals who are not yet drinking (young adults who have recently turned 21, for example), and not at special risk, can be told that "moderate drinking" will probably not be harmful. (Abstinent individuals, however, should not be advised to begin to drink two drinks a day solely to protect against coronary artery disease.) Finally, those who are at higher risk (because of a family history of alcoholism, for example) must be made aware of the tradeoffs involved in decisions to drink.

Chapter 13

Binge Drinking

Binge drinking is defined as "the consumption of five or more drinks in a row on at least one occasion." In national surveys about a third of high school seniors and 42 percent of college students reported at least one occasion of binge drinking within the previous 2 weeks.

While national surveys have documented a significant decline in the use of other drugs by high school seniors and college-age youths, there have been only modest declines in the numbers reporting binge drinking. Teenagers and young adults drink alcoholic beverages at about the same rates they did 5 years ago. Binge drinking increases the risk for alcohol-related injury, especially for young people, who often combine alcohol with other high risk activities, such as impaired driving. According to the Centers for Disease Control and Prevention, the four leading injury-related causes of death among youths under the age of 20 are motor vehicle crashes, homicides, suicides, and drowning. Alcohol is involved in many of these deaths.

Sexual encounters with their inherent risks of pregnancy, sexually transmitted diseases, and HIV exposure, as well as date rape and other violence, can and do occur more frequently while students are consuming large amounts of alcohol by binge drinking.

Binge drinking, or the partying lifestyle of young people, may be related to an environment that appears to support heavy drinking. Youths report that alcohol is more easily available to them today than it was 5 years ago, and there is a high correlation between availability and use. In addition, alcoholic beverages remain inexpensive in

---

Excerpted from (SMA)94-2060.

comparison with other beverages, especially beer when purchased in kegs, often the center of a party.

As young people enter the culture of the college campus, they are confronted with many challenges and opportunities: the opportunity to be independent of parental control; the need to conform; and the insecurity of a new social setting. Forty-one percent of college students engage in binge drinking, as compared to 34 percent of their non-college counterparts.

Another factor that may add to the college setting as a high-risk environment for binge drinking is that youths on college campuses are targets of heavy marketing of alcoholic beverages. Beer companies are especially active in promoting to college students. Student newspapers and campus bulletin boards boast ads for happy hours with price reductions and other incentives that promote heavy drinking. Representatives of the alcohol industry, including producers, wholesalers, and retailers, sponsor campus social, sporting, and cultural events, even on campuses where the majority of participants are under the age of 21.

Prevention strategies in response to binge drinking by young people include actions to reduce alcohol availability, such as increases in price, and responsible beverage service practices, especially at parties. Some communities require keg tagging, which requires kegs to be labeled with a serial number identifying the purchaser in case the keg is discovered at an underage drinking party. Other strategies include restrictions on marketing and promotion practices that glamorize heavy drinking, especially those directed at young people.

References

College Bulletin: Put on the Brakes! Take a Look at College Drinking (1992) CS07.

Office of the Inspector General Report on Youth and Alcohol (1991) RP0799.

CSAP Prevention Resource Guide on College Youth (1991) MS418.

Youth & Alcohol: Selected Reports to the Surgeon General, U.S. Department of Education (1993) PH334.

Chapter 14

Screening for Alcoholism

It is estimated that at least 20 percent of adults who visit a physician have had an alcohol problem at one time. In a survey of patients admitted to an inpatient service, 12 to 30 percent screened positively for alcoholism. Yet, several recent studies indicate that physicians in various health care settings often do not recognize and treat alcoholism. These findings underscore the need for effective and accurate procedures that will enable clinicians to screen for alcoholism.

Alcohol screening identifies individuals in a patient population who have begun to develop or who are at risk for developing alcoholism. Although physicians customarily take a patient's medical history, routine use of a standard alcoholism-detection instrument is valuable because these instruments provide a structured, disciplined, and consistent means to detect individuals at risk.

Two types of alcoholism-screening instruments are available. The first type includes self-report questionnaires and structured interviews; the second type includes clinical laboratory tests which can detect pathophysiology associated with excessive alcohol consumption. Both types of screening instruments should be valid (i.e., measure what the clinician or researcher is attempting to measure) and should yield reliable results (i.e., consistent across raters and time).

Sensitivity and specificity, key properties of every screening test, are related to validity. Sensitivity refers to the test's accuracy in identifying individuals with an alcohol problem (i.e., persons with the disease test

National Institute on Alcohol Abuse and Alcoholism (NIAAA), *Alcohol Alert*, No. 8, PH285, April 1990.

as positive). Specificity refers to the test's effectiveness in identifying people who do not have an alcohol problem (i.e., persons without the disease test as negative).

Two issues should be addressed in the discussion of sensitivity and specificity. First, it is not possible to optimize both properties in a screening instrument. The likelihood of overidentifying alcohol abuse occurs with increased sensitivity; conversely, the possibility of missing people who have an alcohol problem heightens with increased specificity. Second, in determining the utility of a screening test, knowledge of the test's sensitivity and specificity is not sufficient. The prevalence of the particular condition in the screened population also must be taken into account. Sensitivity and specificity are functions of a screening test's cutoff score (a value that clinicians use to define a positive result from a screening instrument). If the base rate of a condition in a population is low, most of the cases identified by a sensitive test will be false positives.

In addition, it is important to note that no "gold standard" exists for evaluating the accuracy of screening instruments. Clinicians compare evidence for alcoholism from medical records and clinical examination with screening results to confirm the accuracy of a particular alcoholism-screening instrument.

The CAGE questionnaire, a mnemonic for attempts to **c**ut down on drinking, **a**nnoyance with criticisms about drinking, **g**uilt about drinking, and using alcohol as an **e**ye-opener, is a self-report screening instrument that appears to be suited to a busy medical setting when there is limited time for patient interviews. The CAGE, which can be self-administered or conducted by a clinician, poses four overt yes-no questions and requires approximately 1 minute to complete. Bush and colleagues used the CAGE to screen 518 patients in a community teaching hospital. At a cutoff score of "2" (in this case, meaning two "yes" answers), the investigators found that the test correctly identified 75 percent of alcoholics (sensitivity) and 96 percent of nonalcoholics (specificity). For routine health screening, the test may identify individuals with alcohol problems that might have been missed otherwise.

The Michigan Alcoholism Screening Test (MAST) is a formal 25-item questionnaire that requires approximately 25 minutes to complete. The MAST focuses on the consequences of problem drinking and on the subjects' own perceptions of their alcohol problems. Recent studies have reported that a cutoff score of "12" or "13" achieves balanced rates of false positives and false negatives. Two shortened forms of the MAST, a 13-item Short MAST (SMAST) and a 10-item brief MAST (b-MAST), have been constructed using items from the original test that are highly discriminating for alcoholism. A cutoff score of "3" is suggested for the SMAST; a cutoff score of "6" is suggested for the b-Mast.

The Self-Administered Alcoholism Screening Test (SAAST) is a 35-item questionnaire or interview with a yes-no format. A score of "10" or greater denotes probable alcoholism. Hurt and colleagues evaluated the use of the test with patients undergoing general examinations and recommended the instrument as an adjunct to a physician interview and an examination. A more recent study reported that the original SAAST and an abbreviated nine-item version are useful for screening medical patients for alcoholism.

The Alcohol Dependence Scale (ADS) is a self-report questionnaire designed to measure elements of the alcohol dependence syndrome described by Edwards and Gross. The test, which yields an index of severity of alcohol dependence, addresses core features of dependence, including an individual's compulsion to drink excessively, repetitive experiences of withdrawal symptoms, and loss of control over drinking. Ross and colleagues compared the merits of the ADS and the MAST as screening tools and determined that the specificity and sensitivity for the two tests were approximately equivalent.

Alcohol is the most widely used drug by young persons between the ages of 12 and 17 years. Routine screening, however, is relatively rare in pediatric practices. Because life problems for adolescents and adults differ, many screening instruments are inappropriate for younger individuals. The Adolescent Drinking Inventory is a self-report instrument developed specifically to screen adolescents. The inventory's 25 questions focus on drinking-related loss of control as well as social, psychological, and physical symptoms of alcohol problems. Allen and colleagues reported that the inventory correctly identified 88 percent of adolescents with alcohol problems and 82 percent of those without alcohol problems.

Heavy alcohol intake during pregnancy can have severe adverse effects on a developing fetus; yet, maternal drinking can be difficult to detect. Sokol and colleagues developed the T-ACE questionnaire to identify pregnant women who consume quantities of alcohol that potentially can damage the fetus (defined in this study as daily intake of 1 ounce of absolute alcohol or greater). The questionnaire takes approximately 1 minute to complete and incorporates the C, A, and E items of the CAGE. The G item is replaced with a question that addresses alcohol tolerance (T). The investigators considered a woman tolerant if she needs more than two drinks to feel the effects of alcohol. Perhaps because many individuals do not understand the implications of tolerance, the tolerance question did not appear to trigger psychological denial. In a study of 971 pregnant women, the T-ACE correctly identified 69 percent of those women who consumed more than an ounce of alcohol per day.

Clinical laboratory procedures, the second type of screening test, frequently are used to corroborate results of physicians' interviews and of self-administered questionnaires. Biochemical markers of heavy alcohol consumption can provide objective evidence of problem drinking, especially in patients who deny any drinking problem. However, the sensitivities and specificities of these biological laboratory markers can be modified by nonalcoholic liver injury, by drug use, and by metabolic disorders or individual metabolic differences.

Several clinical tests may be useful in detecting harmful alcohol use. Increased activity of serum gamma-glutamyltransferase (GGT) is a relatively sensitive index of liver damage in alcoholics and heavy drinkers. However, this test lacks diagnostic specificity because all types of liver damage and a variety of diseases may cause elevated serum activity of this enzyme. Results may be more discriminating when interpreted in conjunction with the measure of mean corpuscular volume (MCV). MCV, an index of red blood cell size, increases with excessive alcohol intake. Although MCV has a high correlation with alcohol consumption, the index, alone, is not a useful screening marker. The liver enzyme aspartate aminotransferase (AST) can be a useful marker for alcohol abuse: The ratio of levels of mitochondrial AST to total AST has been found effective in differentiating alcoholics from other patients and in detecting chronic excessive drinking.

It is important to note that self-report interviews and questionnaires have greater sensitivity and specificity than routine blood tests for biochemical markers. Laboratory tests may be used most successfully in conjunction with self-report instruments to enhance objectivity.

A Commentary by NIAAA Director Enoch Gordis, M.D.

Untreated alcoholism often results in severe or fatal outcomes and can be the underlying cause of other illnesses. Therefore, screening all patients for alcohol problems—particularly in primary health care settings—is a medical necessity.

Structured interviews and self-report instruments are useful for screening. Both are rapid, inexpensive, noninvasive, and relatively accurate tools. A screening instrument should be selected on the basis of staff experience and training, available testing time, and characteristics of the patient population and should be used consistently.

Although laboratory tests such as the GGT can provide useful information to supplement knowledge gained through an interview or self-report, laboratory tests are not adequate when used alone to screen for alcohol problems.

Developing objective markers of alcohol use currently is an important goal of alcohol research. An objective marker should testify to the subject's blood alcohol level over a period of several weeks, even if the subject is abstinent at the time of sampling.

Chapter 15

Alcohol and Cognition

Research shows that alcohol adversely affects the brain. When health professionals encounter patients who are having cognitive difficulties, such as impaired memory or reasoning ability, alcohol use may be the cause of the problem.

When treating patients who have abused alcohol, it may be of value to attempt to identify the level of any impairment and to modify the treatment accordingly.

Some researchers have investigated whether or not there is measurable alcohol-related cognitive impairment among nonalcoholic social drinkers. Their findings suggest a dose-response relationship between alcohol consumption and diminished scores on certain neuropsychological tests. Statistically significant decreases in test performance have been found for people whose self-reported alcohol consumption was in the range of what was considered social drinking. This is not to say these people were clinically impaired, only that they exhibited certain performance deficits that correlated with alcohol consumption. It is important to note that similar correlations from other studies have not been found to be consistently significant. For example, the results of one general population study showed no correlation between self-reported alcohol consumption and neuropsychological test scores; other findings failed to show a simple dose-response relationship. In a recent review of such studies, Parsons

National Institute on Alcohol Abuse and Alcoholism (NIAAA), *Alcohol Alert*, No. 4, PH258, May 1989.

concluded that data on the relationship of cognitive impairment to amount of alcohol consumed by social drinkers are inconclusive.

Alcoholics in treatment present a different picture. Although most alcoholics entering treatment do not have decreased overall intelligence scores, approximately 45 to 70 percent of these patients have specific deficits in problem solving, abstract thinking, concept shifting, psychomotor performance, and difficult memory tasks. Such deficits usually are not apparent without neuropsychological testing. In addition, structural changes in the brains of alcoholics have been reported, as well as reduced cerebral blood flow and altered electrical activity, but there is not yet any clear evidence implicating these changes as the cause of observed cognitive deficits.

For the most severe alcoholics, serious organic cerebral impairment is a common complication, occurring in about 10 percent of patients. The diverse signs of severe brain dysfunction that persist after cessation of alcohol consumption have been conceptualized in terms of two organic mental disorders: alcohol amnestic disorder (memory disorder) and dementia associated with alcoholism. Recently however, it has been recognized that these two disorders are not mutually exclusive and that some features of each often coexist in the same patient. Alcohol amnestic disorder, commonly called Korsakoff's psychosis or Wernicke-Korsakoff syndrome, is characterized by short-term memory impairments and behavioral changes that occur without clouding of consciousness or general loss of intellectual abilities. Dementia associated with alcoholism consists of global loss of intellectual abilities with an impairment in memory function, together with disturbance(s) of abstract thinking, judgment, other higher cortical functions, or personality change without a clouding of consciousness. It has been suggested that subcortical lesions due to nutritional (thiamine) deficiency are characteristic of Korsakoff's, whereas alcoholic dementia is associated more with cortical changes. There is some evidence that a genetic abnormality may predispose some people to Korsakoff's in the presence of excessive alcohol use and malnutrition.

Tarter and Edwards summarize evidence suggesting that neuropsychological impairment in alcoholics may occur for a number of reasons. The toxic effects of alcohol on the brain may cause impairment directly. In addition, some alcoholics may exhibit impairment as an indirect result of alcohol abuse, e.g., they may have experienced a craniocerebral trauma, they may be eating poorly and suffering nutritional deficits (such as thiamine or niacin deficiencies), or they may have cognitive impairments associated with liver disease.

Some alcoholics may have been cognitively impaired before they began drinking. There is some evidence that persons in groups considered to be at risk for alcoholism (e.g., children of alcoholics) are less adept at certain learning tests and visual-spatial integration than are persons in groups not deemed at risk for alcoholism; this area of research is still under active investigation.

Some researchers have observed that cognitive deficits in some alcoholics resemble those seen in normal elderly persons, leading to speculation that alcohol's effect on cognition may be explained as premature aging. However, it is more likely that such deficits are independent of any deficits associated with normal aging.

Laying aside issues of etiology, evidence indicates that some cognitive impairment in alcoholics is reversible. Researchers report apparent "spontaneous" recovery of cognitive function (recovery seen after the passage of time with no active intervention) among abstinent alcoholics, a result that may be due solely to the absence of alcohol but that also may be due in part to other changes, such as better nutrition and opportunities for social interaction provided in an alcohol treatment setting. There is some evidence that cognitive training and practice experience (remedial mental exercises) can facilitate recovery from impairment.

Because even with prolonged abstinence many alcoholic patients with chronic organic mental disorders may exhibit only modest clinical improvement in brain functioning, there is a need for pharmacological interventions to complement behavioral methods. Recent findings that pharmacological intervention may be useful in restoring some cognitive ability are encouraging.

Although degree of cognitive impairment may not be a clinically significant predictor of post-treatment alcohol consumption, identifying cognitive impairment may have implications for successfully treating some patients. Particularly in the first weeks of abstinence during treatment, cognitive impairments may make it difficult for some alcoholics to benefit from the educational and skill development sessions that are important components of many treatment programs. For example, Becker and Jaffe reported that alcoholics who were tested soon after beginning abstinence were unable to recall treatment-related information presented in a film that was part of the regular treatment program. An implication of such findings is that information presented to alcoholics during the period of impairment in the early weeks of abstinence should be repeated at later stages in the treatment program. Alternatively, presentation of treatment-related information should be delayed until tests indicate some improvement in cognitive function.

A Commentary by NIAAA Director Enoch Gordis, M.D.

Awareness of alcohol's effects on cognition can help general health care providers identify alcoholics and refer them to appropriate treatment. Awareness also can assist the efforts of alcoholism treatment personnel to maximize the potential benefit of treatment for their patients.

In general health care situations, practitioners should use standard alcoholism assessment instruments to determine the extent of alcohol use by patients who show signs of cognitive dysfunction. Patients in whom alcohol use is identified as either a primary or a contributing cause of cognitive dysfunction must be referred to alcoholism treatment. Evidence suggests that some cognitive impairment in alcoholics is reversible. Moreover, cognitive deterioration will worsen with continued drinking.

In addition, alcoholism treatment personnel should know that alcohol-induced cognitive impairment may make it difficult during the first weeks of abstinence for some of their patients to benefit from exposure to the full range of treatment services. Although it may not be possible or necessary for treatment programs to administer extensive neuropsychiatric tests to all patients, a simple test of the patient's ability to benefit from the didactic elements of alcoholism treatment can be made. One test might be to determine what a patient remembers from an initial counseling session.

If there is evidence of cognitive deficiency, patients must be allowed time to recover adequate cognitive function so that, at a minimum, information provided during treatment can be retained. However, other important elements of rehabilitation, such as improving patient nutritional status and exposure to physical exercise and resocialization activities, can be undertaken immediately. As cognitive function improves, patients can begin to participate in such treatment components as individual and group therapy, educational programs, and introduction to Alcoholics Anonymous, with a better chance for understanding—and perhaps for acting on—the information provided.

Chapter 16

Blood Alcohol Concentration

Blood alcohol concentration (BAC) is the amount of alcohol in the bloodstream. It is measured in percentages. For instance, having a BAC of 0.10 percent means that a person has 1 part alcohol per 1,000 parts blood in the body.

In a review of studies of alcohol-related crashes, reaction time, tracking ability, concentrated attention ability, divided attention performance, information process capability, visual functions, perceptions, and psycho-motor performance, impairment in all these areas was significant at blood alcohol concentrations of 0.05 percent. Impairment first appeared in many of these important areas of performance at blood alcohol concentrations of 0.02 percent, substantially below the legal standard in most States for drunkenness, which is 0.10 percent.

Approximately half of traffic injuries involve alcohol. About one-third of fatally injured passengers and pedestrians have elevated blood alcohol levels. For fatal intentional injuries, half of homicides involve alcohol, as do one-quarter to one-third of suicides.

The Centers for Disease Control and Prevention (CDC) estimate that about 30,000 unintentional injury deaths per year are directly attributable to alcohol. Another 15,000 to 20,000 homicides or suicides per year are associated with alcohol.

For non-fatal unintentional injuries many studies show that 25 to 50 percent involve alcohol. The same rates are found for a wide range of non-fatal intentional injuries involving alcohol, including assaults,

---

Excerpted from (SMA) 94-2060.

spouse abuse, child molestation, sexual assault, rape, and attempted suicide.

BAC can be measured by breath, blood, or urine tests. BAC measurement is especially important for determining the role of alcohol in crashes, falls, fires, crime, family violence, suicide, and other forms of intentional and unintentional injury. Information on BAC: (1) provides a baseline for evaluating prevention and intervention programs; (2) supplies data needed for planning and providing direct services; and (3) improves estimates of the economic costs of alcohol use.

One problem in obtaining accurate BAC data is a lack of testing in hospital emergency rooms. Research indicates that emergency rooms do not test routinely for alcohol in crash victims. A national survey of trauma centers found that although two-thirds of the centers estimated that the majority of patients had consumed alcohol, only 55 percent routinely conducted BAC tests at patient admissions. A review of emergency room studies indicated that up to one-third of patients admitted to emergency rooms are not tested.

BAC and Impaired Driving

The public most commonly associates BAC with drunk driving. However, it is more accurate to refer to alcohol-impaired driving because one does not have to be drunk (intoxicated) to be demonstrably impaired. Driving skills, especially judgment, are impaired in most people long before they exhibit visible signs of drunkenness. While most States define legal intoxication for purposes of driving at a BAC of 0.10 percent or higher, alcohol may cause deterioration in driving skills at 0.05 percent or even lower. Deterioration progresses rapidly with rising BAC.

In recognition of impairment at lower BAC levels, the National Highway Traffic Safety Administration (NHTSA) refers to traffic crashes as "alcohol involved" or "alcohol related" when a participant (driver, pedestrian, or bicyclist) has a measured or estimated BAC of 0.01 or above. NHTSA defines a "high-level alcohol crash" as one where an active participant has a BAC of 0.10 or higher. *Healthy People 2000: National Health Promotion and Disease Prevention Objectives* calls for all 50 States to lower legal blood alcohol concentration tolerance levels to 0.04 percent for motor vehicle drivers age 21 and older and .00 percent for those younger than 21. Other ways to lower the BAC levels of drivers include:

- Using planning and zoning ordinances to control the type and number of outlets selling alcohol, as well as the particular hours of the day alcoholic beverages are available for sale;

- Raising the priority of law officers' programs designed to deter drinking and driving, including sobriety checkpoints;

- Implementing programs to promote responsible alcoholic beverage service in both commercial and social settings;

- Organizing comprehensive, community-based awareness programs, including mass media promotion, to counter the adverse consequences of alcohol use in high risk situations, including driving;

- Making the enforcement of underage sales and drinking laws a priority.

References

The Technology of Breath-Alcohol Analysis (1992) PH312.

Prevention Resource Guide: Impaired Driving (1991) MS434.

Safer Streets Ahead (1990) PH292.

Chapter 17

Alcohol and Nutrition

Nutrition is a process that serves two purposes: to provide energy and to maintain body structure and function. Food supplies energy and provides the building blocks needed to replace worn or damaged cells and the nutritional components needed for body function. Alcoholics often eat poorly, limiting their supply of essential nutrients and affecting both energy supply and structure maintenance. Furthermore, alcohol interferes with the nutritional process by affecting digestion, storage, utilization, and excretion of nutrients.

Impairment of Nutrient Digestion and Utilization

Once ingested, food must be digested (broken down into small components) so it is available for energy and maintenance of body structure and function. Digestion begins in the mouth and continues in the stomach and intestines, with help from the pancreas. The nutrients from digested food are absorbed from the intestines into the blood and carried to the liver. The liver prepares nutrients either for immediate use or for storage and future use.

Alcohol inhibits the breakdown of nutrients into usable molecules by decreasing secretion of digestive enzymes from the pancreas. Alcohol impairs nutrient absorption by damaging the cells lining the stomach and intestines and disabling transport of some nutrients into

National Institute on Alcohol Abuse and Alcoholism (NIAAA), *Alcohol Alert*, No. 22, PH346, October 1993.

the blood. In addition, nutritional deficiencies themselves may lead to further absorption problems. For example, folate deficiency alters the cells lining the small intestine, which in turn impairs absorption of water and nutrients including glucose, sodium, and additional folate.

Even if nutrients are digested and absorbed, alcohol can prevent them from being fully utilized by altering their transport, storage, and excretion. Decreased liver stores of vitamins such as vitamin A, and increased excretion of nutrients such as fat, indicate impaired utilization of nutrients by alcoholics.

Alcohol and Energy Supply

The three basic nutritional components found in food—carbohydrates, proteins, and fats—are used as energy after being converted to simpler products. Some alcoholics ingest as much as 50 percent of their total daily calories from alcohol, often neglecting important foods.

Even when food intake is adequate, alcohol can impair the mechanisms by which the body controls blood glucose levels, resulting in either increased or decreased blood glucose (glucose is the body's principal sugar). In nondiabetic alcoholics, increased blood sugar, or hyperglycemia—caused by impaired insulin secretion—is usually temporary and without consequence. Decreased blood sugar, or hypoglycemia, can cause serious injury even if this condition is short lived. Hypoglycemia can occur when a fasting or malnourished person consumes alcohol. When there is no food to supply energy, stored sugar is depleted, and the products of alcohol metabolism inhibit the formation of glucose from other compounds such as amino acids. As a result, alcohol causes the brain and other body tissue to be deprived of glucose needed for energy and function. Although alcohol is an energy source, how the body processes and uses the energy from alcohol is more complex than can be explained by a simple calorie conversion value. For example, alcohol provides an average of 20 percent of the calories in the diet of the upper third of drinking Americans, and we might expect many drinkers who consume such amounts to be obese. Instead, national data indicate that, despite higher caloric intake, drinkers are no more obese than nondrinkers. Also, when alcohol is substituted for carbohydrates, calorie for calorie, subjects tend to lose weight, indicating that they derive less energy from alcohol than from food.

The mechanisms accounting for the apparent inefficiency in converting alcohol to energy are complex and incompletely understood, but several mechanisms have been proposed. For example, chronic drinking triggers an inefficient system of alcohol metabolism, the microsomal ethanol-oxidizing system (MEOS). Much of the energy from MEOS-driven alcohol metabolism is lost as heat rather than used to supply the body with energy.

Alcohol and the Maintenance of Cell Structure and Function

Structure

Because cells are made mostly of protein, an adequate protein diet is important for maintaining cell structure, especially if cells are being damaged. Research indicates that alcohol affects protein nutrition by causing impaired digestion of proteins to amino acids, impaired processing of amino acids by the small intestine and liver, impaired synthesis of proteins from amino acids, and impaired protein secretion by the liver.

Function

Nutrients are essential for proper body function; proteins, vitamins, and minerals provide the tools that the body needs to perform properly. Alcohol can disrupt body function by causing nutrient deficiencies and by usurping the machinery needed to metabolize nutrients.

Vitamins. Vitamins are essential to maintaining growth and normal metabolism because they regulate many physiological processes. Chronic heavy drinking is associated with deficiencies in many vitamins because of decreased food ingestion and, in some cases, impaired absorption, metabolism, and utilization. For example, alcohol inhibits fat absorption and thereby impairs absorption of the vitamins A, E, and D that are normally absorbed along with dietary fats. Vitamin A deficiency can be associated with night blindness, and vitamin D deficiency is associated with softening of the bones.

Vitamins A, C, D, E, K, and the B vitamins, also deficient in some alcoholics, are all involved in wound healing and cell maintenance. In particular, because vitamin K is necessary for blood clotting, deficiencies of that vitamin can cause delayed clotting and result in ex-

153

cess bleeding. Deficiencies of other vitamins involved in brain function can cause severe neurological damage.

Minerals. Deficiencies of minerals such as calcium, magnesium, iron, and zinc are common in alcoholics, although alcohol itself does not seem to affect the absorption of these minerals. Rather, deficiencies seem to occur secondary to other alcohol-related problems: decreased calcium absorption due to fat malabsorption; magnesium deficiency due to decreased intake, increased urinary excretion, vomiting, and diarrhea; iron deficiency related to gastrointestinal bleeding; and zinc malabsorption or losses related to other nutrient deficiencies. Mineral deficiencies can cause a variety of medical consequences from calcium-related bone disease to zinc-related night blindness and skin lesions.

Alcohol, Malnutrition, and Medical Complications

Liver Disease

Although alcoholic liver damage is caused primarily by alcohol itself, poor nutrition may increase the risk of alcohol-related liver damage. For example, nutrients normally found in the liver, such as carotenoids, which are the major sources of vitamin A, and vitamin E compounds, are known to be affected by alcohol consumption. Decreases in such nutrients may play some role in alcohol-related liver damage.

Pancreatitis

Research suggests that malnutrition may increase the risk of developing alcoholic pancreatitis, but some research performed outside the United States links pancreatitis more closely with overeating. Preliminary research suggests that alcohol's damaging effect on the pancreas may be exacerbated by a protein-deficient diet.

Brain

Nutritional deficiencies can have severe and permanent effects on brain function. Specifically, thiamine deficiencies, often seen in alcoholics, can cause severe neurological problems such as impaired movement and memory loss seen in Wernicke/Korsakoff syndrome.

Pregnancy

Alcohol has direct toxic effects on fetal development, causing alcohol-related birth defects, including fetal alcohol syndrome. Alcohol itself is toxic to the fetus, but accompanying nutritional deficiency can affect fetal development, perhaps compounding the risk of developmental damage.

The nutritional needs during pregnancy are 10 to 30 percent greater than normal; food intake can increase by as much as 140 percent to cover the needs of both mother and fetus. Not only can nutritional deficiencies of an alcoholic mother adversely affect the nutrition of the fetus, but alcohol itself can also restrict nutrition flow to the fetus.

Nutritional Status of Alcoholics

Techniques for assessing nutritional status include taking body measurements such as weight, height, mass, and skin fold thickness to estimate fat reserves, and performing blood analysis to provide measurements of circulating proteins, vitamins, and minerals. These techniques tend to be imprecise, and for many nutrients, there is no clear "cutoff" point that would allow an accurate definition of deficiency. As such, assessing the nutritional status of alcoholics is hindered by the limitations of the techniques. Dietary status may provide inferential information about the risk of developing nutritional deficiencies. Dietary status is assessed by taking patients' dietary histories and evaluating the amount and types of food they are eating.

A threshold dose above which alcohol begins to have detrimental effects on nutrition is difficult to determine. In general, moderate drinkers (two drinks or less per day) seem to be at little risk for nutritional deficiencies. Various medical disorders begin to appear at greater levels.

Research indicates that the majority of even the heaviest drinkers have few detectable nutritional deficiencies but that many alcoholics who are hospitalized for medical complications of alcoholism do experience severe malnutrition. Because alcoholics tend to eat poorly—often eating less than the amounts of food necessary to provide sufficient carbohydrates, protein, fat, vitamins A and C, the B vitamins, and minerals such as calcium and iron—a major concern is that alcohol's effects on the digestion of food and utilization of nutrients may shift a mildly malnourished person toward severe malnutrition.

A Commentary by NIAAA Director Enoch Gordis, M.D.

The combination of an adequate diet and abstention from alcohol is the best way to treat malnourished alcoholic patients. Nutritional supplements have been used to replace nutrients deficient in malnourished alcoholics in an attempt to improve their overall health. Dosages of nutritional supplements such as vitamin A that exceed normally prescribed levels may result in overdose.

Although various nutritional approaches have been touted as "cures" for alcoholism, there is little evidence to support such claims. However, renewed research attention to the nutritional aspects of alcohol leaves open the possibility that a role for nutritional therapy in alcoholism treatment may yet be defined.

Chapter 18

Alcohol and Cancer

Cancer kills an estimated 526,000 Americans yearly, second only to heart disease. Cancers of the lung, large bowel, and breast are the most common in the United States. Considerable evidence suggests a connection between heavy alcohol consumption and increased risk for cancer, with an estimated 2 to 4 percent of all cancer cases thought to be caused either directly or indirectly by alcohol.

A strong association exists between alcohol use and cancers of the esophagus, pharynx, and mouth, whereas a more controversial association links alcohol with liver, breast, and colorectal cancers. Together, these cancers kill more than 125,000 people annually in the United States. The following sections discuss alcohol's role in these cancers.

What Is Cancer?

Cancer is a group of diseases characterized by cells that grow out of control; in many cases, they form masses of cells, or tumors, that infiltrate, crowd out, and destroy normal tissue. Although the body strictly regulates normal cells to grow within the confines of tissues, cancer cells reproduce independently, uninhibited by tissue boundaries. Cancer develops in three stages: initiation, promotion, and progression. Cancer-causing agents, known as carcinogens, can contribute to the first two stages.

National Institute on Alcohol Abuse and Alcoholism (NIAAA), *Alcohol Alert*, No. 21, PH345, July 1993.

Cancer initiation occurs when a cell's DNA (the substance that genes are made of) is irreversibly changed so that, once triggered to divide, the cell will reproduce indefinitely. The "change" involves mutations to the cell's genes that can occur spontaneously or can be induced by a carcinogen. In some cancers, it has been shown that the mutations occur in oncogenes, genes that normally promote cell division, or in suppressor genes, genes that normally suppress cell division. Thus, it is believed that cancer-causing mutations result in overpromotion or undersuppression of cell reproduction. During cancer promotion, the initiated cell is stimulated to divide. The stimulus can be natural, as when tissue damage requires proliferation of new cells, or it can be caused by a carcinogen. During cancer progression, tumors produced by the replicating mass of cells metastasize, or spread, from the initial or primary tumor to other parts of the body, forming secondary cancers.

Alcohol's Link to Cancer

Two types of research link alcohol and cancer. Epidemiologic research has shown a dose-dependent association between alcohol consumption and certain types of cancer; as alcohol consumption increases, so does risk of developing certain cancers. More tenuous results have come from research into the mechanism by which alcohol could contribute to cancer development.

Epidemiologic Research

The strongest link between alcohol and cancer involves cancers of the upper digestive tract, including the esophagus, the mouth, the pharynx, and the larynx. Less consistent data link alcohol consumption and cancers of the liver, breast, and colon.

Upper digestive tract. Chronic heavy drinkers have a higher incidence of esophageal cancer than does the general population. The risk appears to increase as alcohol consumption increases. An estimated 75 percent of esophageal cancers in the United States are attributable to chronic, excessive alcohol consumption.

Nearly 50 percent of cancers of the mouth, pharynx, and larynx are associated with heavy drinking. People who drink large quantities of alcohol over time have an increased risk of these cancers as compared with abstainers. If they drink and smoke, the increase in risk is even more dramatic.

158

Liver. Prolonged, heavy drinking has been associated in many cases with primary liver cancer. However, it is liver cirrhosis, whether caused by alcohol or another factor, that is thought to induce the cancer. In areas of Africa and Asia, liver cancer afflicts 50 or more people per 100,000 per year, usually associated with cirrhosis caused by hepatitis viruses. In the United States, liver cancer is relatively uncommon, afflicting approximately 2 people per 100,000, but excessive alcohol consumption is linked to as many as 36 percent of these cases by some investigators.

The association between alcohol use and liver cancer is difficult to interpret, because liver cirrhosis and hepatitis B and C virus infections often confound data. Studies of the interactions between alcohol, hepatitis viruses, and cirrhosis will help clarify these associations with liver cancer (see below).

Breast. Chronic alcohol consumption has been associated with a small (averaging 10 percent) increase in a woman's risk of breast cancer. According to these studies, the risk appears to increase as the quantity and duration of alcohol consumption increases. Other studies, however, have found no evidence of such a link.

The inconsistency and weakness of epidemiologic findings suggest that a third confounding factor, such as nutrition, may be responsible for the link between alcohol and breast cancer. However, studies that adjusted for dietary factors such as fat intake found that the association between alcohol and breast cancer remained.

Recent studies suggest that alcohol may play an indirect role in the development of breast cancer. These studies indicate that alcohol increases estrogen levels in premenopausal women, which, in turn, may promote breast cancer.

Colon. Epidemiologic studies have found a small but consistent dose-dependent association between alcohol consumption and colorectal cancer, even when controlling for fiber and other dietary factors. Despite the large number of studies, however, causality cannot be determined from the available data.

Other cancers. A few studies have linked chronic heavy drinking with cancers of the stomach, pancreas, and lungs. However, the association is consistently weak and the majority of studies have found no association.

Mechanisms of Alcohol-Related Cancers

The epidemiologic data provide little insight into whether or how alcohol increases the risk for various cancers. For some cancers, such as mouth and esophageal, alcohol is thought to play a direct causal role. For others, such as liver and breast cancers, alcohol is thought to play an indirect role by enhancing mechanisms that may cause cancer. Studies looking at these direct and indirect mechanisms may shed light on alcohol's role in developing cancers.

Oncogenes. Preliminary studies show that alcohol may affect cancer development at the genetic level by affecting oncogenes at the initiation and promotion stages of cancer. It has been suggested that acetaldehyde, a product of alcohol metabolism, impairs a cell's natural ability to repair its DNA, resulting in a greater likelihood that mutations causing cancer initiation will occur. It has recently been suggested that alcohol exposure may result in over-expression of certain oncogenes in human cells and, thereby, trigger cancer promotion.

Alcohol as a Cocarcinogen. Although there is no evidence that alcohol itself is a carcinogen, alcohol may act as a cocarcinogen by enhancing the carcinogenic effects of other chemicals. For example, studies indicate that alcohol enhances tobacco's ability to stimulate tumor formation in rats. In humans, the risk for mouth, tracheal, and esophageal cancer is 35 times greater for people who both smoke and drink than for people who neither smoke nor drink (30), implying a cocarcinogenic interaction between alcohol and tobacco-related carcinogens.

Alcohol's cocarcinogenic effect may be explained by its interaction with certain enzymes. Some enzymes that normally help to detoxify substances that enter the body can also increase the toxicity of some carcinogens. One of these enzymes is called cytochrome P-450. Dietary alcohol is able to induce cytochrome P-450 in the liver, lungs, esophagus, and intestines, where alcohol-associated cancers occur. Subsequently, carcinogens such as those from tobacco and diet can become more potent as they, too, pass through the esophagus, lungs, intestines, and liver and encounter the activated enzyme.

Nutrition. Chronic alcohol abuse may result in abnormalities in the way the body processes nutrients and may subsequently promote certain types of cancer. Reduced levels of iron, zinc, vitamin E, and some of the B vitamins, common in heavy drinkers, have been experimentally associated with some cancers. Also, levels of vitamin A, hypothesized to have anticancer properties, are severely depressed in the liver and esophagus of rats during chronic alcohol consumption.

A recent study indicates that as few as two drinks per day negates any beneficial effects of a "correct" diet on decreasing risk of colon cancer. Although the study suggests that a diet high in folic acid, a B vitamin found in fresh fruits and vegetables, decreases the risk for colon cancer, it also warns that alcohol consumption may counter this protective action and increase the risk for colon cancer by reducing folic acid levels.

Mechanisms of Liver Cancer. The possible role of alcohol in the development of liver cancer is incompletely understood. In Asia and Africa, hepatitis B virus infection is thought to cause most liver cancer; the association is less frequent in the United States. Eighty percent of patients with liver cancer also have cirrhosis, and between 27 and 80 percent test positive for hepatitis B or C infection. The chronic heavy drinking that causes liver cirrhosis might exacerbate cirrhosis caused independently by the hepatitis B or C viruses. Some studies indicate that alcohol consumption hastens the development of liver cancer in patients with hepatitis C infection, whereas others indicate that alcohol has no compounding effect in such patients.

Suppression of Immune Response. Alcoholism has been associated with suppression of the human immune system. Immune suppression makes chronic alcohol abusers more susceptible to various infectious diseases and, theoretically, to cancer.

Summary

Although epidemiologic studies have found a clear association between alcohol consumption and development of certain types of cancer, study findings are often inconsistent and may vary by country and by type of cancer. The key to understanding the association lies in research designed to decipher how alcohol may promote cancer. Such studies examine alcohol's metabolic effects at the cellular and genetic levels. Research examining the ways in which alcohol may induce cancers has found some potential mechanisms, the most promising of which implicates oncogenes.

A Commentary by NIAAA Director Enoch Gordis, M.D.

As can be seen from this *Alcohol Alert*, the evidence for alcohol's role in promoting some cancers (e.g., cancers of the mouth and throat) is stronger than the evidence linking alcohol use to other cancers, such as breast cancer. Public health policy should reflect the strength of the evidence of alcohol's role in promoting various cancers. Convincing evidence of alcohol's effects on common cancers—even when these effects are minor—has important public health implications. However, it is equally important that the public not be subjected to undue alarm when evidence for an increased risk for cancer due to alcohol use is weak or inconclusive.

Chapter 19

Alcohol and the Liver

Alcoholic liver disease is one of the most serious medical consequences of chronic alcohol use. Moreover, chronic excessive alcohol use is the single most important cause of illness and death from liver disease (alcoholic hepatitis and cirrhosis) in the United States.

The Normal Liver

Normal liver function is essential to life. The liver is the largest organ of the body, located in the upper right section of the abdomen. It filters circulating blood, removing and destroying toxic substances; it secretes bile into the small intestine to help digest and absorb fats; and it is involved in many of the metabolic systems of the body. Digested food substances are carried from the intestine directly to the liver for further processing. The liver stores vitamins; synthesizes cholesterol; metabolizes or stores sugars; processes fats; and assembles amino acids into various proteins, some for use within the liver and some for export. The liver controls blood fluidity and regulates blood-clotting mechanisms. It also converts the products of protein metabolism into urea for excretion by the kidneys.

Alcoholic Liver Disease

The three alcohol-induced liver conditions are fatty liver, alcoholic hepatitis, and cirrhosis.

National Institute on Alcohol Abuse and Alcoholism (NIAAA), *Alcohol Alert*, No. 19, PH329, January 1993.

163

Some degree of fat deposition usually occurs in the liver after short-term excessive use of alcohol. However, fatty liver rarely causes illness.

In some heavy drinkers, alcohol consumption leads to severe alcoholic hepatitis, an inflammation of the liver characterized by fever, jaundice, and abdominal pain. Severe alcoholic hepatitis can be confused with many serious abdominal conditions, such as cholecystitis (inflammation of the gall bladder), appendicitis, and pancreatitis. It is important to be aware of this potential confusion because some of these other conditions require surgery, and surgery is contraindicated in patients with alcoholic hepatitis. These patients have a high death rate following surgery.

The most advanced form of alcoholic liver injury is alcoholic cirrhosis. This condition is marked by progressive development of scar tissue that chokes off blood vessels and distorts the normal architecture of the liver.

A patient may have only one of the three alcohol-induced conditions or any combination of them. Traditionally, they have been considered sequentially related, progressing from fatty liver to alcoholic hepatitis to cirrhosis. However, some studies have demonstrated that alcoholics may progress to cirrhosis without passing through any visible stage resembling hepatitis. Thus, alcoholic cirrhosis can appear insidiously, with little warning.

Fatty liver is reversible with abstinence. Alcoholic hepatitis may be fatal but can be reversible with abstinence. While alcoholic cirrhosis is often progressive and fatal, it can stabilize with abstinence.

Complications of advanced liver disease include severe bleeding from distended veins in the esophagus, brain disorders (hepatic encephalopathy), accumulation of fluid in the abdomen (ascites), and kidney failure.

Not all liver disease that may occur in alcoholics is caused by alcohol. In addition, when alcohol-induced liver disease does occur, it may be accompanied by other conditions, not related to alcohol, that also can cause liver failure. These include nonalcoholic hepatitis and exposure to drugs and occupational chemicals (see below).

Extent of the Problem

Alcohol-related cirrhosis is known to be underreported. However, about 44 percent of all deaths caused by cirrhosis in North America are reportedly alcohol related.

Up to 100 percent of heavy drinkers show evidence of fatty liver, an estimated 10 to 35 percent develop alcoholic hepatitis, and 10 to 20 percent develop cirrhosis.

Daily drinkers are at a higher risk of developing alcoholic cirrhosis than are binge drinkers. In general, patients with alcoholic cirrhosis have been drinking heavily for 10 to 20 years.

Mortality from cirrhosis in the United States varies significantly with gender, race, and age. In 1988, the highest mortality from cirrhosis occurred in nonwhite males, followed by white males, nonwhite females, and white females. Most of the deaths from alcoholic cirrhosis occur in people ages 40-65. Thus, alcoholic cirrhosis kills people in what should be their most productive years.

How Does Alcohol Damage the Liver?

Currently we do not know how alcohol causes cirrhosis. However, there are many mechanisms by which alcohol injures the liver. Many of these mechanisms are poorly understood, in part because no simple animal model has been developed for cirrhosis. In addition, there is considerable variation among individuals in susceptibility to alcoholic liver disease, so that among people drinking similar amounts, only some develop cirrhosis.

Diet

Before the 1970's, alcoholic cirrhosis was believed to arise from nutritional deficiencies common among heavy drinkers. Overwhelming evidence subsequently proved that alcohol itself is toxic to the liver, even when nutrition is adequate. Today, it is believed that nutritional effects and direct alcohol toxicity interact in such complex ways that the influence of the two cannot be separated.

Genetics

Genetic differences might explain why some heavy drinkers develop cirrhosis while others do not. The scar tissue that forms in the cirrhotic liver is composed of the protein collagen. It has been suggested that stimulation of collagen synthesis resulting from activation of the collagen gene may promote liver scarring. In that case, it might be speculated that differences in genes for collagen among

165

individual drinkers may be associated with differences in the development of alcoholic cirrhosis.

Free Radicals and Acetaldehyde

Much of the cell damage that occurs during liver degeneration is believed to be caused by free radicals, highly reactive molecular fragments, liberated during alcohol metabolism. The damage caused by free radicals can include the destruction of essential components of cell membranes. The cell's natural defenses against free radicals include the natural chemicals glutathione (GSH) and vitamin E.

The function of GSH and vitamin E is impaired in alcoholics. For example, chronic alcohol ingestion decreased GSH levels in baboons and humans. Similarly, chronic alcohol feeding significantly increased damage caused by free radicals in liver cells of rats maintained on a diet low in vitamin E.

Acetaldehyde, the primary metabolic product of alcohol in the liver, appears to be a key generator of free radicals. Because of its reactivity, acetaldehyde can promote membrane damage and can stimulate the synthesis of collagen to form scar tissue.

Nonalcoholic Hepatitis

The increased prevalence of hepatitis C viral infection in alcoholics might explain some of the variation in individual susceptibility to alcoholic liver disease. In addition, chronic hepatitis C infection is significantly correlated with the severity of alcoholic cirrhosis and may influence the progression of alcoholic liver disease in some patients.

The Immune System

The immune system responds or contributes to liver cell damage in alcohol-induced liver disease in complex ways, although a causal relationship is unclear. Acetaldehyde has been shown to attach chemically to liver proteins. The altered proteins may then trigger various immune responses. Cellular toxins are released, causing cell damage; certain proteins are deposited along the liver's small blood-carrying channels; and specific white blood cells are activated.

Liver Metabolism

Chronic alcohol administration has been found to increase the rate of oxygen metabolism by the liver. In addition, a series of studies by Israel and colleagues demonstrated similarities in the effects of alcohol and thyroid hormone on liver cells. They called these effects the "liver hypermetabolic state." As a result of these studies, propylthiouracil, a drug used to treat excessive production of thyroid hormone, has been tested for the treatment of alcoholic liver disease (see Treatment below).

Gender

Current evidence suggests that women may be more susceptible than men to alcoholic liver disease; more research is necessary to validate this hypothesis.

Environmental Factors

Chronic alcohol consumption markedly increases the liver toxicity of various industrial solvents, anesthetics, medications, and vitamins. For example, acetaminophen (Tylenol and others), a widely used over-the-counter pain reliever, is generally safe when taken in recommended doses. However, excessive use of acetaminophen has been associated with liver toxicity in people drinking heavily. Alcohol also enhances the toxicity of excess vitamin A, so care must be taken when treating an alcoholic with a vitamin A deficiency.

Treatment

Alcoholic Hepatitis

Mortality from alcoholic hepatitis during the early weeks of treatment is very high. Although the evidence is inconsistent, corticosteroid therapy may improve survival during the early stages of the disease in patients with severe alcoholic hepatitis. Supplemental amino acids may improve a patient's nutrition but not the chances of survival or progression to cirrhosis.

Orrego and colleagues reported that the drug propylthiouracil (PTU) improved survival of patients with all types of alcoholic liver disease. However, other studies have demonstrated no benefit from this therapy in patients with alcoholic hepatitis.

Abstinence is the cornerstone of therapy for patients with prolonged alcoholic hepatitis. Also important are careful control of diet with correction of vitamin deficiencies, and management of medical complications.

If the patient with alcoholic hepatitis lives to leave the hospital, abstinence is essential for long-term survival. Alexander and coworkers found that more than 80 percent of those who abstained or markedly reduced their drinking were alive 7 years later, whereas only 50 percent who continued to drink were alive 7 years later.

Alcoholic Cirrhosis

Treatment for cirrhosis is directed at symptoms and complications, with abstinence a requirement. For terminally ill patients, liver transplantation is the only effective treatment. This procedure in alcoholic cirrhotic patients has demonstrated success and survival rates equal to those for nonalcoholic cirrhotic patients.

Future directions in cirrhosis therapy are suggested by a study showing that lecithin protects against the development of alcohol-induced liver scarring in baboons. This therapy has not yet been studied in humans.

A Commentary by NIAAA Director Enoch Gordis, M.D.

Abstinence from alcohol is the single most important component of treatment for alcoholic liver disease. Continued drinking will worsen the condition of patients with this disease and greatly increase their risk for death. Physicians who treat alcoholic liver disease, no matter how competently, and who do not address their patients' drinking are practicing bad medicine, akin to treating an iron-deficiency anemia and disregarding the colon cancer that is causing it.

Because many alcohol abusers and most alcoholics require some form of treatment to remain abstinent, simply giving advice to "quit" drinking often is not sufficient. Physicians who choose not to manage their patients' alcohol problems may refer these patients to specialized alcohol treatment providers for evaluation and appropriate treatment. In referring a patient to appropriate alcohol treatment, physicians should keep informed of their patients' progress, as relapse may further complicate management of the alcoholic liver disease.

Chapter 20

Alcohol and AIDS

There are two reasons to investigate connections between alcohol, HIV infection, and AIDS: alcohol may adversely affect the immune system, and alcohol may influence high-risk sexual behavior.

Human immunodeficiency virus (HIV) is the agent that causes acquired immunodeficiency syndrome (AIDS). HIV is transmitted through sexual contact with an infected individual, through exchange of infected blood or blood products, or to the newborn from an infected mother. HIV-infected persons may harbor the virus for many years with no clinical signs of disease. Eventually, HIV destroys the body's immune system, mainly by impairing a class of white blood cells whose regulatory activities are essential for immune protection. As a result, people who have AIDS are prone to lung infections, brain abscesses, and a variety of other infections caused by microorganisms that usually do not produce disease in healthy people. Those who have AIDS also are prone to cancers such as Kaposi's sarcoma, a skin cancer rarely seen in non-HIV-infected populations.

One million people in the United States are estimated to be infected with HIV. At least 40,000 new HIV infections are thought to occur among adults and adolescents, and an estimated 1,500 to 2,000 new HIV infections are thought to occur among newborns each year. Currently, 8 to 10 million people worldwide are estimated to be infected with HIV. Of these, 50 percent are expected to develop AIDS within 10 years, and 90 percent may develop AIDS within 20 years of initial

National Institute on Alcohol Abuse and Alcoholism (NIAAA), *Alcohol Alert*, No. 15, PH311, January 1992.

infection. The prognosis for persons with AIDS is grim: AIDS-associated mortality may approach 85 percent within 5 years of diagnosis.

Alcohol and the Immune System

Alcohol can impair normal immune responses that protect the body from disease. Chronic alcohol consumption has been shown to reduce the number of infection-fighting white blood cells in laboratory animals and in humans. Chronic alcohol ingestion or alcohol dependence can depress antibody production and other immune responses in animals and in humans. Alcohol can suppress activities of certain immune system cells, called macrophages, that help keep the lungs free from infection. In addition, alcoholics appear to be more susceptible to bacterial infections and cancer than are nonalcoholics. Studies in animals and in humans indicate that consuming alcohol during pregnancy can decrease immune resistance in the offspring.

Alcohol's generally immunosuppressive effects could mean that 1) drinking may increase vulnerability to HIV infection among people exposed to the virus, and that 2) among people who are already HIV infected, alcohol-induced immunosuppression might add to HIV-induced immunosuppression, and speed the onset or exacerbate the pathology of AIDS-related illness. These are complex ideas and areas of intense investigation, but so far only a few studies have been published. Researchers have learned that alcohol can impair white blood cell responses to HIV. A provocative study that warrants replication found that a single drinking episode depressed certain immune responses of white blood cells taken from healthy volunteers. In addition, white blood cells isolated after this drinking episode were more susceptible to HIV infection than were cells isolated from subjects who did not drink, hinting that even occasional alcohol consumption may increase the likelihood of infection upon exposure to HIV. Whether alcohol use influences the progression of AIDS in persons already infected with HIV has been explored in a recent study of homosexual men. While these researchers found that neither alcohol nor other drugs seem to influence the progression of HIV infection or the development of AIDS, their results await confirmation. Clearly, more research is needed to understand alcohol's role in HIV infection and the course of ensuing disease.

170

Alcohol and Sexual Behavior

Sexual practices considered to be high risk for acquiring HIV from an infected individual include vaginal or anal intercourse without a condom; other sexual practices that facilitate exchange of blood, semen, or other body secretions; and unprotected sexual activities with multiple partners. The frequency with which sexual partners engage in such practices also influences the risk for exposure to HIV.

Alcohol's relationship to high-risk sexual behavior may be explained in two ways. First, alcohol use may be a marker for a risk-taking temperament: those who drink alcohol may also engage in a variety of high-risk activities, including unsafe sexual practices, as a part of a "problem behavior syndrome." Second, alcohol may influence high-risk behaviors at specific sexual encounters by affecting judgment and disinhibiting socially learned restraints. These are not mutually exclusive interpretations.

In addition, these two explanations have different implications for the prevention of high-risk sexual behavior. Among people who have a risk-taking temperament, reducing alcohol consumption may not reduce high-risk sexual behavior. However, among those who are more likely to take sexual risks when they are drinking than when they are not, reducing alcohol consumption should also reduce high-risk sexual behavior.

There are two approaches to studying alcohol's relationship to sexual behavior that may result in HIV infection. One approach examines whether alcohol use in general is correlated with sexual risk-taking behavior in general. In this approach, an observed association between drinking and high-risk sexual activity could imply that these two behaviors are part of a larger risk-taking tendency, or that alcohol itself influences sexual risk-taking, or both. Another approach examines the consequences of alcohol use during specific sexual encounters. An observed connection between alcohol use and sexual risk-taking during specific encounters suggests a direct influence of alcohol on such behavior.

A number of studies have identified associations between drinking and high-risk sexual activity. These studies also have found that an absence of or a reduction in alcohol use is associated with a decrease in high-risk sexual behavior. A study of heterosexual drinking habits and sexual behavior found that women and men who frequently combined alcohol use with sexual encounters were generally less likely to use condoms during intercourse. Similarly, a study of homosexual men found alcohol or other drug use combined with sexual activity to be strongly associated with high-risk sexual behavior: even those who drank only occasionally at the time of sexual encounters were twice as likely to be categorized as "high risk," based on the frequency of involvement in a range of sexual practices within nonmonogamous relationships, than were those who did not drink. Further, those men who did not drink during sexual encounters were three times more likely to be classified in a "no risk" category than were men who combined drinking with sexual activity. Recently, a reduction in alcohol use among homosexual men has been associated with a reduction in high-risk sexual behavior.

Other studies that examine the consequences of alcohol use at specific sexual encounters also have demonstrated a connection between alcohol use and high-risk sexual behavior. Scottish adolescents who drank at the time of first intercourse were less likely to have used a condom than those who did not drink. A survey of adolescents in Massachusetts revealed that teens were less likely to use condoms if sexual activity followed drinking or other drug use. Similarly, adult homosexual men and heterosexual women (but not heterosexual men) reported that they were less likely to use a condom during those sexual encounters in which they felt intoxicated. These reports of simultaneous alcohol use and high-risk sexual behavior suggest that alcohol can directly influence sexual risk-taking. However, these combined behaviors may still reflect a risk-taking tendency in some individuals.

Further research is needed to define conditions under which alcohol use is linked to high-risk sexual activity. Information generated from such studies will be vital for developing and improving programs to prevent HIV transmission.

A Commentary by NIAAA Director Enoch Gordis, M.D.

Science has made remarkable progress in our understanding of HIV and AIDS. Yet we know very little about the role of alcohol in the transmission and acquisition of HIV or in the progression of HIV infection to AIDS. Such knowledge would enhance efforts to prevent HIV exposure and decrease the number of new AIDS cases.

We know that alcohol affects the immune system. This suggests that alcohol could affect the course of HIV infection and AIDS, which is a disease of the immune system. For example, alcohol might affect the body's ability to defend against HIV infection upon exposure to the virus; alcohol might alter the course of infection to the development of AIDS; or alcohol might affect the severity or duration of the special infections, known as opportunistic infections, that characterize AIDS. So far, the research findings in this area are hard to reconcile. On one hand, laboratory evidence shows clearly that alcohol impairs the ability of white blood cells to defend against the human immunodeficiency virus. On the other hand, studies involving human populations have found that neither alcohol nor other drugs modify the course of HIV infection or AIDS. Given the complexity of the human immune system, the contradictions presented by these findings, while puzzling, are not unexpected. One key to solving this puzzle will be more attention, in long-term studies of human populations, to objective evidence of drinking and to laboratory evidence of immune function status.

We know also that alcohol is associated with high-risk sexual activity that potentially can result in exposure to HIV. Some people may be more likely to engage in certain sexual behaviors when drinking as a result of alcohol's disinhibiting effects. (In others, alcohol use and unsafe sexual practices seem to be a part of a "risk-taking temperament," in which unsafe sexual practices may occur whether or not alcohol is consumed.)

Prevention efforts that address the link between alcohol consumption and unsafe sex are being evaluated for their effectiveness in reducing high-risk sexual activity. In addition, researchers are investigating various settings, such as bars and alcohol treatment programs, and certain groups, such as teenagers, where intervention strategies could be employed to decrease alcohol-related high-risk sexual activity. It is hoped that these findings will help target HIV-related prevention strategies in a way that will help to reduce the incidence of new cases of HIV infection, and ultimately reduce the number of persons with AIDS.

Chapter 21

Alcoholism and Co-Occurring Disorders

The term "comorbidity" refers to the presence of any two or more illnesses in the same person. These illnesses can be medical or psychiatric conditions, as well as drug use disorders, including alcoholism. Comorbid illnesses may occur simultaneously or sequentially. The fact that two illnesses are comorbid, however, does not necessarily imply that one is the cause of the other, even if one occurs first.

An understanding of comorbidity is essential in developing effective treatment and prevention efforts. For example, since alcoholism causes liver disease, measures to decrease alcohol consumption will help reduce the incidence of liver disease. With respect to treatment, persons exhibiting comorbid alcohol-related and medical or psychiatric disorders often fall through the cracks of the health care system because of administrative distinctions among addiction, medical, and mental health-related services. Patients are often forced to choose between clinical settings, often resulting in neglect of one condition.

Alcoholism and other disorders might be related in a number of ways, including the following: 1) Alcoholism and a second disorder can co-occur, either sequentially or simultaneously, by coincidence. 2) Alcoholism can cause various medical and psychiatric conditions or increase their severity. 3) Comorbid disorders might cause alcoholism or increase its severity. 4) Both alcoholism and the comorbid disorder may be caused, separately, by some third condition. 5) Alcohol use

National Institute on Alcohol Abuse and Alcoholism (NIAAA), *Alcohol Alert*, No. 14, PH302, October 1991.

or alcohol withdrawal can produce symptoms that mimic those of an independent psychiatric disorder.

Research on the nature of the relationship between comorbid disorders generally relies on surveys of either the clinical population (persons in treatment) or the general population. Most studies of comorbidity are based on clinical samples. This may result in inflated estimates of comorbidity, since persons with multiple ailments may be more likely to seek treatment (Berkson's fallacy). This trend may be countered to some extent by the reluctance of some alcoholism treatment centers to admit persons exhibiting serious psychiatric problems. Thus, the prevalence of comorbid psychiatric disorders among alcoholics in treatment does not reflect the actual prevalence of such comorbidity in the community.

Additional methodological difficulties complicate both clinical and general population investigations. For example, estimates of comorbidity will also vary depending on how alcohol use disorders are defined. Definitions of alcoholism have included 1) formal definitions of abuse and dependence appearing in psychiatric classification systems such as the *DSM-III-R*; 2) alcohol-related symptom ratings; 3) serious manifestations of physiological dependence (i.e., tolerance and withdrawal); and 4) various levels of heavy alcohol consumption. Since alcohol use, alcohol withdrawal, and alcohol abuse and dependence may each relate to comorbid conditions in an entirely different way, it is essential when evaluating comorbidity to clarify which aspects of alcohol use are involved. Similar considerations apply to the evaluation of comorbid disorders. For example, when evaluating depression, it is important to distinguish among sadness, grief, and major depressive disorder.

An important source of comorbidity data is the Epidemiologic Catchment Area (ECA) program of the National Institute of Mental Health. The ECA surveyed more than 20,000 respondents residing in households, group homes, and long-term institutions in five sites across the United States to provide data about the prevalence and incidence of psychiatric disorders, as well as issues related to treatment. (Prevalence is the number of existing cases; incidence is the number of new cases.)

Conclusions about causal relationships between alcohol use disorders and comorbid psychiatric disorders based on ECA data are problematic, since sequencing criteria consisted of age at first symptom of the alcohol use disorder, rather than age at onset of the syndrome. Moreover, the ECA program defined alcohol use disorders as the occurrence of enough symptoms to meet the associated diagnostic criteria over the life course. The sporadic occurrence of isolated symptoms, perhaps years apart, provides an insufficient basis for testing competing hypotheses related to comorbidity.

Because the term "comorbidity" is often not applied to medical conditions, a number of medical conditions that are often comorbid with alcoholism are mentioned below. A discussion of comorbidity with psychiatric disorders will follow.

Medical Conditions

Alcohol has been shown to be directly toxic to the liver. Approximately 90 to 100 percent of heavy drinkers show evidence of fatty liver, an estimated 10 to 35 percent develop alcoholic hepatitis, and 10 to 20 percent develop cirrhosis. Fatty liver is reversible with abstinence, alcoholic hepatitis is usually reversible upon abstinence, and while alcoholic cirrhosis is often progressive and fatal, it can stabilize with abstinence. In addition to liver disease, heavy alcohol consumption causes chronic pancreatitis and malabsorption of nutrients.

The prevalence of alcoholic cardiomyopathy (heart muscle disease) is unknown. Alcohol-induced heart damage appears to increase with lifetime dose of alcohol.

Alcohol can damage the brain in many ways. The most serious effect is Korsakoff's syndrome, characterized in part by an inability to remember recent events or to learn new information. The incidence of alcohol-related brain damage is approximately 10 percent of adult dementias in the United States. Milder attention and memory deficits may improve gradually with abstinence.

Additional diseases strongly linked to alcohol consumption include failure of reproductive function and cancers of the mouth, larynx, and esophagus. Hospitalized alcoholics have also been found to have an increased prevalence of dental problems, compared with nonalcoholic psychiatric patients, including missing teeth and nonrestorable teeth.

Psychiatric Disorders

Despite the study's shortcomings, data from the ECA provide a starting point for assessing the prevalence of some comorbidities (on a lifetime basis). Based on ECA data, alcoholics are 21.0 times more likely to also have a diagnosis of antisocial personality disorder compared with nonalcoholics. Similar "odds ratios" for some other psychiatric comorbidities are as follows: drug abuse, 3.9 times; mania,

6.2 times; and schizophrenia, 4.0 times. There is only a mild increase in major depressive disorder among alcoholics (odds ratio 1.7), and essentially no increase in anxiety disorders.

Antisocial Personality Disorder

The strongest correlate of alcoholism documented in the ECA is antisocial personality disorder (ASPD). Determining the chronological relationships between the two disorders is complicated by the following factors: 1) both disorders typically begin early in life, thus requiring retrospective reporting from adults; 2) there is considerable overlap in the symptoms of the two disorders; 3) alcohol or other drug abuse is itself one of the diagnostic criteria for ASPD; and 4) intoxication leads to behavioral disinhibition, thus lowering the threshold for antisocial behavior.

Comorbid ASPD has prognostic and treatment implications for alcoholics. Patients with ASPD have an earlier age of onset of alcohol and other drug abuse and a more rapid and serious course of illness.

Bulimia

Bulimia is an eating disorder in which patients, usually female, binge on sugar- and fat-rich meals, and purge regularly, as by self-induced vomiting. This disorder is characterized by craving, preoccupation with binge eating, loss of control during binges, an emphasis on short-term gratification, and ambivalence about treatment—symptoms that resemble those of addictive disorders. Bulimics commonly exhibit multiple drug use disorders and have high rates of alcoholism. Between 33 and 83 percent of bulimics may have a first-degree relative suffering from alcohol abuse or alcoholism.

Depression

Although it has been suggested that alcoholism and depression are manifestations of the same underlying illness, the results of family, twin, and adoption studies suggest that alcoholism and mood disorder are probably distinct illnesses with different prognoses and treatments. However, symptoms of depression are likely to develop during the course of alcoholism, and some patients with mood disorders may increase their drinking when undergoing a mood change, fulfilling criteria for secondary alcoholism. When depressive symptoms are

178

secondary to alcoholism, they are likely to disappear within a few days or weeks of abstinence, as withdrawal symptoms subside.

Anxiety

Studies (not using ECA data) indicate that approximately 10 to 30 percent of alcoholics have panic disorder, and about 20 percent of persons with anxiety disorders abuse alcohol. Among alcoholics entering treatment, about two-thirds have symptoms that resemble anxiety disorders. The relation between major anxiety disorders and alcoholism is unclear. Several studies indicate that anxious patients may use alcohol or other drugs to self-medicate, despite the fact that such use may ultimately exacerbate their clinical condition.

The strongest correlation between alcoholism and severe anxiety symptoms occurs in the context of alcohol withdrawal. The severe tremors, feelings of tension, restlessness, and insomnia associated with withdrawal begin to subside after 4 or 5 days, although a vulnerability to panic attacks and to generalized anxiety may continue for months. Because these symptoms decrease with abstinence, they are unlikely to represent an independent anxiety disorder. Interestingly, subjects suffering from both alcoholism and panic disorder are unable to distinguish between a number of symptoms common to both disorders.

Other Drug Abuse

Based on ECA data, alcoholics are 35 times more likely than nonalcoholics to also use cocaine. Similar odds ratios for other types of drugs are: sedatives, 17.0 times; opioids, 13.0 times; hallucinogens, 12.0; stimulants, 11.0; and marijuana and related drugs, 6.0. Surveys of both clinical and nonclinical populations indicate that at least 90 percent of alcoholics are nicotine dependent.

Comorbidity affects the course of illness and the response to treatment of both alcoholism and its comorbid illnesses, whether these occur simultaneously or sequentially. Because alcohol-related comorbidity is so common, research is needed to improve the recognition and appropriate management of alcohol abuse and alcoholism occurring in the context of other disorders.

A Commentary by NIAAA Director Enoch Gordis, M.D.

Treatment for co-occurring illnesses in persons with alcoholism should be a standard part of every alcoholism treatment program. Unfortunately, many patients with such illnesses fall through the cracks; for example, alcoholic patients with psychiatric problems who may be rejected by both alcoholism programs and mental health programs. This situation is unacceptable. In many instances, leadership can help solve this problem. Program directors who are concerned about providing the best care to their patients should work within their service areas to develop comprehensive treatment networks for multiply affected patients. In some cases, this may mean facilitating changes in city, county, or State laws to mandate care for such patients. In other cases, it might mean working to resolve differences in treatment philosophy that make it difficult for patients to be treated for comorbid conditions; for example, the requirement of some alcoholism programs that methadone-maintained individuals be drug free before acceptance for treatment. Patients who are alcoholic and who also suffer from other illnesses deserve the same kind of comprehensive care as a cancer patient with pneumonia, or a diabetic patient with glaucoma.

Researchers interested in the causes of disease will differ on whether studying the patient with co-occurring disease is a promising research strategy. On the one hand, the presence of one illness has been known to modify the course of another for better or worse. Clearly, it would be valuable to understand why. On the other hand, because we barely understand the fundamentals of alcoholism, studying it in the presence of other diseases may introduce complications. For example, diabetes increases an individual's risk for atherosclerosis, but researchers interested in atherosclerosis might not choose to unravel the causes of this disease by studying it primarily in diabetic patients.

Because of the increase in the frequency of polydrug abuse, alcoholism treatment programs must be aware of and prepared to deal with this problem in their patients. It should be noted, however, that the most common pattern of abuse in the United States is still alcoholism alone.

Chapter 22

Alcohol Withdrawal Syndrome

The alcohol withdrawal syndrome is a cluster of symptoms observed in persons who stop drinking alcohol following continuous and heavy consumption. Milder forms of the syndrome include tremulousness, seizures, and hallucinations, typically occurring within 6-48 hours after the last drink. A more serious syndrome, delirium tremens (DTs), involves profound confusion, hallucinations, and severe autonomic nervous system overactivity, typically beginning between 48 and 96 hours after the last drink. Estimates vary on the incidence of serious consequences of alcohol withdrawal. Regardless of actual incidence, recent evidence suggests that it may be important to treat everyone who is suffering from alcohol withdrawal.

In a classic study that has shaped our understanding of alcohol withdrawal for many years, Isbell et al. (1955) found that alcohol-related seizures occur only after stopping heavy drinking. In a recent study that looked primarily at seizures, Ng et al. (1988) challenged Isbell's concept and reported that the risk of first seizure is related to current alcohol use rather than to withdrawal. They concluded, based on self-reports given retrospectively by seizure patients, that the relationship of alcohol use to seizures is causal and dose-dependent. However, emerging neurophysiological findings lend support to Isbell's interpretation of withdrawal.

In the central nervous system, ethanol (in concentrations high enough to intoxicate humans) interferes with the processes that tell

National Institute on Alcohol Abuse and Alcoholism (NIAAA), *Alcohol Alert*, No. 5, PH270, August 1989.

certain nerve cells to activate or become excited. It also enhances those processes that tell certain nerve cells to be restrained. Thus, ethanol acts as a nonspecific biochemical inhibitor of activity in the central nervous system. During withdrawal, a person's central nervous system experiences a reversal of this effect: Excitatory processes are enhanced while inhibitory processes are reduced. Such changes can result in overactivation of the central nervous system when alcohol is withdrawn.

Clinical researchers have measured this overactivation in patients. Even patients with moderately severe alcohol withdrawal can experience sympathetic nervous system overactivity and increased production of the adrenal hormones cortisol and norepinephrine. Both of these hormones can be toxic to nerve cells. Moreover, cortisol can specifically damage neurons in the hippocampus—a part of the brain that is thought to be particularly important for memory and control of affective states. Thus, repeated untreated alcohol withdrawals may lead to direct damage to the hippocampus.

Ballenger and Post (1978) did a retrospective chart review that led them to postulate that repeated inadequately treated withdrawals could produce future withdrawals of increased severity. These authors suggested that this phenomenon may be analogous to kindling as described in the animal literature. In kindling, repeated, weak (subthreshold), electrical or pharmacological stimulation of certain parts of the central nervous system leads to increased sensitivity; an animal eventually exhibits behavioral changes (including seizures) that are more severe on each occasion. The implication is that repeated untreated withdrawals from alcohol have a cumulative effect and create more serious future withdrawals. Only a minority of chronic alcoholics develop a seizure disorder, so an inherited vulnerability may be involved. Many investigators now believe that chronic alcoholics who cannot maintain abstinence should receive pharmacotherapy to control withdrawal symptoms, thereby reducing the potential for further seizures and brain damage.

In a recent review of pharmacological treatments for alcohol intoxication, withdrawal, and dependence, Liskow and Goodwin (1987) concluded that the drugs of choice for treating withdrawal are the benzodiazepines—e.g., the longer-acting benzodiazepines chlordiazepoxide (Librium) and diazepam (Valium) or the shorter-acting benzodiazepines oxazepam (Serax) and lorazepam (Ativan).

Physicians traditionally have used benzodiazepines by administering decreasing doses over the period of alcohol withdrawal. Rosenbloom (1988) recommends this approach, suggesting the use of intermediate half-life benzodiazepines (such as lorazepam), or even shorter half-life drugs (such as midazolam), because these drugs do not linger in the system and allow for doses to be easily titrated to the patient's response. However, Sellers et al. (1983) introduced a different approach. At the start of treatment, doses of diazepam are given every 1 to 2 hours until withdrawal symptoms abate. Because diazepam has a long half-life and produces a psychoactive metabolite (desmethyldiazepam) with an even longer half-life, there is usually no need for further medication. This strategy, called "loading dose," simplifies treatment, protects against seizures, and eliminates possible reinforcement of drug-seeking behavior in patients who otherwise might receive additional medication for relief of symptoms.

Other agents, such as the beta-blocker propranolol, the beta-blocker atenolol in combination with oxazepam, and the alpha-2-adrenoreceptor agonist clonidine, have been tested and shown to alleviate some symptoms of the withdrawal syndrome, but there is no clear evidence of their efficacy in preventing seizures. Potential drugs for future use are calcium channel blockers and carbamazepine, which are now in the early stages of evaluation.

Most clinicians use medications to diminish the symptoms of alcohol withdrawal. However, Whitfield et al. (1978) reported success with nondrug detoxification of a group of ambulatory patients with uncomplicated alcoholism. The treatment consisted of screening and providing extensive social support during withdrawal. The authors concluded that nondrug detoxification offers a reduced need for medical staff, a shortened detoxification period, and no sedative interference with a patient's alertness for participating in an alcohol treatment program.

Several researchers have developed scales for assessing the severity of the alcohol withdrawal syndrome: the Total Severity Assessment and Selected Severity Assessment, the Abstinence Symptom Evaluation Scale, and the Clinical Institute Withdrawal Assessment Scale (CIWA). Originally developed as research tools for studying treatment efficacy, such scales are now finding clinical use. Foy et al. (1988) demonstrated that a modified version of the CIWA can assist in guiding treatment and predicting patients at risk for severe alcohol withdrawal. Such scales also may be helpful when monitoring the adequacy of a loading dose of medication. However, rating procedures are not infallible, and an occasional patient will have a more severe reaction than the scale predicts. Rating procedures cannot replace the clinical judgment of medical staff.

One final point deserves mention. A recent study by Hayashida et al. (1989) compared outpatient with inpatient detoxification. The researchers concluded that outpatient medical detoxification is "an effective, safe, and low-cost treatment for patients with mild-to-moderate symptoms of alcohol withdrawal." However, the data from this study indicate that inpatient detoxification was more effective than outpatient detoxification: At the 6-month followup those treated as inpatients reported significantly greater improvement in their drinking behavior, despite having been measured as more impaired than the outpatient group at the time of admission. This point is not emphasized in the report. Whereas outpatient detoxification may be cheaper for some alcoholics, it is not clear to what extent serious comorbidities, which may be undetected outside a hospital setting, may lead to more severe and expensive problems later.

A Commentary by NIAAA Director Enoch Gordis, M.D.

A variety of techniques exist for managing alcohol withdrawal, some that involve pharmacotherapy with sedatives and some that do not. Based on current literature, it appears that it is probably safe to treat mild withdrawal without drugs. However, research on treating alcohol withdrawal is just beginning to accumulate. Recent research findings show a potential for central nervous system damage to patients who experience repeated withdrawals and suggest that all patients exhibiting alcohol withdrawal symptoms receive pharmacotherapy. As evidence increases, it may well be that pharmacotherapy becomes the recommended choice in all withdrawal cases. Therefore, it is vital that clinicians keep abreast of the literature to ensure that their patients receive the most up-to-date care.

When using sedatives to treat alcohol withdrawal, understanding the relative advantages and disadvantages of different drug administration techniques is important. Administering an initial dose of a long-acting benzodiazepine, like diazepam, with repeated doses every 2 hours until symptoms subside, then stopping the drug, simplifies treatment and frees patients and staff to focus on the recovery process, not drug dosage schedules. However, this method could cause problems if sedation is found to complicate an existing medical condition, such as chronic obstructive pulmonary disease, because the drugs, or their metabolites, remain in the body for several days. On the other hand, by giving repeated doses of a short-acting benzodiazepine (e.g., oxazepam), probably for several days, if complications to medical conditions are found, the drugs can be easily stopped due to their rapid elimination by the body. But this regimen is less easily managed because medication must be given around the clock, and it could result in the patient and staff attending to the drug-taking regimen rather than to recovery.

In deciding which drug administration technique to use for individual patients, there is no substitute for a thorough medical evaluation. There is a welcome trend toward using the CIWA and other clinical scales for measuring withdrawal syndrome severity and for guiding drug treatment decisions; their use should be encouraged. However, no scaling instrument is infallible. Withdrawal severity scales should be used to complement, not replace, a thorough clinical evaluation of the patient's medical status.

Chapter 23

Relapse and Craving

There is evidence that approximately 90 percent of alcoholics are likely to experience at least one relapse over the 4-year period following treatment. Despite some promising leads, no controlled studies definitively have shown any single or combined intervention that prevents relapse in a fairly predictable manner. Thus, relapse as a central issue of alcoholism treatment warrants further study.

Similar relapse rates for alcohol, nicotine, and heroin addiction suggest that the relapse mechanism for many addictive disorders may share common biochemical, behavioral, or cognitive components. Thus, integrating relapse data for different addictive disorders may provide new perspectives for relapse prevention.

Impaired control has been suggested as a determinant for relapse, yet is defined differently among investigators. Keller suggested that impaired control has two meanings: the unpredictability of an alcoholic's choice to refrain from the first drink and the inability to stop drinking once started. Other investigators limit the use of "impaired control" to the inability to stop drinking once started. They suggest that one drink does not lead inevitably to uncontrolled drinking. Research has shown that severity of dependence affects the ability to stop drinking after the first drink.

Several relapse theories utilize the concept of craving. Use of the term "craving" in a variety of contexts, however, has led to confusion about its definition. Some behavioral researchers argue that the idea

National Institute on Alcohol Abuse and Alcoholism (NIAA), *Alcohol Alert*, No. 6, PH277, October 1989.

of craving is circular, hence meaningless, since in their view, craving can only be recognized retrospectively by the fact that the subject drank. They deemphasize physiological urges and stress the relationship between the behavior of drinking and environmental stimuli that prompt the behavior. On the other hand, Ludwig and Stark find no problem with the term "craving": craving is recognized simply by asking whether a subject who has not yet drunk alcohol feels a need for it, much as one can inquire about another person's hunger before he or she eats. Ludwig and associates suggested that alcoholics experience classical conditioning (Pavlovian), by pairing external (e.g., familiar bar) and internal (e.g., negative mood states) stimuli to the reinforcing effects of alcohol. This theory suggests that craving for alcohol is an appetitive urge, similar to hunger, that varies in intensity and is characterized by withdrawal-like symptoms. The symptoms are elicited by internal and external cues that evoke memory of the euphoric effects of alcohol and of the discomfort of withdrawal.

Physiological responses to alcohol cues have been described. For example, research has shown that exposure to alcohol, without consumption, can stimulate an increased salivary response in alcoholics. Similarly, skin conductance levels and self-reported desire for alcohol were correlated for alcoholic subjects in response to alcohol cues; the relationship was strongest for those most severely dependent. Alcoholics demonstrated significantly greater and more rapid insulin and glucose responses than nonalcoholics following the consumption of a placebo beer.

Several relapse prevention models incorporate the concept of self-efficacy, which states that an individual's expectations about his or her ability to cope in a situation will affect the outcome. According to Marlatt and colleagues, the transition from the initial drink following abstinence (lapse) to excessive drinking (relapse) is influenced by an individual's perception of and reaction to the first drink. These investigators formulated a cognitive-behavioral analysis of relapse, positing that relapse is influenced by the interaction of conditioned high-risk environmental situations, skills to cope with the high-risk situations, level of perceived personal control (self-efficacy), and the anticipated positive effects of alcohol. An analysis of 48 episodes revealed that most relapses were associated with three high-risk situations: (1) frustration and anger, (2) social pressure, and (3) intrapersonal temptation. Cooney and associates supported this model by demonstrating that, among alcoholics, exposure to alcohol cues was followed by diminished confidence in the ability to resist drinking.

Marlatt and Gordon argue that an alcoholic must assume an active role in changing drinking behavior. Marlatt advises the individual to achieve three basic goals: modify lifestyle to enhance the ability to cope with stress and high-risk situations (increase self-efficacy); identify and respond appropriately to internal and external cues that serve as relapse warning signals; and implement self-control strategies to reduce the risk of relapse in any situation.

Rankin and colleagues tested the effectiveness of cue exposure in extinguishing craving in alcoholics. The investigators gave severely dependent alcoholic volunteers a priming dose of alcohol, which had been shown to evoke craving. Volunteers were urged to refuse further alcohol; their craving for more alcohol diminished with each session. After six sessions, the priming effect almost completely disappeared. Volunteers who participated in imaginal cue exposure did not have the same outcome. This treatment was performed in a controlled, inpatient setting; the long-term effectiveness of cue exposure for diminishing craving after discharge remains to be demonstrated.

Chaney and associates investigated the effectiveness of skills-training intervention to help alcoholics cope with relapse risk. The alcoholics learned problem-solving skills and rehearsed alternative behaviors for specific high-risk situations. The investigators suggested that skills training may be a useful component of a multimodal behavioral approach to prevent relapse.

A relapse prevention model for alcoholics emphasizes a strategy that helps each individual develop a profile of past drinking behavior and current expectations about high-risk situations. The therapy promotes use of coping strategies and behavioral change by engaging the patient in performance-based homework assignments related to high-risk situations. Preliminary outcome data revealed a decrease in the number of drinks consumed per day as well as in drinking days per week. Forty-seven percent of the clients reported total abstinence over the 3-month followup period, and 29 percent reported total abstinence over the entire 6-month followup period.

Disulfiram (Antabuse) is used as an adjunct to enhance the probability of long-term sobriety. Although patient compliance is problematic, disulfiram therapy has successfully decreased frequency of drinking in alcoholics who could not remain abstinent. A study of supervised disulfiram administration reported significant periods of sobriety of up to 12 months in 60 percent of patients treated.

Preliminary neurochemical studies have revealed that decreased levels of brain serotonin may influence appetite for alcohol. Alcohol-preferring rats have lower levels of serotonin in various regions of the brain. In addition, drugs that increase brain serotonin activity reduce alcohol consumption in rodents. Four studies have evaluated the effect of serotonin blockers—zimelidine, citalopram, and fluoxetine—on alcohol consumption in humans, each using a double-blind, placebo-controlled design. These agents produced a decrease in alcohol intake and, in some cases, a significant increase in the number of abstinent days. These effects, however, were found among small samples and were short lived. Controlled trials in larger dependent populations are needed before serotonin blockers can provide hope as a possible adjunct for relapse prevention.

In both pharmacological and behavioral prevention strategies, it is important to consider severity of alcohol dependence as a critical factor.

A Commentary by NIAAA Director Enoch Gordis, M.D.

The primary goal of alcoholism treatment, as in other areas of medicine, is to help the patient to achieve and maintain long-term remission of disease. For alcohol dependent persons, remission means the continuous maintenance of sobriety. There is continuing and growing concern among clinicians about the high rate of relapse among their patients, and the increasingly adverse consequences of continuing disease. For this reason, preventing relapse is, perhaps, the fundamental issue in alcoholism treatment today.

Modern science, both biological and behavioral, has explored a number of different leads in the quest to prevent relapse. These range from pharmacological agents, such as the serotonin uptake blockers and disulfiram, to behavioral constructs, such as cue extinction and skills training. Although these are promising leads that one day may improve significantly the chances of alcohol dependent persons to continue long-term sobriety, there are no definitive answers yet to this troubling aspect of alcoholism treatment. For example, the interesting work on pharmacological agents to help prevent relapse evolved from the study of brain receptors, and suggests that serotonin may diminish an alcoholic's desire or craving for alcohol. This research, however, must be confirmed by properly conducted controlled clinical trials before widespread application to treating alcohol dependency. Similarly, behavioral approaches have been well described by the talented scientists who undertook the initial studies; however, evidence of the effectiveness of these approaches in preventing relapse in dependent drinkers has not been documented in adequate controlled trials.

Although we are not yet at the point where we can state definitively what works best in preventing relapse, I firmly believe that we are on the brink of a new period in alcoholism treatment research that ultimately will help us to develop this knowledge. For the present, therapists should examine critically the evidence for new nonpharmacological approaches before initiating them. Similarly, good clinical wisdom should discourage the use of unproven pharmacological agents to prevent alcoholism relapse until the efficacy of using such agents in this regard is proven.

Chapter 24

Youth and Alcohol: Dangerous and Deadly Consequences

Foreward

The health toll exacted by underage drinking is clear: 4.6 million teenagers have a drinking problem; alcohol-related accidents are a leading cause of death among young people 15-24 years of age; and about half of all youthful deaths in drowning, fires, suicide, and homicide are alcohol-related.

Purpose

The purpose of this study was to describe the dangerous and often unrecognized consequences of underage drinking.

Background

As part of her campaign against underage drinking, the Surgeon General [Antonia Novello] requested that the Office of Inspector General (OIG) provide information on some of the negative consequences of youth alcohol use. This concern mirrors one of the Department of Health and Human Services Secretary's [Louis Sullivan's] goals which is to reduce the prevalence of alcohol problems among children and

Excerpted from *Youth & Alcohol: Selected Reports to the Surgeon General*, U.S. Department of Education; a complete copy of this report may be purchased from the U.S. Government Printing Office: 1994 380-788/20148.

youth. As part of his strategy to meet this goal, the Secretary sponsored "Healthy People/Healthy Environments: The Secretary's National Conference on Alcohol-Related Injuries" on March 23-25, 1992. This conference served as a call-to-action and a forum for health professionals to help advance the alcohol and injury-related objectives of *Healthy People 2000*. This study is one in a series conducted by the OIG related to youth and alcohol. A related report, "Youth and Alcohol: Drinking and Crime" (OEI-09-92-00260), describes the association between alcohol and youth crime.

Although extensive research exists related to the negative consequences of adult alcohol use, few national studies have attempted to assess the relationship between underage drinking and rape, sexual assault, suicide, and other harmful incidents. Researchers who attempt to link youth alcohol use with injuries and other problems face legal and scientific barriers. For example, one survey found that emergency room physicians rarely will administer blood alcohol tests unless an injury was automobile-related or the test is vital to a patient's treatment.

Most studies and data related to the negative consequences of underage drinking focus on traffic fatalities. For instance, the National Highway Traffic Safety Administration reported that 34.8 percent of drivers ages 18 to 20 and 18.9 percent of drivers ages 15 to 17 who were involved in fatal automobile crashes in 1989 had alcohol in their system. Although few national data concerning other problems exist, researchers focusing on local populations have uncovered startling data concerning alcohol use among youth who experience serious injuries or unintentional death.

Methodology

Using several University of California on-line database services, we conducted a review of medical, legal, psychological, and other social research studies and surveys related to the negative consequences of youth alcohol use. We also referred to articles and data obtained during our previous youth and alcohol studies.

Summary of Research Findings

Crime

The Department of Justice (DOJ) and other researchers at times have attempted to determine the extent to which underage drinking is associated with criminal activity. These researchers have found a strong association between alcohol use and crimes of aggression, such as murder and rape (for further information, see the OIG report "Youth and Alcohol: Drinking and Crime").

- According to a DOJ survey, 31.9 percent of youth under 18 in long-term, State-operated juvenile institutions in 1987 were under the influence of alcohol at the time of the offense.

- A DOJ 11-city survey found that from 4 to 32 percent of male juvenile arrestees admitted using alcohol in the 72 hours prior to their arrest.

- A 1974 survey of youth under 21 in State adult correctional facilities found that approximately 36.4 to 38.6 percent reported drinking at the time of the offense.

One researcher reported that almost 50 percent of German juvenile offenders surveyed in 1971 were intoxicated when they committed criminal offenses. For crimes of aggression—such as murder, robbery, rape, and assault—the rates were "rather higher."

Victims of Crime

Studies of various populations have shown that many victims of violent crime are intoxicated at the time of the incident. While this problem is most frequently noted in rape victims, victims of other crimes exhibit similar high levels of intoxication.

- In a national survey of college students, almost 50 percent who said they had been victims of crime admitted that they had used drugs or alcohol before the crime occurred.

- A study of homicide victims in Atlanta, Georgia, found that 51 percent had blood alcohol levels of .10 percent or greater.

- One social science researcher observed that minors who drink may provoke assailants or otherwise catch the attention of criminals by handling money openly, acting vulnerable, or failing to take normal precautions in public.

Rape and Sexual Assault

Researchers estimate that alcohol use is implicated in one- to two-thirds of sexual assault and acquaintance or "date" rape cases among teens and college students.

- In a survey of students at a southwestern university, 55 percent of sexual assault perpetrators and 53 percent of sexual assault victims admitted to being under the influence of alcohol at the time of the assault.

- According to a school administrator, 100 percent of sexual assault cases at the University of Colorado involve alcohol.

- A study of college women nationally found that alcohol use is one of the strongest predictors of a college woman's rape.

- A survey of high school students found that 18 percent of females and 39 percent of males say it is acceptable for a boy to force sex if the girl is stoned or drunk.

Risky Sexual Behavior

Alcohol use is associated with the early onset of sexual activity and with risky sexual behavior.

- A study of ninth grade students from four urban high schools showed that the best predictor of risky sexual behavior was alcohol and/or drug use.

- Other studies of adolescents have shown that the use of substances, including alcohol and tobacco, are associated with early sexual debut and an inadequate use of contraceptives.

- A 1990 survey of Massachusetts 16- to 19-year-olds found that 49 percent were more likely to have sex if they and their partner had been drinking. In addition, 17 percent used condoms less often after drinking.

- The National Longitudinal Survey of Youth found that substance use and sexual activity are more closely linked for white youth than they are for minority youth.

Suicide

According to one researcher, "Suicide among American teenagers is increasing at an alarming though underestimated rate." Alcohol acts as a contributing factor in the timing and seriousness of youth suicide attempts. Although youth may use alcohol in an attempt to reduce stress and pressure, this frequently results in additional self-destructive behavior.

- In a detailed analysis of youth suicide, one researcher found that drug and alcohol abuse is the most common characteristic of youth who attempt suicide. Seventy percent of youth suicide attempters were frequent drug and/or alcohol users. In addition, he noted a high incidence of drug and alcohol abuse among youth suicide attempters' parents.

- Based on rising youth suicide rates, three researchers conducted a study on 10- to 19-year-old suicide victims in Allegheny County (PA). They found "a striking association . . . between the ingestion of alcohol and the use of firearms as a method of suicide." They conclude that "the epidemic increase in the suicide rate among youth may be associated with an increase in the prevalence of alcohol abuse."

Water-Related Injuries and Drowning

Although swimming, boating, and diving are popular activities among youth, they can be deadly, especially when the participants consume alcohol before or during these water activities. According to national data, drowning is the second leading cause of injury-related death among adolescents and young adults. One researcher named alcohol and/or drug use as the primary factor contributing to adolescent swimming, boating, and diving drownings.

- Two studies that have attempted to link youth alcohol use and drowning found that from 40 to 50 percent of young males who drown used alcohol prior to drowning.

- According to national data, the ratio of young males who drown after boating incidents outnumbers females 12 to 1. Alcohol particularly may affect a youth's balance, resulting in the boat capsizing or the youth falling overboard.

- A detailed study of the factors contributing to youth drowning indicated that alcohol may severely affect a young swimmer's coordination and judgment. Peer pressure may cause youth to attempt to swim beyond their ability. On a dare, a youth might experience overconfidence if under the influence of alcohol. At the same time, the youth might underestimate the length of swim or the water's currents.

- Researchers have documented that 40 to 50 percent of all diving injury victims consumed alcoholic beverages. Again, alcohol may impair judgment, resulting in a youth underestimating the challenge.

Campus-Related Problems

A researcher who reviewed studies on college drinking found that missing classes, missing work, and not studying were the most frequently noted alcohol-related problems. Other researchers have linked alcohol use with more serious campus problems.

- In a national survey, college administrators estimated that student alcohol use leads to 69 percent of damage to residence halls, 34 percent of academic problems, and 25 percent of dropouts.

- A Towson State (MD) University study found that alcohol was a factor in 98 percent of student conduct violation cases.

Chapter 25

Young People's Drinking Habits, Access, Attitudes and Knowledge: A National Survey

Introduction

Purpose

This inspection surveyed junior and senior high (7th through 12th grade) students to determine how they obtain, view, and consume alcohol.

Background

In response to public health concerns and the adverse health consequences of alcohol abuse, Surgeon General Antonia Novello requested that the Office of Inspector General (OIG) survey youth to determine their views and practices regarding alcohol use. These concerns mirror one of Department of Health and Human Services (HHS) Secretary Louis Sullivan's goals which is to reduce the prevalence of alcohol problems among children and youth. The Surgeon General is particularly concerned about the drinking habits of youth, especially the nation's 20.7 million 7th through 12th graders. This report is one in a series prepared by the OIG related to youth and alcohol. It describes survey findings concerning youth perceptions, knowledge, opinions, and drinking habits.

Excerpted from *Youth & Alcohol: Selected Reports to the Surgeon General*, U.S. Department of Education; a complete copy of this report may be purchased from the U.S. Government Printing Office: 1994 380-788/20148.

Youth Consumption and Beliefs About Alcohol

According to the U.S. Department of Education, 20.7 million students attend 7th through 12th grade. Previous national surveys have disclosed that most adolescents have tried alcohol and that many drink frequently. Among high school seniors in the class of 1990, 89.5 percent had used alcohol at least once, and 32.2 percent had experienced a "binge" of 5 or more drinks in a row within the past 2 weeks. While recent surveys of high school students indicate an overall drop in drug use, alcohol use continues at a high rate.

According to another survey, adolescents have started drinking at earlier ages since 1978. Although youth begin using alcohol at earlier ages, their information regarding its contents and effects may be faulty. A recent survey of 4th, 5th, and 6th graders found that only 21 percent consider wine coolers a drug, while 50 percent believe beer, wine, and liquor are drugs.

Youth Access to Alcohol

Youth obtain alcohol from a variety of social and commercial sources. Although the minimum age to buy alcohol in all States is 21, studies show that youth are frequently able to obtain alcohol with little or no problem. While youth frequently find alcohol at parties without parental supervision and at friends' homes, they also obtain alcohol from retail outlets in a variety of ways. Youth may (1) have an older friend purchase alcohol, (2) buy from stores that are known to sell to minors, and/or (3) solicit a stranger to purchase alcohol. In some areas, youth may simply purchase alcohol without being challenged by the vendor. According to a recent study, underage males were able to buy beer in 97 of 100 District of Columbia stores.

Methodology

To establish the universe of 7th through 12th grade students, we compiled data on all secondary (junior and senior high schools), kindergarten through 8th grade (K-8), and kindergarten through 12th grade (K-12) schools in the United States. We weighted the States based upon the total number of schools. The eight randomly selected States were: California, Colorado, Florida, Illinois, Louisiana, New York, Ohio, and Pennsylvania. We obtained data on all target schools in the eight States from the U.S. Department of Education. After weighting each county in each State by the number of students, we randomly selected two counties in each State. We randomly selected two schools from each county list, without weighting, for a total sample of 32 schools.

During March and April 1991, we conducted structured interviews with a random national sample of 956 students in the 7th through 12th grades. We asked all students about their opinions and knowledge of alcohol. We asked about the personal experiences of students who had drunk at least one full alcoholic beverage in the past year. Throughout this report, we refer to these students as "students who drink." Of the students who never drank alcohol or had not had a drink during the past year, we asked about their perceptions and observations of their classmates who drink. We refer to these students as "non-drinkers."

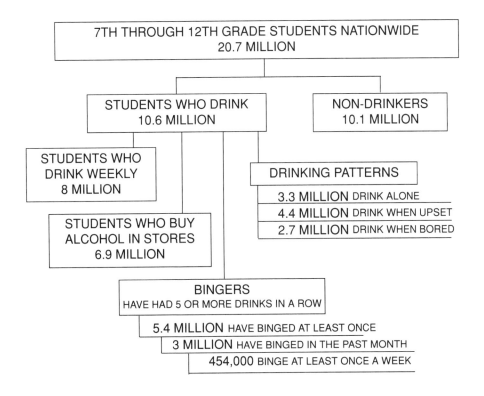

Figure 25.1. Statistical Highlights: Who Drinks?

Findings

Fifty-One Percent of Junior and Senior High School Students Have Had at Least One Drink Within the Past Year

According to our survey, 68 percent of all students have drunk alcohol at least once, and 51.2 percent (10.6 million) have had at least one drink within the past year. The average student who drinks is 16 years old and in the 10th grade. Of the students who drink, 53.8 percent are male and 46.2 percent are female.

We found that students were 13 years old when they took their first drink. This is close to other national surveys that report 12.3 years as an average age.

We found that 8 million, or 38.6 percent of all students, drink weekly. Three million students reported that they do not usually drink each week.

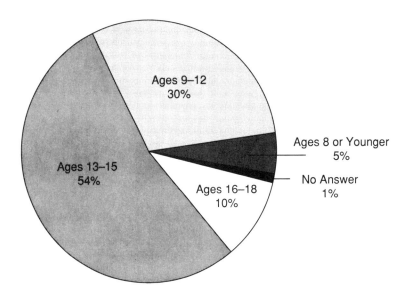

Figure 25.2. *The Majority of Students Have Their First Drink In Their Early Teens.*

Junior and Senior High School Students Drink 35 Percent of all Wine Coolers Sold in the United States and 1.1 Billion Cans of Beer Each Year

We asked students about four types of alcoholic beverages—beer (including all malt beverages), wine coolers, wine, and liquor (including mixed drinks that contain alcohol such as rum or vodka). Some students drink more than one type of alcoholic beverage. We project that:

- 9.2 million students have drunk beer. Of this group, 6 million drink between 0.12 and 33 beers weekly. In some schools, students mentioned that they drink 40-ounce bottles of malt liquor instead of 12-ounce cans or bottles of beer.

- 8.9 million students have drunk wine coolers. Of this group, 4 million drink between 0.16 and 12 wine coolers weekly.

- 6.2 million students have drunk wine. Of this group, 1.4 million drink between 0.25 and 24 glasses of wine weekly.

- 7.2 million students have drunk liquor. Of this group, 3.6 million drink between 0.25 and 24 drinks weekly.

Wine Coolers are the students' "drink of choice." When asked about their favorite alcoholic drink, 42.1 percent of students who drink chose wine coolers. This translates to 4.5 million students who drink nationally. In addition, 51 percent of all students say that wine coolers are the favorite drink among their friends and classmates. Students choose wine coolers because they taste good, are fruity, do not have a strong taste of alcohol, and they think wine coolers do not contain much alcohol.

Junior and senior high school students drink 35 percent of all wine coolers sold in the United States. According to estimated sales figures, 88.8 million gallons of wine coolers were sold in the United States in 1989. Based on an average consumption of 6.4 million bottles weekly (12-ounce size), we estimate that students drink 31.2 million gallons of wine coolers annually. By projecting the total volume of wine coolers students reported drinking, we estimate that students drink 35 percent of the wine coolers sold in this country.

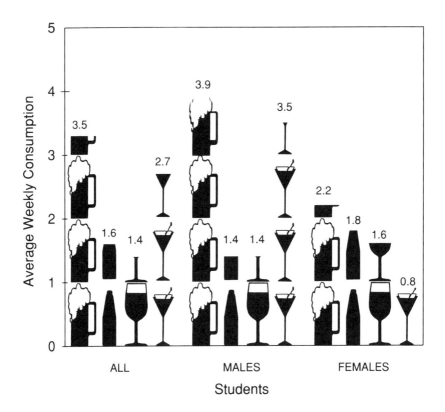

BEER

WINE COOLER

WINE

LIQUOR

Figure 25.3. *Average weekly consumption for each alcoholic beverage type is shown. While wine coolers are the "drink of choice," students drink more beer.*

Junior and senior high school students drink 1.1 billion beers each year. Students drink less than 2 percent of the 62 billion bottles and cans of beer consumed annually in the United States. While this percentage appears small, it is staggering when one considers that minors illegally consume more than a billion beers each year. Students who chose beer as their favorite alcoholic beverage said it tastes good, is easy to get, is cheap, and does not get you drunk as fast as other alcoholic beverages. Several students said that beer is always around or available at parties.

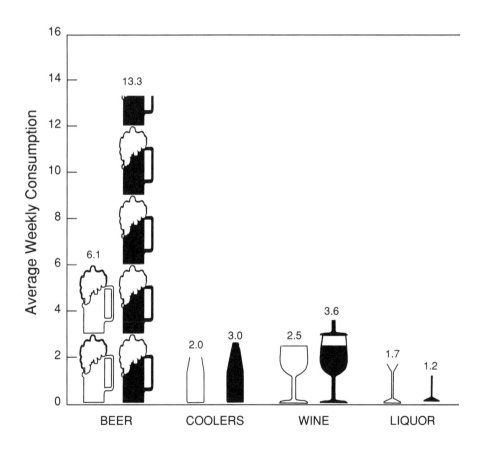

Figure 25.4. *Bingers drink more beer than other alcoholic beverages.*

More Than 5 Million Students Have Binged; 3 Million Within the Last Month; 454,000 Binge at Least Once a Week

Researchers define a "binge" as drinking five or more drinks in a row. Our projections show that 5.4 million students have "binged" at least once. Almost 55 percent of these had binged at least once in the month before the survey. For this group, the number of binges ranged from 1 to 20 per month.

The demographics for students who binge mirror the demographics for all students who drink. Fifty-nine percent are male; 41 percent female. The average binger is a 16-year-old male in the 10th grade. He was 12 years old when he took his first drink, slightly less than the average 13 years for all students who drink. He consumes six drinks each week.

There is a smaller group of students who binge almost every week 454,000 students average 15 drinks weekly. Their average age is 16.6 years, and they are in the 11th grade. Eighty-seven percent are males, and 13 percent are females.

More Than 3 Million Students Drink Alone, More Than 4 Million Drink When They Are Upset, and Less Than 3 Million Drink Because They Are Bored

Scientific research has shown that alcohol is a fast-acting drug. The early phases of drug action tend to have a positive effect on mood and general arousal level. Many students use alcohol as a tool to help them cope with certain feelings and situations. Of the 10.6 million students who drink, (1) 31 percent drink alone, (2) 41 percent drink when they are upset because it makes them feel better, (3) 25 percent drink because they are bored, and (4) 25 percent drink to feel high.

We compared these responses to a smaller group of students who binge. We found that students who binge are more likely to drink alcohol to relax, change their mood, or cope with emotional distress. Of the 5.4 million students who binge, (1) 39 percent drink alone, (2) 58 percent drink when they are upset, (3) 30 percent drink when they are bored, and (4) 37 percent drink to feel high.

DRINKING PATTENS

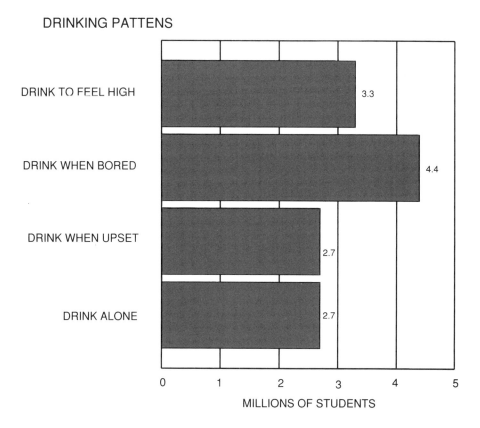

Figure 25.5. Student drinking patterns are reason for concern.

Students Lack Essential Knowledge About Alcohol and its Effects

Nationwide, 5.6 million students are unsure of the legal age to purchase alcohol. The minimum age to purchase alcohol in all States is 21. Nevertheless, a projected 1.6 million students do not even know such a law exists. Many students know about the law, but do not know the minimum age is 21. Their guesses ranged from 14 to 24 years.

In Louisiana, only 46 percent of the students we interviewed knew the correct minimum age. The confusion among these students may be attributed to the State law which prohibits persons under 21 from purchasing, possessing, or consuming alcohol, yet does not prohibit restaurants and bars from selling alcohol to persons over 18. Therefore, someone between 18 and 21 who drinks in a restaurant has committed a violation, but the restaurant or bartender has not. A State Alcohol Beverage Commission official said they are "not prosecuting the underage drinker because the law is superficial. When servers realize this, they are not hesitant to sell to those under 21."

A third of all students do not understand the intoxicating effects of alcohol. We asked students about alcohol's intoxicating effects and whether different stimulants will counteract these effects. More than 2.6 million students do not know a person can die from an overdose of alcohol. More than one-third of students believe that drinking coffee, getting some fresh air, or taking a cold shower will "sober you up."

In addition, a projected 259,000 students think that wine coolers or beer cannot get you drunk, cannot make you sick, or cannot do as much harm as other beverages. Students like wine coolers because they are "like soda—I don't consider them alcohol," and "they . . . don't get you drunk."

Students do not know the relative strengths of different alcoholic beverages. Almost 80 percent of the students do not know that one shot of whiskey has the same amount of alcohol as a 12-ounce can of beer. Similarly, 55 percent do not know that a 5-ounce glass of wine and a 12-ounce can of beer have the same amount of alcohol. One out of three students do not know that all wine coolers contain alcohol.

Student Knowledge Varies Greatly

- *Actual Question; Correct Answer; Percent Correct*

- Mothers who drink alcohol during pregnancy have a higher risk of having babies with birth defects; true; 98%
- Alcohol slows the activity of the brain; true; 96%
- A teenager cannot become an alcoholic; false; 96%
- Alcohol improves coordination and reflexes; false; 93%
- A person can die from an overdose of alcohol; true; 87%
- Many wine coolers actually contain no alcohol; false; 68%
- Drinking coffee, getting some fresh air, or taking a cold shower can help a person "sober up" more quickly; false; 54%
- One can of beer (12 ounces) has more alcohol than a glass of wine (5 ounces); false; 45%
- One shot of whiskey (11% ounces) has twice as much alcohol as a can of beer (12 ounces); false; 21%

Nine Million Students Get Their Information About Alcohol From Unreliable Sources

More than 4 million students learn about alcohol from their friends, whose information may or may not be accurate. Similarly, more than 5 million students say that they "just picked up" what they know by themselves or that nobody taught them. A greater proportion of students who drink than non-drinkers learn about alcohol through unreliable sources. When asked who taught him about alcohol, one student explained, "Nobody. A lot of teenagers who drink it don't know what it is."

As shown in Figure 25.6, non-drinkers are much more likely to learn about alcohol from their family and school than are students who drink. Non-drinkers are also slightly more likely to cite the media as a source of their knowledge.

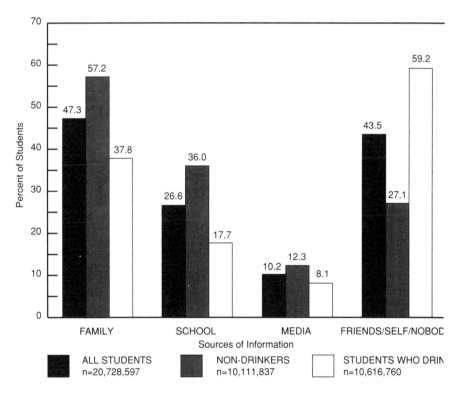

Figure 25.6. Students learn about alcohol from their parents, school, and the media.

More than a quarter of all students cited school, a class, teachers, or a specific school program as teaching them about alcohol. For example, a few students mentioned the Drug Abuse Resistance Education (D.A.R.E.) program. A coordinated effort between local police and schools, D.A.R.E. sends uniformed police officers into the schools to teach 5th- and 6th-grade students about alcohol and other drugs.

Seven Million Students Are Able to Walk Into a Store and Buy Alcohol

Students can buy alcohol in stores. Almost two-thirds or 6.9 million of the students who drink buy their own beverages. Despite the minimum age laws, students as young as 12 or 13 said they can buy alcoholic beverages in a store. As students get older, a larger proportion buy alcohol directly. Students said, "Sometimes they [vendors] do not even ask your age," and "I could go out right now and buy some." Students may (1) use fake identification, (2) buy from stores known to sell to young people or stores with young clerks, or (3) just go in and buy alcohol. Forty-five percent of all students know someone who has used a fake identification to buy alcohol. A small group, 4.5 percent, admit they steal alcohol from stores. Unable to purchase alcohol from stores, students in Philadelphia, Pennsylvania use a black market source. Students mentioned that houses, called "speakeasies," sell alcohol to underage students, and they offer some alcoholic beverages, like Cisco, which are not available elsewhere in the State.

Friends, parties, and stores are the main sources for alcohol. Students who drink usually obtain alcohol from their friends. Their grade in school influences where and how they get alcohol. While 88 percent of 12th graders get alcohol through friends, only 49 percent of 7th graders do. The younger students obtain alcohol from their parents with or without their parents' knowledge. Almost three-fourths of the 7th graders obtain alcohol from their parents, while only a quarter of the 12th graders do.

Almost 65 percent of all students—students who drink and nondrinkers alike—have been to parties where alcohol is served. The number of students attending parties increases with each grade level. More than 79 percent of high school students (9th through 12th grade) have been to parties with alcohol. When asked where they obtain alcohol, 88 percent of the students who drink mentioned parties.

Students Accept Rides From Friends Who Have Been Drinking

In 1989, almost 2,800 students between 15 to 19 years old died in alcohol-related traffic accidents. Forty-five percent of the traffic accidents among this age group are alcohol related, yet students say it is not okay to drink and drive.

Even though 92 percent of all students in our survey said a person should never drink and drive, almost a third have accepted a ride from a driver who had been drinking. This translates to 6.8 million students who are placing their lives in danger. Almost half of the students who drink have been a passenger in a car that a friend drove after drinking.

Parents, Friends, and Alcoholic Beverage Advertisements Influence Students' Attitudes About Alcohol

Parents influence students' attitudes about alcohol. Almost two-thirds of all students say their parents do not approve of underage drinking or would punish them if they drank. Some extreme examples of punishment that students gave are, "I would have a grave," "I would be grounded until I was 42," and "They would beat my behind!"

Many parents are more lenient. Thirty-five percent of the students who drink say their parents tolerate their drinking under certain conditions. These conditions typically limit the amount, frequency, or location of the student's drinking. Examples include, "They tell me not to go overboard and not to get drunk" and "I can have it with my parents." Almost 15 percent of the students who drink reported that their parents trust them or do not say or do anything about their drinking.

Friends influence students by providing both alcohol and occasions to drink. Nationwide, 10.1 million students drink with their friends. The main reasons students gave for drinking involve their friends:

- Almost 8.7 million students drink to have fun.
- Less than 5.5 million students, or half of those who drink, do so because their friends drink.
- More than 6 million drink to be social.

At one of the surveyed schools, the March cover story from the student newspaper discussed student views on drinking beer. The article

211

listed reasons why beer is so popular, including "it makes even the most shy people witty and clever at parties." Some students expressed concerns that the most popular weekend activity is drinking. One student was disappointed that "several of my friends can't be social unless they are drunk (or so they say)."

Advertisements for alcoholic beverages influence students' perceptions about alcohol. Thirty-nine percent of all students named something they like about advertisements for alcoholic beverages. Their likes vary widely. The most common responses were that the advertisements spotlight attractive people and make drinking look like fun. We asked students if anything appealed to them about the advertisements. Student responses included:

- "They are very convincing. They make it look very glamorous."
- "The way they make life look like fun."
- "They look exciting and fun. The message is: It is all right to drink, not that it is bad."
- "Some of them are funny, and some have sexy women."
- "They make you look like you're cool and accepted."
- "Girls in the ads are skinny, and I want to be like that."
- "The slogan 'The Right Beer Now' makes you think 'Is now a good time to drink?'"

Virtually all students have seen advertisements for alcoholic beverages. To find out if students were able to associate a spokesperson, star, or symbol with a particular brand of beer, we asked the students if Spuds MacKenzie is the mascot for Coors Light beer. More than half knew that "Spuds" was not Coors' mascot. Because the majority knew enough to correctly link the symbol and the product, advertisements may be a stronger influence on students than they realize.

Part Three

Other Licit and Illicit Substances of Abuse

Chapter 26

Nicotine/Tobacco

Cigarette smoking is perhaps the most devastating preventable cause of disease and premature death. Nearly 50 million Americans smoke, with as many as one in five teenagers a regular smoker, resulting in nearly 420,000 deaths each year. Smoking is particularly dangerous for teens because their bodies are still developing and changing and the 4,000 chemicals (including 200 known poisons) in cigarette smoke can adversely affect this process. Cigarettes are also highly addictive, both mentally and physically, and can serve as a major gateway to other forms of drug addiction. Adolescent cigarette smokers are 100 times more likely to smoke marijuana and are more likely to use other illicit drugs such as cocaine and heroine in the future.

What Are the Risks Associated with Smoking Cigarettes?

- diminished or extinguished sense of smell and taste
- frequent colds
- smoker's cough
- gastric ulcers
- chronic bronchitis

This chapter contains text from the National Institute on Drug Abuse *Capsules*, C-83-8, revised September 1993; "Prescriptions to Help Smokers Quit," by Ricki Lewis, Ph.D., *FDA Consumer*, December 1992; and excerpts from "Tips for Teens About Smoking," Center for Substance Abuse Prevention, nd.

- increase in heart rate and blood pressure
- premature and more abundant face wrinkles
- emphysema
- heart disease
- stroke
- cancer of the mouth, larynx, pharynx, esophagus, lungs, pancreas, cervix, uterus, and bladder

Although many people smoke because they believe cigarettes calm their nerves, smoking releases epinephrine, a hormone which creates physiological stress in the smoker, rather than relaxation. The addictive quality of the drug makes the user feel he must smoke more to calm down, when in effect the smoking itself is causing the agitation. The use of tobacco is addictive. Most users develop tolerance for nicotine and need greater amounts to produce a desired effect. Smokers become physically and psychologically dependent and will suffer withdrawal symptoms when use is stopped. Physical withdrawal symptoms include: changes in body temperature, heart rate, digestion, muscle tone, and appetite. Psychological symptoms include: irritability, anxiety, sleep disturbances nervousness, headaches, fatigue, nausea, and cravings for tobacco that can last days, weeks, months, years, or an entire lifetime.

Cigarette Smoking

Cigarette smoking has been the most popular method of taking nicotine since the beginning of the 20th century. In 1989, the U.S. Surgeon General issued a report which concluded that cigarettes and other forms of tobacco are addicting, and that nicotine is the drug in tobacco that causes addiction. In addition, the report determined that smoking was a major cause of stroke and the third leading cause of death in the U.S. Despite this warning, the National Household Survey on Drug Abuse shows that more than 50 million Americans continue to smoke cigarettes, making nicotine one of the most addictive drugs in the U.S.

Nicotine is both a transient stimulant and a sedative to the central nervous system. Nicotine is physically and psychologically addictive. The ingestion of nicotine results in an almost immediate "kick" because it causes a discharge of epinephrine from the adrenal cortex. This stimulates the central nervous system, as well as other endocrine glands, which causes a sudden release of glucose. Stimulation

216

is then followed by depression and fatigue, leading the abuser to seek more nicotine.

Extent of Use

National Monitoring the Future Survey

- Prevalence rates for smoking among young people remain high, despite the demonstrated health risk associated with smoking. Since 1975, cigarettes have consistentlyy been the substance most frequently used on a daily basis by high school students.

- Since peaking in the late 1970s, current cigarette smoking among high school seniors has remained around 28-30% through 1992 despite the depreciable downturn which has occurred in the use of most other drugs during this period.

- In 1992, 7.0% of eighth graders, 12.3% of 10th graders, and 17.2% of 12th graders smoked cigarettes daily during the past month Approximately 3% of eighth graders, 6% of 10th graders, and 10% of 12th graders say they smoke half of a pack of cigarettes or more, per day.

- Among college students, 37.3% smoked cigarettes within the past year, 23.5% smoked within the past month, and 14.1% smoked daily. Of those one-to-four years beyond high school but not in college 45.2% smoked cigarettes within the past year, 35.0% smoked within the past month, and 27.5% smoked daily. In addition, 8.9% of college students and 20.5% of non-college students reported smoking 1/2 pack or more per day.

National Household Survey on Drug Abuse

- People aged 26-34 have the highest rates of smoking. For this age group, 38.8% smoked cigarettes within the past year and 33.7% smoked within the past month.

- More than 146 million (71.0%) people 12 years and older have tried smoking cigarettes; 64 million (31.2%) have smoked cigarettes within the past year, and almost 54 million (26.2%) have smoked cigarettes within the past month.

- Almost 28 million (27.9%) males and 26 million (24.6%) females have smoked cigarettes within the past month.

Smoking's Not Smart

The more educated Americans are, the less likely they are to smoke. In 1974, 27.5 percent of college-educated Americans smoked, but in 1990 that figure had declined by nearly half to 14.1 percent. During the same period, among people who hadn't finished high school, smokers dropped only from 43.8 percent to 36.7 percent. This information comes from interviews with 120,000 persons in 55,000 households (Source: PHS annual report, *Health, United States*, 1991; quoted in *FDA Consumer*, December 1992).

Health Hazards

Nicotine has been reported to reduce anxiety and smokers report that they get calming effects from it. Nicotine is absorbed readily from tobacco smoke in the lungs. With regular use, levels of nicotine accumulate in the body during the day and persist overnight. Thus, daily cigarette smokers are exposed to the effects of nicotine for 24 hours each day.

Nicotine taken in by cigarette smoking takes only seconds to reach the brain, but has a direct effect on the body for up to 30 minutes. Cigarette smoke is primarily comprised of a dozen gases (mainly carbon monoxide), nicotine, and tar. The tar in a cigarette, which varies from about 15 mg for a regular cigarette to 7 mg found in a low tar cigarette, exposes the user to a high expectancy rate of lung cancer, emphysema and bronchial disorders. The carbon monoxide in the smoke increases the chance of cardiovascular diseases.

The effects of nicotine escalate bronchial and cardiovascular disorders—chronic bronchitis and emphysema are common diseases among cigarette smokers. The risk of congestive heart failure is also increased by the effects of nicotine.

Nicotine produces effects on mood as well as on the heart, lungs, stomach, neurotransmitters, and sympathetic and parasympathetic nervous systems. Short-term effects of nicotine in cigarette smoke include sweating, vomiting, and throat irritation. Over time, more serious conditions develop including increased heart rate and blood pressure.

The most serious effects of smoking are lung cancer, in which only 12% of people so diagnosed will live for five years, and stroke. Cancer of the esophagus, mouth, lips, and larynx are also associated with cigarette smoking.

Pregnant women who smoke cigarettes run an increased risk of having a stillborn or a premature infant, or an infant with low birthweight. Women who smoke generally have earlier menopause. If women smoke cigarettes and also take oral contraceptives they are more prone to cardiovascular and cerebrovascular diseases than for other smokers—this is especially true for women over 30 years old.

The Environmental Protection Agency recently concluded that second-hand smoke causes lung cancer in adults and greatly increases the risk of respiratory illnesses in children.

Treatment

Research suggests that smoking cessation should be a gradual process, because withdrawal symptoms are less severe in those who quit gradually rather than all at once. Rates of relapse are highest in the first few weeks and months and diminish considerably after three months. The optimal treatment for smoking cessation includes behavioral therapy. Studies have shown that pharmacological treatment combined with psychological treatment, including psychological support and skill training to overcome high-risk situations, result in some of the highest long-term abstinence rates.

Nicotine chewing gum is one medication treatment approved by the Food and Drug Administration (FDA) for the treatment of nicotine dependence. Nicotine in this form acts as a nicotine replacement to help smokers quit the smoking habit. The success rates for smoking cessation treatment with nicotine chewing gum vary considerably across studies but evidence suggests that it is a safe means of facilitating smoking cessation if chewed according to instruction and restricted to patients who are under medical supervision.

Prescriptions to Help Smokers Quit (FDA)

In the 1950s, smoking was depicted as a sophisticated, enjoyable activity, and advertisements brimmed with smiling, happy people puffing away. Although ads still depict smoking as sophisticated and enjoyable, in the 1990s the health dangers of smoking are widely known—and about 76 percent of the nation's approximately 46 million smokers say that they would like to quit, according to a 1991 Gallup poll.

Smoking cessation is a major goal of the U.S. Public Health Service's Healthy People 2000 Program. Cigarette smoking causes lung cancer, heart attacks, and other serious health problems in smokers. It can cause health problems in nonsmokers exposed to "secondhand" smoke as well.

Airlines, restaurants, hospitals, and workplaces are banning smoking or restricting it to designated areas, and pressure to quit is intense.

As former Surgeon General C. Everett Koop, M.D., said, "If you have a spouse who's nagging you at home to quit, children who suggest that you're going to die if you don't, and then your boss says you can't smoke at the worksite, that's a pretty good indication that it's time to try to quit."

But quitting is a lot easier said than done. Each year, about 17 million Americans try to stop smoking, according to the American Cancer Society. Only 1.3 million succeed.

While many people have successfully stopped smoking on their own, many other smokers need help if they're going to succeed in quitting. For a number of years, stop-smoking programs have been available through various organizations such as the American Cancer Society and the American Lung Association.

In recent years, the Food and Drug Administration has approved two types of products to help smokers quit: nicotine chewing gum and the transdermal nicotine patch. Nicorette chewing gum, containing 2 milligrams (mg) of nicotine, was approved by FDA in 1984. Last June, a 4-mg dosage form of the Marian Merrell Dow product was approved.

The newest stop-smoking tool is the transdermal nicotine patch. It looks like a Band-Aid, is changed daily, and delivers nicotine to the bloodstream. Four brands of nicotine patch—Nicoderm, Habitrol, Prostep, and Nicotrol—were approved for marketing by FDA in late 1991 and early 1992. Both the chewing gum and the patch are to be used as aids to a comprehensive smoking-cessation program.

Tobacco is regulated by the Bureau of Alcohol, Tobacco and Firearms. Within the U.S. Department of Health and Human Services, the Office on Smoking and Health has the responsibility for educating the public about the health hazards of smoking. FDA, also an HHS agency, regulates nicotine gum and patches as prescription drugs; a doctor's expertise is needed to identify which patients might benefit from these products, and to prescribe the most effective course of treatment for an individual patient.

Targeting Nicotine

Cigarette smoke contains more than 4,000 chemicals and affects many of the body's chemical messengers, such as neurotransmitters and hormones. These chemical messengers mediate a wide range of bodily responses, such as metabolism and heart and respiratory function. In 1988, the Surgeon General's report on "The Health Consequences of Smoking" identified nicotine as the addictive component of tobacco smoke. Its absence triggers the symptoms of withdrawal—irritability, anger, anxiety, restlessness, inability to concentrate, hunger, and nicotine craving.

The idea behind nicotine replacement therapy, which includes the patch and nicotine gum, is that providing nicotine in a form other than a cigarette can minimize the symptoms of withdrawal while a person is weaned from smoking. During this time, with the help of a counselor or doctor in a smoking-cessation program, the patient learns to live without the habits associated with cigarette smoking, such as having something in the hand or mouth, drawing smoke in and puffing it out, or reaching for a cigarette in response to a behavioral cue, such as a cup of coffee or stress.

"The phone rings, you say, 'Just a second,' and grab a cigarette. You smoke after a meal. The gum and patch are different in that they separate the behavioral cues from the nicotine delivery," says Elbert D. Glover, Ph.D., director of the Tobacco Research Center at the West Virginia University School of Medicine in Morgantown.

A Special Way to Chew

To be most effective, Nicorette must be chewed in a special way. When doctors prescribe nicotine chewing gum, they tell smokers to stop smoking completely and discuss what the maximum number of pieces of gum a day should be.

When the smoker craves a cigarette, he or she places one piece of nicotine gum in the mouth and begins to chew—very slowly. This slowness is important for the proper release of the nicotine and to avoid side effects similar to those experienced when inhaling tobacco for the first time or smoking too fast. These side effects include lightheadedness, nausea, vomiting, throat and mouth soreness, hiccups, and upset stomach.

After about 15 chews, the smoker notes a peppery taste or a tingling in the mouth. This is the signal to "park" the gum by placing it between the cheek and the gums. When the peppery taste or tingling is almost gone, the user starts chewing again. When the taste or tingling returns, the person "parks" the gum in a different place in the mouth. This process continues for about 30 minutes, at which point the nicotine is gone from the gum.

After about two or three months, the smoker should be ready to be weaned from the gum by gradually reducing use. Some ways this can be done are by reducing the number of pieces each day, by chewing some pieces for shorter amounts of time, or by using sugarless gum in place of Nicorette.

Automatic Dosages

A drawback of gum is that, as with smoking itself, the user controls the dose and schedule of nicotine delivery. In contrast, with the 24-hour skin patch, nicotine enters the body automatically, either over a 24-hour period or only while the person is awake, depending on the type of patch used.

All four patch brands come in different dosages so that the amount of nicotine supplied to the patient can be gradually lowered. For example, treatment with Nicoderm (marketed by Marion Merrell Dow) or Habitrol (manufactured by Kabi Pharmacia) begins with a 21-mg per day dose, about equal to the nicotine in a pack of cigarettes. Each patch is worn for 24 hours. After four to eight weeks, the patient switches to a 14-mg patch, and then, two to four weeks later, to the final 7-mg patch. ProStep (marketed by Lederle Labs) is also worn around the clock. It comes in two dosage levels, 22 mg and 11 mg. Nicotrol (manufactured by Parke-Davis), the most recently approved patch, is worn only while awake. It comes in dosages of 15 mg, 10 mg, and 5 mg.

Which patch and dosage is best for any particular individual is a medical decision made by a doctor, taking into account the patient's smoking level and lifestyle and other needs. For example, a person who smokes less than a pack a day probably would not be told to use a patch supplying a higher level of nicotine, such as that delivered by patches supplying one-pack equivalent dosage.

All patches deliver nicotine through the skin and prevent withdrawal symptoms from stopping smoking, but the specific design of each patch and a patient's skin type determines how fast the nicotine enters the body. Glover explains that some patches deliver nicotine rapidly into the skin, from which it enters the bloodstream, whereas other patches control the release from the device itself.

Says Michael Eriksen, director of the national Centers for Disease Control's Office on Smoking and Health in Atlanta, "A nicotine patch is not a magic bullet. It doesn't make you quit—it just replaces the nicotine after a smoker quits. You have to be motivated on your own and then the patch is helpful."

Quit Rates

A typical short-term "quit rate" for 2-mg nicotine gum in well-planned studies in smoking-cessation clinics is 30 to 50 percent of participants. Research is ongoing to determine if rates improve with the 4-mg dosage gum.

To see how the gum was being used—and to determine its success outside the research setting—a team led by Richard E. Johnson, Ph.D., at the Center for Health Research in Portland, Ore., evaluated 2-mg gum use by 612 smokers over an 18-month period at a health maintenance organization. The results, published in the January 1992 *Journal of Family Practice*, showed that many patients chewed sporadically, claiming, "I use the gum in situations where smoking is prohibited" or "when I have cravings." Only 1 in 20 gum chewers also had behavioral therapy to stop smoking. This emphasizes the importance of doctors taking time to fully explain the correct use of the nicotine substitution products and of patients asking their physicians questions, if in doubt about correct use.

Quit rates with the transdermal nicotine patch began making headlines when a report in the Dec. 11, 1991, *Journal of the American Medical Association* discussed findings in nine smoking-cessation clinics across the United States. Three doses of nicotine (21 mg, 14 mg, and a placebo delivering less than 1 mg) in 24-hour patches were compared in a double-blind fashion (neither the patients nor the researchers knew which dosage patients received). Altogether, 756 smokers wore the patches for six weeks, and those who were successful were weaned through decreasing doses during a second six weeks.

The higher the dose of nicotine, the higher the percentage of patients who quit smoking completely in three to six weeks. Sixty-one percent given 21-mg patches, 48 percent of those given 14-mg patches, and 27 percent of those on placebo quit. Counseling consisted of weekly 45- to 60-minute group sessions, including a two-minute review of individual progress and discussions of behavior modification techniques. Patients kept a daily diary to record cigarette use, and weekly clinic visits assessed their progress.

The nine-center transdermal nicotine patch study group concluded, "All transdermal nicotine doses significantly decreased the severity of nicotine withdrawal symptoms and significantly reduced cigarette use by patients who did not stop smoking. Compliance was excellent, and no serious systemic adverse effects were reported."

Success rates vary from clinic to clinic and study to study because the programs and patients differ. "The patch helps those people who are the most nicotine dependent—those who have tried to quit in the past, but found withdrawal to be so severe that they had to go back," says CDC's Eriksen. By the same token, it may be less effective for low nicotine-dependent smokers.

A nicotine-dependence scale developed by Karl-Olov Fagerstrom, Ph.D., a clinical psychologist at the Smoking Withdrawal Clinic at Ulleraker Hospital in Uppsala, Sweden, can help determine whether a particular smoker has a high or low nicotine dependency, and is used in many smoking studies. "The Fagerstrom scale is a simple set of questions. The hallmark question is, do you have a cigarette in the morning within the first 30 minutes of rising? If yes, you're pretty dependent," says Eriksen. Another telling sign is if a person smokes when sick in bed. Other common characteristics of the nicotine-dependent smoker include inhaling, smoking many cigarettes a day, and preferring a high-nicotine brand.

Possible Problems

In addition to effects resembling first smoking experiences when the gum is chewed too fast, as previously discussed, side effects of nicotine chewing gum can include mouth sores, headaches, heart palpitations, and excess saliva. These are most likely to occur during the first few days of use. Less common but more serious side effects have been reported, and these risks should be discussed with a doctor before taking Nicorette.

With the nicotine patch, the most common side effect is skin irritation. In about 14 percent of users, the area where the patch is applied (a hairless, clean dry spot on the upper part of the body) becomes irritated (red and itchy) in the first few hours after application. But allergic reaction to the patch is rare—many of these people who initially experience itching simply try again in a different spot and are fine. In some clinical trials, 35 percent of patients had short-term itching or burning and 6 percent dropped out due to skin reactions. To help prevent skin irritation, directions advise against using the same spot twice within a week.

The physician labeling for the nicotine patch includes the precaution that patients should be urged to stop smoking completely when using the patch, and be told that if they continue to smoke they may experience adverse effects due to peak nicotine levels being higher than those from smoking alone. The labeling says that if there is a significant increase in cardiovascular or other side effects, treatment with the patch should be reduced or discontinued.

Signs of nicotine overdose include headache, dizziness, abdominal pain, drooling, nausea, vomiting, diarrhea, cold sweat, blurred vision, difficulty hearing, mental confusion, weakness, and fainting. Symptoms of severe overdose include tremor, respiratory failure, low blood pressure, and prostration.

Since the marketing of the first two nicotine patches in December 1991, FDA has received reports of patients suffering heart attacks while using nicotine patches, including five from Sturdy Memorial Hospital in Attleboro, Mass. Most had continued to smoke while using the patch, and most had preexisting heart disease. The possibility of excess nicotine aggravating heart disease has been pointed out by many researchers, and patch labels advise users to inform the doctor if there is a history of heart attack, irregular heartbeat, heart pain (angina pectoris), or high blood pressure. An FDA advisory committee considered the information available on the possible relationship between nicotine patch use and heart attacks last July 14 and found the data did not show an increased risk of heart attack with patch use. The committee, therefore, did not recommend any change in labeling.

Nicotine gums and patches should be kept out of the reach of children and pets. If eaten, the patch can cause severe nausea and vomiting, and can be fatal. Swallowing a piece of the gum usually causes no symptoms in persons for whom it has been prescribed, but if a child chews or swallows one or more pieces, a doctor or poison control center should be contacted.

Cigarette smoking during pregnancy can cause miscarriage or low birth weight, and animal studies show that nicotine alone can harm a fetus. Therefore, although quitting smoking by behavioral methods is encouraged, neither nicotine chewing gum nor transdermal nicotine patches are advised for use during pregnancy.

However, scientists are considering whether continuing to smoke during pregnancy poses more risks than using nicotine therapy products. In addition to nicotine, cigarette smoking exposes the fetus to other risks, including doses of thousands of other chemicals such as carbon monoxide, which robs the fetus of oxygen.

At least 5 million smokers have tried the patch, and about 2 million smokers a year have tried the gum. Health-care providers, organizations, family members, and smokers themselves are all hoping that these medications will help more people kick nicotine for good and lead longer, healthier lives.

—by Ricki Lewis, Ph.D.

Ricki Lewis is a geneticist and the author of a college biology text. Judith Levine Willis, editor of *FDA Consumer*, also contributed to this article.

Resources

American Council for Drug Education
204 Monroe Street, Suite 110
Rockville, MD 20850
(301) 294-0600
(800) 488-DRUG

National Cancer Institute
Cancer Information Service
Johns Hopkins Oncology Center
550 N. Broadway Suite 307
Baltimore, MD 21205
(800) 4-CANCER

National Clearinghouse for Alcohol and Drug Information
P.O. Box 2345
Rockville, MD 20847-2345
(301) 468-2600
(800) 729-6686

National Families in Action
2296 Henderson Mill Road
Suite 204
Atlanta, GA 30345
(404) 934-6364

Office on Smoking and Health Centers for Disease Control
Mail Stop K-50
4770 Buford Highway, NE
Atlanta, GA 30341-3724
(404) 488-5708

Listed in your local White Pages:

American Cancer Society
American Lung Association
American Heart Association

More Information Available

For more information on the hazards of tobacco abuse, environmental tobacco smoke, and smoking cessation programs see *Respiratory Diseases and Disorders Sourcebook* (1995)—Volume 6 in Omnigraphics' *Health Reference Series*.

Chapter 27

Spit Tobacco

Teen Consumption Rises

Large-scale consumption of tobacco has been a factor in American culture for centuries, predating Columbus and the early settlers. Prior to the beginning of the 20th century, however, when Americans consumed tobacco, it was primarily in the form of smokeless tobacco (chewing tobacco and snuff) or what is now called spit tobacco (ST). In fact, spit tobacco accounted for nearly 60 percent of the 7.5 pounds of tobacco consumed per adult in the United States in 1900.

Following the introduction and mass-marketing of the first blended cigarette in this country in 1913, consumption of all other forms of tobacco began to decline. Ironically, one of the factors that hastened the decline of spit tobacco and encouraged cigarette consumption was a concern for health. Many people believed that public spitting was responsible for the spread of tuberculosis, a major uncontrolled cause of death at that time. In response, many towns and cities enacted local ordinances that prohibited spitting on public streets and sidewalks.

Today, heightened awareness of the hazards of smoking has led to a renewed consumer interest in spit tobacco, called smokeless tobacco by the industry. Some people think of these products as a safe alternative because of the implicit notion that the major health risk component—the smoke—has been eliminated.

"Focus on Spit Tobacco," *The Challenge: Safe, Disciplined, and Drug-Free Schools*, U.S. Department of Education, Vol. 5, No. 3, 1992.

How Is Spit Tobacco Used?

Spit tobacco includes two main types: snuff and chewing tobacco. Snuff "dippers" place a small amount of shredded or finely ground tobacco (loose or encased in a paper pouch) between their cheeks and gums. Tobacco "chewers" place wads of loose leaf tobacco or plugs of compressed tobacco in their cheek. Both dippers and chewers suck on the tobacco and spit out the tobacco juices and saliva generated.

Nicotine enters the user's bloodstream by being absorbed through the lining of the mouth. In normal use, a snuff dipper places a pinch in the mouth and holds it there for 20 to 30 minutes. The amount of nicotine absorbed is two to three times the amount delivered by a regular-size cigarette. Chewing tobacco has less available nicotine per gram of tobacco compared with moist snuff, but chewers use more tobacco per dose. Thus, users who consume 8 to 10 dips or chews a day receive a nicotine dose equal to that taken by a heavy smoker who consumes 30 to 40 cigarettes daily. Nicotine is absorbed more slowly from spit tobacco than from cigarette smoke; however, more nicotine per dose is absorbed from spit tobacco and it stays in the bloodstream longer.

Who Uses These Products?

Increases in ST consumption that occurred during the 1980s were primarily confined to younger age groups. Prevalence of both chewing and snuff tobacco use among older teens increased between 250 and 300 percent between 1970 and 1985. Almost one in five adolescent male students surveyed recently by the Centers for Disease Control in Atlanta reported using ST on one or more days within the past month.

A 1989 study by the National Collegiate Athletic Association (NCAA) of drug use by college athletes found that use of spit tobacco by college athletes had increased 40 percent compared with a similar study conducted in 1985. More importantly, the NCAA found that the majority of college users began dipping or chewing before they went to college—21 percent in junior high school and 54 percent in senior high school.

Research indicates that the majority of youths who use spit tobacco begin use before the age of 12 with rural males starting more than a year earlier.

Young male spit tobacco users in 1992 consumed an average of three and a half cans of snuff or almost one pouch of chewing tobacco a week. The average use of more than six times per day produces a nicotine intake equivalent to one and a half to two packs of cigarettes.

Short-Term Health Effects

Leukoplakia (white, wrinkled skin patches inside the mouth) and gum recession at the usual site of tobacco placement are the most frequent consequences of short-term spit tobacco use. These conditions occur in 40 to 60 percent of spit tobacco users. Leukoplakia are a serious concern because, over time, they can become malignant.

Long-Term Consequences

In 1981, researchers at the National Cancer Institute published the results of an important study that pointed to a strong statistical link between oral snuff dipping and oral cancer. The following year, Dr. C. Everett Koop, in releasing his first report as surgeon general, reviewed a limited range of data and concluded: "Long term use of snuff appears to be a factor in the development of cancers of the oral cavity, particularly cancers of the cheek and gum." As additional evidence began to accumulate, many health organizations expressed concern that the rapidly observed increase in ST use, particularly in adolescents and young adults, may indicate a future epidemic in oral cancers.

In 1986, the surgeon general issued a report entitled "The Health Consequences of Using Smokeless Tobacco," which virtually eliminated any lingering doubts about the hazards of smokeless tobacco. The report concluded:

> *"Oral use of smokeless tobacco represents a significant health risk. It is not a safe substitute for smoking cigarettes. It can cause cancer and a number of noncancerous oral conditions and can lead to nicotine addiction and dependence."*

The report also noted that evidence related to the carcinogenic potential of chewing tobacco was limited, but the evidence on oral use of snuff was more than sufficient to conclude that it caused cancer.

Currently, at least 75 percent of oral or pharyngeal cancers are attributed to all forms of tobacco use including spit tobacco use. Only one-half of those with oral cancer are alive five years after diagnosis. In addition, most oral cancers are not diagnosed until they have reached an advanced stage, so those whò survive the oral cancer have an exceptionally high risk of developing subsequent cancers.

As a result of the surgeon general's warning, Congress banned advertising of spit tobacco on all broadcast media and required a series of health warnings on spit tobacco products and in print advertising. Consumption of moist snuff, the most dangerous form of spit tobacco, declined in both 1986 and 1987; however, the decline was short lived. Consumption of snuff began to increase again in 1988 and is at record high levels today.

Other adverse health effects associated with long-term spit tobacco use are dental decay, tooth abrasion, and tooth loss.

Strategies to Reduce ST Use

Factors that encourage, establish, and maintain cigarette smoking are essentially identical for spit tobacco; therefore, the same strategies now being recommended to reduce cigarette smoking nationally can also help to prevent or reduce spit tobacco use. These strategies employ a dual approach that targets both the individual and the user's larger social environment.

Like cigarette smoking, spit tobacco use begins primarily in adolescence. Unlike cigarette smoking, however, spit tobacco use is almost exclusively a male phenomenon. Young people who use spit tobacco give as the most influential reason for first trying the product perceived support from their fathers, other male relatives, and their peers. Thirty-seven percent of youths who used spit tobacco said their fathers also used it, and 33 percent had a brother or other male relative who used it. The majority of young people surveyed in 1992 said their parents know about their use of spit tobacco, and 87 percent said they used it regularly at home.

Although a significant number of adolescents may experiment with spit tobacco use—including some adolescent females—most never become regular users and some who do use regularly quit before they become truly dependent. Spit tobacco dependency is not a sudden phenomenon but one that begins gradually with experimentation in early adolescence or even preadolescence. Factors that help move young people from thinking about using to experimenting include the widespread availability of spit tobacco products and the ease with which children can purchase them, promotional distribution of free samples—many of which are given to teens despite local laws—and advertising.

How Schools Can Help

Although most schools have implemented policies prohibiting cigarette smoking on school grounds and at school-related functions, some policies do not specifically include the use of spit tobacco. In order to curb the use of these products effectively, schools need to adopt and enforce strong policies prohibiting the use of spit tobacco by students and staff on school grounds and at school-sponsored activities such as athletic competitions.

School health programs in many regions of the country where spit tobacco use is high (for example in the Southeast and rural areas of the country) are adopting curricula targeted to preventing the use of these substances either as stand-alone units or as part of their general health education programs.

How the Community Can Help

Increasingly, it is evident that schools cannot solve complex social problems by themselves. Measures to reduce spit tobacco use among children must be comprehensive in scope and focused on implementing policies aimed at preventing initiation of spit tobacco use and use of tobacco in general. Among the strategies that can help to curb initiation of tobacco use in all its forms are: stronger enforcement of laws that prohibit persons under the age of 18 from purchasing tobacco; restrictions of advertising that appeals to children and adolescents; bans on vending machine sales; elimination of free samples; and a substantial increase in the federal and state excise taxes on spit tobacco.

Unless we can do substantially more now to discourage teenage use of the dangerous, deadly, and addictive substance, we face the future prospect of paying substantially more in increased health care costs, premature deaths, and needless human suffering in the future.

Additional information for this article is drawn from *Spit Tobacco and Youth*, U.S. Department of Health and Human Services, Office of Inspector General, December 1992.

—*by Donald R. Shopland*

233

Chapter 28

Marijuana

Marijuana remains the most commonly used illicit drug in the U.S. According to the 1992 National Household Survey on Drug Abuse, more than 67.5 million (32.8%) Americans had tried marijuana at least once in their lifetimes, and almost 17.5 million (8.5%) had used marijuana within the past year. In 1985, 51.5 (33.5%) million Americans had tried marijuana at least once in their lifetimes, and 23.7 million (15.4%) had used marijuana within the past year.

Marijuana is a mood-altering drug. It is made from the leaves, small stems, and flowering tops of the hemp plant, *Cannabis sativa.* Although cannabis contains over 400 chemicals, one substance, known as THC, is chiefly responsible for the "high" or intoxication that the drug produces.

What Does Marijuana Do to Work Performance?

While high, the marijuana user often finds it hard to think or talk clearly, to remember, to form sentences and to solve problems. Speech may be choppy and thoughts jump from one subject to another, making conversation difficult to understand. Intoxicated users also have trouble paying attention to their work and making good judgments.

This chapter includes text from "Marijuana Update," National Institute on Drug Abuse, *Capsules*, C-88-06, Revised September 1993; and, "Marijuana—It's Your Business: Drug Awareness," provided by the Drug Enforcement Administration and produced by the American Council for Drug Education, nd.

Studies have shown that marijuana users have problems accurately measuring distance, speed and time. Since the drug slows reflexes and reduces coordination, users find it hard to react quickly when faced with an unexpected situation while driving or operating machinery and equipment.

Recovering marijuana users often talk about their own near misses at work. They describe being nervous when they have to work closely with coworkers who smoke marijuana. One aircraft technician talked about a coworker who was so high he ignored the safety alarms. When crew members pulled him away from the blades of an ascending helicopter, his eyeglasses were sucked up in the chopper's blades. The marijuana user survived, but his behavior caused thousands of dollars worth of damage to the helicopter.

What Effect Does Marijuana Have On Learning?

The intoxication that marijuana produces interferes with learning. Short-term memory and the ability to concentrate—two functions that are needed in order to succeed in school—are especially affected.

Students who are high on marijuana have difficulty recalling both written and orally presented material. They also have trouble communicating their thoughts in a clear way. Not only do their grades fall, but they miss opportunities for learning that may not occur again.

In addition to these problems, students who smoke marijuana regularly display a number of other negative effects in the areas of social and emotional development. These include:

- A loss of motivation and interest in activities they previously enjoyed. This is often called "amotivational syndrome."
- Withdrawal from non-drug using friends.
- Failure to acquire age-appropriate social skills or, as one expert put it, "They simply do not grow up emotionally."
- Increased mood swings and irritability.
- Decreased attention span and increased distracted behavior.

What Effect Does Marijuana Have On Physical Health?

Regular use of marijuana may produce negative effects on the respiratory tract and the reproductive system.

Among heavy users, sore throats, coughs, and bronchitis are common and immediate effects. Since users also inhale deeply and hold the smoke in their lungs for several seconds, experts believe that in the long-term, their lungs may be seriously damaged.

Marijuana users also frequently smoke tobacco cigarettes, drink alcohol and take other mood-altering drugs. This kind of multiple drug use increases the risk of serious health problems.

Women who use marijuana during pregnancy, for example, often fit the multiple drug use profile. As a result, they increase their risk of having a premature or low-birthweight baby. Low birthweight is a leading contributor to infant mortality in the United States.

What Are the Signs of Regular Use?

Occasional use is difficult to detect although marijuana has a distinctive smell which may cling to clothing and hair. Regular users often have chronic hacking coughs or reddened eyes. They may complain of a dry mouth and throat. Many users report problems swallowing and say that their tongues, mouths and throats feel numb.

The following signs and symptoms may indicate a possible behavioral problem or a problem with alcohol or drugs other than marijuana. However, if a friend or loved one exhibits any combination of the characteristics listed, marijuana use may be the explanation:

- Low tolerance for frustration and defiant, rebellious behavior;
- Poor impulse control and unpredictable, wide-ranging mood swings, including sudden outbursts of anger, crying or laughter, and depression;
- Confused thinking—some users cannot remember what they did yesterday;
- Inappropriate responses to authority figures, (for example, supervisors, teachers, coaches, parents);
- Taking advantage of others and constant lying;
- Poor performance on the job or in school;
- Lateness and absenteeism at work;
- Loss of interest in family, non-drug using friends, and healthy, social activities; and
- Brushes with the law for driving violations, vandalism, fighting and shoplifting.

The key is a change in old behavior patterns. Performance slips, friends change, personal hygiene suffers, or the personality seems different.

What Is Marijuana Dependence?

Marijuana dependence occurs when the user relies on the drug to cope with daily life and cannot function confidently without it. In the beginning, marijuana use provides instant pleasure and makes the user feel good. The desire to repeat this pleasant feeling prompts continued use. Soon, the user smokes marijuana as a response to boredom, anxiety, and uncertainty, or as a part of socializing ("partying") with other pot smokers.

Marijuana use can become so compelling that friends, family, and other positive activities begin to lose their importance. Dependent users often say and may believe that they can stop smoking at any time. However, this does not usually happen, especially when users' social lives revolve around partying. They may feel upset, depressed and anxious, and may have problems sleeping when they try to stop smoking the drug. These negative feelings encourage them to return to marijuana use.

With few exceptions, anyone who uses marijuana regularly can become dependent on it. People coping with learning disabilities, attention deficit and hyperactivity disorders and other pre-existing psychological problems such as depression may be at special risk.

What Can a Heavy User Do to Stop?

Like alcoholics, regular marijuana smokers often do not understand the role that the drug plays in their problems. Users must first recognize their dependency on the drug. Sometimes, they need outside help to come to this understanding. Then, they must make a commitment to stop. This means making changes so that life no longer revolves around marijuana. They must form new friendships and participate in drug-free activities. Since this is a difficult task, family members and friends must help in this effort.

Some users may need additional support to become drug-free. Employee assistance programs, local health and mental health departments, and members of the clergy are often able to identify resources for specialized help.

One last caution—marijuana use is almost never a solo act, nor is it a substitute for alcohol. For the most part, regular marijuana users also drink alcohol, smoke tobacco cigarettes and take other mood-altering drugs. Multiple drug use increases the risk of present and future health problems. It also has an immediate impact on behavior because using drugs together results in more serious problems than using one drug alone.

The 1992 Monitoring the Future (MTF) Survey

The National Institute on Drug Abuse's (NIDA) MTF survey assesses drug use among high school seniors and young adults across the country. In 1991, the survey was expanded to include data on eighth and tenth graders.

Since 1979, there has been a downward trend in marijuana use among youth. Annual marijuana use among high school seniors was down to almost 22% in 1992, less than half the rate of 1979, and lifetime use among high school seniors decreased from 60.4% in 1979 to 32.6% in 1992.

	1979	1985	1991	1992
Ever Used	60.4	54.2	36.7	32.6
Used In Past Year	50.8	40.6	23.6	21.9
Used In Past Month	36.5	25.7	13.8	11.9

Figure 28.1. *Percent of High School Seniors Who Have Used Marijuana*

Effects of Marijuana on the Brain

Significant progress has been made by NIDA grantees in determining how marijuana acts on the brain. One study found that in rats chronic THC exposure damages and destroys nerve cells and causes other pathological changes in the hippocampus. In fact, several animal studies have focused attention on the hippocampus, the major component of the brain's limbic system that is crucial for learning, memory, and the integration of sensory experiences with emotions and motivation. Taken together, these results may provide clues to the mechanisms underlying marijuana-induced euphoria.

Researchers have found that THC, the active ingredient in marijuana, changes the way in which sensory information gets into and is acted on by the hippocampus the part of the brain that scientists believe underlies memory. Investigations have shown that neurons in the information processing system of the hippocampus and the activity of the nerve fibers are suppressed by THC. In addition, researchers have discovered that learned behaviors, depending on the hippocampus, also deteriorate.

Effect on the Lungs

Scientists at the University of California, Los Angeles, found that the daily use of one to three marijuana joints appears to produce approximately the same lung damage and potential cancer risk as smoking 5 times as many cigarettes. The study results suggest that the way smokers inhale marijuana, in addition to its chemical composition, increases the adverse physical effects. The same lung cancer risks associated with tobacco also apply to marijuana users even though they smoke far less. The study findings refute the argument that marijuana is safer than tobacco because users only smoke a few joints a day.

Recent Research on the THC Receptor

In 1988 it was discovered that the membranes of certain nerve cells contain protein receptors that bind THC, marijuana's active ingredient. Once securely in place, THC kicks off a series of cellular reactions that ultimately lead to the "high" that users experience when they smoke a marijuana cigarette. It was reasoned that a THC-like compound must exist in the body and bind to these receptors. In 1992, researchers identified a naturally occurring chemical in the body that binds to the these same receptors. Named anandamide, this compound behaves chemically like THC.

Studies will continue with anandamide to understand how it interacts with THC receptors to affect memory, movement, hunger, pain, and other functions that are altered by marijuana use.

Resources for Additional Help and Information

American Council for Drug Education
204 Monroe Street, Suite 110
Rockville, MD 20850
(800) 488-DRUG (3784)
(301) 294-0600

National Clearinghouse for Alcohol and Drug Information
P.O. Box 2345
Rockville, MD 20852
(800) 729-6686

American Lung Association
Consult the telephone directory for your community's local affiliate.

Chapter 29

Inhalants

Caution

Exposure to inhalant fumes can be a serious medical emergency. Do not hesitate to call 911 or Poison Control for immediate help. Inhalant abuse is deadly serious. By starving the body of oxygen or forcing the heart to beat more rapidly and erratically, inhalants can kill sniffers, most of whom are adolescents.

What Are Inhalants

Inhalants are a group of products found in most households and workshops that produce a "high" when they are deliberately inhaled or sniffed. Inhalants in various forms have been and continue to be abused throughout the world.

Among the most commonly abused inhalants today are gasoline, glue, typewriter correction fluid, lacquer thinner, butane, fabric protector, freon, spray paint, cooking spray and nitrous oxide. A group of products called nitrite inhalants (e.g., "snappers," "poppers," "locker room") also are abused. Unlike household solvents and aerosols which

---

This chapter contains text from "Inhalants—It's Your Business: Drug Awareness," provided by the Drug Enforcement Administration and Producd by the American Council for Drug Education, nd; "Inhalant Abuse: Its Dangers Are Nothing to Sniff At," NIH Pub. No. 94-3818; and, "Tips for Teens about Inhalants," Center for Substance Abuse Prevention, nd.

are used primarily by rural and suburban preteens and adolescents, nitrite inhalants are more popular among urbanized, young adults.

What Is an Inhalant High Like?

When sniffed deliberately, inhalants produce an almost instantaneous intoxication similar to alcohol's.

Abusers sniff or "huff" inhalants:

- Directly from the container;
- By spraying the product on a sock, a rag or a roll of toilet paper and breathing in the fumes; or
- By spilling or spraying the product into a plastic bag or balloon and, while holding it over the mouth and nose, breathing in the vapors.

During the 15 to 45 minutes that the intoxication lasts, abusers feel giddy and lightheaded. Once the high ends, many users develop pounding headaches, upset stomachs and bad breath. Most feel dizzy and/or sleepy. Some behave as if they are in a stupor and pass out. These effects usually disappear in one or two hours.

Who Uses Inhalants?

Since inhalants are readily available and inexpensive, they are particularly popular among rural and suburban pre-teens and young adolescents. For years, drug abuse specialists in the Southwest and on Native American reservations have considered inhalant abuse a special problem for their treatment populations, whose remote locations had previously limited their access to mood-altering drugs. However, many experts now believe that inhalant abuse is a hidden problem in many communities, one that is frequently missed in existing hospital- and school-based surveys due to underreporting.

Experts do agree that most youngsters who start using inhalants do so as a group social activity and then stop fairly quickly. Headaches, nausea and fears about serious side effects are reasons commonly given for quitting. Some young people, however, continue to use despite these negative consequences.

Drug counselors say that disadvantaged adolescent boys, with at least one alcoholic parent, who have problems in school and difficulty fitting in with peers are the most likely to become heavily involved with inhalants. However, drugs users of any age and background often will use inhalants when other drugs are unavailable and, as mentioned earlier, nitrite inhalants are a drug of choice among certain populations.

What Effects Do Inhalants Have?

As the warnings on their containers indicate, inhalants are powerful chemicals that have serious and sometimes deadly effects when they are misused. In the short-term, inhalant abusers may experience:

* Impaired judgment;
* Decreased coordination;
* Coughing, nasal irritation and nosebleeds;
* Increased heart rate, irregular heart beat, and heart failure (sudden sniffing death);
* Respiratory depression;
* Suffocation; and
* Hangover.

Problems with coordination are responsible for the numerous accidents, particularly serious falls, that inhalant abusers commonly experience. Poor judgment and relaxed inhibitions often result in reckless behavior that includes destruction of property as well as violence towards self and others. When abusers sniff from plastic bags or balloons they also run the risk of suffocating.

Great Britain has been tracking inhalant-related deaths for several years. They have found that first-time inhalant users account for one-in-five of the deaths recorded, a fact that underscores the hazards of trying inhalants even one time.

Sudden sniffing death (SSD) is another major risk linked to inhalant abuse. SSD can affect both experienced and inexperienced abusers. For reasons that are not yet fully understood, some abusers suffer heart failure after inhaling deeply several times. Some treatment experts believe SSD is more likely to occur if the abuser engages in strenuous physical activity after sniffing, or is surprised or scared while sniffing. For this reason, when parents or others approach suspected abusers, they should do so calmly and cautiously to prevent the possibility of triggering this fatal response.

Possible long-term effects from abusing inhalants include:

* Weight loss;

- Mood swings, depression and paranoia;
- Poor memory, mental confusion and serious brain damage;
- Liver damage; and
- Kidney damage.

Over time, heavy users become tolerant to the effects of inhalants and must use increasing amounts to get high. It is among this group that brain damage is most often seen.

Signs of Possible Inhalant Abuse

In the early stages of use, inhalant abuse is difficult to detect. However, signs of possible use include:

- Chemical odor on body and clothes, or in room;
- Red, glassy or watery eyes and dilated pupils;
- Slurred speech;
- Staggering gait and uncoordination;
- Inflamed nose, nosebleeds, and rashes around nose and mouth;
- Loss of appetite;
- Intoxication;
- Seizure; and
- Coma.

Scope of the Problem

Inhalant abuse came to public attention in the 1950s when the news media reported that young people who were seeking a cheap "high" were sniffing glue. The term "glue sniffing" is still widely used, often to include inhalation of a broad range of common products besides glue, notes Dr. Charles W. Sharp of NIDA's Division of Basic Research.

With so many substances lumped together as inhalants, research data describing frequency and trends of inhalant abuse are uneven and sometimes contradictory. However, evidence indicates that inhalant abuse is more common among all socioeconomic levels of American youth than is typically recognized by parents and the public. For instance, NIDA's Monitoring the Future survey shows that in 1993, one in every five 8th graders, or 19.4 percent, used an inhalant in his or her lifetime.

Inhalants were used by equally high percentages of 10th and 12th graders, according to the NIDA survey. Lifetime inhalant use among 12th graders, which had increased steadily for most of the 1980s, leveled off somewhat at 17.4 percent in 1993. Also, 17.5 percent of 10th graders reported lifetime inhalant use in 1993.

Inhalants are most commonly used by adolescents in their early teens, with usage dropping off as students grow older. For example, while 5.4 percent of 8th graders reported using inhalants within the past 30 days, known as "current" use, only 2.5 percent of seniors reported current use of inhalants.

A major roadblock to recognizing the size of the inhalant problem is the ready availability of products that are inhaled. Inhalants are cheap and can be purchased legally in retail stores in a variety of seemingly harmless products. As a result, adolescents who sniff inhalants to get high don't face the drug procurement obstacles that confront abusers of other drugs.

Inhalant abuse also appears to be a problem worldwide according to research data presented at a recent NIDA technical review, "Epidemiology of Inhalant Abuse: An International Perspective." According to Nicholas Kozel, of NIDA's Division of Epidemiology and Prevention Research, low price and easy availability and access make inhalants as problematic in Africa, Asia and Latin America as it is in the United States.

Types of Inhalants

Inhalants can be broken down into three major categories—volatile solvents, nitrites, and anesthetics.

Volatile solvents are either gases, such as butane gas fumes, or liquids, such as gasoline or paint thinner, that vaporize at room temperature. Since the 1950s, the number of common products that contain volatile solvents has increased significantly. Besides gasoline and paint thinner, products with volatile solvents include spray paint, paint and wax removers, hair spray, odorants, air fresheners, cigarette lighter fuels, analgesic sprays, and propellant gases used in aerosols such as whipped cream dispensers.

Volatile solvents produce a quick form of intoxication—excitation followed by drowsiness, disinhibition, staggering, lightheadedness, and agitation. Because many inhalant products contain more than one volatile solvent, it is difficult to clearly identify in humans the specific chemical responsible for subsequent brain or nerve damage or death.

Some volatile solvents are inhaled by abusers because of the effects produced not by the product's primary ingredient but by propellant gases, like those used in aerosols such as hair spray or spray paint. Other volatile solvents found in aerosol products such as gold and silver spray paint are sniffed not because of the effects from propellant gases but because of the psychoactive effects caused by the specific solvents necessary to suspend these metallic paints in the spray.

Nitrites historically have been used by certain groups, largely gay men, to enhance sexual experience and pleasure. Often called "poppers" or "rush," some nitrite products are sold as room odorizers. But use of nitrites has fallen off dramatically in recent years. This may be partly because products containing butyl, propyl, and certain other nitrites were banned in 1991, although products using chemical variants of the banned substances are still sold.

For the past 13 years, NIDA's Monitoring the Future survey has adjusted for the underreporting of nitrite use, recognizing that many survey respondents did not include information about nitrite use when answering survey questions about inhalant abuse. That's because most respondents fail to consider the use of nitrites as a form of inhalant abuse, unless prompted with specific questions mentioning "poppers," "rush," or other nitrite-specific references, researchers say.

Some observers now believe that adjusting inhalant abuse survey results to combine nitrite use with volatile solvent use can lead to mistaken conclusions when viewing consolidated data over several years. That's because nitrite use is declining while volatile solvent use has been on the rise for a number of years. "In combining solvents with nitrites and then adjusting the data, it appears that inhalant use has not changed over the past 16 years when, in fact, solvent use has steadily increased for a decade and a half and just now may be leveling off," says Dr. Fred Beauvais, a psychologist and NIDA-funded researcher at the Tri-Ethnic Center for Prevention Research at Colorado State University at Fort Collins.

Because the current inhalant profile lumping nitrites with volatile solvents leads to misleading data and inferences, many researchers believe that a scientific description of inhalant abuse should distinguish abuse of volatile substances from abuse of nitrites and perhaps anesthetics.

Within the other major category of inhalants, the anesthetics, the principal substance of abuse is nitrous oxide. A colorless, sweet-tasting gas used by doctors and dentists for general anesthesia, nitrous oxide is called "laughing gas" because it often induces a state of giggling and laughter. Recent anecdotal reports indicate that nitrous oxide is being sold illicitly to teenagers and young adults at outdoor events such as rock concerts and on the street. Nitrous oxide often is sold in large balloons from which the gas is released and inhaled for its mind-altering effects.

But nitrous oxide is no laughing matter. Inhaling the gas may deplete the body of oxygen and can result in death; prolonged use can result in peripheral nerve damage.

Inhalants and their Chemical Contents

Volatile Solvents

Adhesives

- Airplane glue
- Rubber cement
- Polyvinylchloride cement

Aerosols

- Spray Paint
- Hair spray
- Deodorant, air freshener
- Analgesic spray, asthma spray

Solvents and Gases

- Nail polish remover
- Paint remover
- Paint thinner
- Typing correction fluid and thinner
- Fuel gas
- Cigarette lighter fluid
- Gasoline

Cleaning Agents

- Dry cleaning fluid
- Spot remover
- Degreaser

Dessert Topping Sprays

- Whipped cream, whippets

Nitrites and Anesthetics

Nitrite Room Odorizers

- "Poppers" and "rush"

Anesthetics

- Gas
- Liquid
- Local

—Adapted from *Inhalant Abuse: A Volitile Research Agenda*, NIDA Research Monograph 129, 1992.

Dangers of Inhalant Abuse

Although no central system exists in the United States for reporting deaths and injuries from abusing inhalants, several studies have documented the dangers associated with inhalant abuse. A study by Dr. James C. Garriott, the chief toxicologist in San Antonio and Bexar County, Texas, examined all deaths in the county between 1982 and 1988 that were attributed to inhalant abuse. Most of the 39 inhalant-related deaths involved teenagers, with 21 deaths occurring among people less than 20 years old. Deaths of males outnumbered those of females 34 to 5. Many of the abusers met with a violent death possibly related to but not directly caused by the use of volatile solvents. Eleven deaths were caused by suicide (10 by hanging), 9 by homicide, and 10 by accident, including falls, auto accidents, and overdoses.

Most of those people who died in Bexar County had used toluene-containing products, such as spray paints and lacquers, Dr. Garriott reported. The next most frequent cause of death in the Texas study was the use of a combination of chemicals found in typewriter correction fluids and other solvents. Other abused substances that resulted in death included gasoline, nitrous oxide, and refrigerants, such as fluorocarbons (Freon). Freon now has been replaced with butane or propane products in most aerosols.

As reported in the Texas study, the solvent toluene, a common component of many paints, lacquers, glues, inks, and cleaning fluids, is identified frequently in inhalant abuse deaths and injuries. A 1986 study of 20 chronic abusers of toluene-containing spray paints found that after one month of abstinence from sniffing the paint, 65 percent of the abusers had damage to the nervous system. Such damage can lead to impaired perception, reasoning, and memory, as well as defective muscular coordination and, eventually, dementia.

In England, where national statistics on inhalant deaths are recorded, the largest number of deaths in 1991 resulted from exposure to butane and propane, which are used as fuels or propellants. Many researchers believe that abuse of butane, which is used in cigarette lighters, is on the increase in the United States. NIDA's Dr. Sharp says, "It's hard to tell whether this is a passing fancy or whether some youthful abusers actually like to get dizzy on the butane and propane gases."

A recent report of this particular inhalant problem in the Cincinnati region indicates that butane gas is the cause of enough deaths to foster national concern about the abuse of fuel gases, whether or not it is a passing form of inhalant abuse, Dr. Sharp says. He notes that "sniffers seem to go out of their way to get their favorite product." For instance, in certain parts of the country, "Texas 'shoe-shine' [a shoe-shining spray containing toluene] and silver or gold spray paints are local or current favorites," he says.

Since the banishing of fluorocarbons, the most common sniffing death hazards among students in the United States probably are due to butane and propane, Dr. Beauvais says. "Doctors and emergency room staffs need to be aware that the profile of the teenager who inhales volatile solvents is not limited to the ethnic lower socioeconomic classes," he cautions. "Many sources lead us to believe that abuse of these readily available inhalants has reached epidemic proportions, indicating an urgent need for preventive efforts directed at teenagers and their parents with emphasis on the risk of sudden sniffing death."

Who's Abusing Inhalants?

One possible reason for the increased use of volatile solvents is that more girls are joining boys in sniffing solvents. "The rates of solvent use for males and females have been converging over the past 20 years," Dr. Beauvais says. Recent studies in New York State and Texas report that males are using solvents at only slightly higher rates than females are. Among Native Americans, whose solvent abuse rates are the highest of any ethnic group, lifetime prevalence rates for males and females were nearly identical, according to 1991 NIDA data.

There is a public perception that inhalant abuse is more common among Hispanic youth than among other ethnic groups. However, recent surveys have not found high rates of abuse by Hispanics in all geographic areas, Dr. Beauvais points out. "It appears that rates for Hispanics may be related to socioeconomic conditions," he says. "As those conditions vary so will the levels of solvent use. Hispanic youths in poor barrio environments may use solvents heavily, but Hispanic youths in less stressful environments do not."

In fact, inhalant abuse shows an episodic pattern, with short-term abuse outbreaks developing in a particular school or region as a specific inhalant practice or product becomes popular in a fashion typical of teenage fads. This episodic pattern can be reflected in survey results and can overstate the magnitude of what is a continually fluctuating level of abuse, says Dr. Beauvais.

Inhalant abusers typically use other drugs as well. "Children as young as 4th graders who begin to use volatile solvents also will start experimenting with other drugs, usually alcohol and marijuana," says Dr. Beauvais. "Adolescent solvent abusers are typically polydrug users and are prone to use whatever is available, although they do show a preference for solvents." However, solvent abuse often is held in low regard by older adolescents, who may consider it unsophisticated, a "kid" habit, he adds.

Not only juveniles are abusing inhalants. Current reports indicate that college age and older adults are the primary abusers of butane and nitrous oxide.

Are Inhalants Addictive?

When inhalant use continues over a period of time, a user will probably develop a tolerance to inhalants. This means that the user will need more frequent use and greater amounts of a substance to achieve the effect desired. This, in turn, leaves a user at much greater risk of suffering from possible negative effects of the drug, such as liver, lung, and kidney impairment, brain damage, nervous system damage, and even death.

Physical dependence can also result, and when a user tries to give up the inhalant habit, withdrawal symptoms such as hallucinations, headaches, chills, delirium tremors, and stomach cramps may occur.

Resources

Aerosol Education Bureau
1001 Connecticut Ave., N.W., Suite 1120
Washington, DC 20036

American Council for Drug Education
204 Monroe Street, Suite 110
Rockville, MD 20850
(301) 294-0600
(800) 488-DRUG

Center for Substance Abuse Treatment
National Drug Information and Treatment
Referral Hotline
11426-28 Rockville Pike, Suite 410
Rockville, MD 20852
(800) 662-HELP
(800) 66-AYUDA (Spanish speaking callers)

Families Anonymous, Inc.
P.O. Box 528
Van Nuys, CA 91408

Families in Action
2296 Henderson Mill
Suite 204
Atlanta, GA 30345
(404) 934-6364

International Institute for Inhalant Abuse
799 E. Hampden Avenue
Suite 500
Englewood, CO 80110
(800) 832-5090
(303) 788-4617

National Council on Alcoholism and Drug Dependence (NCADD)
12 West 21st Street
New York, NY 10010
(800) 622-2255
(212) 206-6770

National Clearinghouse for Alcohol and Drug Information
P.O. Box 2345
Rockville, MD 20847-2345
(800) 729-6686
(301) 468-2600

Solvent Abuse Foundation for Education (SAFE)
750 17th Street, N.W., Suite 250
Washington, DC 20006
(202) 332-7233
(202) 429-0655 FAX

Chapter 30

Nonmedical Use of Prescription Drugs and Drug Diversion

The Nonmedical Use of Prescription Drugs in the United States

The following paper was written by:

Edgar H. Adams, Sc.D.
Senior Scientist
Office of the Director
National Institute on Drug Abuse
5600 Fishers Lane
Rockville, MD 20857

Andrea N. Kopstein
Division of Epidemiology and Prevention Research
National Institute on Drug Abuse
5600 Fishers Lane
Rockville, MD 20857

Pharmaceuticals have brought major changes in the health and quality of life of the population of the United States and the world. Among these changes have been such milestones as the eradication

Excerpts from *Impact of Prescription Drug Diversion Control Systems on Medical Practice and Patient Care*, National Institute on Drug Abuse Research Monograph Series, NIH Pub. No. 93-3507.

of polio and small pox, and, on a broader spectrum, the ability to cure infections with antibiotics. The development of psychoactive drugs has brought similar benefits, ranging from the effective relief of pain to the control of mental illness to a point where massive deinstitution-alization became possible.

Each year, more than 1.5 billion prescriptions or an average of 6.7 prescriptions per person are dispensed from drug stores in the United States. The psychotherapeutic drugs, analgesics (excluding nonnar-cotic analgesics) and sedative hypnotics account for approximately 215 million prescriptions a year (Burke et al. 1991). There is no doubt that these potent psychoactive medications are abused by some people. These drugs may be diverted from the manufacturing or distribution levels obtained through dishonest or duped doctors or from dishon-est or duped pharmacists. They may also be obtained via pharmacy thefts, prescription forgery, or by illegal importation from foreign sources.

Data from the National Household Survey on Drug Abuse (NHSDA), the primary measure of the use and abuse of drugs in the United States, indicate that in the United States in 1991, approxi-mately 172 million household residents reported that they had ever used alcohol, 68 million reported the use of marijuana, 25 million re-ported ever using any psychotherapeutic drug, and 24 million reported ever using cocaine (NHSDA Population Estimate 1991). If current use (any use in the past month) is considered, 103 million used alcohol, approximately 10 million used marijuana, 3 million used a psycho-therapeutic drug and approximately 2 million used cocaine. It should be noted that the psychotherapeutic category is summed over four classes of medicinal agents: stimulants, sedatives, tranquilizers, and analgesics. Of these, only the current use of analgesics (1.4 million) exceeds 1 million.

The issue has been raised regarding the extent to which these data reflect abuse. In the NHSDA, the question on nonmedical use of drugs is phrased as follows:

This is a very important point about the next set of questions. We are interested in the nonmedical use of these prescription type drugs. Nonmedical use of these drugs is any use on your own, that is either: without a doctors prescription, in greater amounts than prescribed, more often than prescribed, or for any reasons other than a doctor said you should take them—such as for kicks, to get high, to feel good, or curiosity about the pills effect.

The breadth of this definition has caused some to question whether self-medication is being measured rather than abuse.

This paper uses data from the NHSDA and the Drug Abuse Warning Network (DAWN). The primary measures associated with drug abuse are used to describe the current prevalence of abuse of illicit psychotherapeutic agents. The NHSDA also attempts to measure the consequences associated with drug use by collecting data on self-reported problems attributed to selected drugs. These problems include such things as becoming depressed or losing interest in things, having arguments or fights with family and friends, feeling alone or isolated and other problems. In total, eleven types of problems are included.

National Household Survey on Drug Abuse

The NHSDA has been conducted since 1971 and sponsored by NIDA since 1974. The 1991 survey represents the 11th survey in the series. A significant change in 1991 was an increase in the sample size so that data were collected from over 32,000 individuals, compared to approximately 9,000 interviews in 1990. Other changes in 1991 include the collection of data from persons living in some group quarters, e.g., civilians living at military installations, those living in college dormitories, and homeless shelters (homeless people not in shelters were not included). Also, Alaska and Hawaii were included for the first time. The response rate of approximately 84 percent is consistent with the response rates obtained with previous surveys. As in the past, the data are based on self-reports and do not include incarcerated populations.

More than 37 percent of the household population in the United States have tried drugs. The seriousness of the drug problem in the United States is reflected in part in polls conducted in the early 1970s as well as the early 1990s that cite drug abuse as one of the major problems facing our country. The good news is that while drug abuse remains a significant problem, the size of the problem appears to be diminishing. However, in some cases the gains of the last several years appear to have stabilized. For example, the estimates of any current illicit drug use in the population were the same in 1991 as in 1990; this was also true for marijuana and cocaine. This should be interpreted with some caution since the time period covered is only one year. The same is true of the nonmedical use of any psychotherapeutic agent. The significant decrease in past year use of these agents between 1988 and 1990 was not maintained in 1991.

	1988 Number*	%	1990 Number*	%	1991 Number*	%
Lifetime	23,536	11.9	24,025	11.9	25,463	12.6
Past Year	11,399	5.7	8,567	4.3	9,161	4.5
Past Month	3,393	1.7	2,858	1.4	3,062	1.5

* In thousands Source: NIDA National Household Survey on Drug Abuse Population Estimates 1989, 1990, 1991

Figure 30.1. *Trends in Nonmedical Use of Any Psychotherapeutic Agents 1988-1991.*

This pattern of stability is also exhibited for each of the classes of psychotherapeutic agents. In 1991, there were no significant changes in either the past month or past year's use in stimulants, sedatives, tranquilizers, or analgesics between 1990 and 1991.

	1988 Number*	%	1990 Number*	%	1991 Number*	%
Stimulants	1,755	0.9	957	0.5	668	0.3
Sedatives	784	0.4	568	0.3	755	0.4
Tranquilizers	1,174	0.6	568	0.3	889	0.4
Analgesics	1,151	0.6	1,534	0.8	1,403	0.7

* In thousands

Source: NIDA National Household Survey on Drug Abuse Population Estimates 1989, 1990, 1991

Figure 30.2. *Trends in Past Month Use of Selected Psychotherapeutic Agents, 1988-1991.*

	1988		1990		1991	
	Number*	%	Number*	%	Number*	%
Stimulants	4,957	2.5	3,109	1.5	2,709	1.3
Sedatives	3,099	1.6	2,233	1.1	2,130	1.0
Tranquilizers	4,407	2.2	2,538	1.3	3,408	1.7
Analgesics	5,342	2.7	4,999	2.5	5,090	2.5

* In thousands

Source: NIDA National Household Survey on Drug Abuse Population Estimates 1989, 1990, 1991

Figure 30.3. Trends in Past-Year Use of Licit Psychotherapeutic Agents, 1988-1990.

Drug Abuse Warning Network (DAWN)

DAWN collects data on drug-related emergency episodes in the total coterminous United States and 21 metropolitan areas. In 1986, the conversion of DAWN to a probability sample was initiated. Weighted data are currently available from 1988 forward, making long-term trend analysis impossible. Previous analyses of long-term trends using consistent reporting panels indicated an increase in the number of total DAWN episodes between 1985 and 1989, but a decrease in the number of episodes associated with controlled prescription drugs (Figure 30.4) (Adams 1991). In 1985, controlled prescription drugs accounted for approximately 38 percent of the episodes compared to 21 percent in 1989.

	1985	1986	1987	1988	1989
Total DAWN Episodes	76,391	87,388	103,500	114,411	109,400
Controlled Prescription Drug Episodes	28,840	27,430	27,219	25,292	23,020

* Based on data from 441 consistently reporting facilities with adjustments for nonresponse.

Figure 30.4. Emergency Room Data: Total Number of Emergency Room Episodes and Episodes Associated With Controlled Prescription Drugs According to Year, 1985-1989*.

259

Figure 30.5 shows the top 20 drugs reported to the DAWN in 1990. Included in the top 20 are 15 licit pharmaceutical products, including over the counter products such as aspirin and acetaminophen.

Drug Name	# of Mentions	# of Suicide Mentions	Revised # Mentions
Alcohol-in-combination	115,162	49,125	66,037
Cocaine	80,355	5,203	75,152
Heroin/Morphine	33,884	1,154	37,720
Acetaminophen	25,422	20,938	4,484
Aspirin	19,188	15,525	3,663
Ibuprofen	16,299	N/A	N/A
Alprazolam	15,846	10,976	4,870
Marijuana/Hashish	15,706	1,124	14,582
Diazepam	14,836	8,604	6,232
Amitriptyline	8,642	6,535	2,107
Acetaminophen with Codeine	8,222	N/A	N/A
O.T.C. Sleep Aids	7,984	6,733	1,251
Lorazepam	7,625	4,857	2,768
D-Propoxyphene	7,417	1,164	6,253
Fluoxetine	6,917	6,205	712
Diphenhydramine	6,483	5,059	1,424
Methamphetamine/Speed	5,236	661	4,571
Oxycodone	4,526	2,528	2,076
PCP and PCP Combinations	4,408	244	4,154
Lithium Carbonate	44,025	N/A	N/A

Source: DAWN Annual Emergency Room Data 1990

Figure 30.5. *Drug Abuse Warning Network Weighted Emergency Room Estimates, 1990.*

These data are often cited as evidence of the diversion and abuse of these products. In fact, the inclusion of many of these agents in the top 20 is due to an anomaly in DAWN that, unfortunately may now be more misleading than informative. The anomaly occurs because the DAWN data include suicide attempts and gestures as one of the motivations listed for DAWN cases. So, while DAWN data are often quoted as reflecting diversion and prevalence of abuse, they reflect neither. The impact of the suicide attempts and gestures category on the top 20, especially licit pharmaceutical agents, is apparent from Figure 30.5. For example, the number of acctaminophen cases drops from 25,422 to 4,484 and fluoxetine drops from 6,917 to 712. The arguments for excluding suicide cases from the analysis of DAWN data have been expressed previously (Adams 1988, 1991). Furthermore, the DAWN data are a measure of the consequences of abuse and not prevalence, as is sometimes implied. Increases in DAWN cases may reflect an increase in the number of users, but they may just as well reflect a shift in patterns of use (e.g., from snorted cocaine to smoked crack).

Other Consequences

As previously noted, the NHSDA contains a measure of the problems associated with the use of drugs. The problems range from health, work or school problems to drug-related problems with other people, feelings of depression, isolation, anxiety, and irritability. Respondents were asked to identify the specific drugs which caused any identified problem. These data are summarized in Figure 30.6. A review of the data suggests an internal consistency between the pharmacology of the drug and the problems reported. For example, difficulty in thinking clearly and having arguments and fights with family and friends are mentioned more frequently for alcohol than feeling nervous and anxious and irritable and upset for cocaine. Among past year cocaine users almost 15 percent reported one or more of these problems in the 1990 NHSDA. For the licit psychotherapeutic agents, it was necessary to combine the data from 1988 and 1990 in order to get reliable estimates of the problems attributed to these agents. Only 0.2 percent of past year sedative users and 0.1 percent of past year tranquilizer users reported at least one of the 11 problems. Two percent of past year stimulant users experienced at least one problem, while problems reported by analgesic users were so infrequent that the estimates were unreliable, even with the 2-year file.

| | Percent Reporting at Least |
Drug	One of Eleven Problems
Cocaine (1990)	15%
Psychotherapeutic Agents (1988-1990)	
Analgesics	*
Tranquilizers	0.1%
Sedatives	0.2%
Stimulants	2.0%

* Estimate unreliable

Source: National Household Survy on Drug Abuse

Figure 30.6. *Problems Associated with Past Year Drug Use.*

Discussion

The use and abuse of licit psychotherapeutic agents obtained outside of normal medical channels is part of the drug abuse problem in this country. In 1991, an estimated 3 million Americans reported the nonmedical use of one of these agents at least once during the month prior to being interviewed. A critical question regarding this number is the proportion that reflects "abuse," however abuse is defined.

The report of the Shafer Commission includes data from a survey of 3,291 persons age 12 and above conducted in the fall of 1972 (National Commission on Marijuana and Drug Abuse 1973). Respondents were asked to identify various situations as drug abuse or not drug abuse. The report concluded that there was a tendency to identify nearly any situation as drug abuse. For example, 82 percent of the respondents said taking more of a nonprescription medication than the label directed was drug abuse, while 35 percent said that having a cocktail or highball with lunch or dinner and in the evening was abuse. However, the following were most often connected with abuse: use for pleasure, use to help cope with the day, taking more than prescribed or directed, and occasional use of heroin.

The current definition of nonmedical use includes the references to taking a drug in greater amounts than prescribed or more often than prescribed. It seems likely that a significant proportion of people reporting nonmedical use in the NHSDA may be obtaining the psychotherapeutic agents through licit channels. If abuse is related to problems attributed to the use of these agents, then the overall problem from a health perspective is relatively small. The problems are a fraction of those associated with marijuana, cocaine, alcohol or tobacco. The DAWN data are supposed to reflect consequences associated with the abuse of drugs, but for the licit psychotherapeutics they are misleading. The primary reason for this is the inclusion of suicides as described above.

From a law enforcement perspective, the diversion of these licit psychotherapeutic agents from legitimate practice, whether through forgeries, scams, or theft, is illegal. Representatives of the law enforcement and health communities often cite, albeit inappropriately, DAWN data as evidence of the size of the prescription drug abuse problem.

The importance of understanding the magnitude of the problem and the source from which the drugs are obtained is reflected by the fact that unlike heroin, for example, these are licit products that are subject to varying degrees of bureaucratic regulation and control. In fact, ten or more States are now spending millions of dollars in attempting to control the diversion of these products through the monitoring of physicians and patients.

In States where multiple copy prescription programs have been implemented, 35 to 50 percent reductions in the prescribing of the medicinal agents covered by the program have been noted. Some have argued that the reduction reflected the extent of overprescribing, while others argue that there is a chilling effect that is having a negative impact on patient care. Oklahoma has implemented an electronic data transfer program that does not require the use of a special form although the information sent to the State is the same as in a triplicate program. Preliminary analysis seems to suggest that this program does not have a chilling effect on prescribing.

To date, the only empirical evidence would seem to suggest that a chilling effect does, in fact, exist and that there is a negative impact on patient care. In Texas, a study demonstrated a reduction in the prescribing of Schedule II drugs and a corresponding increase in the prescribing of Schedule III analgesics (Sigler et al. 1984). In New York State there has been an increase in the prescribing of outdated, less effective, and more lethal drugs such as meprobamate and chloralhydrate instead of benzodiazepines (Weintraub et al. 1991). In another study conducted in New York, two-thirds of the population felt that sending copies of prescriptions to the State was a violation of privacy, and 30 percent of the respondents stated that they would not take the best drug prescribed if it fell under the triplicate prescription program (Adams and Palmerini 1992).

Unfortunately, there is a paucity of data either at the national or State level that can address these issues. The current circumstances only reinforce the need for the health and law enforcement communities to work in concert. They must agree on the data that is needed, the best way to collect it and use it, and to design programs that effectively reduce prescription drug abuse without impairing health care.

Drug Diversion Control Systems, Medical Practice, and Patient Care

The following paper was written by:

Gene R. Haislip, J.D.
Deputy Assistant Administrator
Office of Diversion Control
Drug Enforcement Administration
Washington, DC 20537

Introduction

In recent years, some persons and corporate representatives have expressed concern that government-imposed controlled substances controls, especially multiple copy prescription systems, adversely affect the quality of patient care. The experience and available information, however, support the position that the reverse is the case, that such controls help ensure the quality of patient care and that it is negligent and criminal prescribing that supports excess drug sales, which are adversely affected. Research in every area affecting the health and welfare of citizens is desirable and it is no less the case in the area under review. However, this should not obscure the fact that a great store of knowledge, wisdom, and experience exists, nor should it be misused as an excuse to delay needed social action. Moreover, to evaluate drug diversion control systems on the basis of their impact on medical practitioners tends to obscure the correct focus of these systems. Their impact on medical practitioners and patient care is only one part of a larger purpose, which is to protect the public from the consequences of drug traffic and abuse. Nevertheless, control systems do have an impact on improving medical practice and patient care and it is worthy of attention. But, before proceeding in this area, it is desirable to focus at least briefly on the principal concern for which control systems are created.

The Problem of Diversion

The diversion of licit drugs into the illicit drug traffic continues to be a major component of the national drug problem. Evidence of this can be found by looking at national estimates of hospital emergency room mentions for the top 20 controlled substances from the Drug Abuse Warning Network (DAWN). Approximately one out of every three mentions (33.5 percent) in 1990 was for a licitly manufactured substance. The dominant group for licit drugs continues to be the benzodiazepines. In 1990, there were eight among the fourteen licit drugs. Over the past few years, they have accounted for approximately 60-65 percent of the mentions for licit drugs. However, there are also four narcotic analgesics among the top 20 controlled drugs. One of these is hydrocodone, which has shown a 56 percent increase In mentions in 1990. The influx of licit drugs into illicit channels is further demonstrated by examining emergency room episodes for cocaine and heroin. Among the drugs mentioned most often in combination with these are diazepam, alprazolam, methadone, and oxycodone. This statistical evidence is further corroborated by the Community Epidemiology Work Group and actual day-to-day State and DEA (Drug Enforcement Administration) case investigations.

Federal and State Criminal Investigations

Today there are approximately 845,000 DEA registrants that fall within the closed system of distribution of controlled substances. The overwhelming majority take their responsibilities seriously. Unfortunately, however, a small percentage of registrants break their public trust and engage in supplying the lucrative illicit market. The basis of this market is, as every pharmacologist knows, that these legitimate drugs produce consequences essentially identical to the purely illicit drugs and are sold for the same extraordinary profit. Relatively few Federal, State, and local law enforcement resources are dedicated to apprehending diverters of controlled pharmaceuticals, and yet we have some notable statistics to share. In 1987, DEA diversion investigators, often working in conjunction with their State and local counterparts, reported 63 criminal convictions. In 1990, the number of convictions grew to 192. Further, in 1990, criminal court fines levied against pharmaceutical diverters exceeded $2 million. Finally, another gauge of the extent of diversion of controlled pharmaceuticals and the cooperative Federal and State response is the number of civil actions against registrations. From October 1987 through September 1990, the DEA's Office of Chief Counsel handled over 1,000 show cause proceedings to revoke, suspend, or deny Federal controlled substances registrations.

The Function of Standards and Controls

Before proceeding to examine the impact of the laws designed to control the distribution of these drugs, it is appropriate to mention the principles on which they are based. The basic function of government-imposed standards and controls is to improve the quality of goods and services by establishing minimum requirements to protect the public from inferior, negligent, or fraudulent practices, e.g., automobiles which malfunction, drugs which do more harm than good, airline pilots who fly under the influence of intoxicants, or physicians who improperly prescribe or profiteer from the weakness or ignorance of the public, etc. Controls are limited, however, to establishing a minimum acceptable level of goods and services and do not guarantee excellence. Nevertheless, excellence in good medicine is encouraged when it does not have to compete with unlicensed service which may be offered at a much reduced price.

An additional issue that is of concern to governments and taxpayers is cost-effectiveness. This is a socioeconomic issue which relates to cost as compared with (1) other alternatives, (2) the availability of funds for the intended purpose, and (3) the severity of the social problem which they are intended to correct.

These are principles to bear in mind in any examination of the issues under discussion. It is evident that any future research will be dealing with some aspect of the application of these principles. It is also evident that the possibilities for such research are enormous and could consume the work of decades. It is for this reason that decisions of the day, as always, must inevitably be made on the basis of experience, wisdom, and the best available evidence.

Oversupply and Excessive Demand

When we behold the diversity of the world and its history, we must stand in awe. Not one thing is simple. Not one thing can be damned but what some useful result can be made of it. Not one thing can be praised but what some evil or stupidity can be found in it. It is no less so in the matters under review. We have in view a complex process of controls and standards operating within a dynamic and complex socioeconomic system consisting of industry, commerce, the health professions, the public, and government. Although it may not have been scientifically validated, I am confident in asserting that virtually all people hate to be sick or to feel bad. Those who are, or fear the possibility, hunger after health and happiness and its assurance. Medicine is viewed as the panacea; medicine for what ails, medicine to prevent the possibility of ailment.

This need for medicine has led scientists and doctors to produce wonders in the world, the virtual elimination of smallpox, polio, and numerous other sources of tragedy and horror. It is estimated that U.S. companies alone spend approximately $8 billion per year to support these efforts. This desire for medicine has led even larger numbers of people into avenues of profiteering, some of which were bogus and some of which were destructive: the sale of addictive medicines, "fat clinics" whose activity produces amphetamine dependence and brain damage, heroin for morphine addiction, "stress clinics" whose trade results in addiction, stress management for young women which produces middle-aged benzodiazepine "junkies," or the dumping in developing countries of out-of-date surplus antibiotics which destroy livers while providing corporate tax deductions. The excessive desire for medication has often led to an equally excessive supply. A couple of recent examples relating to the consumption and utilization of controlled substances will help to illustrate this latter point.

Prior to the passage of the Federal laws, it was estimated that approximately eight billion 10 mg doses of amphetamine and methamphetamine were manufactured, prescribed and consumed in the United States. This resulted in the massive abuse of stimulants throughout the country. They were obviously available everywhere and under all sorts of conditions, particularly through weight reduction clinics. As a result of the application of quota reductions and a variety of enforcement measures, the quantity now available within the legitimate sector is approximately one-half of 1 percent of the previous amount. This has had tremendous impact on patient care as well as general protection of the public. Consider the vast numbers of persons who have not become drug-dependent, have not been killed in accidents, do not pose social problems, have not wasted their money, or died of overdose. The tremendous quantities of these stimulants which were previously available would equate to 6 to 20 million stimulant-dependent persons, depending upon dosage per day. This compares with present figures of 29 to 115 thousand persons for whom they are currently prescribed. Thus, the impact of controls on patient care has truly been significant.

The drug methaqualone provides another interesting example. At one point, in 1981, the number of deaths and injuries which were reported in connection with this drug were equal to those involving heroin. It was soon discovered that the great majority (perhaps 95 percent) of the world's legitimate production of this substance was being sold into the illicit traffic under the pretext and assumption of legitimacy. During the late 1970s and early 1980s, a phenomenon known as "stress clinics" operated in the United States. The financiers behind these clinics were nonmedical personnel who sought to profiteer from the prescription and sale of Quaaludes under the guise of treating patient stress. Clinics were set up in Chicago, New York, Ft. Lee (NJ), Boston, Miami, Los Angeles, and in other cities. Doctors were hired at all these clinics to write prescriptions for one drug—Quaaludes. Again, the evidence was clear that most of the Nation's legitimate manufacture was actually being used for this disguised illicit purpose.

After extensive investigation over many years, and after many arrests of doctors, pharmacists, and other conspirators, three ringleaders were convicted in March of 1983 of operating a Continuing Criminal Enterprise (CCE) and sentenced to 15, 12, and 10 years in prison with no possibility of parole. Finally, the drug was taken off the market by Act of Congress in 1984.

The Impact of Commercial Interests

Mind-altering drugs create dependence and a desire on the part of substantial numbers of persons to engage in their habitual consumption in the absence, and in excess, of any legitimate medical need, with resulting injury and costs to both the society and the individual. This social behavior is the basis of a demand for such substances in excess of need. This is precisely illustrated in the examples cited. If permitted to do so, the market will expand production and sales to meet this demand, thus generating profits far in excess of those associated with legitimate medical and social needs.

This fact is the basis on which all substance controls are predicated. Controls act to reduce the permissible circumstances for consumption, thus restricting the volume of sales, and thereby conflicting with powerful commercial interests. Thus, we often see that commercial interests seek to resist or reduce controls, utilizing all the arguments and tactics clever lawyers can devise. A good example of this was the Federal effort to bring benzodiazepines under control. This action was first proposed in January 1966 and due to a series of hearings, delays, legal motions, and appeals, was not finalized until July of 1975, only a short time before the patent expired. Oftentimes much of the industry involved in the supply of controlled substances behaves in this way. Such generalizations have to be qualified since the pharmaceutical industry is by no means homogenous. For example, some manufacturers have occasionally sought appropriate control status for new products. The attitudes of corporate management are as diverse as those of individuals, and the behavior of some should not be used to characterize all. In the area of controlled substances, commercial interests sometimes manifest themselves in several important ways that may threaten the integrity of the health professions and the quality of patient care. These include (1) extensive organized efforts to influence physician behavior, (2) large expenditures on advertising, and (3) well financed political networking and lobbying activities to influence government at all levels.

The relationship between the medical practitioner, the drug manufacturer, and patient drug consumption is complex. Companies use a variety of techniques to increase product utilization by medical practitioners. In the case of new drugs, this is inevitable because the developer possesses the majority of the knowledge concerning the product and has usually performed all or most of the research concerning it. However, promotion is largely the work of corporate sales departments, advertising, and detail men. Available studies show that this activity often goes far beyond technical explanation regarding indication for use of the drug, into all of the marketing techniques associated with non-drug products. According to the recent report of the AMA Council on Ethical and Judicial Affairs (1990), companies sponsor medical conferences that may include free lunches, dinners, hospitality suites, cash payments to attenders, or full cost of family transportation to a resort area with extra days for vacation. Some companies have provided gifts or cash payments for every patient who was started on a particular drug. In 1987, the pharmaceutical industry spent $5,000 per U.S. physician to promote its products, or 25 percent of total sales revenues. Moreover, in recent years some firms have shown a strong desire to extend prescription drug advertising directly to the consumer in order to stimulate sales. Thus, we see the persistence of commercial pressure to extend prescription drug consumption through a variety of techniques that go well beyond professional education.

Political networking is another means of protecting sales and especially of resisting control measures which threaten them. Thus, for example, most of the lobbying activity in opposition to control measures such as the multiple copy prescription systems is organized and initiated by manufacturers. This includes the sponsorship of seminars and meetings and other devices designed to create the appearance of alarm on the part of the medical professional, which might otherwise be absent. The availability of financial resources allows the employment of consultants whose reputation and influence within organized medicine and government facilitate these efforts. These are all practices which should be further researched by those concerned with patient care and public welfare.

A resort to dilatory tactics is the final defense of commercial interest professionals and executives. This may take the form of involved legal proceedings to contest control actions or perhaps simply a call for more research. In the present circumstances, for example, there is now a great desire to research the impact of multiple copy prescription programs prior to any further legislative action. These systems have existed since 1940 and have been further enacted throughout the 1980s, but this sudden concern has arisen only since the action of the State of New York in now including benzodiazepines under its triplicate prescription requirement. It is now obvious that this action dramatically reduced the sale and utilization of these drugs. Some of their manufacturers claim that this is because many physicians are now intimidated in prescribing them by fear of government oppression. But New York State's action only created a reporting requirement. It did not change either State or Federal medical standards or in any way affect the approval for marketing of benzodiazepines.

Claims of reduced availability of drugs have, in fact, been made regarding the impact of controls on the prescribing and dispensing of narcotics for the treatment of cancer pain. Yet, the record discloses national quotas for production of narcotics have steadily increased over the past 10 years. In the case of morphine, the increase has been by more than 400 percent. It appears that these claims, as they relate to drug controls, are bogus and designed to play upon our natural sympathies.

Fear of Disclosure

Although demands for research are sometimes used as a dilatory tactic, some are fearful of what the collection of data might actually disclose. For example, not long ago I had occasion to address a conference concerned with the administration of methadone maintenance programs, a difficult undertaking requiring the highest degree of patience, dedication and professionalism. In the course of my remarks, I reminded the conferees of the high number of death and injury reports in the DAWN system associated with methadone, an entirely legal drug under stringent quota control, all of which is supposed to be prescribed for medical need. The evidence does indeed suggest that it may be the most lethal of controlled drugs, legitimate or otherwise, on a dosage level kilogram-for-kilogram basis. It is not a popular thing to say, but it nevertheless needs to be examined and appreciated especially by those who utilize the drug. I subsequently learned that these remarks were not appreciated by some, and that one large, well-known institution which conducts maintenance programs thereafter declined to participate in the DAWN data collection system, citing my remarks as a reason not doing so.

Certainly we have ample evidence that some practitioners fear the creation of data systems which will expose the nature of their prescribing activity. This is because a small percentage of such persons may flood a community with diverted drugs through profiteering or excessive prescribing contrary to legitimate medical standards. For example, by utilizing national drug distribution data, we discovered an area in Texas which reported an enormous consumption of the Schedule II stimulant known as Preludin. A certain Dr. Thomas was the subject of a lengthy DEA/Texas Department of Public Safety investigation which disclosed that he was responsible for the dispensing of 46 percent of Preludin in the State, or approximately 33,600 dosage units per month. Prescriptions were issued at the physician's office in Nacogdoches, Texas, or from various motels in the Dallas, Texas area. On April 15, 1983, John Hall Thomas, M.D. a physician from Nacogdoches, Texas, was sentenced to five years in prison following his conviction for illegally prescribing Preludin.

In 1986, national distribution data disclosed that Pennsylvania accounted for the consumption of approximately 25 percent of all Schedule II amphetamine and methamphetamine manufactured in the U.S. and nearly 33 percent of all the Schedule II phenmetrazine (Preludin) although it had only 4.8 percent of the Nation's population.

Operation Quaker State was initiated by the DEA to reverse the upward spiraling trend. Between 1986 and 1988, over 43 separate investigations were initiated and completed against Pennsylvania physicians and pharmacies. Over 60 onsite investigations were conducted after the new 1987 Pennsylvania anorectic law was passed as a result of this DEA initiative. In addition to numerous criminal and civil convictions, a number of highly successful registrant cancellations were accomplished. By 1989, distribution of these drugs in Pennsylvania had returned to a normal level.

From the above, it may be seen that there are quite a few persons interested in hiding their activity from official scrutiny. The collection of prescription data does have an inhibiting effect on their activities, but not for the reasons usually cited by critics of data collection. These systems make more visible the malpractice and criminal profiteering which were previously safely hidden from authorities. The accomplices and willing victims of such persons never complain to authorities and may operate without discovery indefinitely without such data systems. Filling out forms for the use of government and law enforcement personnel can never be popular with anyone, whether it is for income taxes or controlled drugs. But it is only those who have no legitimate justification for their income or behavior who are inhibited by them.

In summary, then, experience supports the following conclusions with regard to the impact of drug controls on patient care:

1. The actual and potential demand for controlled substances exceeds legitimate need, thus necessitating the application of a variety of controls to ensure that production, sales, and supply do not exceed this need. The dependence-producing character of controlled substances and the potential for profits for both licit and illicit suppliers creates pressure to expand their availability beyond need, as illustrated in the examples cited.

2. Controls are intended to protect the entire public, of which patients are a smaller but critically important subset.

3. Controls should accord with the standards of legitimate patient care and medical practice.

4. Administrative and enforcement practices should not exceed these parameters.

5. Controls serve to protect patients from either willful or negligent abuse and excess, even though they may be willing to consent to such conduct by virtue of ignorance or dependence.

6. Controls help establish minimum standards of patient care and help sustain the public trust in the medical professions.

7. Data requirements relating to drug distribution, prescribing, and utilization do not establish standards of medical care, but do assist enforcement and licensing authorities in discovering incidents in which they are not being adhered to.

Chapter 31

Drug Misuse Among the Elderly: A Covert Problem

Abstract

Drug misuse and chemical dependency in the elderly is often un-recognized until an acute reaction occurs. The financial and psychological costs to individuals and society for drug-related problems will likely increase as unprecedented numbers of people are surviving into their later years. Presently, the elderly consume 25% to 30% of all prescription drugs. This consumption rate becomes even more problematic when prescription drugs are combined with alcohol or other drugs, including over-the-counter medications. In examining the dimensions of this covert problem, the biological changes accompanying age, as well as the often overlooked sociological and psychological variables, need to be explored. Intervention and prevention, to be effective, must take cognizance of a wide range of socially relevant issues implicated as causally important.

In many respects, contemporary industrial societies have become drug oriented. We are constantly barraged with messages promoting the use of drugs to alleviate discomfort or to stimulate and enhance pleasurable experiences. One result of the "pill for every ill" mentality is an increasing incidence of drug misuse and dependency across the entirety of social and demographic categories. Dependence on and abuse of both licit and illicit drugs may occur for many reasons and serve many purposes. Mule, in attempting to explain the causal chain, proposes a sociocultural, macro-level etiology, asserting "drug dependency speaks loudly and emphatically about the ills of our technological culture overburdened by political conflicts, racism, hypocrisy, and economic imbalance."[1]

At the micro level, changes in the structure and roles of contemporary families have been posited as factors in drug misuse patterns. The elderly are consequently affected by changes in the family. Today, more elderly are living alone and assuming more responsibility for their health care. Thus, it is imperative that health professionals closely monitor drug-taking patterns of the elderly whose optimum well-being is often dependent upon and affected by both prescription and nonprescription drugs.

In 1985, $28.5 billion was spent on prescribed and nonprescribed medications.[2] Currently, it is estimated that 25%-30% of all prescription drugs are taken by older adults.[3,4] According to Gans, some 30% of this age group are taking eight or more prescription drugs daily. He also estimates that by the year 2020, 50% of all prescription drugs will be taken by the elderly.[5]

This article will address drug use and misuse patterns of people in the later years of the life cycle. Specifically, it will: review the magnitude of drug use with prescription and over-the-counter (OTC) drugs taken alone or in combination with alcohol; discuss physiological factors that enhance drug sensitivity in the elderly; and explicate the psychological and sociological dimensions that may contribute to misuse and dependency. In conclusion, some prevention and drug management guidelines will be recommended for professionals who practice with this population.

Definitions of Drug Misuse and Dependency

To clarify the problem being discussed, it is first necessary to define the terms. Although, in the strictest sense, misuse and drug dependency are not synonymous, for the purposes of this article the terms will be used interchangeably. This is based on the premise that a drug dependency problem is a form of drug misuse, and certainly drug misuse can develop into a dependency state. Glantz, however, advocates using the term "drug misuse" when referring to the elderly.[6] He defines misuse as the inappropriate use of drugs intended for therapeutic purposes.

The elderly often misuse psychoactive drugs, but they also misuse drugs that traditionally have not been considered drugs of abuse.[6,7] Although they may not become intoxicated or obtain a "high," the intentional misuse of non-psychoactive substances, such as laxatives or OTC analgesics, may be said to provide some sort of gratification or the behavior would probably not be repeated. Drug misuse involves several dimensions including under- and over-medication, inappropriate self-prescribing, drug swapping, and drug hoarding. Regardless of terms applied, the drugs most frequently found to be misused by the elderly include cardiac medications, antihypertensives, laxatives, analgesics, nutritional products, and psychoactive agents.[8] The implication for both health-care providers and society is that the magnitude of the problem will grow larger in the future as the at-risk population increases simultaneously with the expanding market of prescription and nonprescription drugs.

A High Risk Group

Substance abuse is currently receiving considerable attention, most of which is focused on the consumption of illegal substances and alcohol by teenagers and younger adults. Comparatively, the elderly have received minimal attention in studies of drug misuse and dependency.[9,10] Despite this neglect, it is a serious problem and will no doubt increase with the "graying of America." A high-risk population for drug-related problems is emerging as unprecedented numbers of people are surviving into their later years. By the year 2025, older people will account for up to 21.1% of the US population, numbering some 58.6 million.[11] Those over 85 years of age whose health-care needs are disproportionate to their numbers will double by the end of the 1990s. In addition, the elderly population is currently and will surely remain predominantly female as women live longer than their male counterparts. In the United States, between the ages of 65-69 years, there are 1.3 women for every man; by age 75-79, there are 1.6 women; and by age 85, there are 2.3 women for every man.[12] These statistics are relevant to the topic here as women experience more health problems, seek health-care consultation more often, and consume more drugs than their male counterparts.

In addition to demographic changes, there are some major social and psychological changes that are likely to amplify the magnitude of drug-related problems. Among these changes are: an increase in OTC drugs (prescription drugs changed to OTC status); an increase in the number of elderly living near or below the poverty level; changes in Medicare coverage; an elderly population that will make more decisions about health care and engage in increased self-medication; increased cost for professional consultation; and an aging population that may have been drug dependent in their youth.[13]

Specification of the prevalence of drug use in the elderly is important for several reasons. Multiple drug use is a frequent phenomenon, with older people taking an average of five drugs, and some taking as many as eight different preparations.[7] For this population, morbidity and mortality rates are more adversely affected by drug interactions, reactions, and misuse. Accident statistics for all age groups illustrate that adverse consequences are frequently associated with inappropriate medication used alone or in combination with alcohol.[14] The elderly not only consume a disproportionate share of medications, but it is also estimated that up to 10% of community dwelling elderly have an alcohol problem as well.[15] Drug dependency, particularly with psychoactive medications alone or combined with alcohol, results in economic losses that accrue to society as a whole and can no longer be overlooked for this segment of the population. The implications are particularly relevant since retirement age has become more flexible and segments of the older population are choosing to remain in the labor force. Their ability to participate productively is seriously challenged when alcohol and prescription and OTC medications are commonly present in their lives.

Eckardt maintains that a decline in alcohol consumption may occur with aging.[16] The extent of alcohol consumption by the elderly is difficult to determine because of isolation, the reluctance of relatives and friends to believe that an elderly person is drinking, and often the inability of health-care providers to diagnose an alcohol problem. Pascarelli and Fisher suggest alcohol abuse may approach 21% in certain high-risk groups such as single men and veterans.[17] Gomberg surveyed the literature on the incidence of drinking problems in the elderly and found the incidence to range from a low of 2.2% to 25% and 70% for selected high-risk hospitalized males.[18]

Drug or substance misuse is implicated not only in economic loss but often precipitates dysfunctional family and social relationships. This is particularly so with alcohol. The older alcoholic is often isolated and estranged from family and community support systems. Having retired, the workplace no longer provides an opportunity for affirming contact and social support. This loss of social support is often compounded by frequent life crises due to either infirmity or death of a spouse or significant other. While drug-taking behavior among the elderly has not yet been specified in as great detail, the patterns of alcohol abuse identified by Mishara and Kastenbaum may be helpful in understanding psychosocial problems.[19] They suggest that alcohol consumption produces nine symptoms among older drinkers: hangovers and blackouts; psychological dependence on alcohol; health problems and accidents related to alcohol use; financial problems; problems with families and spouses; problems with friends or neighbors; job-related problems; personality changes; and legal problems. Having surveyed the available data on alcohol, they go on to express concern regarding the paucity of information about the combination of medication use and alcohol for this age group.

Drug Sensitivity and Aging

Drug sensitivity among the elderly differs substantially than that of their younger counterparts. With age, the range between the therapeutic and adverse effect ratio of drugs appears to be narrow. Because of age-related physiological changes, older persons experience increased biological sensitivity and greater individual variability to the effects of drugs and alcohol. Straus discusses how nutritional practices, caffeine consumption, and cigarette smoking, may influence individual reaction and sensitivity to drugs.[20]

Although it is often difficult to separate the effects of aging from the effects of disease, a person's response to medications and alcohol changes over time. Changes in sensitivity to various drugs, as well as modifications in the way the body handles them, can have a profound impact on their effects.[21] These modifications refer to alterations in the rate and extent of absorption, distribution, metabolism, and excretion of drugs. Consequently, physiological changes in older adults that result in less effective clearance of drugs may cause problems of drug toxicity and dependence.

With age, body fat increases while total body water and lean body mass decrease. As a result, water soluble drugs, such as alcohol, tend to produce higher blood levels in older individuals because there is less body water, ie, a decreased volume of distribution, in which to disperse.[21] Fat soluble drugs, such as tranquilizers and sedative-hypnotics, do not produce higher blood levels but have prolonged effects due to greater disposition, ie, increased volume of distribution, to fat tissue.

The liver and kidneys are the primary organs responsible for breaking down and removing most drugs from the body. Enzyme action in the liver provides the principal mechanism for transforming drugs to metabolites that are more readily excreted by the kidney. Some drugs do not undergo metabolic transformation and are excreted directly by the kidney. Due to decreased cardiac output and other age- or disease-related factors, these organs may begin to function less effectively. As a result, drugs or their active metabolites may be cleared from the body more slowly. This means an older person may need a lower dose or a longer interval between doses to achieve the desired therapeutic effect.

In addition, there are other changes that occur with age that impact an individual's ability to take medications appropriately. For example, loss of visual acuity can make it hard for an older adult to distinguish colors of medications or their shapes. Vision changes may also make the label on the prescription vial difficult, if not impossible, to read. Decrements in hearing ability can interfere with attempts to inform the older adult about the proper use of the medication.

Cognitive functioning is yet another important factor influencing drug-taking patterns. Short-term memory loss can result in missed or doubled-up doses. Health-care providers must anticipate some degree of sensory or cognitive impairment that may affect medication practices. It is essential, therefore, that they consider age-related dosage adjustments and less complicated dosage regimens when prescribing for the elderly.

Medication Patterns of the Elderly

Of all segments of the population, the elderly are the most likely to experience a drug-induced illness.[5] There is no doubt that multiple drug use is more frequent with the elderly and accounts for increased morbidity and mortality. Based on the magnitude of drug use, it is not surprising that one sixth of all hospital admissions of patients over age 70 years are attributed to adverse drug reactions.[5] Over 15 years ago, Wynne and Heller reported that one in five patients entering the geriatric units of general hospitals displayed a drug-related problem.[22] There is every reason to assume that these patterns have not been reversed.

In general, older women report higher use of medications, including the consumption of psychoactive drugs.[23] Psychoactive medications, if misused or combined with other substances such as alcohol, can produce serious consequences for anyone, but particularly for the older person. Some psychoactive drugs cause paradoxical reactions in the older person. For example, Petersen and Thomas found 80.9%

of acute drug reactions among the elderly involved misuse of a psychoactive prescription drug.[23] Some hypnotics produce reactions of excitement, confusion, and incontinence, along with increased daytime drowsiness and sedation.[24] Antianxiety agents and hypnotics containing benzodiazopines can be particularly troublesome, as they are eliminated more slowly in the elderly, potentially resulting in increased drowsiness, confusion, disorientation, disinhibition, agitation, and belligerence. Many antidepressant drugs may also precipitate hypotension, cardiac arrhythmias, constipation, urinary retention, dryness of the mouth, and glaucoma.[25]

Approximately one third of all expenditures for medications by the elderly is for OTC drug products.[26] Evidence from one community study indicates that 69% of persons over the age of 60 years use OTC drug products regularly.[27] Simonson observed that an overwhelming majority of elderly take OTC medications at least occasionally, with some using as many as ten different medications.[28] This high consumption rate can be attributed, to some extent, to the increased incidence of health problems such as constipation, arthritis, and insomnia with advancing age.

The magnitude of all types of drug use is extensive. A Michigan study looking at drug-use patterns of healthy elderly found 71% used prescription drugs, 54% used OTC drugs, and 20% used home remedies. In addition, approximately 50% of the sample indicated they used OTC analgesics, laxatives, and antacids four to five times a week.[29] In a study of older Washington, DC residents, Guttmann found 62% reported prescription drug use, and 69% were taking OTC drugs daily.[27] Likewise, Chien and associates reported high usage rates for prescription drugs, OTC drugs, or both.[30] Ostrom et al studied elderly residents living independently in two urban high-rise apartments and found 75% used prescription drugs and 82% used OTC drugs regularly.[31] They also discovered that 51% stored noncurrent prescription drugs for later use. In an early study by Schwartz et al, 30% of the patients were found to be taking prescription drugs prescribed for someone else.[32]

One reason cited for the elderly using a large number of OTC drugs is that these drugs are less expensive and more accessible than prescription medications. Therefore, an older person with an arthritic condition living on a limited income may choose to self-medicate with OTC products rather than incur the expense and inconvenience of a professional consultation.[33] In 1987, approximately 12% of the noninstitutionalized elderly in the United States lived below the poverty level. For elderly women, the poverty rate is 25%.

Stress, Support, and Well-Being as Components of Drug-Taking Behavior

Aside from age-related physiological and pathological changes that produce increased symptomatology and a resulting dependency on drugs as a treatment modality, there exists a whole spectrum of psychosocial factors to be considered. To date, there has been relatively little research explicating the role these factors may play in the extent of drug dependency in the elderly. Researchers and professionals in social gerontology, however, have traditionally investigated the quality of life, lifespan developmental changes, and sociodemographic factors that can be related to maladjustment. These dimensions, along with such variables as stress, self-esteem, social support, locus of control, and mastery, need to be considered in the context of drug-taking behavior.

The deleterious effects of stress and the lack of supportive personal relationships have been found to be important factors that affect the morale and adjustment of older persons. In essence, maintaining one's sense of well-being throughout the lifespan is contingent upon supportive personal resources. In the absence of such resources, the ability to exercise control over one's social and physical world is diminished and negative effects are more likely. There is no doubt that affirming social feedback is necessary for older persons to maintain a sense of mastery over their lives.[35] Thus, there appears to be a relationship between social resources and support and one's psychological or emotional state leading to maladaptive behaviors.[35,36]

The difficulty with evaluating the extent of social support is that it can be analyzed in either quantitative or qualitative terms. It can be seen in terms of the networks of available individuals whom one can call upon for goods and services. Alternatively, support can be perceived as emotional bolstering and intimate bonding which provides a sense of belonging and membership.[37] Depending on the perspective taken, the evaluation of support can be dramatically different. In general, however, the less extensive the social resources upon which individuals can lean during times of crises or stress, the more likely they are to manifest various forms of maladaptive behavior.

Another factor frequently thought to mediate the perception of stress is locus of control. Individuals who feel that control of events resides within themselves seem to cope better in stressful situations than do individuals who view events as generally beyond or outside their control.[38] The exact nature of the relationship is not as clear as many assume, however. According to Lefcourt,[39] Phares,[40] and others, the relationship may not be linear. It is possible that individuals who fall in one or the other extreme may have more difficulty dealing with stress than those who lie in the middle range.

Other psychosocial parameters that may affect drug misuse and dependency in the elderly are loneliness and self-esteem. Russell has demonstrated correlations between individuals who score low on the revised UCLA Loneliness Scale as being satisfied with their interpersonal contacts versus those who score high and report frequent feelings of loneliness.[41] With the dramatic shift in living arrangements, more older people are living alone than ever before. In 1900, in the US, over one third of single elderly lived with others, but in 1975, only 7% resided with children or others.[42] Due to increased life-expectancy of females, women living alone outnumber men by a considerable margin. The obvious question is whether their living alone constitutes loneliness. Further, if they are lonely, does this fact in any way affect their drug-taking behavior?

Rosenberg,[43] Wylie,[44] and Breytspraak and George[42] have, in fact, demonstrated the relevance of low self-esteem as a variable which may be implicated in drug misuse and other deviant behavior. Kaplan and colleagues[45] have also reported self-esteem to be a consistent factor in predicting drug misuse. Individuals with low esteem participate in more deviant drug behaviors than do their more assured counterparts. An appropriate question to pose is, "Are elderly persons with low esteem more likely to engage in inappropriate drug-taking patterns?"

Prevention and Intervention

From the vantage point of prevention and intervention, a wide range of issues remain to be explored. From this cursory overview, it is not difficult to understand the potential risk of an older person developing a drug misuse or dependency problem when they are confronted with significant changes in their lives. It is not yet understood what effect, if any, living arrangements may have on drug-taking behaviors. Institutionalization comprises one dimension of the issue while congregate versus community residence is yet another. Many of these changes, along with illness or death of a significant other, poverty, isolation, and the expected physiological alterations, may promote feelings of depression and a loss of control. In either instance, what is in fact inappropriate drug use may appear to be a viable coping strategy.

Professionals having contact with older persons must be cognizant that drug misuse and dependency are potential problems for all social classes and must be addressed from an anticipatory preventive perspective. For this population, thorough drug histories should be taken during every health-care encounter, with particular attention given to the use of OTC drugs, psychoactive agents, and alcohol. In light of the pressing need to identify and understand predisposing factors that structure one's lifestyle, it is paramount that sociodemographic variables such as economic status, living arrangements, social support, and gender be considered. Also, elements of self-identify such as self-esteem and locus of control need to be included in the assessment.

We have not yet begun to appreciate how social sanctions may enter into the drug-taking behavior of a given age group such as the elderly or how societal reaction may channel differential access, knowledge, attitudes, or subjective views of appropriate behavior. In short, it is not enough to solely address drug behavior, isolated from the constellation of causal factors that play a role. Those interested in prevention and/or intervention must consider also how their personal reactions to, or treatment of, the elderly may facilitate aberrant drug-taking behavior. For example, health-care providers who hasten to prescribe psychoactive medication to older women may be doing so on the basis of their own stereotypes as much as actual medical conditions.

Reactions to alcohol use may similarly reflect sex-typed conditioning.[46] There is a need for a better understanding of the role of the health-care provider's expectations in shaping treatment regimens. For example, in terms of educational intervention, some researchers have found the elderly are about one half as likely to receive counseling on the use of prescription drugs as their younger counterparts.[47]

Regardless of unexplored issues, immediate and cost-effective intervention and prevention can begin if professionals incorporate the following suggestions into their practice: alert older persons and their families about the potential danger associated with excessive drug and alcohol use; confront them when there is an existing problem; provide a supportive milieu for drug treatment and education programs; promote group or peer counseling programs to effectively deal with psychosocial changes of aging; modify prescription regimens for this age group; and explore client's psychosocial status during each encounter.

References

1. Mule J: *Behavior in Excess*. New York, The Free Press, 1981.

2. Waldo DR, Levit KR, Lazenby H: National health expenditures 1985. *Health Care Financing Review* 1986; 8(1):1-21.

3. Lamy P: Geriatric drug therapy. *Am Fam Physician* 1986; 36(6):118-124.

4. Hecht A: Medicine and the elderly. *FDA Consumer* 1983; Sept:20-21.

5. Problems with prescription drugs highest among the elderly. *Am Fam Physician* 1983; 28(6):236.

6. Glantz M: Predictions of elderly drug abuse, in Peterson D, Whittington F (eds): *Drugs, Alcohol and Aging* Dubuque, IA, Kendall Hunt Publishing Co, 1982, pp 117-126.

7. Braude MC: Drugs and drug interactions in the elderly woman, in Ray BA, Braude MC (eds): *Women and Drugs: A New Era for Research*. Washington, DC, National Institute of Drug Abuse, 1986.

8. Barone JA, Holland M: Drug use and abuse in the elderly. *US Pharmacist* 1987; May:82-96.

9. Juergens J, Smith M, Sharpe T: Determinants of OTC drug use in elderly. *Journal of Geriatric Drug Therapy* 1986; 1(1):31-46.

10. Atkinson RM (ed): *Alcohol and Drug Abase in Old Age*. Washington, DC, American Psychiatric Press, Inc, 1984.

11. Brotman HB: *Data from Summary Table 13 Based on Middle Series Projections, 1982-2050*. Washington, DC, US Census Bureau, 1982.

12. Senate US Printing Office: *How Older Americans Live: An Analysis of Census Data by Special Committee on Aging*, DHHS Publication No 99-9. Washington, DC, US Government Printing Office, 1985.

13. Coons SJ, Hendricks J, Sheahan SL: Self-medication with nonprescription drugs. *Generations* 1988; 12(4):22-26.

14. Stephens CJ: Alcohol consumption and casualties: Drinking in the event. *Drug Alcohol Depend* 1987; 20(20):115-127.

15. Schuckit M: Geriatric alcoholism and drug abuse. *Gerontologist* 1977; 17(2):168-174.

16. Eckardt MJ: Consequences of alcohol and other drug use in the aged, in Behnke JA, Finch CE, Moment GD (eds): *The Biology of Aging*. New York, Plenum Press, 1978, pp 191-204.

17. Pascarelli E, Fisher W: Drug dependence in the elderly. *International Journal Aging and Human Development* 1974; 5(4):347-356.

18. Gomberg ES: Drinking and problem drinking among the elderly, in Glantz M, Petersen D, Whittington F (eds): *Drugs and the Elderly Adult* Government Printing Office, Washington, DC, Research Issues, 32, DHHS No (Adm) 83-1269, 159-163, 1980.

19. Mishara BL, Kastenbaum R: *Alcohol and Old Age*. New York, Grune & Stratton, 1980.

20. Straus R: Risk factors in geriatric drug use: Bio-behavioral issues, in Moore S, Teal F (eds): *Geriatric Drug Use: Clinical and Social Perspectives*. New York, Pergamon Press, 1985.

21. Carruthers SG: Clinical pharmacology of aging, in Cape RDT, Coe RM, Rossman I (eds): *Fundamentals of Geriatric Medicine*. New York, Raven Press, 1983.

22. Wynne RD, Heller F: Drug overuse among the elderly: A growing problem. *Perspective on Aging* 1973; 11:15-18.

23. Petersen D, Thomas C: Acute drug reactions among the elderly. *J Gerontol* 1975; 30(5):552-556.

24. Castleden CM, Houston A, George CF: Are hypnotics helpful or harmful to elderly patients? *Journal of Drug Issues* 1979; 9(1):55-61.

25. Salzman C, Bessel VK: Psychotropic drug prescriptions for elderly patients in a general hospital. *J Am Geriatr Soc* 1980; 28(1):18-20.

26. Gibson RM, Waldo DR: National health expenditures. *Health Care Financing Review* 1980; 3:1-54.

27. Guttmann D: Patterns of legal drug use by older Americans. *Addictive Diseases: An International Journal* 1978; 3(3):337-356.

28. Simonson W: *Medications and the Elderly: A Guide for Promoting Proper Use*. Rockville, MD, Aspen, 1984.

29. Seniors and Substance Abuse Task Force: *Substance Abuse Among Michigan Senior Citizens: Current Issues and Future Decisions*. Lansing, Ml, Michigan Offices of Services for the Aging, 1978.

30. Chien C, Townsend E, Townsend A: Substance use and abuse among the community elderly: The medical aspect. *Addictive Diseases: An International Journal* 1978; 3(3):357-372.

31. Ostrom J, Hammarlund R, Christensen D, et al: Medication usage in an elderly population. *Medical Care* 1985; 23(2):157-164.

32. Schwartz D, Wang M, Zietz L: Medication errors made by chronically ill patients. *Am J Public Health* 1962; 52(12):2019-2029.

33. Kofoed LL: OTC drug overuse in the elderly: What to watch for. *Geriatrics* 1985; 40:55-60.

34. Social Security Administration: Social Security Bulletin, Annual Statistical Supplement, 1988. Government Printing Office, Washington, DC, FFA Publication #13-11700:115.

35. Billings AG, Moos RH: Psychosocial stressors, coping and depression, in Beckmam EE, Lebee WR (eds): *Handbook of Depression*. Homewood, IL, Dorsey Press, 1985.

36. Lin N, Dean A, Ensel WM (eds): *Social Support, Life Events and Depression*. New York, Academic Press, 1986.

37. Antonucci TC: Personal characteristics, social support, and social behavior, in Binstock RH, Shanas E (eds): *Handbook of Aging and the Social Sciences* New York, Van Nostrand Reinhold Co, 1985, pp 94-128.

38. Rotter JB: Generalized expectancies for internal versus external control of reinforcement. *Psychological Monographs: General and Applied* 1966; 80:1-28.

39. Lefcourt H: *Locus of Control: Current Trends in Theory and Research*. New York, John Wiley, 1976.

40. Phares E: *Locus of Control in Personality*. Morristown, NJ, General Learning Press, 1976.

41. Russell D: The measurement of loneliness, in Peplau LA, Perlman D (eds): *Loneliness: A Sourcebook of Current Research*. New York, Wiley Interscience, 1982.

42. Breytspraak LM, George LK: Self-concept and self-esteem, in Mangen DJ, Peterson WA (eds): *Research Instruments in Social Gerontology: Clinical and Social Psychology*. Minneapolis, University of Minnesota Press, 1982, vol 1.

43. Rosenberg M: *Conceiving the Self*. New York, Basic Books, 1979.

44. Wylie R: *The Self-Concept*. Lincoln, NE, University of Nebraska Press, 1974.

45. Kaplan HB, Johnson RJ, Bailey CA: Self-rejection and the explanation of deviance: Refinement and elaboration of a latent structure. *Social Psychology Quarterly* 1986; 49(2):110-128.

46. Gomberg ES: Historical and political perspectives of women and drug use. *Journal Social Issues* 1982; 38:9-23.

47. Morris LA, Grossman R, Bardall G, et al: A survey of patient sources of prescription drug information. *Am J Public Health* 1984; 74:1161-1162.

—by Sharon L. Sheahan, MSN, CFNP;
Jon Hendricks, PhD;
and Stephen Joel Coons, PhD

Sharon L. Sheahan is Associate Professor, College of Nursing, University of Kentucky, Lexington; Jon Hendricks is Chairman, Department of Sociology, Oregon State University, Corvallis; Stephen Joel Coons is Assistant Professor, College of Pharmacy, University of Kentucky, Lexington.

Chapter 32

Anabolic Steroids:
A Threat to Body and Mind

The Price of Perfection

Shock waves went through the sports world when Canadian track superstar Ben Johnson was denied his gold medal at the 1988 Olympics after tests showed he had taken anabolic steroids. The incident called international attention to the use of anabolic steroids among world-class athletes to gain competitive advantage.

Still, athletes and nonathletes alike persist in taking them. Teenagers are taking anabolic steroids not just to excel in sports but to enhance their self-images by perfecting their physiques. There are even reports of male adults in physically demanding professions like law enforcement using them to appear tougher and more formidable.

As the drug grows in popularity so does awareness of the serious side effects it may cause. One of the most alarming is the threat of AIDS. HIV—human immunodeficiency virus—can be transmitted if shared needles are used to inject the drug.

But potential harm to physical and psychological health is only one aspect of this troubling trend.

A Question of Values

The nonmedical use of anabolic steroids raises more ethical and moral issues. Engaging in steroids use is illegal. Users are likely to find

DHHS Pub. No. (ADM) 91-1810.

291

themselves acquiring these drugs through illicit—and expensive—channels. The heavy demand for anabolic steroids has given rise to a black market, with sales estimated at as much as $400 million a year. Moreover, supplies, which are often illegally manufactured and do not meet established standards, may be contaminated.

Athletes who use these drugs are cheating. They gain an unfair advantage over opponents and violate the ban on steroids imposed by most major sports organizations.

Another Addictive Substance?

Can anabolic steroids be added to the list of addictive drugs? Early signs point to addictive patterns among users. At the very least, users demonstrate an unwillingness to give up anabolic steroids even in the face of possibly dire consequences to their health.

Stopping the Trend

As the health risks of anabolic steroids become more apparent, efforts to curtail their use—through education, legislation, and medical practices—are intensifying.

For those already hooked, kicking the steroids habit is the best chance to escape devastating side effects. For potential users, the solution, of course, is to never take the drug at all. There are other ways to be a winner athletically and socially without harming health and without cheating.

Using Anabolic Steroids

Valid Medical Uses

Steroids are drugs derived from hormones. Anabolic steroids comprise one group of these hormonal drugs. In certain cases, some may have therapeutic value.

The U.S. Food and Drug Administration has approved the use of selected anabolic steroids for treating specific types of anemia, some breast cancers, osteoporosis, endometriosis, and hereditary angioedema, a rare disease involving the swelling of some parts of the body.

Some medical specialists believe that anabolic steroids can improve the appetite and improve healing after surgery, but the FDA has withdrawn approval for such uses since the claims are vague and largely unsubstantiated.

What Are Anabolic Steroids?

Anabolic steroids—or more precisely, anabolic/androgenic steroids—belong to a group known as ergogenic, or so-called "performance-enhancing," drugs. They are synthetic derivatives of testosterone, a natural male hormone.

"Anabolic" means growing or building. "Androgenic" means "masculinizing" or generating male sexual characteristics.

Most healthy males produce between 2 and 10 milligrams of testosterone a day. (Females do produce some testosterone, but in trace amounts.) The hormone's anabolic effects help the body retain dietary protein, thus aiding growth of muscles, bones, and skin.

The androgenic characteristics of testosterone are associated with masculinity. They foster the maturing of the male reproductive system in puberty, the growth of body hair and the deepening of the voice. They can affect aggressiveness and sex drive.

Do They Really Work?

Anabolic steroids are designed to mimic the bodybuilding traits of testosterone while minimizing its "masculinizing" effects. There are several types, with various combinations of anabolic and androgenic properties. The International Olympics Committee to date has placed 17 anabolic steroids and related compounds on its banned list.

Athletes who have used anabolic steroids—as well as some coaches, trainers, and physicians—do report significant increases in lean muscle mass, strength, and endurance. But no studies show that the substances enhance performance.

Anabolic steroids do not improve agility, skill or cardiovascular capacity. Some athletes insist that these substances aid in recovery from injuries, but no hard data exists to support the claim.

Sports Organizations Outlawing Anabolic Steroids

The International Olympics Committee banned steroids use by all athletes in its member associations in 1975. Since then most major amateur and professional organizations have put the drugs on their list of banned substances. They include:

- National Football League
- National Collegiate Athletic Association
- International Amateur Athletic Federation
- International Federation of Body Builders

A Brief History

Winning Through Doping

The drive to compete—and to win—is as old as humankind. Throughout history, athletes have sought foods and potions to transform their bodies into powerful, well-tuned machines.

Greek wrestlers ate huge quantities of meat to build muscle, and Norse warriors—the Berserkers—ate hallucinogenic mushrooms to gear up for battle.

The first competitive athletes believed to be charged with "doping"—taking drugs and other nonfood substances to improve performance—were swimmers in Amsterdam in the 1860s. Doping, with anything from strychnine and caffeine to cocaine and heroin, spread to other sports over the next several decades.

Enter Anabolic Steroids

The use of anabolic steroids by athletes is relatively new. Testosterone was first synthesized in the 1930s and was introduced into the sporting arena in the 1940s and 1950s When the Russian weightlifting team—thanks, in part, to synthetic testosterone—walked off with a pile of medals at the 1952 Olympics, an American physician determined that U.S. competitors should have the same advantage.

By 1958 a U.S. pharmaceutical firm had developed anabolic steroids. Although the physician soon realized the drug had unwanted side effects, it was too late to halt its spread into the sports world.

Early users were mainly bodybuilders, weightlifters, football players, and discus, shot put, or javelin throwers—competitors who relied heavily on bulk and strength.

During the 1970s demand grew as athletes in other sports sought the competitive edge that anabolic steroids seemed to provide.

By the 1980s, as nonathletes also discovered the body-enhancing properties of steroids, a black market began to flourish for the illegal production and sale of the drugs for nonmedical purposes.

The Position of the Medical Community

The American Medical Association condemns the use of anabolic steroids by athletes. Other medical associations have joined with the AMA in deploring steroids abuse, including the:

- American Academy of Pediatrics
- American College of Sports Medicine
- American Osteopathic Academy of Sports Medicine

Abusing Anabolic Steroids

Who Takes Them—And Why?

Today it is not only the college football player or the professional weightlifter or the marathon runner who may use anabolic steroids.

It may be an 18-year-old who loathes his skinny body. Or a 15-year-old in a hurry to reach maturity.

Or a policeman who wants more muscle power on the job.

And the use of anabolic steroids is not confined to males. Professional and amateur female athletes—track and field competitors, swimmers, bodybuilders—feel the pressure to triumph, too.

Increasing numbers of adolescents are turning to steroids for cosmetic reasons. In a 1986 survey, as many as 45 percent of 200 high school users cited appearance as a primary reason for taking steroids.

Young people who use steroids defy easy categorizing. They come from cities and rural areas, from poor families and wealthy ones. They are of all races and nationalities. The common link among them is the desire to look, perform and feel better—at almost any cost. Users—and especially the young—are apt to ignore or deny warnings about health risks. If they see friends growing taller and stronger on steroids, they want the same benefits. They want to believe in the power of the drug.

How Prevalent Is Use?

Surveys and anecdotal evidence indicate that the rate of nonmedical steroids use may be increasing.

In 1990, a NIDA survey of high school seniors showed that nearly 3 percent—5 percent of males and 0.5 percent of females—reported using steroids at some time in their lives.

The same survey showed that steroids were used within the last year by nearly as many students as crack cocaine and by more students than the hallucinogenic drug PCP.

Use among college females appears to have increased somewhat. A study of 11 universities in 1984 found that steroids users were reported in only one women's sport—swimming—at a rate of 1 percent.

295

In a follow-up survey in 1988, 1 percent of women in track and field and basketball also reported taking steroids.

Use among adult or professional athletes has not been well documented, although anecdotal evidence clearly supports the suggestion that anabolic steroids have enjoyed popularity among football players, weightlifters, wrestlers, and track and field competitors, among others.

A Glossary of Terms

Drug and steroids use in sports has spawned a glossary of its own:

- *Blending*—Mixing different drugs.
- *Bulking up*—Increasing muscle mass through steroids.
- *Cycling*—Taking multiple doses of steroids over a specified period of time, stopping for a time and starting again.
- *Doping*—Using drugs and other nonfood substances to improve athletic performance and prowess.
- *Ergogenic drugs*—Performance-enhancing substances.
- *Megadosing*—Taking massive amounts of steroids, by injection or pill.
- *Plateauing*—When a drug becomes ineffective at a certain level.
- *Roid rages*—Uncontrolled outbursts of anger, frustration or combativeness that may result from using anabolic steroids.
- *Shotgunning*—Taking steroids on a hit-or-miss basis.
- *Stacking*—Using a combination of anabolic steroids, often in combination with other drugs.
- *Tapering*—Slowly decreasing steroids intake.

Megadosing

Anabolic steroids are usually taken in pill form. Some that cannot be absorbed orally are taken by injection. The normal prescribed daily dose for medical purposes usually averages between 1 and 5 milligrams.

Some athletes, on the other hand, may take up to hundreds of milligrams a day, far exceeding medically recommended dosages. Operating on the erroneous more-is-better theory, some athletes indulge in a practice known as "stacking." They take many types of steroids, sometimes in combination with other drugs such as stimulants, depressants, pain killers, anti-inflammatories, and other hormones.

Many users "cycle," taking the drugs for 6 to 12 weeks or more, stopping for several weeks and then starting another cycle. They may do this in the belief that by scheduling their steroids intake, they can manipulate test results and escape detection. It is not uncommon for athletes to cycle over a period of months or even years.

Health Hazards

Raising a Red Flag

Although controlled studies on the long-term outcome of megadosing with anabolic steroids have not been conducted, extensive research on prescribed doses for medical use has documented the potential side effects of the drug, even when taken in small doses. Moreover, reports by athletes, and observations of attending physicians, parents, and coaches do offer substantial evidence of dangerous side effects.

Some effects, such as rapid weight gain, are easy to see. Some take place internally and may not be evident until it is too late. Some are irreversible.

The Dangers

Dangers to Men. Males who take large doses of anabolic steroids typically experience changes in sexual characteristics. Although derived from a male sex hormone, the drug can trigger a mechanism in the body that can actually shut down the healthy functioning of the male reproductive system. Some possible side effects:

- Shrinking of the testicles
- Reduced sperm count
- Impotence
- Baldness
- Difficulty or pain in urinating
- Development of breasts
- Enlarged prostate

Dangers to Women. Females may experience "masculinization" as well as other problems:

- Growth of facial hair
- Changes in or cessation of the menstrual cycle

297

- Enlargement of the clitoris
- Deepened voice
- Breast reduction

Dangers to Both Sexes. For both males and females, continued use of anabolic steroids may lead to health conditions ranging from merely irritating to life-threatening. Some effects are:

- Acne
- Jaundice
- Trembling
- Swelling of feet or ankles
- Bad breath
- Reduction in HDL, the "good" cholesterol
- High blood pressure
- Liver damage and cancers
- Aching joints
- Increased chance of injury to tendons, ligaments, and muscles

Special Dangers to Adolescents

Anabolic steroids can halt growth prematurely in adolescents. Because even small doses can irreversibly affect growth, steroids are rarely prescribed for children and young adults, and only for the severely ill.

The Office of the Inspector General in the U.S. Department of Health and Human Services has gathered anecdotal evidence that preteens and teens taking steroids may be at risk for developing a dependence on the drugs and on other substances as well.

The Threat of AIDS

People sometimes take injections of anabolic steroids to augment oral dosages, using large-gauge, reusable needles normally obtained through the black market. If needles are shared, users run the risk of transmitting or contracting the HIV infection that can lead to AIDS.

The Psychological Effects

Scientists are just beginning to investigate the impact of anabolic steroids on the mind and behavior. Many athletes report "feeling good" about themselves while on a steroids regimen. The downside, according to Harvard researchers, is wide mood swings ranging from periods of violent, even homicidal, episodes known as "roid rages" to bouts of depression when the drugs are stopped.

The Harvard study also noted that anabolic steroids users may suffer from paranoid jealousy, extreme irritability, delusions, and impaired judgment stemming from feelings of invincibility.

Are Anabolic Steroids Addictive?

Evidence that megadoses of anabolic steroids can affect the brain and produce mental changes in users poses serious questions about possible addiction to the drugs.

While investigations continue, researchers at Yale University have found that long-term steroids users do experience many of the characteristics of classic addiction: cravings, difficulty in ceasing steroids use and withdrawal symptoms.

Pennsylvania State University researchers studied a group of high school seniors who had developed a psychological, if not physical, dependence on anabolic steroids. Adolescent users exhibit a prime trait of addicts—denial. They tend to overlook or simply ignore the physical dangers and moral implications of taking illegal substances.

Certain delusional behavior that is characteristic of addiction can occur. Some athletes who "bulk up" on anabolic steroids are unaware of body changes that are obvious to others, experiencing what is sometimes called reverse anorexia.

Supply and Demand: The Black Market

Many users maintain their habit with anabolic steroids acquired through a highly organized black market handling up to $400 million worth of the drugs a year.

Until recently most underground steroids were legitimately manufactured pharmaceuticals that were diverted to the black market through theft and fraudulent prescriptions. More effective law enforcement coupled with greater demand forced black marketers to seek new sources.

Now black-market anabolic steroids are either made overseas and smuggled into the United States or are produced in clandestine laboratories in this country. These counterfeit drugs may present greater health risks because they are manufactured without controls and thus may be impure, mislabeled, or simply bogus.

Sales are made in gyms, health clubs, on campuses, and through the mail. Users report that suppliers may be drug dealers or they may be trainers, physicians, pharmacists, or friends.

It's not hard for users to buy the drugs or to learn how to use them. Many of them rely on an underground manual, a "bible" on steroids that circulates around the country.

Safe—And Healthy—Alternatives

Anabolic steroids may have a reputation for turning a wimp into a winner or a runt into a hulk, but the truth is that it takes a lot more to be a star athlete.

Athletic prowess depends not only on strength and endurance, but on skill and mental acuity. It also depends on diet, rest, overall mental and physical health, and genes. Athletic excellence can be, and is, achieved by millions without reliance on dangerous drugs.

Fighting Back

Testing

The major national and international sports associations enforce their ban against anabolic steroids by periodic testing. Testing, however, is controversial.

Some observers say the tests are not reliable, and even the International Olympic Committees tests, considered to be the most accurate, have been challenged. Athletes can manipulate results with "masking agents" to prevent detection, or they can take anabolic steroids that have calculable detection periods.

Despite the problems, testing remains an important way of monitoring and controlling the abuse of steroids among athletes. Efforts are underway to make testing more accurate.

Treatment

Treatment programs for steroids abusers are just now being developed as more is learned about the habit.

Medical specialists do find persuasion is an important weapon is getting the user off the drug. They attempt to present medical evidence of the damage anabolic steroids can do to the body. One specialist notes that medical tests, such as those that show a lowered sperm count, can motivate male athletes to cease usage.

300

One health clinic considers the anabolic steroids habit as an addiction and structures treatment around the techniques used in traditional substance abuse programs. It focuses on acute intervention and a long-term follow-up, introducing nonsteroid alternatives that will maintain body fitness as well as self-esteem.

Legislation

Both Federal and State governments have enacted laws and regulations to control anabolic steroids abuse.

In 1988, Congress passed the Anti-Drug Abuse Act, making the distribution or possession of anabolic steroids for nonmedical reasons a Federal offense. Distribution to minors is a prison offense.

In 1990, Congress toughened the laws, passing legislation that classifies anabolic steroids as a controlled substance. The new law also increases penalties for steroids use and trafficking. To halt diversion of anabolic steroids onto the black market, the law imposes strict production and recordkeeping regulations on pharmaceutical firms.

Over 25 states have passed laws and regulations to control steroids abuse, and many others are considering similar legislation.

Education

Prevention is the best solution to halting the growing abuse of anabolic steroids. The time to educate youngsters is before they become users.

Efforts must not stop there, however. Current users, as well as coaches, trainers, parents, and medical practitioners need to know about the hazards of anabolic steroids. The young need to understand that they are not immortal and that the drugs can harm them. An education campaign must also address the problem of covert approval by some members of the medical and athletic communities that encourages steroids use.

The message needs to be backed up by accurate information and spread by responsible, respected individuals.

For Further Information

NIDA Hotline—1-800-662-HELP

Operated by the National Institute on Drug Abuse, this is a confidential information and referral line that directs callers to drug abuse treatment centers in their local community.

301

NCADI—1-800-729-6686

The National Clearinghouse for Alcohol and Drug Information (NCADI) provides information on all drugs, including alcohol. Free materials on drug abuse are also available. If you wish to write NCADI, the address is P.O. Box 2345, Rockville, MD 20852.

Resources

American College of Sports Medicine, "Position Stand on The Use of Anabolic/Androgenic Steroids in Sports," 1984.

American Osteopathic Academy of Sports Medicine, "Policy Statement and Position Paper: Anabolic/ Androgenic Steroids and Substance Abuse in Sport," May 1989.

Buckley, W.E.; Yesalis, C.E.; Vicary J.R.; Streit, A; Katz D.L.; Wright, J.E., "Indications of Psychological Dependence Among Anabolic/Androgenic Steroids Abusers." Adaptation from a paper, "Anabolic steroids Use: Indications of Habituation Among Adolescents," *Journal of Drug Education*, 1989.

Carolan, N.J., "The Treatment of the Anabolic steroids Addict," Unpublished paper, 1991.

Cicero, T.J., and O'Connor, L.H., "Abuse Liability of Anabolic Steroids and Their Possible Role in the Abuse of Alcohol, Morphine and Other Substances," *NIDA Research Monograph 102*, 1990.

Dyment, P.G., and Goldberg, B., Committee on Sports Medicine, "Anabolic Steroids and the Adolescent Athlete," *Pediatrics*, January 1989.

Frankle, M.A., "Anabolic-Androgenic Steroids: A Guide for the Physician," *The Journal of Musculoskeletal Medicine*, November 1989.

Friedl, K.E., "Reappraisal of the Health Risks Associated with the Use of High Doses of Oral and Injectable Androgenic Steroids," *NIDA Research Monograph 102*, 1990.

Hecht, A., "Anabolic Steroids: Pumping Trouble," *FDA Consumer*, September 1984.

International Federation of Bodybuilders, "The Battle Against Steroids Goes On: Position Paper of the I.F.B.B," 1990.

Kashkin, K.B., and Kleber, H.D., "Hooked on Hormones? An Anabolic Steroid Addiction Hypothesis," *Journal of the American Medical Association*, December 1989.

Katz, D.L., and Pope, H.G., "Anabolic/Androgenic Steroid-Induced Mental Status Changes," *NIDA Research Monograph 102*, 1990.

Kennedy, N., "Steroid Studies: Estimated Percentages of Use," Appendix B of the Research Subcommittee of the Interagency Task Force on Anabolic Steroids, National Institute on Drug Abuse, 1990.

Lombardo, J.A., "Anabolic/Androgenic Steroids," *NIDA Research Monograph 102*, 1990.

Miller, R.W., "Athletes and Steroids: Playing a Deadly Game," *FDA Consumer*, November 1987.

National Institute on Drug Abuse, "Anabolic Steroids: Is Bigger Better or Just Big Trouble?," *NIDA Notes*, Spring/Summer 1989.

National Institute on Drug Abuse, "Study of Athletes Shows Aggression and Other Psychiatric Side Effects From Steroid Use," *NIDA Notes*, Spring/Summer 1989.

Norris, J.A., "FDA Warns: Steroids May Be Hazardous to Your Health," *Schools Without Drugs: The Challenge*, U.S. Department of Education, November 1987.

Office of Inspector General, U.S. Department of Health and Human Services, "Adolescents and Steroids: A User Perspective," August 1990.

Office of Inspector General, U.S. Department of Health and Human Services, "Adolescent Steroid Use," 1990.

Stehlin, D., "For Athletes and Dealers, Black Market Steroids Are Risky Business," *FDA Consumer*, 1987.

U.S. Food and Drug Administration, "The Blackmarketing of Anabolic, Ergogenic and Related Prescription Drugs for Athletic Enhancement: An FDA Overview," *FDA Consumer*, 1987.

U.S. General Accounting Office, "Drug Misuse: Anabolic Steroids and Human Growth Hormone," August 1989.

Yesalis, C.E.; Anderson, W.A.; Buckley, W.E.; and Wright, J.E., "Incidence of Non-Medical Use of Anabolic Steroids," *NIDA Research Monograph 102*, 1990.

Chapter 33

Steriod Substitutes

German sprinters Katrin Krabbe and Grit Breuer never made it to the 1992 Summer Olympics in Barcelona, Spain.

United States hammer thrower Jud Logan and shot putter Bonnie Dasse went but were sent home early.

Also sent home from the Olympics were Wu Dan, a Chinese women's volleyball player; Madina Biktagirova, a Unified Team marathoner; and Andrew Davies and Andrew Saxton, both British weight lifters.

All tested positive for banned drugs, but, surprisingly to some fans, none of the drugs were anabolic steroids.

Krabbe, Breuer, Logan, Dasse, Davies, and Saxton tested positive for clenbuterol, a veterinary drug. Dan tested positive for strychnine, a poison that is a stimulant in small doses; and Biktagirova tested positive for norephedrine, a mild stimulant. Though the three drugs are not steroids, all are abused in sports because athletes believe they enhance performance.

From athletes in international competition to college and high school athletes to the teenager who simply wants to "bulk up," people of all ages and abilities have found alternatives to replace anabolic steroids.

Regulated by the Drug Enforcement Administration, anabolic steroids were placed in the Controlled Substances Act's Schedule III (which includes some narcotic drugs, stimulants and depressants) by the Anabolic Steroids Act of 1990. Unlawful distribution and possession

"No-Win Situation for Athletes," *FDA Consumer*, December 1992.

with the intent to distribute anabolic steroids is a federal crime, punishable by up to five years in prison.

Since the law was enacted, many athletes have avoided anabolic steroids because of the penalties associated with their abuse, says Donald Leggett, a compliance officer in the Food and Drug Administration's Center for Drug Evaluation and Research. "They have looked at other chemicals that perform in a similar fashion but are not technically regulated as or called anabolic steroids."

Those alternatives include prescription, veterinary, investigational, and unapproved drugs, and dietary supplements.

Dietary supplements are regulated as foods. No data has been submitted to FDA to prove bodybuilding claims for these substances, and the short- and long-term effects of their use are unknown.

"Many alternatives are labeled as 'dietary supplements' even though they make anabolic and other athletic enhancement claims. Such attempts to market directly to the public may represent a circumvention of the safety and efficacy provisions required of drugs. Thus, the short- and long-term effects of their use are generally unknown," Leggett says.

When supplement manufacturers make bodybuilding and drug-type claims, FDA can, and often does, issue warning letters to the manufacturer or prosecute for consumer fraud. FDA's Center for Drug Evaluation and Research recently won several court cases involving consumer fraud by supplement manufacturers, Leggett says.

The consumer is defrauded by believing these supplements will build muscles or promote testosterone production, when in fact they do no such thing, he says.

In a study, published in the Aug. 26, 1992, *Journal of the American Medical Association*, of bodybuilding magazine advertisements, Rossanne M. Philen, M.D., and colleagues, report that they counted 89 supplement brands, 311 products, and 235 ingredients, most of which were unspecified amino acids. More than 22 percent of the products had no ingredients listed in their advertisements.

The study also found that many steroid-type ingredients, called sterols, were being advertised. With the exception of ecdysterone, the sterols were all plant derivatives. Ecdysterone is an insect hormone with no known use in humans.

The abuse of many of these ingredients, as well as prescription, veterinary, investigational, and unapproved drugs, concerns FDA.

Agency investigators have collected more than 3,000 drug samples from the black market over a 10-year period, according to Leggett.

Many of those samples, he says, were not steroids but other, potentially more dangerous, prescription drugs.

Some steroid alternatives popular among athletes include the investigational drugs clenbuterol and gamma hydroxybutyric acid, or GHB, and approved prescription drugs such as human growth hormone and erythropoietin, better known as EPO.

Clenbuterol

Clenbuterol is used in several European countries by animal trainers to build muscle mass and strength in exhibition livestock. It has never been approved for any use in the United States.

Athletes use clenbuterol because they think it has the same mass and strength-building capability in people as it does in animals.

But clenbuterol also has serious, immediate side effects in humans. In Spain, between March and July 1990, 135 people became ill after eating beef liver that contained clenbuterol residues. Their symptoms included fast heart rate, muscle tremors, headache, dizziness, nausea, fever, and chills. Symptoms appeared from 30 minutes to six hours after they ate the liver and lasted for nearly two days.

Like most other steroid alternatives, the long-term effects of clenbuterol are not fully known. But, Leggett says, some serious cardiovascular complications may result from their use.

In many instances, veterinary drugs are used simply because they are easier than human drugs to obtain, Leggett says. "Historically, there are places in this country, particularly in rural areas, where just about anyone could walk in and purchase a veterinary equivalent of a [human] drug that would require a doctor's prescription."

Gamma Hydroxybutyric Acid

Gamma hydroxybutyric acid, better known as GHB, is another steroid alternative used widely by teenagers and athletes of all abilities.

GHB is an investigational new drug that powerfully and rapidly induces sleep and depresses the central nervous system in animals and humans, according to Leggett.

The drug has been illegally marketed as a steroid alternative both openly and "in the back room" in gyms, spas, and health food stores and advertised in bodybuilding magazines. Promoters claim it stimulates production of human growth hormone and thus produces muscle mass and weight loss. It has also been promoted as a sleep aid and touted as a street drug.

But GHB is extremely dangerous.

A Duluth, Ga., teenager, getting ready for his high school prom on May 11, 1990, drank a concoction of water and Somatomax PM, a powdery substance containing GHB his friend had bought at a health food store. Instead of getting the "high" he had expected, he was in a coma 20 minutes after taking the drink. Fortunately, his parents soon found him, and with emergency treatment he recovered.

There were 80 hospitalizations from GHB use reported through November 1990, according to a national Centers for Disease Control study published in the Nov. 30, 1990, issue of *Morbidity and Mortality Weekly Report*.

Patients reported that within 15 to 60 minutes of taking one-half to three teaspoons of GHB, they developed symptoms such as vomiting, drowsiness, dizziness, tremors, seizure-like movements, unconsciousness, slowed heartbeat, lowered blood pressure, breathing difficulty, and breathing cessation. Patients recovered, usually with emergency room care, in 2 to 96 hours. There have been no reported deaths.

Human Growth Hormone

Human growth hormone, or HGH, is another popular steroid alternative. Produced naturally by the human body, HGH's only approved medical use is to treat pituitary dwarfism, but it is under investigation to treat other disorders.

Human growth hormone, manufactured using recombinant DNA technology, is identical to the natural hormone. Some athletes believe that HGH promotes muscle growth and muscle strength although researchers have not confirmed these claims.

Lyle Alzado, a former Los Angeles Raiders defensive lineman, said in a July 4, 1991, *New York Times* article that human growth hormone has become the drug of choice for today's athlete, primarily because it is undetectable in drug tests. Alzado died May 14, 1992, from a rare form of brain cancer, central nervous system lymphoma, which he attributed to his prolonged use of steroids and HGH.

Too much human growth hormone, produced by a hyperactive pituitary gland or a tumor, is the cause of acromegaly, a condition characterized by excessive growth of the bones of the hands, feet and face. Acromegaly is ultimately fatal because of resulting heart disease and other metabolic problems.

Erythropoietin

Erythropoietin, or EPO, is another steroid alternative used in the international sports community although it has seen limited abuse in the United States.

EPO, approved for treating anemias associated with chronic renal failure and zidovudine (AZT) therapy in HIV-infected patients, stimulates bone marrow to produce red blood cells. The hormone appeals to athletes because they tire less easily when taking it and because it is undetectable by tests presently used.

"It [EPO] increases the red blood cell count, and therefore the athlete is able to absorb more oxygen and increase stamina—the oxygen-carrying capacity of the blood system is just unbelievable," Leggett says.

But EPO use is not without risk. As the body's red blood cell count rises and the blood thickens, blood clots, heart attack, or stroke could result.

Abuse of EPO is especially risky among marathoners and long-distance bicyclists. As these athletes compete, Leggett explains, they lose body fluids, including blood fluids. Reducing blood fluids concentrates the already abnormally high red blood cell count, which can lead to polycythemia, an abnormal increase in circulating red blood cells.

"EPO can turn their blood to the consistency of Jell-O," he says.

Severe Penalties

Here are some potential health effects of drugs and other substances—ranging from the mildest to the most severe—used as alternatives to anabolic steroids.

- greasy skin
- headache
- severe acne
- premature balding
- bloating associated with water retention
- dizziness
- chills
- drowsiness
- nausea
- vomiting
- muscle tremors

- fever
- fast heart rate
- slowed heart rate
- bloody diarrhea
- seizure-like movements
- lowered blood pressure
- breathing difficulty
- breathing cessation
- blood clots
- cardiovascular problems
- liver disease
- cancer
- heart attack
- stroke
- death

Deadly Potential

FDA is particularly concerned with athletes' abuse of prescription drugs because they usually take the drugs without a physician's supervision and in higher doses than recommended for their limited medical uses.

"We consider these things to have the potential for hazard when they're not monitored or taken in accordance with the supervision of a licensed practitioner," Leggett says.

"Many of these people take way above and beyond the directions for use simply because they feel 'the more the better.' That was true of anabolic steroids, too. The people who are taking these drugs are essentially saying, 'If one teaspoon is recommended, I'm going to take five and grow five times as fast.'"

With that philosophy, the potential for an overdose is very high—and so is the potential for death.

FDA is also concerned about the prescription, veterinary, investigational, and unapproved drugs used as steroid alternatives primarily because little is known of the short- and long-term effects these drugs may have on humans, especially when taken in higher-than-recommended doses or in combination with other drugs.

Comparing anabolic steroids to those steroid alternatives, Leggett says, "We approved all of these anabolic steroids for domestic use in treating diseases like anemias, osteoporosis, and certain cancers. We know what to expect from their label dosage and overdoses.

310

"We have no idea what a normal dosage or overdose is for many of the steroid alternatives or what might be their effect. This is because we've never seen any clinical studies reflecting their use in humans. So, we're completely without a baseline there."

Some short term reactions from using steroid alternatives are similar to those associated with anabolic steroid abuse. These reactions include: bloody diarrhea, nausea, vomiting, severe acne, premature balding, bloating associated with water retention, and greasy skin.

"Those are all soft effects, which may or may not be very serious," Leggett says. "But if the preliminary effects from using steroid alternatives are similar to those associated with anabolic steroid abuse, then there is the potential for some of the long-term effects, too. Effects long-term steroid abusers experience include cardiovascular problems, liver disease, certain cancers."

Clenbuterol, gamma hydroxybutyric acid, human growth hormone, and erythropoietin, all banned in international competition, are some of the more popular steroid alternatives athletes are now abusing. But, Leggett says, this list is likely to grow as athletes experiment with different and new chemicals.

As athletes strive for bigger, more muscular bodies through chemicals, Leggett, expecting the worst, says, "I'm sure they'll come up with something someday that's even more disastrous than the few [drugs] we've seen in recent years."

—by Kevin L. Ropp

Kevin L. Ropp is a staff writer for *FDA Consumer*.

Chapter 34

Cocaine

What Is Cocaine?

Cocaine is one of the most powerfully addictive drugs of abuse. Most clinicians estimate that approximately 10 percent of the people who begin to use the drug "recreationally" will go on to serious, heavy use. Once having tried cocaine, an individual cannot predict or control the extent to which he or she will continue to use the drug.

Cocaine is a powerful and fast-acting central nervous system stimulant or "upper" that comes from the processed leaves of the coca plant which is native to South America. Users snort cocaine (inhale it through the nose), inject it into their veins, or smoke it to obtain an intense "high" or euphoria.

Cocaine is not a new drug. Over a hundred years ago it was extremely popular in the United States and was used in a variety of products, including patent medicines (Coca-Cola was one of the best known), tonics, ointments and throat lozenges. By 1914, fears about the drug's power and concern about the number of people who became dependent on cocaine, or suffered other toxic consequences, led most states and the federal government to prohibit or restrict its use.

This chapter contains text from "Cocaine and Crack—It's Your Business: Drug Awareness," provided by the Drug Enforcement Administration and produced by the American Council for Drug Education, nd; and National Institute on Drug Abuse *Capsules* C-86-4, May 1986, and C-82-2 revised September 1993.

Cocaine Freebase

Freebase is a form of cocaine that is smoked. It is extremely dangerous, yet increasing in popularity. In 1982, almost 7 percent of clients admitted to treatment facilities were freebasing cocaine, up from 1 percent in 1979. Of the almost 11,000 hospital emergency room visits reported to NIDA's Drug Abuse Warning Network in 1984, 6.1 percent involved cocaine smoking, up from 2.2 percent in 1983.

Freebase is the result of a chemical process whereby "street cocaine" (cocaine hydrochloride) is converted to a pure base by removing the hydrochloride salt and many of the "cutting" agents. The end product, freebase, is not water soluble. Therefore, the only way to get it into the system is to smoke it.

Freebase is smoked in a water pipe. It's more dangerous than "snorting" cocaine because it reaches the brain within seconds, resulting in a sudden and intense high. The euphoria a user experiences, however, quickly disappears and the user faces an enormous craving to freebase again and again. Consequently, freebasers often increase the dose and the frequency of the dose, resulting in a severe addiction which may include physical debilitation and financial ruin.

The reported symptoms of freebasing cocaine include weight loss, increased heart rate and blood pressure, depression, paranoia, and hallucinations. Manic paranoia or depressive psychoses have been seen in some heavy users. There is also some concern that smoking freebase may have a specific effect on the lungs.

What Is Crack?

"Crack" is the street name for an inexpensive, easy-to-use, smokable form of cocaine that looks like tiny chunks or rocks. Users smoke crack cocaine in small pipes, and in tobacco and marijuana cigarettes. If a person already smokes tobacco cigarettes, using crack is simple to do.

Crack is widely available and costs as little as $3 per dose, placing it within reach of even the youngest teen; the poorest youth.

When users smoke crack, they get high very rapidly. Until recently, the only way to achieve this effect was to use cocaine intravenously. One of the most dangerous aspects of crack is the fact that this intense and rapid "rush" now can be achieved through smoking—a form of drug use that is mistakenly considered safer than injection.

314

Combined with its low cost, the crack form of cocaine makes this potent drug dangerously available to people who would not ordinarily put a needle in their arm.

How Does Cocaine Affect the User?

Cocaine in all its forms makes users feel energetic, alert and self-confident. When the rush or high wears off, however, a depressed, let-down feeling called a "crash" can follow. This is more likely to occur when the drug is used repeatedly (binging), as cocaine is generally used. Users feel tired, irritable, nervous or out of sorts when they crash and experience an intense craving to use cocaine again.

With continued use, many users become extremely anxious and depressed when they aren't snorting, injecting or smoking cocaine. Some become paranoid and suspicious with repeated use of the drug. They start believing people are "out to get them" and take steps to protect themselves from these imaginary threats. Other users have hallucinations where they see and feel things that aren't there. Some experts believe cocaine causes changes in the brain that make users hunger for the drug. Whether the brain is permanently affected or not, the high that cocaine provides and the discomfort that follows when the rush wears off compels many users to return to the drug repeatedly.

What Physical Effects Does Cocaine Have?

Regardless of how it is used—whether smoked, snorted or injected—cocaine may produce:

- Increased blood pressure and heart rate, and constricted blood vessels. These physiological changes can produce heart attacks;
- Strokes;
- Nausea, headaches, sweating and, in some cases, seizures;
- Chest pain, breathing difficulties, and respiratory failure;
- Trouble sleeping, loss of appetite, reduced sex drive; and
- Drug dependence.

In addition to its other effects, when sniffed, cocaine may produce:

- Loss of sense of smell and nose bleeds, and sores around the nose and upper lip;

- Problems swallowing and hoarseness; and
- Sinus problems.

In addition to its other effects, when injected, cocaine may produce:

- AIDS, hepatitis, and other infections and sores at the injection site; and
- Endocarditis.

In addition to its other effects, when smoked cocaine may produce:

- Severe chest pain, wheezing, black phlegm and chronic cough;
- Parched lips, tongue and throat, and extreme hoarseness;
- Bleeding in the lungs and coughing up blood;
- "Crack lung" (pneumonia-like symptoms, but no evidence of pneumonia when x-rays are taken); and
- Singed eyebrows and eyelashes, and burns on fingers and other parts of the body.

Pregnant women who use cocaine in any form take special risks. They are more susceptible to the drug's negative effects on the heart. They are also more likely to experience premature separation of the placenta, spontaneous abortion and premature delivery than are non-users.

Cocaine may cause blood clots in the brain of the fetus. It also may interfere with the normal development of the fetus.

Cocaine babies are often small in size. Such low-birthweight babies often have more health and developmental problems than normal-sized babies.

Breastfeeding mothers who smoke, snort or inject cocaine pass the cocaine on to their babies. Cocaine in breast milk makes nursing babies irritable and fussy.

What Other Effects Does Cocaine Have?

No matter how cocaine is taken, with time most regular users or those who binge weekly or even a few times per month suffer from some or all of the following:

- Anxiety;
- Depression;

- Loss of pleasure in acts that are normally pleasurable;
- Lack of energy;
- Paranoia; and
- Hallucinations.

Also, as the need for cocaine becomes a main concern, heavy users lose the ability to make good decisions about the demands of daily life. Health and safety, job and family responsibilities, and personal relationships all suffer. Users talk about "falling in love with cocaine and doing anything to buy it." The craving to use is so powerful that scientists consider cocaine one of the most reinforcing drugs known.

What Effects Does Cocaine Have on the Workplace?

Cocaine is a dangerous substance that causes serious physical, mental and social problems. However, when people first use it, they feel upbeat and recharged. They think the drug makes them smarter and helps them work better than they did before. By the time cocaine's negative effects begin appearing, many users are already dependent on it.

Cocaine users pose serious problems on the job. They often miss work, arrive late, and steal from employees and coworkers. Lack of food and sleep makes them short-tempered and, in some cases, dangerous. The paranoia that cocaine (and crack) cause may lead to misunderstandings and violence against other employees.

Extent of Cocaine Use

The Monitoring the Future Survey

This survey assesses the extent of drug use among adolescents and young adults across the country.

- Data shows that cocaine use among high school seniors has been on a downward trend since its peak in 1985. The proportion of seniors who have used cocaine at least once in their lifetimes has dropped from 17.3% in 1985 to 6.1% in 1992. Current use of cocaine decreased from 6.7% in 1985 to 1.3% in 1992. In 1992, 3.3% of 10th graders had tried cocaine at least once down from 4.1% in 1991. Despite the declines among 10th and 12th graders, the percentage of eighth graders who had ever tried cocaine rose significantly from 2.3% in 1991 to 2.9% in 1992.

- Of college students one to four years beyond high school, in 1992, 3.0% used cocaine within the past year and 1.0% used cocaine in the past month—a decrease from 6.9% in 1985.

- In 1992, 5.9% of young adults one to four years beyond high school but not in college used cocaine within the past year and 1.7% used cocaine in the past 30 days.

The National Household Survey

- In 1992, almost 23 million Americans age 12 and older had tried cocaine at least once in their lifetimes; almost 5 million had used cocaine during the past year, and more than 1 million used cocaine in the past month. These are significant decreases in cocaine use since its peak in 1985.

- Use of crack cocaine has also declined. In 1992, almost 2.8 million people had used crack cocaine at least once in their lives, down from 3.9 million in 1991. In 1992 about 800,000 people had used crack within the past year, down from about 1 million in 1991.

The Drug Abuse Warning Network (DAWN)

DAWN collects data on drug abuse morbidity and mortality through reports from hospital emergency rooms and a selected sample of medical examiners in 21 metropolitan areas. Data from the DAWN system continues to show increases in adverse health consequences associated with the use of cocaine.

- The estimated number of cocaine-related emergency room mentions has fluctuated since 1988 when it totalled 101,578. That number increased to 110,013 in 1989 and then decreased significantly to 80,355 in 1990. However, in 1991 the number of cocaine-related emergency room mentions increased significantly again to 102,727.

- The number of cocaine-related deaths nearly quadrupled between 1984 and 1990. Cocaine was the substance most frequently mentioned in drug-related deaths in 1991. Among cocaine-related deaths: 72% of decedents were male; 28% were female, 38% were white; 45% were black; and 15% were Hispanic.

Added Dangers

Cocaethylene

When people mix cocaine and alcohol consumption, they are compounding the danger each drug poses and unknowingly forming a complex chemical experiment within their bodies. NIDA (National Institute on Drug Abuse) funded researchers have found that the human liver combines cocaine and alcohol and manufactures a third substance, cocaethylene, that intensifies cocaine's euphoric effects, while possibly increasing the risk of sudden death.

Pregnant Women

Estimates vary on the extent of drug abuse by pregnant women. One NIDA study reported that in 1991 almost 4.5 million women had used an illicit drug within the past month. Of this group, it was estimated that more than 400,000 had used cocaine.

When a pregnant woman uses drugs, she and her unborn child are exposed to significant health risks. During pregnancy, almost all drugs cross the placenta and enter the bloodstream of the developing baby. The most serious possible adverse affects on the unborn child's health include premature delivery and low birthweight. Other possible problems include ectopic pregnancy, still birth, Sudden Infant Death Syndrome, and small gestational size. The pregnant woman who uses drugs is herself at increased risk of hemorrhage, spontaneous abortion, toxicity, sexually transmitted diseases, and nutritional deficiencies. In addition, drug use by pregnant women puts women and their children at risk for HIV/AIDS.

Resources for Additional Information and Help

American Council for Drug Education
204 Monroe Street, Suite 110
Rockville, MD 20850
(800) 488-DRUG (3784)
(301) 294-0600

CSAP National Resource Center for the Prevention of Perinatal Abuse
of Alcohol and Other Drugs
9300 Lee Highway
Fairfax, VA 22031
(800) 354-88224
(703) 218-5600

Cocaine Anonymous:

For groups in your area, please consult your local telephone directory

National Clearinghouse for Alcohol and Drug Information
P.O. Box 2345
Rockville, MD 20852
(800) 729-6686
(301) 468-2345

Hotlines

1-800-COCAINE (262-2463)
1-788-2800

Chapter 35

Crack Cocaine: A Special Challenge

The Crack Cocaine Story

The emergence of crack cocaine in the mid-1980s signaled a dramatic new challenge to nationwide prevention efforts. Previous strategies had focused on preventing the initiation of drug use or diverting the progression from experimentation to regular, frequent drug taking. Crack cocaine use prevention, by contrast, would mean changing the behavior of committed drug users and addicts—convincing this skeptical population that crack cocaine is a substantially worse threat to their survival than drugs they had previously taken. Although crack cocaine may be a gateway or initial drug for some, most new crack cocaine users are long-term, heavy users of illicit drugs and alcohol. Many lessons have been learned in the last decade about prevention, but the challenge remains: reducing crack cocaine use depends on the development and implementation of imaginative new responses to the special demands of the populations most at risk.

The crack cocaine epidemic in the United States emerged in 1985 with great speed and power, becoming a major national concern within a year. Three unusual phenomena distinguished crack cocaine from previous illicit drugs. First, the crack cocaine epidemic occurred during a long-term downward trend in overall drug use in the United States. Second, cocaine was not a new drug; what was new was that cocaine was being smoked, instead of snorted or injected. Third, crack

Excerpted from DHHS Pub. No. (ADM) 91-1806.

cocaine use—in contrast to the use of alcohol, marijuana, and snorted cocaine (the major American drugs of abuse prior to the onset of crack cocaine)—was concentrated primarily in urban areas among ethnic/racial populations and was associated to an unusual degree with violent crime.

Why Crack Cocaine Is Different

The first reported use of crack cocaine was in the Bahamas in 1983. By 1985, it was readily available on the streets of New York City and spreading to other parts of the United States. As it reached each community, its rapid and intense high and its addictive capacity instantly marked it as a drug of major concern.

The hallmark of crack cocaine, perhaps more than any other drug, is its ability to induce persistent, intensive drug-seeking behaviors. Crack cocaine offers its users an intense high in a very short time. A drug absorbed through the lungs after smoking quickly reaches the brain, rapidly producing the sought-after high. Cocaine taken intranasally attains a peak high in 10 to 15 minutes and lasts about an hour; intravenous use peaks in 3 to 5 minutes and lasts 30 to 45 minutes; but a crack cocaine high is achieved in 10 to 15 seconds and lasts about 15 minutes. Crack cocaine users typically smoke repeated doses or "hits" of the drug to extend the high, sometimes for many hours. Crack cocaine is absorbed over the entire surface of the lungs, an area roughly the size of a football field. The dosing of snorted cocaine is self-limited by reactive constriction of nasal blood vessels, but because there is no similar shutoff process for crack cocaine, a far higher dosage is permitted to reach the brain far more quickly.

In the brain, crack cocaine directly affects the pleasure centers, which are thought to be controlled primarily by the neurotransmitter dopamine. Animal studies have shown that the reinforcing properties of cocaine are enormous, producing a powerful craving that leads the user to abandon all else in a compulsion to obtain more of the drug. Heavy crack cocaine users often forgo food and sleep to stay high, and they frequently suffer malnutrition and exhaustion as a result.

Accompanying the craving for the drug is the euphoria that users say it produces. The intensity and rapid onset of euphoria, combined with the strong craving that may develop, account for crack cocaine's high potential for addiction.

Crack cocaine is capable of producing both a physical and a psychological addiction. As tolerance for the drug develops, the user needs more and more crack cocaine to experience the same degree of effects. The effect that crack cocaine produces may be accompanied by confusion, increased heart rate and blood pressure, and sweating. Withdrawal from the drug after prolonged use produces feelings of anxiety, irritability, insomnia, and depression. Some users find these sensations frightening and choose to avoid the drug because of its powerful side effects.

Smoking crack cocaine also heightens certain important effects that are relatively mild when cocaine is snorted—increased heart rate, blood pressure, and temperature—which can lead to seizures, heart attack, stroke, and death. A fatal overdose is possible with even a small amount of crack cocaine at the first use of the drug. Medical effects of crack cocaine use include chronic respiratory problems (most commonly a persistent cough), chronic fatigue, and insomnia. Long-term psychological effects of crack cocaine use include behavior and personality changes including impulsive, even violent, behavior and paranoia. Panic attacks are also occasional reactions to chronic crack cocaine use. All of these effects adversely influence a crack cocaine user's relationships, responsibilities, and overall physical and mental health.

Crack cocaine has a high entrepreneurial attraction. It is sold in affordable amounts and produces its own repeat clientele through its addictive properties. Although street-level dealers, usually youth, may start out as nonusers, many become addicted as a result of crack cocaine's ready availability and peer encouragement. Initial profits may dissipate, ultimately leaving the dealer both an addict and in serious debt. Especially in large urban centers, this situation is extremely volatile, typically contributing to a pattern of crime and violence as well as to family and community disruption.

Conclusion

Placed in the context of the history of drug use in the United States, crack cocaine use and the epidemic of the mid-1980s appear to be further episodes in the enduring search for more intense drug experiences by young adult and adolescent populations. However, in this episode the drug is especially cheap, addictive, and associated with dramatic psychological, physiological, and social consequences. The history of drug abuse suggests that, as the use of crack cocaine diminishes with time, it is likely to be replaced with another potent drug, also initially perceived as manageable. Given this likelihood, and the heavy toll a drug such as crack cocaine can take on American families and communities, it is essential to study the lessons of the crack cocaine epidemic to avoid repeating them.

Chapter 36

Heroin

Health Hazards

Heroin is an illegal and highly addictive narcotic. Addictive or dependence-producing properties are exhibited by (1) persistent regular use of a drug, (2) attempts to stop such use which lead to significant and painful withdrawal symptoms, (3) continued use despite damaging physical and/or psychological problems, (4) compulsive drug-seeking behavior, and (5) need for increasing doses of the drug.

Heroin exerts its primary addictive effect by activating both the region of the brain that is responsible for producing the pleasurable sensation of "reward" and the region which produces the classic physical dependence syndrome. Together these actions account for the user's loss of control and the drug's habit-forming action.

Many health problems related to heroin use are caused by uncertain dosage levels (due to fluctuations in purity), use of unsterile equipment, contamination of heroin by cutting agents, or use of heroin in combination with other drugs such as alcohol or cocaine. Typical problems include skin abscesses, inflammation of the veins, serum hepatitis, and addiction with withdrawal symptoms.

Heroin and AIDS

Utilization of unsterile needles by multiple individuals (needle sharing) increases the risk of exposure to HIV, the causative agent

National Institute on Drug Abuse (NIDA), *Capsules*, C-86-7; subheads added.

for Acquired Immune Deficiency Syndrome (AIDS). Heroin itself, as well as a drug-abusing lifestyle, may depress the body's ability to withstand infection.

While intravenous drug users account for approximately 25 percent of all reported AIDS cases, their proportion of the AIDS population appears to be increasing. In the first half of 1985, intravenous drug users accounted for 33 percent of all new AIDS cases. Moreover, 54 percent of newborns contracting AIDS have a parent who is an intravenous drug user, and intravenous drug users account for a similarly disproportionate share of the percentage of heterosexually transmitted AIDS cases.

Symptoms and Signs of Heroin Use

The reported symptoms and signs of heroin use include euphoria, drowsiness, respiratory depression, constricted pupils and nausea. Withdrawal symptoms include watery eyes, runny nose, yawning, loss of appetite, tremors, panic, chills, sweating, muscle cramps and insomnia. Elevations in blood pressure, pulse respiratory rate and temperature occur as withdrawal progresses.

Symptoms of heroin overdose include shallow breathing, clammy skin, convulsions, and coma. Death may result.

Other Related Risks

By modifying the molecular structure of certain controlled substances, underground chemists have been able to create new forms of drugs grouped under the term "designer drugs." Some of these, the fentanyl analogs, are capable of producing effects many times greater than those achieved with heroin. Others, the meperidine analogs such as MPTP, have been implicated in a growing number of drug reactions which mimic Parkinsonism and which may result in death.

Heroin use during pregnancy is associated with stillbirths, placental abruptions, and sudden infant death. Unless the mother is receiving treatment, her baby is likely to show symptoms of withdrawal and to be below normal birth weight.

Prevalence of Use

While heroin use continues to be a major concern in several cities, estimates indicate that the total number of addicts has been reduced since the early 1970s. During the past 8 years, the number of addicts has held relatively constant at around half a million.

Eighty-four percent of admissions [into treatment programs] were 25-44 years of age in 1981, compared to 75 percent in 1979. This reflects, in part, a stable and aging pool of users.

Risk Factors

The consumption of alcohol in combination with heroin street preparations of uncertain composition is one of the major causes of heroin-related deaths. The occasional user faces increased danger of accidental overdose because he/she does not have tolerance to the drug.

The number of heroin-related deaths may increase with an increase in the purity and availability of heroin street preparations.

User Characteristics

In each of the four recognized heroin epidemics occurring in the last 2 decades, the age at first use for those new users entering drug abuse treatment generally increased. For example, in the 1967-1971 epidemics 3 percent of the new users were in the 12-17 age bracket as opposed to 9 percent in the latest epidemic.

While more of the new users were Black than white in the heroin epidemic of 1967-1971, in subsequent epidemics the racial composition reversed with more white initiates than Black [initiates] entering drug abuse treatment.

Approximately 36 percent of heroin users entering drug treatment programs are women (1984). Moreover, nearly a third of these women are involved in prostitution, making them particularly vulnerable to HIV infection and its transmission. Thus, over 80 percent of heterosexually-linked AIDS cases are female.

Patterns of Use

According to the hospital drug emergency mentions reported to the total DAWN system in 1985, the preferred method of administering heroin is by injection (90.5 percent of the heroin patients showed this route of administration).

Few street heroin users utilize sterilized equipment, thus "track marks," or the skin discolorations caused by unsterilized needles and the injection contaminants, are visible at injection sites.

The relative price of heroin in terms of purity and availability is believed to influence drug preference for many users. Dilaudid, amphetamines, and cocaine we frequently abused by heroin users in preference to poor quality heroin.

Cocaine was the leading secondary drug reported by heroin clients in treatment data reported to NIDA (1984); 19 percent of heroin users reported cocaine as a secondary drug.

Prevalence of Health Consequences

During the past few years, heroin abuse has been a regional problem. Certain areas experienced increases in heroin-related emergencies or deaths, while other areas showed a declining or stable trend.

Demographically, more than 60 percent of the emergency room episodes in 1985 involving heroin and reporting to the DAWN system occurred among individuals 30 years old or older. Fifty-three percent were Black, 30 percent white, and 13 percent were Hispanic. Seventy percent were male.

Similar distributions were seen among DAWN deaths involving heroin by sex and age, i.e., the majority were male (82 percent), 68 percent were 30 years old or older, about equal proportions were white (44 percent) or Black (40 percent). Fifteen percent were Hispanic.

As "speedballing," or the combined use of cocaine and heroin has become more common, so have the health consequences associated with the injection of this combination of drugs. Cocaine and heroin mentions in DAWN emergency rooms more than tripled between FY 1981 and FY 1985.

In 1985, almost 41 percent of the heroin-related emergency room cases reported the use of heroin in combination with other drugs. The most prevalent combinations were heroin and cocaine, and heroin and alcohol.

Between 1981 and 1985 heroin-related deaths almost doubled, from 700 to approximately 1300. Almost 85 percent of the heroin-related deaths occurred in combination with other drugs. The combination of heroin and alcohol accounted for almost 50 percent of the cases.

Supplies of Heroin

The cultivation of opium and its refinement into heroin is a worldwide problem. Production sites are widely distributed and often found in areas which are not policed or effectively controlled by central governments. Consequently, curbing the diversion of heroin to America is a high U.S. priority which involves favorable U.S. decisions on foreign aid and other matters to countries which cooperate in promoting a vigorous drug enforcement program within their borders.

According to the Drug Enforcement Administration's Heroin Signature Program, the proportion of Southwest Asian (SWA) heroin available in the U.S. increased slightly, representing half of the total U.S. supply. Mexican heroin remained at about one-third nationally, while Southeast Asian (SEA) heroin accounted for about 17 percent of the total available.

According to reports from the National Institute on Drug Abuse's (NIDA) Community Epidemiology Workgroup in June 1986, fourteen cities reported the growing availability of a potent form of heroin known as "black tar," "gumball," or "tootsie roll." Previously, the presence of this substance had only been reported in the western section of the country. The source country for this form of heroin is Mexico.

Chapter 37

Methamphetamine

Methamphetamine Abuse

Methamphetamine is a drug that can strongly activate the sympathetic division of the nervous system. Methamphetamine falls within the amphetamine family which refers to a group of chemically related drugs all of which produce similar behavioral and physiological effects. Every drug in the amphetamine group is a psychostimulant, or a drug that increases the activity of the brain. Unlike other frequently abused drugs, methamphetamine does not occur in nature but is synthesized in a laboratory.

Street methamphetamine is referred to as speed, crank, crystal, ice, meth, chalk, chicken powder, peanut butter-crank, go-fast, crystal-meth, shabu-shabu, glass, go, zip, chris, and christy. The name used for methamphetamine depends on the physical form (crystal versus powder), the geographical area, and the dealer.

The name "ice" has been used by dealers to represent methamphetamine, as well as other substances including methamphetamine mixed with heroin, cocaine, or other adulterants, 4-methylaminorex, quartz, and rock salt.

This chapter contains text from National Institute on Drug Abuse (NIDA) *Capsules*, C-89-06, January 1990; and "Fact Sheet: ICE," U.S. Department of Justice, Drugs and Crime Data Center and Clearinghouse, nd.

Ice vs. Meth

Methamphetamine originated in Japan in 1919. Ice is a new, smokeable form of methamphetamine. While Ice and "Crystal Meth" are chemically the same, they are structurally different. Ice is a crystalline form of methamphetamine which is high in purity (90-100%). It is similar in size and appearance to quartz or rock salt. Crystal Meth, while it is called "crystal", is usually obtained in a powder form and in varying levels of purity. Both Ice and Crystal Meth can be smoked. While the effects of Crystal Meth last two to four hours, the duration of an Ice-high is said to last anywhere from 7 to 24 hours. Crystal Meth is typically injected, snorted, or ingested orally (in pill form).

Use of any form of methamphetamine results in intense euphoria and tremendous energy. There have been reports of paranoid and violent behavior with prolonged usage. Because the purity of Ice is greater, these effects are intensified. Ice has also been reported to cause nausea, vomiting, rapid respiratory and cardiac rates, increased body temperature, and coma at high dosage levels. Overdoses are common since it is difficult for the users to control the amount of smoke being inhaled. Since 1985, there have been 32 deaths attributed to Ice in Honolulu. In the first six months of 1989, there were 12 deaths.

Dangers of Methamphetamine Abuse

Like cocaine, methamphetamine chemically affects the brain's reward system, causing excessive stimulation and producing euphoria. Methamphetamine enters the brain more rapidly than other members of the amphetamine group because it is more soluble in the brain's membranes, thereby readily producing a "rush" of euphoria when injected or smoked. Many people who try methamphetamine go on to compulsive abuse of this drug.

Typically, small doses of methamphetamine have prominent central stimulant effects including stimulated movement and speech, feelings of excitement and euphoria, and decreased appetite. Prominent peripheral effects include increases in blood pressure and heart rate. Users report a "pounding heart" sensation, palpitations, hot flashes, dryness of the mouth, and sweating.

Excessive doses can produce mental confusion, severe anxiety, aggressiveness, tremors, chest pain, hypertension, cardiac arrhythmias, elevated body temperature, convulsions, cardiovascular collapse, and death. Repeated doses typically produce nervousness and insomnia. A more extreme manifestation of chronic toxicity is a state of paranoia called amphetamine psychosis which closely resembles paranoid schizophrenia. Psychotic symptoms include hallucinations, paranoid delusions, delusions of parasites and bugs in the skin (resulting in picking at and damage to the skin), and excitement.

Because tolerance develops with continued use, the chronic user progressively increases the dose to obtain desired effects. Methamphetamine abusers may systematically increase their dose 50 to 100 times the initial amount over time, up to several hundred milligrams per day, which would be fatal to the nonuser.

Continued moderate to chronic use of methamphetamines may lead to permanent damage to the brain or death. Chronic use may produce irreversible nerve damage and reductions in central concentrations of dopamine, the neurotransmitter associated with muscular movements and locomotion.

Withdrawal symptoms are the inverse of the acute effects of stimulants. They include emotional depression, decreased energy, lack of interest in the environment, and inability to experience pleasure. The withdrawal of methamphetamine, as with cocaine withdrawal, is accompanied by intense craving for the drug. The severity of withdrawal symptoms depends on the extent of stimulant abuse.

Methods of Use

NIDA's Division of Epidemiology and Prevention Research (DEPR) conducts ongoing surveillance programs that closely monitor trends of methamphetamine use. In 1988, there were 3,030 mentions for methamphetamine/speed use among drug abuse-related emergency room cases in the Drug Abuse Warning Network (DAWN) system which includes selected hospitals within 21 metropolitan areas.

Smoking was the route of administration for 2.8 percent of the emergency room cases. The largest number of cases reported injection as the route of administration. This is of particular concern given the association between intravenous drug use and the spread of the human immunodeficiency virus (HIV).

Recent reports from Hawaii show crystal methamphetamine, referred to as ice and crystal, being smoked almost exclusively. The drug is in the form of a large, usually clear, crystal of high purity, smoked in a glass pipe. The smoke is odorless and the residue of the drug stays in the pipe. The cost of methamphetamine crystal in Hawaii fluctuates, but in general a gram sells for $300-$400. A gram of cocaine in Oahu sells for $100.

The smoking route of administration is physiologically the most direct pathway to the brain. Smoked drugs reach the brain within seconds and manifest their effects immediately, similar to what is seen with intravenous injection. This provides an intense "high" and, therefore, a strongly reinforcing memory of euphoria. In contrast, oral and intranasal drug use have slower and prolonged absorption rates.

While the effects of cocaine may be measured in minutes, the effects of methamphetamine (smoked or injected) last for many hours. Most often, methamphetamine is smoked in runs or periods of continuous use averaging 5 days in length, with an average of 4 days cessation between the periods of smoking. Usually the days of non-smoking are spent sleeping interspersed with periods of ravenous hunger.

Conclusion

Methamphetamine abuse has very serious public health implications. Considerable evidence suggests that permanent neurological changes and deficits can result from chronic methamphetamine use. The smoking route of administration compounds these effects and promotes rapid addiction.

As of this writing, widespread smoking of methamphetamine appears to be largely restricted to Hawaii. However, the increased indicators of methamphetamine use in certain areas of the U.S. mainland raises concern about, at the very least, the transmission of this mode of use to those with a history of methamphetamine abuse. As with cocaine, the smoking route of administration can lead to additional serious adverse health and social consequences.

Chapter 38

Designer Drugs

A Designer Drug is an analogue, a chemical compound that is similar in structure and effect to another drug of abuse but differs very slightly in structure. Designer drugs are produced in clandestine laboratories to mimic the psychoactive effects of controlled drugs. Theoretically, the number of potential synthetic analogues that can be made and distributed is very large. The most commonly know types of synthetic analogue drugs available through the illicit drug market include analogues of fentanyl and meperidine (both synthetic opioids), analogues of phencyclidine (PCP), and analogues of amphetamine and methamphetamine (which have hallucinogenic and stimulant properties). The street names of designer drugs vary according to time, place, and manufacturer, and change frequently.

Fentanyl Analogues

Fentanyl was introduced in 1968, by a Belgium pharmaceutical company as a synthetic narcotic to be used as an analgesic in surgical procedures because of its minimal effect on the heart. In the early 1980s, however, crude clandestine laboratories began manufacturing fentanyl derivatives which were pharmacologically similar to heroin and morphine. These fentanyl analogues create addiction similar to the opiate narcotics and present a significant drug abuse problem including an increased potential for overdose. The most commonly

National Institute on Drug Abuse (NIDA) *Capsules*, C-86-5, revised September 1993.

known fentanyl analogue is alpha-methylfentanyl, which is known on the streets as China White. Other fentanyl analogues on the street include Synthetic Heroin, Tango and Cash, and Goodfella.

Health Hazards

As with other narcotic analgesics, respiratory depression is the most significant acute toxic effect of the fentanyl derivatives. Fentanyl analogues are 80 to 1,000 times more potent than heroin, depending on how they are made, and are 200 times more potent than morphine. They are intended to duplicate the euphoric effects of heroin. Fentanyl analogues have a very rapid onset (one to four minutes), and have a short duration of action (approximately 30-90 minutes) which varies according to the particular drug. Because of the potency and quick onset, even a very small dose of a fentanyl analogue can lead to sudden death.

The most common route of administration is by injection. Authorities report that the victim can die so suddenly from respiratory paralysis that the needle may still be present in the dead user's arm. The antidote naloxone may be used in an overdose situation to counter respiratory depression when the victim is found in time. Recent data indicate that smoking and sniffing are two means of ingestion that are becoming more popular—perhaps due to the attempt on the part of the user to avoid the transmission of HIV/AIDS.

Supply

Fentanyl analogues are marketed as potent heroin alternatives to the heroin-using population. China White, (alpha-methylfentanyl) which appeared in Orange County, CA in 1979, was the first synthetically produced fentanyl that resulted in overdose deaths. Between 1980 and 1985, China White and several other fentanyl analogues were responsible for 100 unintentional overdose deaths in California. In 1982, China White was placed under Schedule I of the Controlled Substance Act (CSA), along with other drugs that have the highest potential for abuse and have no recognized legitimate medical use except for experimental purposes. In 1985, 3-methylfentanyl (TMF), another lethal analogue, along with two other similar derivatives were also classified as schedule I under the CSA.

In 1988, 3-methylfentanyl (TMF) was identified in 16 unintentional overdose deaths in Allegheny County, PA. Multiple drug use was common in most of these cases. Since TMF is a powerful opiate, it is possible that it compounded the suppressant respiratory effects of the other drugs ingested, thereby causing death. In 1991, the fentanyl analogue Tango and Cash was implicated in at least 28 deaths primarily in New York and in other Northeast areas. In 1992, China White was found to be the cause of death in 21 overdoses during two months time, in Philadelphia, PA. To date, fentanyl analogues are responsible for the drug overdose deaths of more than 150 people in the U.S.

Meperidine Analogues (MA)

Meperidine, known by the trade name of Demerol, is a narcotic controlled under Schedule II of the CSA (meaning that it has a high potential for abuse as well as recognized medical use). Over the past decade, the illicit use of meperidine has increased during the periods when heroin was scarce. Two meperidine analogues that have appeared on the streets include 1-methyl-4-phenyl-4-propionoxypiperidine (MPPP) and 1-(2-phenylethyl)-4-acetyloxypiperdine (PEPAP). They are often marketed as New Heroin. MPPP is popular among drug users because when it is injected, it produces an euphoria similar to that produced by heroin. An impurity formed during the clandestine manufacture of MPPP, called MPTP (1-methyl-4-phenyl-1,2,3,6,-tetrahydro pyridine), has been shown to be a potent neurotoxin and has caused irreversible brain damage in several individuals. The damage is manifested in a syndrome resembling a very severe Parkinsonism, that results in increased muscular tone, difficulty in moving and speaking, drooling, and cogwheel rigidity of the upper extremities. Tremor in such patients characteristically involves the proximal muscles and is more pronounced than the typical involuntary rest tremor occurring in idiopathic Parkinsonism. MPTP was identified primarily in California in the early 1980s.

Methamphetamine Analogues

Several dozen analogues of amphetamine and methamphetamine are hallucinogenic, many of which have been scheduled under the CSA. The methamphetamine analogues currently of concern include 3,4-methylenedioxyamphetamine (MDA) and 3,4-methylenedioxymethamphetamine (MDMA).

MDA, known by the street name "love drug", became a drug of abuse in the 1960s. MDA produces a heightened need for interpersonal relationships and users report an increased need to talk to and be with other people. MDA became more widely abused in the early 1980s on college campuses and by psychiatrists until scientists discovered that MDA damages the brain's serotonin neurons, thereby producing brain damage. It consequently became classified as a CSA Schedule I drug. Effects of MDA use resemble those of amphetamine intoxication: hyperactivity, hyperthermia, tachycardia, hypertension, and seizures.

MDMA, often known on the streets as "Ecstasy" or "Adam," is structurally similar to methamphetamine and mescaline, and stimulates the central nervous system and produces hallucinogenic effects. MDMA was first synthesized in the early 1900s as an appetite suppressant, although it was never used as such. It was first synthesized illegally in 1972, but was not widely abused until the 1980s.

MDMA is also closely related to the amphetamine family, as it can result in a variety of acute psychiatric disturbances, including panic, anxiety, depression, and paranoid thinking. Physical symptoms include muscle tension, nausea, blurred vision, faintness, chills, and sweating. MDMA also increases the heart rate and blood pressure. MDMA has been shown to destroy serotonin-producing neurons in animals. These neurons play a direct role in regulating aggression, mood, sexual activity, sleep, and sensitivity to pain. MDMA has also been reported to cause jaw clenching, tremor, and hallucinations.

Both MDMA and MDA have been shown to be neurotoxic. In animal studies, the doses of MDA which produce neurotoxicity are only two or three times more than the minimum dose needed to produce a psychotropic response. This suggests that individuals who are self-administering the drug may be getting a neurotoxic dose. The relationship between the neurotoxic dose and the psychotropic dose of MDMA is currently under investigation. Because of its neurotoxic effects and it abuse potential, MDMA was placed in Schedule I of the CSA on an emergency basis in July, 1985.

The Drug Enforcement Administration reports that MDMA is available in at least 21 states and Canada. It is especially popular with college students and young adults. According to NIDA's Monitoring the Future Survey, 3.2 percent of young adults aged 19-28 and 2.0 percent of college students have tried MDMA at least once in their lifetimes.

Various claims have been made by a small number of psychiatrists for the usefulness of MDMA in enhancing psychotherapy. No evidence has been presented to document these few anecdotal reports.

PCP Analogues

PCP is registered under Schedule III of the CSA. Over the past eight years, PCP analogues have been identified in confiscated street samples but the use of these drugs is not widespread.

Chapter 39

Methcathinone

Methcathinone is a highly addictive illegal drug with the street name "CAT." It is usually homemade from ingredients, including dangerous acids, obtained with little difficulty in most communities.

Users are drawn to Cat because it produces a burst of energy and a feeling of invincibility, accompanied by a state of well-being and euphoria. They pay for their high, however, in the crash that inevitably follows.

The first instance of the illegal manufacture of Cat in the United States is believed to have occurred in Michigan in the late 1980s or early 1990s.

Effects

Damage to the brain and body can be devastating, especially when users progress to the point where they binge on the drug for several days. While in this state, paranoia engulfs them, and they suffer hallucinations and experience excruciating nervousness and anxiety. Appetite decreases or disappears entirely during the binge, often leading to long-term weight loss. The body becomes dehydrated, and an array of other unpleasant symptoms are experienced:

* Pounding heart
* Headaches, stomachaches
* Shakes

"You Can't Trust Cat," a fact sheet provided by the U.S. Drug Enforcement Administration, nd.

When the binge is over, usually because the supply of meth-cathinone has been exhausted, depression clamps down. Users become irritable and argumentative. They drive associates away as they cope with acute social withdrawal.

When sleep finally comes, it may last 24 hours. Rest does not always restore a sense of well-being, however. Users may be drained of energy for as long as several weeks.

How It Is Used

Cat is typically snorted like cocaine, although injection by needle is preferred by some. It is also possible to take Cat orally, by mixing it with a beverage such as coffee or soda drinks.

Ingredients

The recipe for methcathinone includes some relatively benign ingredients but also the following:

- **Sodium dichromate**, commonly used to refine petroleum
- **Sulfuric acid**, usually in the form of battery acid
- **Sodium hydroxide**, obtainable over the counter as lye-based granular drain cleaners
- **Toluene**, a paint thinner
- **Muriatic acid**, used by masons to scrub dried mortar off the face of bricks

Risk to Children

While Cat appeals mainly to those in their 20s and 30s, there have been users as young as 15. Because the drug is relatively inexpensive, law enforcement authorities are concerned that it may find a market among even younger children.

Environmental Effects

Illicit production of methcathinone produces a carcinogenic toxic waste as a byproduct. Although producers of the drug typically make it for use in a close-to-home market, they show little concern for the pollution they spread.

The toxic waste left after the finished product emerges is often dumped in waterways, contaminating fish, well water and wildlife.

If instead it is flushed down the drain, it contaminates septic systems. If simply dumped on fields or vacant land, it contaminates acreage used for crops or grazing, or it taints land upon which homeowners may build.

There is no safe way to dispose of the toxic waste except through legitimate toxic waste disposal facilities.

Penalties

Persons who manufacture methcathinone or assist others in doing so, perhaps by serving as go-betweens to buy ingredients, are being prosecuted under a number of federal statutes. Manufacturing or possession with intent to distribute, for instance, is a violation of Section 841 (a) (1) of Title 21 of the United States Code and is punishable by a prison term of up to 20 years and a fine of up to one million dollars.

Chapter 40

Lysergic Acid Diethylamide (LSD)

LSD is one of the major drugs comprising the hallucinogen class. LSD was discovered in 1938 by Dr. Albert Hofmann, and is one of the most potent mood-changing chemicals. It is manufactured from lysergic acid which is found in ergot, a fungus that grows on rye and other grains. LSD is classified under Schedule I of the Controlled Substances Act, which includes drugs with no medical use and/or high potential for abuse.

LSD, commonly referred to as "acid," is sold on the street in tablets, capsules, or occasionally in liquid form. It is odorless, colorless, and tasteless and is usually taken by mouth. Often it is added to absorbent paper, such as blotter paper, and divided into small decorated squares, with each square representing one dose.

The Drug Enforcement Administration reports that the strength of LSD samples obtained currently from illicit sources ranges from 20 to 80 micrograms of LSD per dose. This is considerably less than the levels reported during the 1960s and early 1970s when the dosage ranged from 100 to 200 micrograms, or higher, per unit.

Adverse Effects of LSD

The effects of LSD are unpredictable. They depend on the amount taken, the user's personality, mood and expectations, and the surroundings in which the drug is used. Usually, the user feels the first

This chapter contains text from National Institute on Drug Abuse (NIDA) *Capsules*, C-92-01, June 1992; and "It Never Went Away," Department of Justice, Drug Enforcement Administration, nd.

effects of the drug 30-90 minutes after taking it. The physical effects include dilated pupils, higher body temperature, increased heart rate and blood pressure, sweating, loss of appetite, sleeplessness, dry mouth and tremors.

Sensations and feelings change much more dramatically than the physical signs. The user may feel several different emotions at once or swing rapidly from one emotion to another. If taken in a large enough dose, the drug produces delusions and visual hallucinations. The user's sense of time and self change. Sensations may seem to "cross over," giving the user the feeling of hearing colors and seeing sounds. These changes can be frightening and can cause panic.

Users refer to their experience with LSD as a "trip," and to acute adverse reactions as a "bad trip." These experiences are long—typically they begin to clear after about twelve hours. Some LSD users experience severe, terrifying thoughts and feelings, fear of losing control, fear of insanity and death, and despair, while using LSD. Some fatal accidents and have occurred during states of LSD intoxication.

Many LSD users experience flashbacks, a recurrence of certain aspects of a person's drug experience without the user having taken the drug again. A flashback occurs suddenly, often without warning and may occur within a few days or over a year after LSD use. Flashbacks usually occur in people who use hallucinogens chronically or have an underlying personality problem, however, people who are apparently normal also have flashbacks.

Bad trips and flashbacks are only part of the risks of LSD use. LSD users may manifest relatively long-lasting psychoses, such as schizophrenia or severe depression. It is difficult to determine the extent and mechanism of the LSD involvement in these illnesses.

Most users of LSD voluntarily decrease or stop its use over time. LSD is not considered to be an addicting drug since it does not produce compulsive drug seeking behavior like cocaine, amphetamine, heroin, alcohol, or nicotine. However, in common with many of the addicting drugs, LSD produces tolerance, so that some users who take the drug repeatedly, progressively take higher and higher doses in order to achieve the state of intoxication that they had previously achieved. This is an extremely dangerous practice, given the unpredictability of the drug.

The National Institute on Drug Abuse (NIDA) is funding studies focusing on neurochemical and behavioral properties of LSD. This research will provide a greater understanding of the mechanisms of action of the drug.

Who Uses It?

LSD has always appealed primarily to white, middle-class users. In the Sixties, it took root on college campuses and it is still there.

The worrisome thing to many drug authorities is that in the past few years a significantly younger LSD customer has appeared as the drug has made inroads in many U.S. high schools. And some of the youthful users are sellers as well.

Users under 20 accounted for 49.8 percent of the LSD emergency room cases counted in 1990 by the Drug Abuse Warning Network. DAWN reported that another 33 percent were in the 20 to 30 age group. Thus, four out of five of those whose bad trips end in emergency rooms are 30 or under.

The annual National High School Senior Survey, funded by the U.S. Department of Health and Human Services, indicates that high school seniors are turning to LSD even as they are turning away from marijuana and cocaine. In the 1990 survey, 8.7 percent of the seniors—in other words, *nearly a tenth of the total sample*—said they had tried LSD at least once. For 1.9 percent, the most recent episode had occurred in the past month.

The new, younger generation of buyers weren't around in the Sixties. They know nothing of LSD's bad reputation and mistakenly perceive it as a no-risk alternative to cocaine and marijuana.

It is because LSD is attracting younger users that the Drug Enforcement Administration has targeted it for increased enforcement efforts.

Many authorities worry that if LSD strengthens its beachhead in high school it will inevitably trickle down to junior high school and elementary school, where blotter with pictures of Donald Duck and teddy bears would have special appeal. Unlike some other drugs, it is within financial reach of many children at $3 or $4 a hit.

As to why LSD users take the drug, there seems to have been a shift in motive from the Sixties to the Nineties. Many early users were consciously seeking a quasi-religious experience. Today's young users seem interested simply in getting high.

Extent of Use

NIDA funds surveys to collect data about the extent of drug use and trends in the United States. Findings from the National Household Survey on Drug Abuse and the National High School Senior

Survey have shown dramatic decreases in the use of most drugs. While recently there have been anecdotal reports and media reports that the use of LSD is increasing, NIDA's surveys show that prevalence rates for LSD use in 1991 are still generally lower than rates of use in the 1970s.

National Household Survey on Drug Abuse

The National Household Survey reports the nature and extent of drug use among the American household population ages 12 and over. The 1991 survey measured the extent of the use of hallucinogens which include such drugs as LSD, PCP, mescaline, and peyote.

In 1991, the rate for lifetime prevalence of hallucinogen use among the population aged 12 and older was 8.2 percent. Lifetime prevalence was highest among the two age groups, 18-25 (13.2%) and 26-34 (15.6%).

National High School Senior Survey

Beginning in 1975, over 16,000 high school seniors nationwide have been surveyed yearly to determine trends in drug use and to measure attitudes and beliefs about drug abuse. Since 1975, the percentage of seniors who have used LSD has remained relatively stable. Among the class of 1975, 11.3% of seniors had used LSD by the time they reached their senior year of high school. In 1991, 8.8% had experimented with LSD. Annual prevalence of LSD use among high school seniors was 7.2% in 1975 and 5.2% in 1991. In 1991, 46.6% of seniors perceived great risk in using LSD once or twice and 84.3% say they see great risk in using LSD regularly. Over 90% of seniors disapprove of people trying LSD once or twice or in taking LSD regularly. Almost 40% of seniors say it would be fairly easy or very easy for them to get LSD if they wanted some.

Drug Abuse Warning Network

NIDA's Drug Abuse Warning Network (DAWN) collects data on all types of drug abuse-related emergency room episodes. Among patients seeking treatment in emergency rooms for LSD-related episodes in 1990: 72% were male and 28% were female; 38% were 12-17 year olds and 37% were 18-25 year olds; 77% were white, 5% were African American, and 5% were Hispanic.

Prevention Tips

School and law enforcement authorities should, first, be alert to the likelihood that LSD may well already be in their midst.

Local prevention programs that have given LSD a low priority may need to be overhauled.

School administrators, drug counsellors and police department drug prevention officers, can find reliable information and put it in as many hands as possible. In particular, they can heighten the awareness of parent groups and service organizations, then call on these same groups to give the message wider dissemination.

DEA's Demand Reduction Program has more than 20 agents in major cities throughout the country who can assist local authorities with LSD prevention programs. These agents, who specialize in drug prevention and education, are called Demand Reduction Coordinators. They may be reached by calling DEA in any of more than 100 cities (usually listed under "U.S. Government" in the telephone directory) and asking for the nearest Demand Reduction Coordinator.

Chapter 41

Phencyclidine (PCP)

Phencyclidine, commonly referred to as PCP, was developed in, 1959 as an anesthetic and was later used in veterinary medicine as a powerful tranquilizer. Use of PCP in humans was discontinued in 1965, as it was found that patients often became agitated, delusional, and irrational while recovering from the anesthetic effects of PCP. It is classified as Schedule III of the Controlled Substances Act. PCP is illegally manufactured in clandestine laboratories and is sold on the street by such names as Angel Dust, Crystal Supergrass, Killer Joints, Ozone, Wack, and Rocket Fuel. The variety of street names for PCP reflects its bizarre and volatile effects.

PCP is a white crystalline powder which is readily soluble in water or alcohol. It has a distinctive bitter chemical taste. PCP can be mixed easily with dyes and turns up on the illicit drug market in a variety of tablets, capsules, and colored powders. It is normally used in one of three ways—snorted, smoked, or eaten. When it is smoked, PCP is often applied to a leafy material such as mint, parsley, oregano, or marijuana.

Extent of Use

NIDA's Monitoring the Future Survey shows that use of PCP by high school seniors has declined steadily since 1979. In 1979, 7.0% of

National Institute on Drug Abuse (NIDA), *Capsules*, C-86-8, revised Sepetember 1993.

seniors had used PCP in the past year, and in 1992, 1.4% of seniors had used PCP in the past year. In addition, 2.4% of seniors used PCP within the past month in 1979, compared to 0.6% in 1992.

According to the 1992 National Household Survey on Drug Abuse, 4.0% of the population aged 12 and older have used PCP at least once. Lifetime use of PCP was significantly higher among those aged 26-34 (8.7 %), than for those aged 18-25 (4.6 %) and those aged 12-17 (1.1 %).

Health Hazards

PCP was first introduced as a street drug in the late 1960s and quickly gained a reputation as a drug that could cause bad reactions and was not worth the risk. Many people, after using the drug once, will not knowingly use it again. Yet others use it consistently and regularly. The reasons that are often cited by users as factors in their continued PCP use are: feelings of strength, power, invulnerability, and a numbing effect on the mind that often results in anger, rage, and in the disappearance of unpleasant memories. Recent studies, including those of men arrested for criminal activity, indicate that if PCP induces violent or criminal behavior, it does so infrequently.

At low to moderate doses, physiological effects include a slight increase in breathing rate and a more pronounced rise in blood pressure and pulse rate. Respiration becomes shallow, and flushing and profuse sweating occur. Generalized numbness of the extremities and muscular incoordination may also occur. Psychological effects include distinct changes in body awareness, similar to those associated with alcohol intoxication. Use of PCP among adolescents may interfere with hormones related to normal growth and development as well as with the learning process.

At high doses, there is a drop in blood pressure, pulse rate, and respiration. This may be accompanied by nausea, vomiting, blurred vision, flicking up and down of the eyes, drooling, loss of balance, and dizziness. Psychological effects at high doses include illusions and hallucinations. PCP can cause effects that mimic certain primary symptoms of schizophrenia, such as delusions, mental turmoil, and a sensation of distance from one's environment. Often times, speech is sparse and mangled.

People who use PCP for long periods of time report memory loss, speech difficulties, depression, and weight loss. When given psychomotor tests, PCP users tend to have lost their fine motor skills and short-term memory. Mood disorders have also been reported. PCP has sedative effects, and interactions with other central nervous system depressants such as alcohol and benzodiazepines can lead to coma or accidental overdose.

Research Advances

Research is underway to explain the biological actions of PCP and the architecture of a receptor known as NMDA receptor complex. The NMDA complex has been implicated in the process of cell death in the nervous system. PCP has been found to block the NMDA operated ions channels, thereby indirectly blocking the receptor that responds to glutamate, a normal chemical messenger. This may give a clue to deciphering the cause of schizophrenia.

In addition, research has to determined that PCP can protect the brain from permanent damage after a stroke or heart attack. Basic brain research on the actions of amino acids and the effects of commonly abused drugs led to this discovery that PCP can stop the uncontrolled activity that destroys nerve cells. This discovery is expected to help people who suffer from any trauma that interrupts the supply of oxygen to the brain. Researchers are now looking for drugs that can work like PCP without producing the psychological effects.

Supply

PCP had a brief period of popularity in the late 1960s, when it was trafficked as a "Magic Peace Pill." The Drug Enforcement Administration reports that abuse of the drug resurfaced from 1975 to recently because of the low price and powerful effects. From the period of 1981 through 1985, trafficking of PCP escalated significantly, particularly among persons under the age of 21. Narcotics reports show that the number of PCP laboratories seized since the mid-1980s is considerably less than the high number reported in 1978.

Part Four

Special Problems Related to Substance Abuse during Pregnancy

Chapter 42

How to Take Care of Your Baby Before Birth

If you want your baby to be strong and healthy...

There are many good things you can do right now to keep yourself healthy. These things can help your baby grow strong and healthy, too.

- Visit your doctor at least once a month for the first 7 months, and more often after that.
- Eat right. Include plenty of milk, fish, meat, fruits, vegetables, whole wheat bread, and cereals.
- Take time to exercise, rest, and get enough sleep.
- Learn all you can about taking care of your baby. Look for childbirth classes in your community.
- Tell your problems to your doctor, your school counselor or religious leader, or the librarian in your neighborhood.

While you are pregnant...

- Don't use alcohol and other drugs. When you use drugs, so does your baby. Alcohol and other drugs can harm your baby.
- Don't drink beer, wine, wine coolers, or liquor.
- Don't smoke cigarettes or marijuana (pot).
- Don't use crack/cocaine, heroin, inhalants (such as gasoline or ammonia), or drugs sold on the street.
- Don't even take drugs you can buy in a store, such as aspirin, laxatives, or vitamins, unless your doctor says it is okay.

DDS Pub. No. (ADM) 91-1557.

If you use drugs or drink alcohol now, your baby might have health problems later. Using drugs can make your baby sick, small, or slow to learn.

If you are drinking alcohol or using other drugs...

STOP NOW. It's not too late to quit. Don't drink any more alcohol or use any more drugs. If you stop drinking alcohol or taking drugs now, you can give your baby a better chance to be born healthy.

If you want to quit taking alcohol or other drugs...

Talk with a doctor or nurse. They can help you or tell you how to get help. Dial 411 for the telephone number you need. Here are some groups that can help:

- Health department or clinic
- Alcoholics Anonymous (AA)
- Narcotics Anonymous (NA)
- Church groups

Call 1-800-662-4357 if you want to talk to someone about a problem with alcohol or other drugs.

You can help your baby to grow strong and healthy...

- Visit your doctor regularly.
- Take care of yourself. Eat good food, exercise, and get enough sleep.
- Talk to somebody you trust about problems.
- Learn all you can about babies.
- Take childbirth classes.
- Remember that alcohol and other drugs can make your baby sick.
- Get help from a clinic, organization, or support group.

To learn more, call or write:

National Clearinghouse for Alcohol and Drug Information
P.O. Box 2345
Rockville, MD 20852
1-800-729-6686 (free call)

Chapter 43

Drug Abuse and Pregnancy

Increasing numbers of women are abusing drugs during pregnancy and thus endangering the well-being and lives of their children as well as themselves. The spreading abuse of phencyclidine (PCP), cocaine, and its potent form "crack," added to the more well known addictive narcotics such as heroin, has intensified concerns about the implications of maternal drug use for unborn children.

Some harmful effects are generally recognized. Cocaine use, for example, increases risk of hemorrhage and premature delivery, threatening the lives of mother and child. Babies exposed to narcotics in the womb are frequently born addicted, and the misery they suffer from withdrawal makes them difficult to care for, creating special demands on mothers who are often unable to take care of their children adequately. Other effects are less certain. Head size is often smaller in infants exposed to narcotics. While growth erases some of the physical differences, there may be subtle, long-term deficits in mental or neurological functioning in infants exposed to drugs in the womb.

Scientists are just beginning to explore how various drugs may affect the development of physical coordination, language, and emotional interactions. NIDA, through its clinical, epidemiological, and basic research programs, is increasing knowledge of immediate and long-term effects of drug use during pregnancy. NIDA grantees and others are designing and evaluating therapeutic programs to help these mothers and their children overcome the harm caused by drugs.

National Institute on Drug Abuse (NIDA), *Capsules*, C-89-04, June 1989.

Scope of the Problem

Evidence of increasing drug use among pregnant women comes from many parts of the country. NIDA estimates that of the women of childbearing age (15-44 years of age), 15 percent are current substance abusers. Approximately 34 million consume alcoholic beverages, more than 18 million are current cigarette smokers, and more than 6 million are current users of an illicit drug, of which 44 percent tried marijuana and 14 percent tried cocaine at least once.

A 1988 survey conducted by the National Association for Perinatal Addiction Research and Education, of 36 hospitals from across the country and representing approximately 155,000 pregnancies annually, found that on average, 11 percent of pregnant women used heroin, methadone, amphetamines, PCP, marijuana, and most commonly, cocaine. The researchers estimate that each year, as many as 375,000 infants may be affected by their mother's drug use.

Dr. Barry Zuckerman and his colleagues at Boston University School of Medicine and Boston City Hospital conducted a study of 1,226 women who gave birth at the hospital between 1986 and 1988. Of this group, 27 percent of the women had smoked marijuana and 18 percent used cocaine. They found that marijuana users gave birth to babies who are three ounces lighter and one-fifth of an inch shorter than babies born to women who did not use marijuana, while the cocaine use was associated with still shorter and lighter infants.

Dr. Loretta P. Finnegan, director of the Family Center of Jefferson Medical College of Thomas Jefferson University in Philadelphia reports that in 1985, 7 percent of women at the center were found to have cocaine in their urine, and now urine screens show that 58 percent are using the substance.

Effects on the Pregnant Mother and the Fetus

Until relatively recently, NIDA's research on the effects of maternal drug use on fetal and infant development has focused on narcotics and drugs like methadone that is used in the treatment of narcotic addiction. As the abuse of cocaine, PCP, and other drugs grew, NIDA expanded this research program to non-narcotic drugs. NIDA's research in this area is intended to estimate incidence, prevalence, and patterns of use of illicit drugs among pregnant women, to identify the consequences of maternal drug use on the newborn, to identify the mechanisms underlying organic and behavioral effects resulting from exposure to drugs, and to develop strategies and procedures to prevent, ameliorate, or reverse these toxic effects and their developmental consequences.

A NIDA-supported study by Dr. Ira J. Chasnoff and his colleagues at Northwestern University's Perinatal Center for Chemical Dependence found that women injecting cocaine intravenously during pregnancy immediately experienced complications, including premature separation of the placenta from the womb, which causes hemorrhaging that threatens the lives of both mother and fetus. Another study found that cocaine-addicted women were twice as likely to suffer premature separation of the placenta as women dependent on other drugs and four times as likely as drug-free women to experience this complication. However, this risk is reduced if the pregnant woman discontinues cocaine use early in pregnancy. Isolated cases of birth defects have been associated with cocaine use during pregnancy; however, additional studies are needed to confirm these observations.

Cocaine can also precipitate miscarriage or premature delivery because it raises blood pressure and increases contractions of the uterus. Maternal cocaine use also endangers the fetus directly. Studies show that the drug constricts arteries leading to the womb. This constriction diminishes the amount of blood, and hence oxygen, that reach the fetus. In one extreme case, cocaine apparently caused fetal stroke.

Effects on Infants

Knowledge of drug effects during the early months of life comes largely from studies of children born to women dependent on narcotics. Infants exposed to these drugs in the womb are often born addicted and undergo a characteristic withdrawal sequence called the Neonatal Abstinence Syndrome (NAS). Newborns with NAS show increased sensitivity to noise, irritability, poor coordination, excessive sneezing and yawning, and uncoordinated sucking and swallowing reflexes. If these symptoms persist, they require medication. NIDA-funded researchers are testing carefully controlled doses of phenobarbital, tincture of opium, and other substances to help infants withdraw from narcotics.

Research using ultrasound measurements also raises questions about the rate of brain growth in narcotic-exposed babies. The head circumference tends to be slightly smaller, although this difference soon disappears. By the time infants are six months old, there is little difference between drug-exposed babies and others in brain measurement. But concerns remain, since prenatal harm to these areas of the brain could affect mental functioning, such as memory, in later childhood. Some researchers find, moreover, that certain differences between drug-exposed and other infants persist, adding to concerns about long-term effects.

Other findings include increased risk for Sudden Infant Death Syndrome in which incidence among cocaine exposed infants in the Chicago study was 17 percent as compared to 1.6 percent in the general population and four percent in infants of mothers maintained on methadone. Assessment at four months of age indicate that the cocaine-exposed infants are at considerable risk for motor dysfunction. Data on 30 full-term cocaine-exposed infants and 50 full-term non-drug exposed infants indicate a significant difference in mean total risk scores with 72 percent of the control group infants in the "no risk" category, while 43 percent of the cocaine-exposed infants, were designated "high risk" for motor developmental dysfunction. The infants will be followed to three years of age.

Long-Term Effects

The epidemic of drug abuse among pregnant women is recent enough that investigators are only now having the opportunity to follow groups of children over several years and thus generalize about more far-reaching effects. Some of the preliminary findings are encouraging. Children at age two to five born to methadone-maintained women seem comparable in intelligence to youngsters of drug-free mothers. However, despite scoring in the normal range for overall intelligence, these children seem to run increased risk of learning disabilities and delayed motor, speech, and language development.

Effective drug intervention programs for drug-dependent mothers and their children may be essential to promoting the youngster's emotional and intellectual well-being. Dr. Judy Howard at the University of California, Los Angeles, is assessing the benefits of a program using a pediatrician, a public health nurse, and a social worker to contact homes regularly to offer information, advice, and referrals to medical and other services. In addition, an infant development specialist works with the children on development skills while a specialist helps mothers and foster parents become sensitive to the child's state of well-being.

The increasing use of drugs by women of childbearing age, the greater numbers of children being born to drug-abusing women, and the environment in which these infants are reared all lend added urgency to conduct additional research in these critical areas.

Chapter 44

Guidelines for Pregnant Substance-Abusing Women

Overview

Traditionally, alcohol and other drug treatment programs served adult males, and few women received the treatment they needed. The scarcity of treatment services for women continues today. It is imperative that programs include services designed specifically for women, particularly pregnant women.

Profile of the Women Being Served

Reliable national estimates of the prevalence of alcohol and other drug use by pregnant women are not available. Several factors limit the accuracy and usefulness of current estimates, including differences in the populations studied, the lack of representativeness of samples used, and differences in the methods employed to determine drug use. Results of specific studies, such as those reported below, illustrate to some degree the nature and extent of the problem.

- Data from one study of 36 hospitals, mainly in urban areas, were extrapolated to arrive at an estimate of 375,000 infants

This chapter contains excerpts from DHHS Pub. No. (SMA) 93-1998: *Pregnant Substance-Using Women*. To receive a copy of the complete report write: Substance Abuse and Mental Health Services Administration, Center for Substance Abuse Treatment—Publications, Rockwall II Building, 10th Floor, 5600 Fishers Lane, Rockville, MD 20852-9949.

exposed in utero to illegal drugs each year, or 11 percent of all births.

- A study conducted in Pinellas County, Florida, of urine samples from more than 700 women enrolling in prenatal care during a 1-month period in 1989 found little difference in the prevalence of drug and alcohol use between women seen at public clinics (16.3 percent) and those seen at private offices (13.1 percent), as well as similar rates of substance abuse among white women (15.4 percent) and black women (14.1 percent).

- A study based on a review of medical records in eight hospitals in Philadelphia in 1989 found that 16.3 percent of women had used cocaine while pregnant.

- A study that assessed drug use, utilizing urine samples obtained at admission for delivery in all seven hospitals in Rhode Island, showed that 3 percent of women used marijuana.

- Fifty-nine percent of the women in a Boston City Hospital study acknowledged that they had consumed alcohol during their pregnancies.

To meet the need for estimates of the prevalence of alcohol and other drug use by pregnant women that are generalizable to the Nation, the National Institute on Drug Abuse has recently sponsored a national, hospital-based study known as the National Pregnancy and Health Survey. Until these and other data become available, service providers should be alert to patterns of alcohol and other drug use occurring locally among women of all socioeconomic and ethnic groups. Those with clinical experience in treating substance-using women have found that the therapeutic needs of women, especially those with children, are markedly different from the needs of men. Substance-using women come from every ethnic and socioeconomic group and have a multitude of needs. Moreover, a substantial portion of the women who seek publicly supported treatment for their addictions share a core group of problems that reflect problems of the communities in which they live. Unless these core problems are addressed, women will be unable to take full advantage of the therapeutic process. Many women who seek treatment for their alcohol and other drug problems through publicly funded programs share the following characteristics:

- Function as single parents and receive little or no financial support from the birth fathers.
- Lack employment skills and education and are unemployed or underemployed.
- Live in unstable or unsafe environments, including households where others use alcohol and other drugs. Many women are at risk of being homeless and some are homeless.
- Lack transportation and face extreme difficulty getting to and from a variety of appointments, including treatment.
- Lack child care and baby-sitting options and are unable to enroll in treatment.
- Experience special therapeutic needs, including problems with codependency, incest, abuse, victimization, sexuality, and relationships involving significant others.
- Experience special medical needs, including gynecological problems.

Access to Services

Pregnant, substance-using women may access health care services from a variety of sites, including emergency rooms, pregnancy testing sites, clinics treating sexually transmitted diseases, community health centers, and clinics of the Special Supplemental Food Program for Women, Infants, and Children (WIC). Occasionally, alcohol and other drug treatment program staff are the first to notice that a woman is pregnant. Regardless of where she accesses care, appropriate referrals for prenatal care should be provided, and she should be assisted to follow through on these referrals.

Access to care must be simplified for a woman when she enters the system. She should receive whatever support is needed—whether it is financial assistance, help in setting up appointments, or transportation and child care services. Whenever possible, a case manager should schedule a specific prenatal appointment for the woman and initiate other needed services. In addition, a psychiatric assessment should be done to identify cases of alcohol and other drug use and psychiatric illness.

It may be difficult to convince a pregnant, substance-using woman to seek prenatal care. The concept of preventive health care, as opposed to emergency-necessitated health care, may be a foreign concept to her. More importantly, she may have a basic distrust or dislike of the health care system in general, and doctors in particular. Her feelings of fear and guilt, and possible negative past experiences, may cause her to expect poor treatment. Sometimes she provokes a hostile interchange with health care professionals.

Women need to receive health care services in an environment that is nonjudgmental, nonpunitive, nurturing, and culturally and linguistically sensitive. It is essential for all members of the health care team, from the clerical staff to the physicians, to recognize the importance of providing prenatal, postnatal, and pediatric services in a caring way. Staff must avoid comments designed to make the patient feel guilty or ashamed, such as the use of pejorative words like "wino" or "junkie." Each health care visit is an opportunity to provide positive reinforcement to the substance-using patient.

Continuum of Care

The pregnant, substance-using woman requires a continuum of care that includes a broad range of support services provided over an extended period of time. This continuum of care should reflect the complexity of her multiple roles as a person in recovery, parent, partner, and frequently, single head of a household. Ideally, support services should be provided as long as the woman and her family need and can benefit from them, potentially until her last child reaches adulthood. In reality, support services may be available for a period of a few months to several years.

The case management function is essential for the recovery and well-being of the substance-using woman and her family. Virtually any agency can provide case management services, although the lead agency typically assigns an appropriate staff person to this role, such as a social worker or nurse. The case manager assists the patient in accessing services, and monitors her participation and progress in using health care, alcohol and other drug treatment, and other social services.

The multiple services coordinated by the case manager are generally provided by a variety of agencies. Many of these services are initiated during or even prior to pregnancy and should continue after delivery for as long as they are appropriate. The consortium of service providers may change over time, depending on the family's individual circumstances and resources.

The case manager should be aware that differences in philosophies may exist between health and social service agencies and the alcohol and other drug treatment field. Behaviors that health and social service agencies view as helping and supportive are often viewed as codependent behaviors by the treatment field. As agencies work together on behalf of patients, they too must recognize and handle complex and legitimate differences in philosophies and practices.

Case Management

Case management is a vital function that helps to ensure that patients receive and appropriately utilize a variety of services necessary for their improved functioning. Case management should be initiated prenatally and continue throughout the postpartum period for all substance-using women. Services should be provided and maintained as appropriate for the individual woman and her family. The case manager should support and guide the patient to address issues concerning her recovery from alcohol and other drug abuse, develop psychosocial and parenting skills, and meet her survival needs. Key case management functions include:

- A review and assessment
- An individual care plan
- Discussion of the plan with the patient
- Referrals to other agencies, groups, or institutions
- Monitoring of the patient's progress
- Ongoing case management support
- A review of the patient's individual care plan

Comprehensive Service Delivery

The delivery of comprehensive services to substance-using women and their families should continue postpartum. The greatest success is achieved by and for these women when a continuum of care is available to address their special needs as women, mothers, spouses, and heads of households. The following services are often needed:

- Health care services
- Alcohol and other drug treatment services
- Survival-related services
- Psychosocial services
- Parenting and family services

Medical Stabilization and Withdrawal

The initial stabilization as well as the medical withdrawal of pregnant women from their drug(s) of abuse are recognized means of reducing the acute illness associated with the use of alcohol and other drugs. The initial stabilization of the patient should be accomplished within 10 days of first contact or earlier if medically necessary.

During the period of stabilization, caregivers need to monitor the mother and fetus for adverse signs of drug withdrawal, establish a basis for ongoing alcohol and other drug treatment and recovery, and initiate a relationship between the mother and available supportive services within the community. The lead agency is generally responsible for assigning an appropriate staff person to undertake case management functions. The role of the case manager is to monitor and promote completion of this initial phase.

Medical Withdrawal from Alcohol

It should be assumed that pregnant women who consume over 8 ounces of [absolute] alcohol (1 pint of liquor) daily have developed tolerance. However, tolerance may develop at lower levels of consumption in some women and in women using multiple drugs.

The sudden cessation of drinking can result in withdrawal symptoms, some of which may be threatening to the mother and the fetus. It is imperative that medical withdrawal of an alcohol-dependent, pregnant woman be conducted in an inpatient setting and under medical supervision that includes collaboration with an obstetrician. These conditions will ensure

- Close observation and monitoring of maternal alcohol withdrawal status
- Continual monitoring of fetal well-being

Symptoms of Alcohol Withdrawal

Early symptoms of alcohol withdrawal generally appear 6 to 48 hours after drinking has stopped but can occur up to 10 days after the last drink. Withdrawal symptoms may include:

- Restlessness
- Tachycardia
- Irritability
- Hypertension
- Anorexia
- Insomnia
- Nausea

- Nightmares
- Vomiting
- Impaired concentration
- Sweating
- Impaired memory
- Tremor
- Elevated vital signs

More severe symptoms of alcohol withdrawal may include:

- Increased tremulousness
- Increased agitation
- Increased sweating
- Delirium (with confusion, disorientation, impaired memory and judgment)
- Hallucinations (auditory, visual, or tactile)
- Delusions (usually paranoid)
- Grand mal seizures

Note: Withdrawal symptoms do not necessarily progress from mild to severe. In some individuals, a grand mal seizure may be the first sign of withdrawal. Seizures usually occur 12 to 24 hours after cessation or reduction of drinking. One-third of all patients who have seizures develop delirium tremens.

Most programs choose to treat the pregnant, alcohol-dependent woman with short-acting barbiturates or benzodiazepines. Chlordiazepoxide (Librium) and other benzodiazepines, such as diazepam (Valium) and barbiturates (Phenobarbital, Seconal), are valuable for symptomatic treatment during medical withdrawal from alcohol. They are also potentially teratogenic. Some clinicians, therefore, recommend avoiding their use if at all possible. The risks versus the possible benefits of their use need to be assessed.

Disulfiram (Antabuse) is contraindicated during pregnancy. Its use has been associated with clubfoot, VACTERL syndrome (a pattern of congenital anomalies), and phocomelia of the lower extremities. The woman who conceives while taking this drug should receive counseling before deciding to continue the pregnancy.

Maternal and Fetal Effects of Alcohol

Alcohol use during pregnancy may be associated with a variety of serious health consequences for the woman, the fetus, and the subsequent infant.

Possible maternal complications of excessive alcohol consumption:

- Nutritional deficiencies
- Pancreatitis
- Alcoholic ketoacidosis
- Precipitate labor
- Alcoholic hepatitis
- Deficient milk ejection
- Cirrhosis

Possible effects on the fetus:

- Fetal Alcohol Syndrome (FAS)—prenatal/postnatal growth retardation; central nervous system deficits including developmental delay and neurological/intellectual impairments; facial feature anomalies, including microcephaly

- Fetal Alcohol Effects (FAE)—cardiac abnormalities; neonatal irritability and hypotonia; hyperactivity; genitourinary abnormalities; skeletal and muscular abnormalities; ocular problems; hemangiomas

- No effect

Opioid Stabilization

The following approaches are used to manage the pregnant, opioid-addicted woman. The first approach is methadone maintenance combined with psychosocial counseling. This is a well-documented approach to improve outcomes for both the woman and her fetus.

The second approach is slow medical withdrawal with methadone. The safety of this second approach has not been documented.

Opioid Withdrawal Signs and Symptoms

Mild withdrawal signs and symptoms include:

- Generalized anxiety
- Opioid craving
- Restlessness
- Slight aching of muscles, joints, and bones
- Lower back pain

Mild to moderate withdrawal signs and symptoms include:

- Tension
- Yen sleep (mild insomnia)
- Mydriasis (pupils dilated)
- Lethargy
- Diaphoresis (increased perspiration)

Moderate withdrawal signs and symptoms include:

- Chills alternating with flushing and diaphoresis (sweating)
- Nausea and/or stomach cramps
- Rhinorrhea (runny nose)
- Moderate aching of muscles, joints, and bones
- Lower back pain
- Anorexia
- Nausea and/or stomach cramps
- Yawning
- Lacrimation (tearing)
- Goose flesh (earlier if client is in a cold, drafty room)
- Elevated pulse and blood pressure

Moderate to severe withdrawal signs and symptoms include:

- Diarrhea
- Tachycardia (pulse over 100 BPM)
- Vomiting
- Increased respiratory rate and depth
- Tremors

Severe withdrawal signs and symptoms include:

- Doubling over with stomach cramps
- Kicking movements
- Elevated temperature (usually low grade, less than 100°F)

NOTE: Withdrawal signs and symptoms differ in their order of appearance from one individual to another. Some individuals may not exhibit certain withdrawal signs and symptoms. Signs may also include uterine irritability, increased fetal activity, or rarely, hypotension.

Symptoms of Opioid Withdrawal Syndrome

Despite its dramatic appearance, the opioid withdrawal syndrome is rarely life-threatening or permanently disabling to an adult. However, there is good evidence that the fetus may be more susceptible to withdrawal symptoms than the mother. In the mother, the initial signs of opioid withdrawal progress to increasingly painful physical symptoms. In addition to these signs, patients show compelling psychological cravings for drugs, as well as drug-seeking behavior.

Methadone substitution is the standard treatment for heroin addiction. Methadone treatment alternatives consist of (1) high-dose blockage; (2) low-dose maintenance; and (3) medical withdrawal.

Medical withdrawal of the opioid-dependent woman is not recommended in pregnancy because of the increased risk to the fetus of intrauterine death. Methadone maintenance is the treatment of choice. In addition to methadone maintenance, a comprehensive approach is needed that will provide the patient with counseling and other services.

The administration of methadone, combined with any opioid agonist/antagonist such as pentazocine (Talwin), will precipitate withdrawal. Any pregnant woman receiving methadone should be advised against taking opioid agonist/antagonists under all circumstances.

Neonatal abstinence syndrome (NAS) may or may not be related to maternal dose of methadone; NAS may also be related to fetal gestational age and infant weight. However, studies in both pregnant women and other adults have shown that larger doses of methadone result in a decreased use of other drugs.

Maternal and Fetal Effects of Opioids

These effects may be the result of concomitant maternal lifestyle factors rather than the direct result of drug use.

Possible effects on the pregnancy:

- Toxemia
- Intrauterine growth retardation
- Miscarriage
- Premature rupture of membranes
- Infections
- Breech presentation (abnormal presentation due to premature delivery)
- Preterm labor
- No effect

Possible effects on the mother:

- Poor nourishment, with vitamin deficiencies, iron deficiency anemia, and folic acid deficiency anemia
- Medical complications from frequent use of dirty needles (abscesses, ulcers, thrombophlebitis, bacterial endocarditis, hepatitis, and urinary tract infection)
- Sexually transmitted diseases (gonorrhea, chlamydia, syphilis, herpes, and HIV infection)
- Hypertensive disorder
- No effect

Possible effects on the fetus and newborn infant:

- Low birth weight
- Prematurity
- Neonatal abstinence syndrome
- Stillbirth
- Sudden infant death syndrome
- No effect

Guidelines for Methadone Maintenance

Methadone maintenance is strongly encouraged for all pregnant, opioid-dependent women. It provides the following advantages:

- Reduces illegal opioid use as well as use of other drugs
- Helps to remove the opioid-dependent woman from the drug-seeking environment and eliminates the necessary illegal behavior
- Prevents fluctuations of the maternal drug level that may occur throughout the day
- Improves maternal nutrition, increasing the weight of the newborn
- Improves the woman's ability to participate in prenatal care and other rehabilitation efforts
- Enhances the woman's ability to prepare for the birth of the infant and begin homemaking
- Reduces obstetrical complications

There are no specific guidelines established for methadone dosages for pregnant women. In general, the clinical trend is toward use of an individually determined, most effective dose that is adequate to prevent withdrawal symptoms. The following guidelines have been used for pregnant and nonpregnant substance users:

- The high-dose methadone blockage dosage is between 50 and 150 mg per day.

- The low-dosage methadone maintenance dosage is less than 60 mg per day.

  Based on current and emerging research, the National Institute on Drug Abuse (NIDA) suggests that maintenance doses below 60 mg are not effective and hence not appropriate. Arbitrary low-dose policies for pregnant and nonpregnant patients is often associated with increased drug use as well as reduced program retention. Based on current informed consensus, the most prudent course is to rely on individually determined methadone dosing that is measured by the absence of subjective and objective abstinence symptoms and the reduction of drug hunger.

  An increased methadone dosage may be needed in later stages of pregnancy to prevent withdrawal. (The greater plasma volume and renal blood flow of pregnancy can contribute to a reduced level of methadone in the blood. As a result, the woman's maintenance dose may be insufficient to prevent cravings.) Either administer methadone twice a day to give a more even blood level throughout the day or raise the single daily dose.

Guidelines for Medical Withdrawal from Methadone

Medical withdrawal of the pregnant, opioid-dependent woman from methadone is not indicated or recommended. Few women will have the motivation or the psychosocial supports to accomplish and maintain total abstinence. The goal, therefore, is to achieve the best therapeutic dose possible with which the woman feels comfortable. The neonatal abstinence syndrome can be treated with minimal complications.

Despite the above caution, at times, medical withdrawal may need to be considered due to logistical or geographic barriers. In these cases, the decision to undertake such a program must be a joint decision between the obstetrician, the woman, and her counselor, with the understanding that few women will be appropriate candidates for this approach.

The woman should understand that she must prove she is a candidate for medical withdrawal by complying with prenatal and therapy appointments and supplying clean urines. If at any time the woman is unable to comply with these requirements, no further decrease in dosage of methadone should be ordered.

Timing of withdrawal. There are no research data that suggest withdrawal in one trimester is worse than in others. Some clinical practitioners indicate concerns regarding methadone withdrawal prior to 14 weeks or after 32 weeks. These concerns are based on the theoretical possibility of an increased incidence of spontaneous abortion and premature labor. Other clinicians believe that withdrawal can be performed in all trimesters.

Patients should be allowed to discontinue withdrawal at any time, for any reason, without feelings of guilt. They should then be placed into a methadone maintenance program at a therapeutically sound dose. Clinicians need to be particularly aware that a decrease in methadone dosage could precipitate a relapse to drug use. Patients in continuous treatment who return to illegal drug use should be placed back on methadone. Methadone is preferable to the use of illegal street drugs.

Withdrawal schedule. Medical withdrawal from methadone is usually done in decrements of 2 to 2½ mg every 7 to 10 days. This procedure should only be done in conjunction with an obstetrician who can monitor the effects on the fetus. Intrauterine demise (death of the fetus in utero) has been documented as a complication of medical withdrawal even when done under optimal conditions, such as hospitalization and close fetal monitoring.

Note: At the time of publication, there was no protocol for medical withdrawal from methadone that had been evaluated in an appropriate number of women with suitable scientific and medical rigor.

Opioid Withdrawal Using Clonidine

The long-term effects of the use of clonidine in pregnancy are still unknown. Although clonidine hydrochloride has been used safely and effectively for rapid medical withdrawal in the management of opioid withdrawal in nonpregnant, opioid-dependent individuals, there are no data concerning its safety in pregnancy. Further research in this area needs to be performed before this technique can be recommended as a standard of care for pregnant women.

Cocaine Withdrawal

There are no well-documented studies regarding the safety or efficacy of using drugs to medically withdraw pregnant, cocaine-using women. The evidence is extremely limited for all methods of medical withdrawal. Inpatient treatment is the ideal whenever possible, although these facilities may not always be available. Medical withdrawal is just the first step in the continuum of care for pregnant, cocaine-dependent women. Referral to ongoing alcohol and other drug treatment and relapse prevention services is essential.

Symptoms of Cocaine Withdrawal

Withdrawal from cocaine dependence is characterized by depression, anxiety, and lethargy, which begin to resolve after approximately 1 week. Less common are signs of a paranoid psychosis during withdrawal from chronic use of high doses of cocaine. In cocaine withdrawal, medication is rarely needed for the serious sequelae that are associated with alcohol, barbiturate, and opioid withdrawal.

Maternal and Fetal/Infant Effects of Cocaine

Possible effects of maternal cocaine use during pregnancy:

- Intrauterine growth retardation (IUGR)
- Abruptio placentae
- Premature labor
- Spontaneous abortion
- No effect

Possible effects on the fetus and newborn infant that have been reported:

- Increased congenital anomalies
- Mild neurodysfunction
- Transient electroencephalogram abnormalities
- Cerebral infarction and seizures
- Vascular disruption syndrome
- Sudden infant death syndrome
- Smaller head circumference
- No effect

Guidelines for Withdrawal From Cocaine: Treatment Options

There are no data about the effectiveness of the following guidelines in pregnancy. In those guidelines that substitute other drugs, many of the drugs are problematic to the newborn and some have not been confirmed to be safe. Some centers do not generally use antidepressants for cocaine withdrawal depression. However, other programs prescribe antidepressants for the first 5 days to try to reduce the high dropout rate that occurs during this period. Sedatives and/or antidepressants may cause excessive drowsiness in a cocaine-dependent woman.

Cocaine-dependent women who require sedatives and/or antidepressants for any significant length of time often have an endogenous depressive disorder. Psychiatric consultation is usually indicated.

Dosing Strategy

To withdraw a pregnant woman dependent on cocaine, the following are options.

- *No medications.* Pregnant patients who are withdrawing from cocaine should not be medicated except in cases of extreme agitation and by individual order of the health care provider.

- *Anxiolytics.* If medication is needed, low doses of diazepam (Valium) or chlordiazepoxide (Librium) (25 mg by mouth, 4 times a day, x 6 doses) may be used.

- *Antidepressants.* A typical withdrawal guideline for cocaine-dependent women uses doxepin (Sinequan) or desipramine (Norpramin). For example,
  —Days 1-2: Doxepin 25 mg (one tablet) by mouth 2 times a day, 50 mg maximum.
  —Days 3-5: Doxepin 25 mg (one tablet) by mouth 2 times a day, then discontinue.
  —Further therapy should be determined by the treating physician after an initial period of observation.
  —No drug therapy is usually indicated after the first 5 days.

- *Barbiturates.* For cocaine withdrawal symptoms:
  —Days 1-2: Phenobarbital 30 to 60 mg every 4 hours as needed.
  —Days 3-4: Phenobarbital 30 to 60 mg every 6 hours as needed.

- *Bromocriptine.* Bromocriptine, a drug used to treat menstrual abnormalities and infertility in women, has provided striking and consistent relief from cocaine craving among inpatients. Research indicates that cocaine, when used by the first-time user, seems to stimulate dopamine and also blocks the reuptake of dopamine, which produces the cocaine high. The brains of regular users of cocaine cannot make dopamine as quickly as the cocaine demands; the result is an eventual depletion that creates the crashing and craving effects. The use of bromocriptine in pregnancy is not recommended because of the lack of proven efficacy and unknown effects, both short and long term, on the fetus.

- *Acupuncture.* Acupuncture has been used in the treatment of cocaine addiction. Traditional use of acupuncture for other disorders has usually been contraindicated in pregnancy. At the time of publication, the National Institute on Drug Abuse has not concluded its evaluation of the efficacy of this treatment.

Sedative-Hypnotic Medical Withdrawal

Inpatient medical withdrawal from barbiturates, benzodiazepines, and other sedative-hypnotic drugs is recommended because continual monitoring of the mother and the fetus is required. Drug doses must be tapered so that mother and fetus arrive at a drug-free state without experiencing an uncontrolled withdrawal.

Barbiturates and benzodiazepines are the most commonly abused sedative-hypnotics. There are marked similarities between the withdrawal syndromes seen with both of these drugs. Patients abruptly withdrawn from large doses of benzodiazepines may sustain withdrawal symptoms that closely resemble those associated with barbiturate physical dependence. Because of these similarities, only the barbiturate abstinence syndrome is presented in this guideline.

Symptoms of Barbiturate Abstinence Syndrome

The barbiturate abstinence syndrome begins 6 to 24 hours after the last dose, and symptoms are generally more severe with the short-acting barbiturates. Signs and symptoms of barbiturate abstinence include:

- Tremulousness
- Diaphoresis
- Anxiety
- Postural hypotension
- Insomnia
- Grand mal convulsions (between days 3 and 7)
- Agitation
- Anorexia
- Delirium
- Nausea and vomiting
- Tendon hyperreflexia

If untreated, withdrawal symptoms can progress to hyperpyrexia, electrolyte abnormalities, cardiovascular collapse, and death.

381

Management of Withdrawal

Management of withdrawal in patients who may or may not be pregnant can include:

- Substitution of a long-acting agent (phenobarbital, diazepam, clonazepam), and subsequent withdrawal of this agent
- Slow withdrawal of the addicting agent

Risk categories for severe withdrawal:

- Low risk: Sporadic use of a drug or use for relief of cocaine-induced anxiety or insomnia.

- Moderate risk: Daily use of a drug for at least 2 to 4 months at a therapeutic level; concomitant alcohol abuse at low doses; history of mild withdrawal symptoms.

- High risk: Prolonged daily use of a drug at higher than therapeutic doses; higher use of alcohol; history of serious withdrawal symptoms.

- Highest risk: Previous withdrawal seizures or a history of a seizure disorder that is exacerbated by sedative-hypnotic withdrawal.

Some considerations for withdrawal from sedative-hypnotic drugs during pregnancy:

- Severe withdrawal from barbiturates can produce status epilepticus and maternal and fetal respiratory arrest. Immediate obstetrical intervention and hospitalization are warranted.

- Use of dilantin and other anticonvulsants have been considered for a patient with a history of withdrawal seizures. However, these drugs have been associated with congenital anomalies. Therefore, their use in pregnancy must be based on an assessment of the risks versus the benefits. Although there are concerns of teratogenicity regarding benzodiazepines and barbiturates, these appear to have a lower risk versus benefit ratio.

Mental Health Considerations

Mental disorders in pregnant, substance-using women often go undetected by health care providers and alcohol and other drug treatment staff. It is essential that a dual diagnosis be made, when appropriate, and addressed in subsequent treatment planning. The complex combination of pregnancy, addiction, and mental illness requires a carefully coordinated approach. The following general guidelines can be useful in assessing the mental health of pregnant, substance-using women.

Mental Health Assessment

Distinguish between drug-induced psychiatric symptoms and a major mental disorder. Symptoms such as anxiety, agitation, and paranoia can be manifestations of a state of drug intoxication or of the withdrawal syndrome itself and at times require no medications. Ongoing psychosocial support may help minimize many of these symptoms.

On the other hand, confirmed mental illness may necessitate the continuation of medications, such as antidepressants or antipsychotics, which have been previously effective in treating the underlying disorder. It is mandatory that a diagnosis of mental illness be ruled out before such medication is stopped. It must be remembered that evidence is inconclusive regarding the safe use of any psychotropic medication in pregnant women. A thorough assessment of the risks versus the benefits must be made prior to administering these medications.

Establish any previous history of psychiatric illness before developing the medical withdrawal treatment plan. Efforts should be made to contact previous therapists, treating agencies, and mental health facilities for this crucial information.

Establish communication early in treatment with mental health personnel involved in the patient's care. These individuals often can provide important history, help build an alliance with the patient, support discharge planning, and provide assistance in the event of an acute management crisis.

383

Individualize medical withdrawal plans for each patient. Carefully review standard guidelines and amend them if there are significant psychiatric problems to be treated.

Set up arrangements to involve mental health personnel, where appropriate, in establishing diagnoses and in developing the treatment plan.

Continue prescribed medications and provide appropriate followup for patients who enter alcohol and other drug treatment programs with well-documented, diagnosed psychiatric illnesses that require psychopharmacologic medication. Continue any prescribed medications, such as methadone and chlordiazepoxide, except as advised by the patient's health and mental health care providers. Patients should be supported in this decision by treatment programs. Some support groups may inappropriately encourage women to abandon all medications.

Do not avoid seeking therapy for the patient because of the complex combination of pregnancy, addiction, and psychiatric problems. Careful planning and staff coordination are usually effective in treatment.

Use well-validated psychiatric assessment scales in the diagnosis and followup of individual patients.

Consider issues of codependency, adult children of alcoholics/other addictions, and deep trauma from childhood in the evaluation of patients.

Guidelines for Medical Withdrawal

Orders for medication should be individualized to minimize the types and doses prescribed. Psychotropic drugs may need to be prescribed throughout medical withdrawal. The use of psychotropic drugs must be considered on a case-by-case basis, taking into consideration their effects on the mother and fetus, particularly with respect to interactions with methadone and possible congenital abnormalities. Behavioral management techniques should be developed to minimize the need for these medications. Providing adequate staff, structure, limits, and support are important treatment methods.

Other Issues

Agitation and oppositional or impulsive behavior can be manifestations of cognitive impairments, such as attention deficit disorder, limited intelligence, mild retardation, or psychotic illness. Patients with these behaviors can appear to have difficulty comprehending or complying with treatment expectations. Awareness of these deficits can help staff manage these problems and adapt treatment methods to minimize or avoid unnecessary confrontations.

Chapter 45

Neurologic Abnormalities in Infants of Substance-Abusing Mothers

Apparently healthy infants of substance-abusing mothers have elevated blood levels of the neurotransmitter norepinephrine, according to California neonatologists and pediatricians. The researchers suggest that the high norepinephrine levels may be responsible for some of the neurologic abnormalities in these infants.

Dr. Sally L. Davidson Ward, assistant professor of pediatrics at the University of Southern California (USC) School of Medicine and Childrens Hospital of Los Angeles, and her colleagues found almost twice as much norepinephrine in the blood of substance-exposed babies as in infants of mothers who did not use any substances of abuse. In contrast, no differences were detected in the blood levels of epinephrine and dopamine, two related neurotransmitters, Dr. Ward says.

With associates at USC, the Los Angeles County/USC Medical Center, and the Martin Luther King Hospital in Los Angeles, Dr. Ward studied 15 healthy babies and 22 otherwise healthy offspring of substance-abusing women. All of these mothers had used cocaine and a variety of other drugs during pregnancy but, according to Dr. Ward, "cocaine was the common denominator."

"The cocaine-exposed babies had no chemical evidence of cocaine in their bodies yet they cried uncontrollably and appeared jittery and were almost continuously in motion," Dr. Ward says. Unlike control babies they were small and had low birthweights despite being term babies. Another characteristic—excessive muscle tone, or hypertonicity—produced abnormal stiffness in their upper bodies. "Together with a

Research Resources Reporter, February 1992.

high level of physical activity, this upper-body stiffness often causes the babies to injure themselves as they move about in their cribs. When they become agitated, cocaine-exposed babies tremble and shake," Dr. Ward says, "and the movements can abrade their skin. Even bedclothes can hurt them."

Blood specimens were obtained from the infants when they were 1 to 4 months old, "at least 1 month after exposure to cocaine," Dr. Ward notes. The blood samples were analyzed for epinephrine, nore-pinephrine, and dopamine differences that might be associated with cocaine or cocaine withdrawal. In addition, the receptors by which those neurotransmitters attach to lymphocytes and blood platelets were also measured. Ideally the neurotransmitter receptors should have been measured in the brain, but that is of course not possible to do in live persons. Other investigators have reported, however, that the receptor concentration on blood cells reflects the concentration in the brain, according to Dr. Ward.

Although the scientists found norepinephrine at nearly twice its normal level in the blood of cocaine-exposed infants, they found no significant differences in the number of receptors in the two groups of babies. "This seems a paradox," Dr. Ward says. "With an increase in the amount of norepinephrine circulating in these cocaine-exposed babies one would expect to see a homeostatic decrease in the number of norepinephrine receptors. The number of receptors ordinarily de-clines when the neurochemicals saturate the nerve endings; con-versely, receptor number rises when the neurochemical level decreases.

"But we did not find that. The number of norepinephrine receptors was the same in the blood of high-norepinephrine, cocaine-exposed babies as it was in the control infants." Dr. Ward adds that she and her associates think they may be detecting an increased sensitivity of the entire system of neurotransmitter-receptor interactions. "Of course we are measuring neurochemical evidence from the peripheral nervous system, not the actual receptors in the brain that have been measured by other investigators in animals exposed to cocaine," she says.

Neurologic abnormalities may occur even when cocaine use stops after the first trimester, according to Dr. Ward. Cocaine damage to the fetus is attributed in part to the vasoconstrictive effect of norepineph-rine and directly to cocaine itself; cocaine narrows maternal and fe-tal blood vessels that carry oxygen-rich blood to the fetal brain and developing internal organs. Dopamine and probably norepinephrine are also thought to inhibit breathing, Dr. Ward says. "It's not fully understood, but we think that breathing problems may place cocaine-exposed infants at a relatively high risk of sudden infant death syndrome (SIDS)," she adds.

Dr. Ward says that babies exposed to opiates—notably heroin and methadone—during fetal life are also at risk of SIDS; they display some of the same symptoms these babies have, but for a shorter time. For cocaine-exposed babies the problems persist at least through the first year of life.

"The hypertonicity we see in these babies is there long after the cocaine itself is gone. Why are these babies still troubled, why are the effects there after the cocaine is long gone? These are the questions we are trying to answer," she says.

"Of course, the ideal medicine for these babies is preventive medicine," says Dr. Ward. "The statistics are alarming. There are close to a half-million cocaine-exposed babies born in the United States each year." She notes that more than 4 percent of pregnant women aged 12 to 34 years used cocaine during pregnancy, according to the 1990 Household Survey of the National Institute on Drug Abuse. Dr. Ward believes the best approach to the problem is drug rehabilitation in nonjudgmental settings for cocaine-addicted women before they begin a pregnancy.

—by Jane Collins

Additional Reading

1. Ward, S. L. D., Schuetz, S., Wachsman, L., et al., Elevated plasma norepinephrine levels in infants of substance-abusing mothers. *American Journal of Diseases of Children* 145:45-48, 1991.

2. Dixon, S. D., Effects of transplacental exposure to cocaine and methamphetamine on the neonate. *Western Journal of Medicine* 150:436-442, 1989.

3. Woods, J. R., Plessinger, M. A., and Clark, K. E., Effects of cocaine use on uterine blood flow and fetal oxygenation. *Journal of the American Medical Association* 257:957-961, 1987.

4. Chasnoff, I. J., Burns, W. J., Schnoll, S. H., and Burns, K. A. Cocaine use in pregnancy. *New England Journal of Medicine* 313:666-669, 1985.

The research described in this article was supported by a Biomedical Research Support Grant from the National Center for Research Resources; the American Lung Association of Los Angeles County; the Greater Los Angeles and Washington: State Chapters of the National Sudden Infant Death Syndrome Foundation; the Los Angeles County Orange County and Inland Empire Chapters of the Guild for Infant Survival; the Junior Women's Club of Orange; and the Ruth and Vernon Taylor Foundation.

Chapter 46

Medical Management of the Drug-Exposed Infant

Medical management of the drug-exposed infant has emerged in recent years as a major challenge to health care professionals. This chapter presents the TIP [Treatment Improvement Protocol] consensus panel's recommendations and guidelines for diagnosis of in utero drug exposure, medical assessment of the neonate, effects of exposure to different types of drugs, guidelines for appropriate treatment, promotion of positive parent-infant interaction, and discharge criteria and instructions. As a foundation for its guidelines in these specific areas, the consensus panel recommends the following:

Surveillance. Clinicians should be aware of shifting local trends due to user preferences and street market availability of particular drugs within the community. Networking with local emergency and trauma services, drug treatment providers, social service agencies, and the criminal justice system provides neonatal caregivers with an opportunity for community surveillance. However, each nursery also should monitor the changing patterns of drug exposure in its newborn population. Further, the quality of data on drug abuse patterns obtained from maternal histories or anonymous toxicology screens should be continually monitored.

This chapter contains excerpts from DHHS Pub. No. (SMA) 93-2011: *Improving Treatment for Drug-Exposed Infants*. To receive a copy of the complete report write: Substance Abuse and Mental Health Services Administration, Center for Substance Abuse Treatment—Publications, Rockwall II Building, 10th Floor, 5600 Fishers Lane, Rockville, MD 20852-9949.

Preconception. Ideally, obstetricians, family practitioners, midwives, family planning clinicians, and other clinicians providing health care to women of childbearing age should provide counseling regarding abstinence from alcohol and other drugs prior to and during pregnancy.

Reducing Barriers to Access. Federal, State, and local agencies should reduce barriers to the use of family planning services and increase access to early prenatal care and other health services, including drug rehabilitation.

Interdisciplinary Treatment. Interdisciplinary intervention for the mother and her offspring (and the father, when possible) should be available at all points of access to care. Professionals involved in this care should include obstetricians, neonatologists, pediatricians, nurses, nutritionists, mental health professionals, social workers, substance abuse counselors, and child development specialists, at a minimum.

Staying Abreast of New Information. The medical literature is replete with research and anecdotal observations on the effects of drugs and alcohol on the infant. Long-term studies of exposure to opiates are sparse, and few systematic studies of long-term alcohol effects are available. Recent research has documented the possible long-term effect of maternal marijuana use on the infant. Longitudinal followup investigations on the effects of *in utero* cocaine exposure are in progress.

Attempts to assess the effects of drug exposure on newborns are confounded by numerous medical and environmental variables. However, acknowledging these limitations, the TIP consensus panel offers these guidelines to the medical management of drug-exposed infants. *In utero* exposure to opiates (heroin and methadone) and cocaine is emphasized. Many of the suggested approaches are also applicable to infants exposed prenatally to other drugs, including alcohol. It is very important to remember that alcohol use frequently coexists with other forms of substance abuse. A brief discussion of alcohol-related effects on infants is included for information.

Alcohol Use in Pregnancy

Abuse of alcohol is a significant societal problem in the United States; approximately 18 million Americans are chronic consumers of alcohol. Current estimates indicate that between 8 and 11 percent of women of childbearing age are either problem drinkers or alcoholics. Alcohol abuse exists within all socioeconomic levels of society. Review of drinking habits during pregnancy should form an essential part of perinatal history taking.

No safe level of alcohol consumption during pregnancy has been determined. Alcohol exposure *in utero* may result in a spectrum of abnormalities of fetal growth and development. Maternal consumption of 2 to 3 ounces of alcohol daily, often in association with "binge drinking," is frequently associated with fetal alcohol syndrome (FAS). Lesser intake of alcohol may produce subcombinations of signs of FAS; these lesser signs have been called fetal alcohol effects (FAE).

The effects of alcohol abuse during pregnancy can be summarized as follows:

Adverse Pregnancy Outcome, including an increased risk of spontaneous abortion.

FAS. The worldwide incidence of FAS is 1-3 births per 1,000 live births. To make the diagnosis of FAS, one abnormality from each of the following categories must be present:

- Prenatal or postnatal growth retardation; failure to thrive (weight, length, and/or head circumference less than the 10th percentile).

- Central nervous system dysfunction, including intellectual, neurologic, and behavioral deficits manifested as mild to moderate mental retardation, hypotonia (poor muscle tone), irritability in infancy, and later hyperactivity in childhood. Mental abnormality occurs in 85 percent of FAS children, and although IQ scores vary, affected children rarely show normal mental ability.

- Facial dysmorphology (structural abnormalities) including at least two of three characteristics: 1) Microcephaly (head circumference less than the 10th percentile). 2) Microphthalmia (abnormal smallness of the eye) or short palpebral fissures, ptosis (dropping eyelid), strabismus (imbalance of the eye muscles), or epicanthal folds (folds of the skin of the upper eyelid over the eye). 3) Poorly developed philtrum, thin upper lip (vermilion border), short upturned nose, or flattening or absence of the maxilla (upper jaw).

FAE. Lesser degree of effect.

Diagnosis of In Utero Drug Exposure

Maternal Substance Use History

A maternal AOD [Alcohol and Other Drug] use interview should be conducted at the earliest point of access into the health care system. (If possible, information about paternal substance use should also be obtained by interviewing the father or questioning the mother.) Despite concerted efforts by health care professionals to promote prenatal care, the mother may not have received such care and the delivery hospitalization may be the only opportunity to elicit information on the nature and extent of the infant's *in utero* exposure to drugs and alcohol. The mother's concern for her infant's health may encourage valid responses; conversely, fear of legal reprisals or loss of custody of the infant may cause the mother to deny drug use.

Treatment Planning

Treatment planning for mothers and involvement of representatives from all participating agencies should include referral to an appropriate AOD abuse treatment program and continued involvement with medical and psychosocial agencies. Adequate arrangements should be made to ensure that the mother can get to the treatment facility, which may, in certain instances, require the provision of transportation for the mother to the location. An indepth treatment plan should be developed for the infant through multidisciplinary efforts of doctors, nurses, social workers, and others. The mother and father should be given the opportunity and urged to take part in treatment planning. If assessment reveals that the infant may be at risk for future harm due to the mother's potential for abuse or neglect, a report should be made to the child protective services agency so that further evaluation can occur. At a minimum, the treatment team must develop a clear followup plan for the infant upon discharge from the hospital, and must arrange for careful monitoring of compliance with the plan.

Toxicology Screening of Mothers and Infants

Maternal AOD use history should be complemented by toxicology screening of the mother and/or infant at the time of delivery only in certain situations (when a complete drug history cannot be obtained and the mother is manifesting symptoms of possible addiction and withdrawal and when the infant is showing withdrawal signs.)

Legal and Ethical Considerations

The diagnosis of infants with in utero drug exposure has significant legal and ethical ramifications. [For a discussion of these issues, refer to the complete copy of *Improving Treatment for Drug-Exposed Infants*, DHHS Publication No. (SMA) 92-1022 available from the Substance Abuse and Mental Health Services Administration's Center for Substance Abuse Treatment.]

Medical Assessment of the Drug-Exposed Neonate

Physical Examination

A thorough physical examination of the neonate should include accurate assessment of weight, length, and head circumference and a standardized assessment of gestational age. Special attention should be paid to signs of intrauterine growth retardation, microcephaly or decreased head circumference, prematurity, congenital infection, and major and minor congenital malformations. Various tools and scoring systems can be used to chart and compare the infant's neuromuscular and physical maturity and size to normal ranges for infants (Ballard et al., 1977; Ballard et al., 1979; Brazelton, 1984; Lubchenco et al., 1966).

Screening for Congenital Infection

Drug-exposed infants are at increased risk of acquiring infections transmitted from mothers whose lifestyles include unsafe sexual practices or intravenous drug abuse. Assessment of the mother for sexually transmitted diseases and human immunodeficiency virus (HIV) should be incorporated into the prenatal care setting and delivery hospitalization.

In Utero *Exposure To Opiates Effects And Treatment*

Effects of In Utero *Heroin Exposure*

The effects of heroin on the neonate are as follows:

Low Birth Weight. The low birth weight is due primarily to symmetric intrauterine growth retardation. Low birth weight may also be due to prematurity. In either case, low birth weight results in the slowing of both body and head growth.

Meconium Aspiration. Meconium aspiration may be caused by hypoxia in association with antepartum or intrapartum passage of meconium secondary to fetal stress.

Neonatal Abstinence Syndrome (Withdrawal). Neonatal abstinence syndrome occurs in about 60 to 80 percent of heroin-exposed infants. Its onset is usually within 72 hours of birth, with possible mortality if the syndrome is severe and untreated. The syndrome involves several body systems. Central nervous system (CNS) signs of abstinence include irritability, hypertonia, hyperreflexia, abnormal suck, and poor feeding. Skin abrasions may result from general hyperactivity. Seizures are seen in 1 to 3 percent of heroin-exposed infants. Gastrointestinal signs include diarrhea and vomiting. Respiratory signs include tachypnea, hyperpnea, and respiratory alkalosis. Autonomic signs include sneezing, yawning, lacrimation, sweating, and hyperpyrexia. If the infant is hypermetabolic, the postnatal weight loss may be excessive and subsequent weight gain suboptimal unless higher caloric intake is provided. In cases demonstrating signs suggestive of the abstinence syndrome, other diagnoses should also receive the clinician's full attention. For example, sepsis, metabolic disorders, and CNS hemorrhage or ischemia should be considered in making the differential diagnosis.

Premature infants seem to manifest fewer overt symptoms of opiate abstinence syndrome. These differences may be due to the developmental immaturity of the preterm CNS, which might ameliorate the clinical appearance of abstinence symptoms, or to variations in total drug exposure due to a shortened gestation.

Delayed Effects. Delayed effects include subacute withdrawal with symptoms such as restlessness, agitation, irritability, and poor socialization that may persist for 4 to 6 months.

Sudden Infant Death Syndrome (SIDS). Epidemiologic studies suggest an association between SIDS and interuterine exposure to opiates (including methadone), but somewhat weaker links between SIDS and cocaine exposure.

Effects of mother's behavior. Adverse effects may be due to the life circumstances and behavior of the mother who uses heroin. Lack of prenatal care, poor nutrition, medical problems and the abuse of other drugs pose significant risk to the mother and the fetus. In addition, heroin use can cause sexual disinhibition, which increases the possibility of the mother's engaging in behaviors that place her at high risk for contracting HIV, such as sharing needles. Or the addicted mother may engage in sex for drugs with partners infected with HIV and other sexually transmitted diseases (STDs).

Effects of In Utero *Methadone Exposure*

Maternal methadone maintenance is a valuable treatment modality when administered under medical supervision. Although methadone poses some threat to the fetus, it is important to contrast the benefits of methadone in pregnancy with the risks associated with the continuing use of heroin. For this reason, methadone maintenance is often recommended for pregnant opioid-dependent women.

Benefits of methadone maintenance during pregnancy:

- Assists women in staying heroin free
- Leads to more consistent prenatal care
- Lessens possibility of fetal death
- Lessens decreased fetal growth and improves growth of newborn
- Reduces risk of HIV infection
- Enables the woman to breastfeed her infant

Risks of In Utero *Methadone Exposure*

Despite the significant advantages of methadone to an opioid-dependent pregnant woman, dangers to the fetus and to the newborn still exist, as described below.

Low Birth Weight. *In utero* exposure to methadone may lead to low birth weight caused by symmetric fetal growth retardation involving fetal weight, length, and head circumference. There is a lack of consensus on the appropriate methadone dosage schedule during pregnancy. Some studies indicate that a higher dose in the first trimester leads to a more optimal birth weight. Thus, a higher dosing schedule during this period may be considered.

Neonatal Methadone Abstinence Syndrome. Although the neonatal methadone abstinence syndrome is similar to that of heroin, it is typically more severe. Whether severity is related to maternal dosage is controversial. Late withdrawal can occur at 2 to 3 weeks of age, and subacute withdrawal can persist until 6 months of age. These phenomena may be related to variations in the metabolism of methadone due to placental transfer or neonatal metabolism. Methadone is also known to accumulate in CNS tissue.

Seizures. Seizures attributed to withdrawal will be seen in some drug-exposed infants. For example, in one study of 301 neonates passively addicted to narcotics, 18 had seizures attributed to withdrawal. Some studies have shown that infants exposed to methadone may have an increased incidence of seizures. Others in the field believe that it is actually the use of diazepam and phenobarbital that increases the incidence of seizures in methadone-exposed babies. The latter recommend the use of paregoric.

Thrombocytosis. At 4 to 10 weeks, methadone-exposed neonates are at risk to develop thrombocytosis, which may persist for 6 to 10 months. [Thrombocytosis is an abnormal increase in the number of blood platelets.]

Hyperthyroid State. Elevation of T_3 and T_4 during the first week of life has been documented.

SIDS. When controlled for other high-risk variables, the rate of SIDS among opiate-exposed infants is about 3-4 times higher than in the general population. The increased rate of SIDS is less impressive for cocaine-exposed infants.

Treatment Protocol for Opiate-Exposed Infants

Neonates exposed *in utero* to opiates should be examined systematically for signs of neonatal abstinence syndrome to assess the need for intervention.

Paregoric has been found to decrease seizure activity, increase sucking coordination, and decrease the incidence of explosive stools. Phenobarbital is also a commonly used agent, and may be especially helpful in cases of polydrug abuse. Other specific agents have been considered in the treatment of neonatal abstinence syndrome, but experience with morphine, methadone, chlorpromazine, and rauwolfia is much too limited to support their use. Diazepam has been used to treat neonatal abstinence, but this agent controls seizures poorly and may lead to respiratory depression in the neonate.

Naloxone is sometimes given to newborns to reverse the perinatally acquired effects of analgesics administered to the mother during labor and delivery. Naloxone is contraindicated in opiate-exposed infants with respiratory depression due to its potential for precipitating a severe narcotic withdrawal. Naloxone is not specifically contraindicated for infants born to cocaine-using mothers, but providers should be aware that such mothers may be polydrug abusers who have also used opiates and that in this circumstance, naloxone may precipitate narcotic withdrawal in the infant.

Modification of the infant's environment—by placing the infant in a dimly-lit, quiet room; swaddling him or her; and using a nonoscillating waterbed if available—may be useful. However, this environmental modification does not eliminate the need for close observation of the infant. Drug-exposed infants in a prone or lateral position are generally comforted best. But caretakers should note an ongoing debate over prone versus supine positioning as possible factors in SIDS.

In Utero *Exposure To Cocaine: Effects And Treatment*

Effects of Cocaine Exposure on the Neonate

The abuse of cocaine became an alarming problem during the last decade. It is estimated that up to 8 million Americans use cocaine regularly and 30 to 40 percent of cocaine addicts are women. Cocaine use by pregnant women has multiple adverse influences on the mother's health, pregnancy outcome, and the well-being of the infants.

As with heroin addiction, adverse effects may be due to the life circumstances and behavior of the mother as well as to the pharmacologic properties of cocaine itself.

Lack of prenatal care, poor nutrition, medical problems, and abuse of other drugs and alcohol pose significant risk to the mother and the fetus. In addition, cocaine use increases the possibility of the mother's engaging in behaviors such as unprotected sex that place her at risk for contracting HIV.

The pharmacologic action of cocaine inhibits uptake of norepinephrine in the synaptic cleft, thus leading to vasoconstriction, hypertension, and tachycardia. In animal models, cocaine increases uterine vascular resistance and decreases uterine blood flow with resulting fetal hypoxemia.

Therefore, cocaine may play an etiologic role in causation of *abruptio placentae*, premature labor, intrauterine growth retardation, and fetal vascular disruption. Cocaine exposure causes a direct neurotoxicity manifested by neurobehavioral disturbances that are usually less striking than those associated with opiate abstinence syndrome.

These neurobehavioral disturbances may be transient, and usually do not require treatment. An encephalopathic syndrome—including irritability, tremulousness, lethargy, somnolence, labile state, decreased habituation, and visual tracking difficulties—has been described in cocaine-exposed newborn infants by many investigators. In addition to clinical signs of cocaine-induced neurotoxicity, transient encephalographic abnormalities can be demonstrated in this population of infants. Besides clinical and encephalographic abnormalities, echoencephalographic abnormalities are found in some cocaine-exposed infants. Lesions varying from ischemic injury with cavitation to intraventricular hemorrhage and ventricular dilation are observed in 8-14 percent of the study population. Cerebral infarctions have also been described in other reports. In some infants, physiologic dysfunction is indicated by alterations in vital signs including tachycardia and hypertension, and cardiac arrhythmias. The risk of sudden infant death syndrome in this population of infants may be increased, but large epidemiologic studies are needed in order to differentiate between effects of cocaine and other factors, such as low socioeconomic status, polydrug abuse, and smoking.

Long-term effects of intrauterine cocaine exposure, as well as polydrug exposure, are described in anecdotal reports, and include attention deficits, flat apathetic moods, decreased fantasy play, and other observations. However, long-term followup studies of cocaine-exposed children are scarce at present.

Subtle neurobehavioral aberrations may persist beyond the neonatal period. Cocaine may produce long term neurodysfunction, which is now being described anecdotally among the first cohort of babies exposed to crack *in utero* as they enter nursery school. The biologic vulnerability of infants exposed to crack *in utero* is modulated by the environment. The poor psychosocial, nutritional, medical, and socioeconomic status of the mother can all contribute to long-term neurodysfunctional sequelae in the infant. Additional risk factors—including intrauterine growth retardation, CNS pathology, prolonged hospitalization, and lack of intellectual nurturing—must be taken into consideration in evaluation of long-term neurobehavioral outcome of cocaine-exposed infants.

Possible Complications of Material and Neonatal Effects of Cocaine Use that May Occur in Pregnancy

Maternal Complications:

- Poor nutritional status
- Increased fisk for infections
- Hypertension/tachycardia/arrhythmias/myocardial infarctions
- Central nervous system hemorrhage
- Depression and low self-esteem
- Increased tendency to engage in risk behaviors for HIV

Pregnancy, Labor and Delivery complications:

- Spontaneous abortion
- Poor weight gain
- Abruptio placentae
- Fetal demise
- Precipitous delivery

Neonatal Complications:

- Intrauterine growth retardation
- Microencephaly or reduced head circumference
- Prematurity
- Congenital malformations/vascular disruption
- Congenital infections
- Cardiovascular dysfunction/arrhythmias

- Feeding difficulties/necrotizing enterocolitis
- Central nervous system hemorrhagic-ischemic lesions
- Neurobehavioral dysfunction
- Seizure activity
- Sudden infant death syndrome (SIDS)
- Increased possibility of HIV involvement

Treatment for Cocaine Exposed Neonates

Treatment for the neonate demands an appropriate nursery environment, comprehensive assessments, pharmacologic intervention, and clinical diagnostic studies.

Optimal Nursery Environment. Such an environment features sound primary nursing care, gentle handling by as few care takers as possible, and an avoidance of stimuli such as light and noise that will irritate the baby. To facilitate and promote optimal infant growth and development, nursery personnel should carefully monitor feeds, initiate strategies to facilitate intake for those infants experiencing feeding difficulties, observe for feeding intolerance or necrotizing enterocolitis, provide opportunities to interact with parents and environment as the infant is able to tolerate them, and provide primary nursing to facilitate parent-infant interactions.

Brazelton Neonatal Behavioral Assessment Scale. Use of the Brazelton Neonatal Behavioral Assessment Scale (Brazelton, 1984) is encouraged. This scale has been used extensively to evaluate newborn behavior such as habituation and responsivity to stimuli (faces, voices, light, bell, rattle, etc.); state (sleeping, alertness); characteristics of changes in state (irritability, inconsolability); and neurological and motor development. Although clinical expertise is demanded to administer the Brazelton Scale, programs will find it useful in evaluating infants exposed to drugs.

Neonatal Neurotoxicity Assessment. While asymptomatic infants do not need to be systematically assessed for neonatal neurotoxicity, consideration should be given to developing scoring criteria for those infants who are symptomatic. In the presence of significant withdrawal symptoms, other etiologies, including polydrug and alcohol exposure and metabolic problems, should be explored.

Pharmacotherapy. If irritability persists in an infant, a short course of phenobarbital is recommended.

Central Nervous System Imaging. Cranial sonograms are not routinely recommended, but recent literature is suggestive of CNS abnormalities, including hemorrhagic ischemic lesions in some drug-exposed infants. As yet, evidence is insufficient to support a mandate for cranial sonograms in all cocaine-exposed infants. However, special consideration should be given to specific neuroimaging of cocaine-exposed preterm infants, infants whose head circumference falls below the 10th percentile on standardized fetal growth curves, and infants with abnormal neurologic signs, neurobehavioral dysfunction, or seizure activity.

Assessment for Congenital Malformations/Vascular Disruptions. Clinicians should have a heightened awareness of the possibility of uncommon but significant congenital malformations or vascular disruptions reported in cocaine-exposed neonates. Systems that may be affected include the genitourinary tract, cardiovascular system (congenital heart malformations), gastrointestinal tract, and skeletal system. Echocardiography and abdominal ultrasound are not currently recommended as routine assessments in cocaine-exposed infants, but should be performed based on clinical indications.

Sudden Infant Death Syndrome. As indicated earlier, SIDS is a multifactorial problem, and opiate exposure is known to increase the neonate's risk of SIDS. There is some controversy over the incidence of SIDS in cocaine-exposed infants, but crack cocaine does appear to raise the risk slightly over controls. Data also suggest that cocaine-exposed infants may exhibit respiratory dysfunction. There are no indications that apnea monitoring decreases the incidence of SIDS. Routine home apnea monitoring for drug-exposed infants is therefore not recommended.

Promoting Positive Mother-Infant Interaction

Hospitals can promote positive interaction between parents and infants by adopting liberal visiting policies and mother-infant interaction time for newborn nurseries. Two other areas of concern are breastfeeding and instruction of mothers in handling drug-exposed infants.

Breastfeeding Drug-Exposed Infants

Breastfeeding is a key area of concern, especially among substance-using women. The advantages of breastfeeding are many, and are well documented. Benefits include the fact that breastfeeding strengthens the bond between the mother and the infant—an advantage that is of vital importance. Despite the instances described below, when breastfeeding is contraindicated, the decision on the part of service providers to advise women against breastfeeding should not be made without careful thought and training, taking into account the particular circumstances of the individual woman. Service providers must often become active breastfeeding advocates, encouraging the mother to breastfeed despite initial resistance to do so and educating her on breastfeeding's advantages to both herself and the newborn.

Nonetheless, there are instances when breastfeeding of drug-exposed infants is contraindicated. Since most drugs are secreted in breast milk, it has often been the practice to advise drug-using mothers not to breastfeed. Women who have been actively using drugs through the pregnancy and after the delivery have been discouraged from breast-feeding because of a number of factors including possible drug toxicity from diverse agents in varying levels, including the risk of exposure to drugs used intravenously, and the mother's medical and nutritional problems associated with continued drug use. Cocaine readily passes into breast milk and may lead to neonatal neurotoxicity, including irritability, tremors, brisk reflexes, mood lability, and even seizures. In addition, breastfeeding is contraindicated if the mother is HIV positive. (It should be noted, however, that the HIV status of the mother may not be known to the care provider or the mother.)

Despite these warnings, the well-known advantages of breastfeeding have led to a reconsideration of breastfeeding in selected substance-using women. There are two kinds of situations, highlighted below, in which care providers might wish to recommend that substance-using women breastfeed their babies: when the woman is on methadone or abstinent.

- In many instances, women who are methadone-maintained should be encouraged to breastfeed, particularly if the woman is known to be HIV-negative and free of other drug use. The fact that breastfeeding is not contraindicated among methadone-maintained patients is an advantage to methadone that is sometimes underemphasized, yet is of crucial importance.

- The recovering user of other substances (including cocaine), who has complied with rehabilitation and been documented to be AOD-free for a suitable period of time before delivery, may be able to breastfeed the infant, provided she continues to abstain from AODs and consents to frequent, random toxicology screens.

In sum, the recommendation regarding whether a substance-using woman should breastfeed her newborn should be made on an individual basis, taking a variety of factors into account. Service providers should receive ongoing training on the issue to keep up with the latest developments in the field.

Instructions in Infant Handling

Parents and other providers of primary care should be taught:

- To assess the baby, interpret his or her cues for more or less interaction, and synchronize one's behavior with that of the infant.
- To organize care and handling so that the baby is not bombarded by multiple stimuli that overwhelm her or his limited ability to habituate.
- To utilize graduated interventions in quieting the fussy, irritable baby.
- To appreciate the infant's unique competencies: The baby's ability to see, hear, and interact with the environment.

Discharging the Drug-Exposed Infant from the Hospital

It is often quite difficult to follow an AOD-using mother and her newborn after release from the hospital, and thus it is vital that the infant and the mother not be discharged too early. According to the Newborn Assessment Score, most babies (96 percent) are symptom-free of withdrawal seizures by the third or fourth day after birth and might otherwise be ready to be discharged from the hospital. However, a small but significant percentage of babies present with withdrawal seizures within 7 to 10 days after birth. For this reason, it is important to closely monitor the drug-exposed infant to determine if he or she needs to remain in the hospital after 4 days. Other medical, social, or environmental issues may further prolong the need for hospitalization.

Discharge Criteria

The infant's discharge should occur after the following criteria are met:

- The infant is taking oral feeds and gaining weight satisfactorily.
- The infant is physiologically stable (has normal vital signs including blood pressure).
- The infant is showing neurobehavioral recovery (can reach full alert state, responds to social stimuli, and can be consoled with appropriate measures).
- All necessary assessments have been completed, since adherence to followup schedules cannot be ensured.

Discharge Instructions

- The parent(s) or alternate primary care provider should receive anticipatory guidance (oral and written) regarding late and subacute withdrawal, seizures, behavioral interventions, and medications (side effects, route of administration, dose, etc.).

- A home evaluation should be performed on all drug-exposed infants or those with multiple risks by a public health nurse or a protective social service worker within 7 days of discharge, when feasible.

- A follow-up appointment for pediatric care should be scheduled within 2 to 4 weeks.

- Mothers and fathers who are not already enrolled in drug abuse treatment and need to be should be referred to an accessible and suitable treatment program prior to the infant's discharge.

- Facilitation of mother's postpartum gynecologic care and family planning should be incorporated into discharge planning of the infant.

- To promote quality improvement, discharge planning instructions should be documented in medical records, and a discharge summary of the hospital course should be given to parents or alternate primary caregiver.

Chapter 47

Followup and Aftercare of Drug-Exposed Infants

Drug-exposed infants should not be viewed as a homogeneous group but as individual at-risk infants presenting with a broad spectrum of possible effects, ranging from healthy term newborns with no apparent effects to high-risk births with significant effects. Living in a drug-abusing family is, in itself, a significant risk factor, regardless of prenatal exposure. Maternal drug use (and paternal drug use as well) represents a health, biological, and psychosocial risk to the developing fetus and a social risk to the young child. The primary focus of the addicted woman is characteristically on her drug of choice, not on her child. A child whose mother abuses drugs often lives in a chaotic environment. Prenatal drug exposure and suboptimal home environments are highly correlated. In combination, they have a synergistic and devastating effect on the child's health and development.

Because the infant exists as part of a mother-child dyad, effective treatment must occur within the context of that relationship, as the mother often serves as the gatekeeper for the child's access to services. Knowledge of other siblings, extended family, the father, friends, neighbors, and other caregivers is also crucial to treatment. Followup and aftercare services should also be based on a multicultural and multilinguistic model that takes into account the cultural backgrounds

---

This chapter contains excerpts from DHHS Pub. No. (SMA) 93-2011: *Improving Treatment for Drug-Exposed Infants*. To receive a copy of the complete report write: Substance Abuse and Mental Health Services Administration, Center for Substance Abuse Treatment—Publications, Rockwall II Building, 10th Floor, 5600 Fishers Lane, Rockville, MD 20852-9949.

of the mother, the father, and the extended family, as well as the service providers. Staff should reflect the different cultural and racial backgrounds of the communities being served. When appropriate, bilingual staff should be hired or other provisions made so that the inability to speak English is not a barrier to care. In sum, to be effective, treatment must occur within the cultural context of the mother and father, the extended family, and the community.

Knowledge of specific drug exposure is necessary for the appropriate medical management and treatment during the newborn period; the type of pharmacotherapy used in treating neonatal abstinence varies according to the specific drugs or combinations of drugs used by the mother. But followup and aftercare should not be based on a deficit model that assumes and screens for specific abnormalities caused by specific drugs. Rather, followup and aftercare should be based on a multirisk model that takes into account not only the prenatal drug exposure but also the medical status of the mother and the caregiving environment of the infant.

All health care and other service providers should consider the possibility that a number of environmental factors may contribute to specific deficits that have been attributed to drug exposure, as outlined below.

Experience with drug-using mothers and their children has demonstrated that drug exposure is only one of a number of risk factors that may affect the lives of the mothers and children. Other risk factors include:

- Chronic poverty
- Poor nutrition
- Inadequate or no prenatal health care
- Sexually transmitted diseases, including HIV exposure
- Domestic violence
- Child abuse or neglect
- AOD abuse within the family (including the father and the extended family)
- Homelessness, transient or inadequate living arrangements, or substandard housing
- Unemployment
- History of incarceration
- Low educational achievement
- Poor parenting skills
- Discrimination based on race, gender, or culture.

The lack of sufficient training among providers also affects the quality of the followup care given to drug-exposed infants and families. To counter the drug-exposed child's early disadvantages, service providers must be prepared to intervene early, often, and from many perspectives. Above all, health care and other service providers should not adopt the attitude that all drug-exposed infants are doomed to an unhappy, unhealthy life. Many, if not most, can eventually lead productive lives, given adequate intervention, education, and treatment services. The following recommendations address interventions for infants and toddlers, the transition to the preschool period, and training for child-oriented professionals. In general, many services require pediatric supervision by a specially trained physician.

Early Interventions for Infants

Components

Because of their distinctive needs, drug-exposed infants should receive more than the standard medical followup. Such followup should preferably be carried out under the supervision of a specially trained pediatrician. Followup interventions include but are not limited to:

- Nutrition (especially if inadequate sucking reflex is evident)
- Psychomotor assessment and monitoring of development
- Vision and hearing screening
- Speech and language assessments and therapy
- Emotional development assessments and therapy
- Play therapy
- Early educational needs assessments
- Physical therapy
- Immunization

Referrals

All health care and other service providers, including physicians, should stay abreast of available community services for drug-exposed infants and their families. Administrators should develop clear procedures to ensure that referrals are made to the appropriate resources. (For example, procedures might clarify whose responsibility it is to make referrals, such as case managers or social workers.)

Examples of routine health care referrals for drug-exposed infants and their families should include referrals to Federal programs such as:

- Early Periodic Screening, Diagnosis and Testing Program
- Maternal and child health services
- Community health centers
- Healthy Start Program.

Although federally supported, these programs vary from State to State and city to city. In addition, regulations and resources associated with these programs may be subject to change each fiscal year. It is important for programs and individual providers serving this population to be aware of these Federal and State resources and to utilize them. Developing and maintaining contact with a public agency (such as the local maternal and child health office, usually housed under the jurisdiction's public health department) can facilitate the process of keeping abreast of programs and resources appropriate for AOD-using mothers and infants.

In addition, in order to provide appropriate referral and followup services to drug-exposed infants and their families, providers and administrators should develop personal contacts among: physicians, social workers, alcohol and other drug counselors, speech and language specialists, early childhood educators, child development specialists, community volunteers, child protective services staff, and others. The new Substance Abuse Block Grant regulations require programs receiving block grant funds set aside for pregnant women and women with dependent children to provide a comprehensive range of services to women and their children, either directly or through linkages with community-based organizations. Thus, contacts with appropriate personnel in these AOD treatment programs should help other agencies with the provision of appropriate referrals.

The appropriateness of certain referrals will vary with the income of the mother, among other factors. For instance, referrals for mothers below the poverty level will usually differ from referrals for mothers who are in a middle-income bracket.

Outcomes

Intervention strategies for drug-exposed infants should promote the following outcomes:

- Self-regulation: the ability to regulate activity, attention, and affect.
- Secure relationships with mother and other significant caregivers.
- Developmentally appropriate progress in motor, cognitive, and speech and language skills.

Delivery System

The Federal early intervention system, mandated under the Individuals with Disabilities Education Act (IDEA), should be used when ever possible to deliver these family-focused services to both infant and mother. (IDEA was formerly known as P.L. 99457, The Education of the Handicapped Act Amendments of 1986. In 1990, the title of the Act was changed, and some changes were made as well in the content of the law. For instance, greater emphasis is now placed on the transition component from toddlers to children aged 3 to 5. The numbers of the law were also dropped when referring to the Act, since the numbers change each time the law is reauthorized. In 1992, the Act is authorized under P.L. 101476.)

IDEA, which focuses on disabled and "at-risk" children aged 6 and younger and their families, establishes two new Federal programs. One (Part H) addresses disabled and at-risk infants and toddlers from birth to 3 years of age; the other program (Part B) addresses disabled children aged 3 to 5. The law provides States with Federal funds to plan and implement early intervention services for children, aimed primarily at coordination. Each State must designate a single lead agency, assisted by a 25-member interagency council. Close coordination among health, social services, and educational agencies is required. The State must establish a public awareness program, a system to locate eligible children, procedural safeguards, data collection, and a State definition of developmental delay. Because designated Federal dollars are for coordination, States must develop strategies for funding direct services. The local school system can be contacted for help in identifying the lead agency responsible for coordination of Part H (infants to toddlers) as well as Part B (children aged 3 to 5) of IDEA.

Eligible children must include those who experience developmental delays as well as children with diagnosed physical or mental conditions, such as Down's syndrome or spina bifida, which are likely to cause delays. States also have the option of including children who are medically or environmentally at risk of substantial delay. Thus, States can, but are not required to, include all children born to mothers who have used drugs *in utero*. However, if an infant is developmentally delayed as a result of this drug exposure, the infant must be included in the program.

The Act also requires an Individualized Family Service Plan (IFSP), which must be developed by a multidisciplinary team and reviewed at least once every 6 months. The following section on the service plan describes what the IFSP must include.

Despite the significance of IDEA, there is a concern that many early intervention programs are designed for infants with more obvious impairments and do not address the more subtle and shared needs of drug-exposed infants and their parents. New models of service delivery and curriculum development must be created to meet the needs of these multirisk infants within the mainstream of early childhood education. Intervention strategies can also be delivered through:

- Home visits (by early intervention programs or home health services)
- Parent-child services delivered within an integrated treatment program of drug treatment and pediatric care
- Parent-child groups that are center- or community-based.

Service Plan

The intensity and format of interventions should be based on the needs of the individual child and family, using a format such as the Individual Family Service Plan (IFSP), developed through early intervention programs. The IFSP must include statements regarding:

- The child's present developmental status and
- The family's strengths and needs.

Major outcomes expected to be achieved for both the child and the family are:

- Timelines for measuring progress
- Specific early intervention services (including health care services) necessary to meet the distinctive needs of the child and the family

412

- Projected startup dates and the expected duration of service provision
- Name of the case manager
- Steps for transition from early intervention into the preschool program.

However, there is a concern among some in the field that the utility of the required IFSP is questionable and problematic.

Additional Casefinding

When an infant receives early intervention services, providers should explore the possibility that siblings may also have been exposed to drugs *in utero*, have been living in a home affected by drug use, and have unidentified or unaddressed service needs.

Supportive Services

Quality child care should be provided for the infant and siblings when the mother or the mother-infant dyad are in treatment. Likewise, transportation services for mothers and their children should be provided to facilitate treatment and other community services.

Schedule

Followup and aftercare services should be regularly scheduled.

Recommendations for Universal Hepatitis B Immunization

Hepatitis B immunization is now universally recommended. In order of priority, the following groups should be immunized: high-risk children and all infants, adolescents living in high-risk areas, and all adolescents. A summary of recommendations follow.

All pregnant women should receive routine serologic screening for HBsAg. All newborn infants should be immunized with the HBV vaccine.

Infants born to women who are HBsAg-negative should be administered the first dose prior to discharge from the hospital. The second dose should be administered at 1 to 2 months of age. The third dose should be administered at 6 to 18 months of age. Those infants not receiving a dose of vaccine at birth should be administered three doses by 18 months of age. The minimal interval between the first two doses is 1 month. The minimal interval between the second and third dose is 2 months, although 4 months or more may be preferable. An alternative scheduling at months 1, 4, and between months 6 and 18 is acceptable—provided the infant's mother is HBsAg-negative—but is not a preferred schedule.

Infants born to HBsAg-positive women must be immunized at or shortly following birth, and should receive one dose of HBIG as soon as possible after birth. The second vaccine dose should be administered at 1 month, and the third dose at 6 months. Their serologic status should be checked at 9 months of age.

Infants born to women whose HBsAg status is unknown at the time of delivery should be immunized at birth with the dose of vaccine recommended for infants born to HBsAg-positive mothers. In order to determine the subsequent management of the infant, including the need to administer HBIG, the mother should be screened for HBsAg as soon as possible.

Older children, adolescents, and adults who are at increased risk of HBV infection should be immunized with HBV vaccine. The routine immunization of all adolescents against HBV should be encouraged and implemented when feasible.

Interventions for Toddlers

Early Childhood Programs

For toddlers who have been receiving early intervention services and whose behavior and development are within normal limits, interventions would include quality, developmentally based early childhood programs like Head Start (modified for younger children with appropriate staffing and curriculum), preschool programs, and parent-child groups.

Quality early childhood programs offer children and their parents the opportunity to be exposed to other adults who have different approaches to childrearing, to try out new activities and learning experiences within a supportive environment, to participate as part of a group, to interact with peers, to receive feedback from others about their behavior, and to experience success and a sense of accomplishment. Children at risk for school failure because of their drug exposure or drug-using home environment can master these critical tasks within an integrated early childhood program.

Individual Therapy

Some children may not have received early intervention, or may still need individual therapy. Interventions, including speech and language services and physical and play therapy should be based on individual profiles of abilities and weaknesses. Low child:teacher ratios (1:1 being optimal) are recommended to allow for quality programming and an individualized focus.

Self-Regulation

Early childhood marks the beginning of self-regulation. Specific strategies to support self-regulation include:

- An orderly, consistent, child-appropriate environment.
- Predictable routines and consistent schedules.
- Clear expectations and rules.
- Clear patterns for transitions (such as a daily routine, warning signals, and signals to move to next activity).
- Offering choices to children.
- Praising a child's efforts, not just successes, each day.
- Using anticipatory guidance to avoid difficult situations.
- Explaining how a child's actions affect others.

Relationships

Strategies to support secure relationships with ongoing caregivers include:

- Individual attention, encouragement of mutual respect, and celebration of each person to build healthy self-esteem.
- Activities that foster self-esteem in both mother and child.
- Labeling of feelings, so the child can learn to identify and express a range of emotions.
- Clear boundaries within adult-child relationships.

Transition to the Preschool Period

Transition from the toddler to preschool period should involve careful planning and preparation with the mother and child to ensure compliance with the new program. Early intervention and developmentally based parent-child and early childhood programs should continue to provide services within a family-centered model, and should feature low child to teacher ratios of 4:1 for multirisk children. In addition, class size should remain small, with no more than eight children and two teachers per classroom. Lower ratios and small class size ensure that the children receive the individualized attention critical to their educational development.

To deal adequately with the complex problems of multirisk children in a school setting:

- Teeded therapeutic services should be provided: speech and language services; physical therapy; cccupational therapy; play therapy.

- Teachers should be provided with training to: understand addiction issues in general; understand women's addiction issues and family systems; understand cultural and racial factors in the family's background; recognize behavioral cues in individual children to promote the child's self-regulation; provide a consistent, predictable, well-structured environment to promote the child's self-regulation; plan for transitions to promote the child's self-regulation; address issues relating to addiction, abuse, and violence.

Quality Assurance Checklist

To ensure the quality of followup and aftercare services to the drug exposed child, the hospital AOD abuse treatment program should provide the following services:

- Qualified staff and inservice education programs.
- Interdisciplinary staff that includes AOD treatment providers.
- Appropriate AOD treatment services for the mother as well as the father.
- Significant involvement of mother and child dyad; if the father is present, he should be involved.
- Child to staff ratio not exceeding 3:1 up to 3 years of age in the early intervention program.
- Transportation.
- Regular medical exams according to schedule.
- Up-to-date immunizations.

- Weekly monitoring visits during first 3 months, and monthly visits up to 18 months; visits should be conducted by the organization responsible for case management.
- Availability of visiting nurses.
- Regular reports to and from social services.
- Ongoing relationship with child protective services.
- Long-term retention of mothers in the program.
- Mechanism for peer review.

Training for Child Oriented Professionals

Health professionals often lack training and experience working with substance-abusing women, addicted families, prenatal drug exposure, and effective intervention strategies. Educators and health care providers must understand addiction, family functioning, and be able to communicate effectively with families.

Child-oriented professionals need specific training and supervision in: taking AOD histories; addiction models and issues for women; family systems—especially regarding the addicted family; prenatal drug exposure (medical, developmental, and behavioral outcomes); child development; family-focused interventions; parent-child interactions; intervention strategies for mothers and children (and fathers); HIV and its relationship to AOD abuse; treatment and referral strategies; and the impact of culture and ethnicity on service delivery.

All professionals working with addicted people and their children must have access to regular clinical supervision. Clinical supervision provides information, support, and stress management.

Part Five

Prevention

Chapter 48

What Is Prevention?

The first step in prevention is to define the problem we are trying to address. Although the popular media and some professionals commonly refer to "our Nation's drug problem," it is clear that many of our most pressing "drug" problems are caused by the use of alcohol. Most Americans now recognize that alcohol is a drug. But to highlight the importance of addressing alcohol use, abuse, and related problems, many professionals now favor the phrase "alcohol and other drugs" (AOD) rather than referring to alcohol separately. For this reason the abbreviation "AOD" is used frequently throughout this chapter.

Second, we must understand that efforts to address alcohol and other drug problems will succeed only if they are part of a national effort to improve health and increase wellness. Clearly, alcohol and other drugs cause a variety of health problems, and reducing their use would have a significant impact on the Nation's health. The reverse is also true. As Americans become more aware of the importance of healthy lifestyles, and as wellness (not just freedom from disease) becomes a national goal, the probability that Americans will risk the consequences of alcohol and other drug use and abuse will decrease. Thus, efforts to reduce these problems must be integrated with the other activities designed to promote good health.

Excerpted from DHHS Pub. No. (ADM) 90-1657, *Citizen's Alcohol and Other Drug Prevention Directory*. A complete copy of this directory may be purchased from the Superintendent of Documents, U.S. Government Printing Office, Washington, DC 20402.

Finally, experience teaches that money alone cannot solve pressing national problems. Although the recent increases in both Federal and private-sector funding to address alcohol and other drug problems are an important step forward, it will ultimately be the efforts of concerned parents, teachers, youths, and other citizens that will turn the tide of alcohol and other drug problems. Indeed, some of the most promising approaches to alcohol and other drug problems have been developed by individuals working at the grassroots level, volunteering their time and energy because of an overriding concern for the health, safety, and welfare of the members of their communities. This spirit of volunteerism is the cornerstone of an aggressive and continuing national effort to combat alcohol and other drug problems and the terrible toll these problems levy on our current health and welfare and on our future.

The Continuum of Strategies

Efforts to address alcohol and other drug problems are usually categorized into *prevention, intervention, treatment,* and *aftercare.* These categories correspond roughly to the stage to which problems with alcohol and other drug use have progressed.

Prevention approaches may be applied to society as a whole in an attempt to foster a climate in which:

- Alcohol use is acceptable only for those of legal age and only when the risk of adverse consequences is minimal;
- Prescription and over-the-counter drugs are used only for the purposes for which they were intended;
- Other abusable substances (e.g., gasoline, aerosol propellants) are used only for the intended purposes; and
- Illegal drugs are not used at all.

Prevention approaches are also aimed at individual citizens to provide them with the knowledge and skills to avoid alcohol and other drug problems. These prevention approaches are appropriate for individuals and groups who have never used alcohol or other drugs or whose use is at a very early stage—before serious problems have occurred.

Rather than addressing alcohol and other drugs directly, some prevention efforts attempt to alter factors that place individuals and groups "at risk." Individuals may be influenced by "risk factors" such as academic failure. Or the risk factor may be something in their personal relationships (for example, another family member may have alcohol or other drug problems). Society as a whole also has risk factors (for example, the lack of economic opportunity or the easy availability of alcohol and other drugs).

The 1986 Anti-Drug Abuse Act identified groups of individuals who are at high risk because of social or environmental conditions. These groups are children of alcoholics and drug abusers; victims of sexual, physical, or psychological abuse; school dropouts; pregnant teens; economically disadvantaged youths; youths with mental health problems; youths who have attempted suicide; and disabled youths. Programs specifically designed for these groups have become a major focus of recent Federal programs.

Prevention approaches can also be used to reduce the negative consequences of alcohol and other drug use and abuse. For example, while ideally we want to prevent people from driving while under the influence of alcohol and other drugs, impaired driving still occurs. Persuading people to use seatbelts can prevent injuries and fatalities resulting from impaired driving. Similarly, teaching intravenous drug users how the AIDS virus can be transmitted by sharing needles can reduce needle sharing and the occurrence of AIDS.

Intervention (sometimes referred to as early intervention) refers to program strategies that are aimed at persons who have begun to use alcohol and other drugs or have begun to experience some problems as a result. The goal of intervention programs is to reduce the level of such use and to prevent alcohol and other drug problems from progressing further.

Treatment is usually provided to those individuals who have many serious problems caused by their use of alcohol or other drugs or who are addicted to or dependent on drugs. Because most individuals whose use of alcohol and other drugs is habitual or addictive cannot stop on their own, treatment programs are often highly structured and involve intensive therapy.

Aftercare (sometimes referred to as rehabilitation) is in many ways a part of treatment. Once an individual has become free of alcohol and other drugs, the program must help the treated person to reenter society without returning to the destructive patterns that made treatment necessary. In some cases, alcohol and other drugs may have so severely disrupted an individual's social, emotional, intellectual, and spiritual growth that it is more correct to think of aftercare as "habilitation" rather than rehabilitation. In other words, some individuals may have to learn for the first time the basic skills and abilities needed to live productive and rewarding lives free from alcohol and other drugs.

In examining this service continuum, we must be aware that prevention efforts are most effective when intervention, treatment, and aftercare services are also available. For example, an education program on alcohol and other drugs in the schools is likely to show a number of students that they are developing alcohol and other drug problems or that a parent is dependent. To help these students, adequate counseling, assessment, and referral resources (intervention) must be available in the school or community. If the student or family member acknowledges the need for treatment, affordable and appropriate treatment and aftercare programs must be available.

The Need for Comprehensive Approaches

The origins of alcohol and other drug use are complex and deeply imbedded in our culture, our social structure, and our economic systems. Effective prevention approaches must address this complexity. Historically, single-focus prevention programs have failed to bring about desired results. Experts now recognize that the most effective approaches to prevent alcohol and other drug problems are comprehensive, coordinated, and include the entire social system.

As an example, let us consider the problem of underage drinking. Recently, the purchase of alcoholic beverages was made illegal for people under 21 years of age in every State. But at the local convenience store, beer may be just as cheap as soft drinks, and sales clerks may not check the identification of young purchasers very carefully. Some adults—even parents—continue to buy alcohol for young people. Some law enforcement officers take a tolerant view of underage drinking and are more inclined to send an intoxicated minor home than to press charges for possession or for driving under the influence. At home, young people may be exposed to endless hours of television programs and commercials that portray drinking as socially acceptable and desirable. Thus, the positive effects of the uniform alcohol purchase age may be undermined because other elements of the social and cultural environment do not support the strong anti-use message communicated by the law.

Cultural norms and values, national policies, State and local laws, law enforcement practices, school policies, the behavior of parents, and the beliefs and attitudes of individuals may all contribute to alcohol and other drug problems. These same forces must be brought to bear if these problems are to be solved. Efforts in one segment of society can easily be canceled out or undermined if they are not supported by other segments. On the other hand, if all segments of society work together, effective prevention programs can be brought about.

This is not to say that individual programs, agencies, or citizens should not take action just because all segments of society have not yet been persuaded to join in the national effort to prevent alcohol and other drug problems. But we must be aware of the complexity and interdependence of our society in planning our prevention efforts.

Furthermore, we must be aware of the cultural and ethnic diversity of our citizens. Because of this diversity, there can be no "one size fits all" prevention program or strategy. Prevention activities must be consistent with the priorities, values, world view, and ways of communicating that exist in each community. Thus, some approaches will be more appropriate in one community than in another, and some programs and strategies may have to be tailored to fit a given ethnic or cultural group.

Prevention Strategies

Over the past two decades, a wide variety of approaches to prevention have been developed. In general, these approaches have focused on a limited number of presumed causes of alcohol and other drug problems or on narrowly defined groups of people. Thus, few current approaches are comprehensive. On the other hand, these approaches are the building blocks from which a comprehensive prevention strategy can be built. Although few approaches can, alone, be expected to have a dramatic impact on alcohol and other drug problems, a thoughtfully selected package of mutually supportive approaches has a good chance of succeeding.

Before discussing specific program approaches, it is necessary to consider the issue of effectiveness. After all, the question of "What works?" should be primary in selecting program strategies. However, because alcohol and other drug problem prevention is relatively new, very little is known about the effectiveness of many prevention approaches.

425

For the most part, we must make "best guesses" concerning the programs and strategies most likely to have a positive impact on alcohol and other drug problems. Nevertheless, we should be encouraged by recent downturns in alcohol and other drug use and related problems in some populations. The aggregate effects of current prevention efforts can be credited, at least in part, for these positive changes.

Strategies Focused on Individuals

Historically, the majority of prevention programs focused on the knowledge, attitudes, and skills of individuals. Early prevention programs assumed that individuals would avoid alcohol and other drugs if only they "knew better." The focus of these programs was to provide factual information about alcohol and other drugs, or sometimes to provide overblown accounts of the dangers of alcohol and other drug use (scare tactics). Although information is clearly an important component of prevention efforts, we have come to realize that information alone is unlikely to have much impact on behavior.

More recently, prevention programs that focus on individuals have attempted to teach a variety of "life skills," including coping skills, decision-making skills, communication skills, and skills to resist peer and other social pressures to use alcohol and other drugs (resistance training). These programs often attempt to enhance self-esteem on the theory that people who feel good about themselves will not need alcohol and other drugs. Most current school-based prevention programs include some combination of life skills, resistance training, and self-esteem enhancement.

Another popular prevention approach that focuses on individuals is "alternatives programs." These programs assume that individuals will avoid alcohol and other drugs if they have better ways of meeting their psychological and emotional needs. Alternative programs can be divided into three basic categories: (1) those that provide alternative "highs" or adventure (e.g., wilderness challenges); (2) those that provide opportunities for meaningful involvement (e.g., community service programs); and (3) those that provide opportunities for alcohol and other drug-free recreation (e.g., prom week celebrations).

Some recent prevention programs have focused on the characteristics of individuals that place them at increased risk of alcohol and other drug problems. Programs have been developed to provide specialized services for children who fall into the risk categories defined in the Anti-Drug Abuse Act of 1986. These programs may also attempt

426

to change social environments, such as schools and classrooms, so that these risk factors occur less frequently in the general population. Programs focused on at-risk individuals are appealing because they address important root causes of alcohol and other drug problems.

Strategies Focused on the Family

Prevention theorists now recognize that experiences in the family are potent determinants of alcohol and other drug problems. Families that are loosely structured and where communication is poor, and families in which the parents behave inconsistently, do not supervise their children closely, and use harsh physical punishment, appear to increase the risk of alcohol and other drug problems in children. A number of programs have been developed to improve parenting skills either in the general population or in families experiencing problems. Programs to improve parenting skills have been shown to change parental behavior and to change some behaviors in children that may lead to alcohol and other drug problems. Such programs hold considerable promise as one component of a comprehensive prevention effort.

Some family programs focus on parents as role models for their children. These programs encourage parents to reduce their own use of alcohol and other drugs and to avoid involving children in related behaviors (e.g., opening beer, pouring drinks, lighting cigarettes). Specialized programs have also been developed for families in which one or both parents are alcohol or other drug abusers. Such programs address both parental alcohol and other drug abuse and the special family problems that result from this abuse.

A key challenge for family prevention programs is getting those families most at risk to participate. In general, the parents who volunteer for parent education are those parents who are already doing a relatively good job of raising their children. Thus, although family programs hold considerable promise, their impact will be greatest when they are able to reach those families who need them most.

Strategies Focused on the Peer Group

Early adolescence is a time of maximum conformity and acute self-consciousness, and the need to fit in with the group is a strong motivator for many young people. Not surprisingly, then, youths who use alcohol and other drugs tend to associate with other users and tend to believe that their friends approve of such use. Some recent prevention programs have attempted to alter peer group norms through publicity campaigns with positive health messages, peer leadership training, clubs and organizations devoted to promoting a no-use lifestyle, and exposure to attractive youths who don't use and can serve as role models.

Programs to alter peer group norms are appealing because it is now widely accepted that alcohol and other drug norms exercise strong control over behavior. We must recognize, however, that norms tend to change slowly. Efforts to change norms are likely to take some time to show a positive impact. On the other hand, changes in norms are probably necessary for a lasting reduction in alcohol and other drug problems.

Strategies Focused on the Schools

Historically, schools have been major sponsors of alcohol and other drug prevention programs including education, alternatives, and peer programs. Until recently, however, little attention has been given to the school itself and the impact of its policies, organization, and climate on alcohol and other drug use.

Many schools and districts are now developing and implementing alcohol and other drug use prevention policies. These policies can reduce alcohol and other drug use by providing a public statement of norms and expectations, helping with the early identification of alcohol and other drug use, referring alcohol- and other drug-involved youths to appropriate programs, and limiting the availability of alcohol and other drugs, at least on campus. In addition, the development and publication of school policies can help to raise awareness among teachers, students, parents, and the community of the school's no-use philosophy. Some schools are also training teachers, counselors, school health staff, and other school personnel to recognize symptoms of intoxication and of alcohol and other drug involvement so that students showing such signs can be helped.

While school policies are important, they do not address many of the root causes of alcohol and other drug use. Prevention theorists also recognize that fundamental changes in schools can have a significant effect on school failure and behavioral problems among students and can increase attachment to school and commitment to education. These improvements can, in turn, reduce the rates of alcohol and other drug problems among students. Among the many changes schools are trying are collaborative, schoolwide planning by faculty, parents, and students; increasing adult-to-student ratios; reducing student anonymity; providing a variety of different activities for students; emphasizing teacher praise and reinforcement of positive behavior; cooperative learning approaches in which students learn teamwork and help each other to succeed; and establishing clear expectations about student behavior.

These programs require schools to make a real commitment to change, but they hold great promise for improving the lives of students not only by reducing alcohol and other drug abuse but by making school a place to experience success, not failure, and by increasing students' commitment to the pursuit of positive social rewards.

Strategies Focused on the Workplace

In recent years, increased attention has been paid to the role of the workplace in alcohol and other drug use prevention and intervention. Initial attention was drawn to the workplace because of safety and productivity problems resulting from alcohol and other drug use on the job. It is now recognized that work-based programs and policies can not only improve work performance, but can also improve the lives of workers and their families. Such programs can contribute to overall worker health and wellness through information campaigns, incentives for seatbelt use and smoking cessation, workplace exercise programs, and so on.

One important component of work-based programs is employer policies concerning alcohol and other drug use or impairment during working hours or use of illegal drugs on or off the job. Such policies have been recognized as an important strategy for reducing accidents and absenteeism and increasing productivity. They are also an important means of reinforcing alcohol and other drug prevention messages from other social institutions.

Many large companies have employee assistance programs. These programs help employees who are having difficulties with their own or a family member's alcohol or other drug use. Generally, such programs allow self-referrals as well as referrals by supervisors who have noticed signs, such as absenteeism or declining productivity, that may indicate an alcohol or other drug abuse problem.

Finally, work-based programs may promote responsible practices in those work settings that sell or serve alcoholic beverages. Several major corporations now sponsor employee training that includes

awareness of legal responsibilities, methods for recognizing false identification and discouraging "second party sales" (i.e., adults buying
alcohol for underage individuals), and methods for refusing service
to intoxicated patrons. In some communities, such training is also
available to small businesses through local alcohol beverage control
agencies, the police, or business organizations.

Strategies Focused on Higher Education

For most Americans, alcohol and other drug use peaks during early
adulthood (18-25 years of age). For this reason, there has been increasing concern over the use of drugs, especially alcohol, on college campuses. Distributors of alcoholic beverages are aware of the high
consumption levels of college students and have aimed aggressive
marketing efforts at this population. Beer advertisements account for
a large percentage of the advertising revenues of many college newspapers, and the alcohol industry promotes its products through free
posters, support of campus activities, and student "representatives"
on campus.

Concerned college administrators and students have responded to
the high level of student alcohol consumption in a number of ways.
Fraternities and sororities have worked with administrators to develop policies and procedures to limit the availability of alcohol at
"Greek" functions. Some campuses have refused to allow alcohol beverage promotions on campus, and many campuses have banned alcohol consumption in sports arenas and stadiums. Student groups have
sponsored campaigns to raise awareness of the dangers of alcohol and
other drugs, and some student health services include alcohol and
other drug use screening as a regular part of student health examinations and other patient contacts. An important challenge for the
future will be the expansion of these and other strategies to reach
larger numbers of our Nation's college students.

Strategies Focused on the Community

Communities are beginning to recognize the extent to which they
can influence the environment in which people live and their potential power to prevent alcohol and other drug problems. Community
action can take a number of different forms. Community leaders can
work to ensure that a variety of prevention strategies are in place and
working in a coordinated fashion. They can make prevention a priority

in their allocation of resources. They can foster and publicize community norms that value wellness and demonstrate a lack of tolerance for the use and abuse of alcohol and other drugs.

Programs are also designed specifically for community action. These include zoning regulations that control the number and location of alcohol sales outlets, increased emphasis on alcohol beverage control enforcement, alcohol and other drug-free zones around schools, and roadblocks to detect drinking or drugged drivers. Some communities have even used zoning regulations to close crack houses or to deter the sales of illegal drugs. Another strategy that is becoming widespread is "community-oriented policing," which includes foot patrols and other techniques to enhance communication and trust between neighborhood residents and law enforcement officers.

Communities are recognizing the importance of community development as part of an overall response to alcohol and other drug problems. When neighborhoods are disorganized, when overall crime rates are high, and residents have limited opportunity for economic success and positive social involvement, rates of alcohol and other drug problems increase. Communities are also beginning to recognize the importance of the physical environment in decreasing these problems. Well-lighted streets free of debris and litter are less likely to attract drug dealers and users or to provide an inviting setting for AOD-related crime.

Summary

When we think of prevention, we often think of educational programs in schools. Yet opportunities to contribute to alcohol and other drug problem prevention exist at all levels of society. Moreover, although prevention has historically focused on the attitudes, knowledge, and skills of individuals, some of the most promising prevention approaches attempt to alter the environments in which individuals live, work, and grow. Overall, communities have a wide variety of approaches from which to choose and many options that can be tailored to local needs, values, and culture.

Resources for Prevention

Citizens concerned about alcohol and other drug problems often feel isolated and frustrated by a lack of resources. In fact, numerous resources are available at the Federal, State, and local levels to assist in prevention efforts. This section discusses some of these resources and how citizens can put them to work in their communities.

Government Resources

Many Federal agencies now play some role in the prevention of alcohol and other drug problems. However, for local communities, the most relevant and accessible of these agencies is the Office for Substance Abuse Prevention (OSAP). OSAP stimulates and supports key prevention projects; identifies, develops, and distributes information concerning prevention research and practice; and administers a national training system to increase the knowledge and skills of prevention practitioners. OSAP serves as a catalyst for collaborative efforts among government, corporate, and voluntary organizations, both at the national level and at regional, State, and local levels. [To contact OSAP write or call: ADAMHA/OSAP, 5600 Fishers Lane, Rockwall II Building, Rockville, MD 20857; (301) 443-0373. Also, see Chapter 51 in this volume for a list of some other specific government and private organizations able to provide help and information.]

Other Federal agencies with resources to offer to local alcohol and other drug prevention efforts include the Department of Education, the Department of Justice, and the National Highway Traffic Safety Administration of the Department of Transportation. These agencies sponsor local prevention initiatives through grant-in-aid programs, develop and disseminate prevention materials and model programs, and conduct information-sharing conferences.

In each State and U.S. Territory, an agency of State government is responsible for coordinating alcohol and other drug abuse prevention and treatment services. In most States, the responsibility for alcohol and other drugs is combined, although in one State, a separate drug and alcohol agency has been established.

Many county and local governments employ an alcohol and other drug prevention and/or treatment planner or coordinator, and many communities now have task forces or committees that coordinate alcohol and other drug abuse initiatives to ensure consistency and avoid duplication. Local law enforcement agencies can also serve as prevention resources and provide such services as presentations to parents and youths, school-based alcohol and other drug use education, and "Neighborhood Watch" programs. Other local government agencies that should not be overlooked in planning prevention efforts include parks and recreation departments that may assist in the development of alcohol and other drug-free events and recreation, local departments of mental health that can provide information and early intervention services, and alcohol beverage control boards that may help with programs to restrict sales of alcohol to minors.

Nongovernment Resources

Many national organizations are actively involved in the Nation's efforts to reduce alcohol and other drug use and related problems. These organizations develop prevention materials, disseminate programs, conduct national media campaigns, lobby for alcohol and other drug abuse legislation, and provide training and technical assistance. In addition, many have chapters that are active in prevention initiatives in local communities.

Many of the agencies and institutions in local communities also play a key role in alcohol and other drug abuse prevention. Schools and the workplace offer access to large numbers of community members and provide opportunities for a variety of prevention initiatives. Other community agencies and institutions can also make a significant contribution to prevention.

An often ignored resource for alcohol and other drug abuse prevention is the health care system. Physicians, nurses, and other health professionals can serve as informational resources; can identify alcohol and other drug problems among their patients; can counsel youths and adults concerning the risks of use; and can serve as highly credible advocates for community and State policies, regulations, and laws that promote health and wellness.

Another important resource for alcohol and other drug abuse prevention is religious institutions. Many community members look to their churches and synagogues for leadership in morality and ethics, and religious institutions have historically played a leadership role in promoting the spiritual and emotional health of their membership. In some communities, religious institutions may also be the primary source of social and recreational activities and can be a vehicle for increasing opportunities for alcohol- and other drug-free recreation for both youths and adults.

Local businesses also have an important role to play in alcohol and other drug abuse prevention. Businesses can sponsor programs for their employees and can help to reduce the availability of alcohol to minors. In addition, businesses can provide support for local prevention efforts in the form of donated materials and services (e.g., printing, mailing, production of public service announcements), and by encouraging their employees to volunteer to work on alcohol and other drug abuse prevention projects.

Many local service organizations have taken an active interest in alcohol and other drug issues. Some of these organizations have developed or sponsored education on these issues, alternatives programs, and teen leadership programs. These organizations can also contribute to the person-power necessary to launch an effective, community-wide prevention effort.

People Resources

Ultimately, the reduction of alcohol and other drug problems relies largely on the efforts of ordinary citizens. The past decade has demonstrated that alcohol and other drug problems can be reduced when parents, other concerned citizens, and youths take a stand and refuse to tolerate the continued deterioration of their homes, schools, and communities. The mobilization of public opinion has been partly responsible for recent reductions in alcohol-related traffic crashes. Public intolerance of smoking has contributed to a social climate that discourages this once common behavior. In the last few years, we have seen a dramatic reduction in illicit drug use, which indicates that our efforts in this area are beginning to pay off. Working together, individual citizens can make a difference in all aspects of America's alcohol and other drug abuse problem.

Chapter 49

Frequently Asked Questions about Preventing Alcohol, Tobacco, and Other Drug Problems

What Is Prevention?

Prevention is the sum of our efforts to ensure healthy, safe, and productive lives for all Americans. As applied to alcohol, tobacco, and other drugs (ATOD), prevention means keeping the many problems related to the use and abuse of these substances from occurring.

Successful ATOD problem prevention means that underage youth, pregnant women, and others at high risk do not use alcohol, tobacco, or other drugs. They do not cause harm to themselves and to those around them.

Prevention reduces the risk of danger and fosters a safe environment. Successful prevention leads to reductions in traffic fatalities, violence, HIV/AIDS and other sexually transmitted diseases (STDs), rape, teen pregnancy, child abuse, cancer and heart disease, injuries and trauma, and other problems associated with substance abuse. Thanks to prevention, our children stay in school. Our workers stay on the job. Prevention works! Let's make prevention work for everyone!

Why Is Prevention of ATOD Problems Important?

ATOD problems cost years of quality life. And, they cost money. For example, alcohol and other drug problems cost each man, woman,

DHHS Pub. No. (SMA) 93-2045.

435

and child in America $800 a year, or nearly $200 billion. If alcohol were never used carelessly in our society, about 100,000 fewer people would die annually from unnecessary illness and injury. Each year, smoking takes the lives of about 400,000 and passive smoking about 50,000.

In addition, prevention efforts strengthen our communities, schools, families, and individuals. Drug dealers are less likely to infiltrate strong communities. Schools with strong policies against smoking and drinking are healthier. Family members who serve as healthy role models help inoculate their offspring. Mentors offer support for healthy individual development.

These facts also help explain why ATOD problem prevention is important:

- Nearly 7 out of 10 manslaughter offenses occur after a person has been drinking or using other drugs.
- Smoking and use of other tobacco products cause cancer and heart disease. Alcohol also is a factor in these diseases.
- The use and abuse of these substances frequently contribute to teen pregnancy, HIV/AIDS/STD transmission, child abuse, and other social problems.
- According to one analysis, persons who abuse alcohol and other drugs use two and one half times the medical benefits as non-abusers; and children of substance abusers also use more health care services.

Violence and disease represent large costs to taxpayers struggling with a record-setting deficit and ever increasing health care costs. Prevention means less money must be spent on preventable diseases. Incarceration is one part of the cost of violence and crime associated with ATOD problems. Violence diverts law enforcement personnel, clogs the courts, causes economic loss and mental anguish for victims, and dulls the potential of our Nation and our people.

Without prevention, young people make unhealthy and unsafe choices, jeopardizing our future abilities to compete in the global marketplace. We are unable to foster vital communities and ensure our Nation's vitality. Alcohol, tobacco, and other drug problems reduce human capital—people who can be working, paying taxes, making neighborhoods safe, and enhancing our ability as a country to compete in a new global economy.

What Is the Importance of Prevention in Health Care Reform?

Prevention is a major key to reduced health care costs. We can reduce costs associated with:

- Spinal cord and head injuries resulting from alcohol- and drug-impaired driving.
- Health, education, and rehabilitation costs associated with children born with Fetal Alcohol Syndrome or who are addicted, at birth, to illegal drugs.
- Chemotherapy and radiation for treatment of cancer occurring in passive smokers.
- ATOD-related emergency room visits.
- Imaging for broken bones and internal injuries associated with alcohol and other drug use.
- Burn treatment and rehabilitation for persons injured by cigarette-caused fires.

According to one analysis, we could reduce the Nation's expenditures on health care by $90.4 billion if alcohol and other drug problems were prevented.

What Do We Now Spend on ATOD Problem Prevention Efforts?

Currently, the Federal Government spends only about $50 per person each year on prevention, treatment, and interdiction related to fighting drug problems (including $3.7 billion to State and local governments).

How Can Prevention Efforts Reduce Costs and Boost the Economy?

In two ways. As stated above, prevention can help reduce health care costs. Second, if we can keep our children in school and learning the skills they need, and if we can keep our workers productive in the workforce, we will boost revenues in a highly competitive environment. We will produce the goods and services needed to expand our resources to reduce the deficit.

How Do We Know that Prevention Works?

Percentages of the population engaging in high-risk behaviors are decreasing. For instance, in 1979, nearly 20 percent of all adolescents ages 12 to 17 were drinking regularly. By 1991, that number dropped to under 10 percent. The incidence of liver cirrhosis also has dropped significantly. Alcohol-related traffic fatalities decreased by 10 percent, representing large numbers of young lives saved.

Why Should We Continue to Invest Resources in Prevention?

There are two very important reasons. First, we have to set up more intensive and repetitive interventions among those who have not been easily persuaded by previous efforts. For example, there are still over 4 million youngsters who drink illegally. There are young people and adults who are at very high risk, for example, school failures, runaways, those who have been abused, children of substance abusers, and those living in high-risk environments. We have not yet achieved great success with these high-risk audiences despite demonstrations of promising approaches.

Second, if prevention efforts are not continued at an intensive level, the gains fall off. Young people entering school today, for instance, believe that smoking is harmful, but the rates of smoking begin to increase without "resistance" skill training and practice and policies that restrict availability, and other prevention efforts. Because prevention efforts have decreased, significant gains have not been made in reducing the use of tobacco products by youths.

More clearly, we can see that if we do not continue prevention efforts, diseases return. The recent resurgence of TB and measles underlines what happens when prevention efforts are not sustained.

How Does Prevention Work?

Several strategies are used effectively, especially in combination:

- *Information Dissemination*—This strategy provides awareness and knowledge of the nature and extent of ATOD use, abuse, and addiction and their effects on individuals, families, and communities, as well as information to increase perceptions of risk associated with ATOD use. It also provides knowledge and awareness of prevention policies, programs, and services. It helps set and reinforce norms (for example, underage drinking and drug dealers will not be tolerated in this neighborhood).

- *Prevention Education*—This strategy aims to affect critical life and social skills, including decision making, refusal skills, critical analysis (for example, of media messages), and systematic and judgmental abilities. Children learn to comprehend and integrate no-use messages.

- *Alternatives*—This strategy provides for the participation of targeted population in activities that exclude ATOD use by youth. Constructive and healthy activities offset the attraction to, or otherwise meet the needs usually filled by, ATOD use.

- *Problem Identification and Referral*—This strategy calls for identification, education, and counseling for those youth who have indulged in age-inappropriate use of tobacco products or alcohol, or who have indulged in the first use of illicit drugs. Activities under this strategy would include screening for tendencies toward substance abuse and referral for preventative treatment for curbing such tendencies.

- *Community-Based Process*—This strategy aims to enhance the ability of the community to provide prevention and treatment services to ATOD disorders more effectively. Activities include organizing, planning, enhancing efficiency and effectiveness of services implementation, interagency collaboration, coalition building, and networking. Building healthy communities encourages healthy lifestyle choices

- *Environmental Approach*—This strategy sets up or changes written and unwritten community standards, codes, and attitudes—influencing incidence and prevalence of ATOD problems in the general population. Included are laws to restrict availability and access, price increases, and community-wide actions.

Who Should Practice Prevention?

Everyone. Policy makers can deliberate after assessing the impact of policy decisions on alcohol, tobacco, and other drug problems, for example: zoning regulations for liquor stores, excise taxes on alcohol and tobacco, and the access to alcohol by youth at sports stadiums. Educators can weave prevention themes and messages into their skill-building exercises—regardless of content—in science, math, reading, and social studies. The faith community can help set low-risk community norms. Youth-serving organization leaders can offer alternatives or mentoring programs. Parents and older siblings can serve as role models and reinforce healthy lifestyle choices and have a good dialogue about drugs, AIDS, and other sensitive topics. Grandparents can help children practice refusal skills. Media representatives can develop stories celebrating youth who have chosen not to drink, smoke, or use drugs; stations can air public service announcements and programs. Governments can transfer knowledge about what works, with whom, and under what conditions. Law enforcement personnel can enforce laws related to driving under the influence and underage sales of tobacco and alcohol. Health care providers can conduct 5-minute screenings at life-cycle points in their patients' lives, for example, when children enter school, when they get sports or camp physicals, when they enter college, when they get married, when they consider pregnancy, when they enter the job market, when they experience a crisis, or when they retire. Pharmacists can provide information about the harms associated with alcohol abuse, tobacco, and illicit drug use, as well as mixing medications with alcohol and tobacco. Businesses can sponsor alternative programs for youth, skill-building seminars, and mentoring programs. Volunteers can become a "friend" to a child of a substance abuser. Child welfare workers can look for signs of alcohol or drug abuse in the home and make referrals.

What Is the Center for Substance Abuse Prevention Seeking to Promote?

A society of people who make low-risk or no risk decisions about alcohol, tobacco, and other drugs. Such decisions greatly reduce the incidence and prevalence of injury, disease, and death associated with the use and abuse of these substances. And, these decisions produce a society that encourages early identification and treatment of those who already have ATOD problems.

How Is CSAP's Position on Drinking Alcoholic Beverages Different from Temperance and Prohibition Models?

For those 21 and over, CSAP discourages high-risk drinking and drinking that places the drinker or others at risk from harm—such as drinking by drivers, pregnant women, or people who are alcohol dependent or alcoholic. CSAP follows the U.S. Dietary Guidelines of the U.S. Departments of Health and Human Services and Agriculture that recommend men limit themselves to two drinks per day and women to one drink per day. CSAP also supports those who voluntarily abstain from alcohol and other drugs for health, safety, religious, or cultural reasons.

What Are the Major Needs for Substance Abuse Prevention?

- Better studies to assess exactly what prevention services and policies work best for whom and under what conditions. For example, what works best for high sensation-seeking youth? What works best in communities beset with high levels of unemployment, poverty, and crime? What works best with men who have few personal support systems?

- Additional resources for implementation of prevention policies and practices at the community level, especially where hopelessness, despair, and poverty prevail.

- Expanded resources for addressing the myths and misconceptions about ATOD use (for example, that alcohol intoxication is funny or is seen as a rite of passage for the young) and to increase the realistic perception of harm.

- More culturally appropriate prevention messages and mechanisms to reach audiences with less exposure to traditional information channels.

- Ways to change norms—especially within high-risk environments, for example, college and university campuses, military installations, and high crime areas.

- A reduction in the disproportionate share of messages aimed at promoting alcohol and tobacco products among low-income populations.

- A decrease of availability and access to alcohol and tobacco products by youth.

Who Benefits from Prevention?

Everyone benefits from prevention. We already practice many types of prevention—when we brush our teeth, fasten our safety belts, and look both ways before crossing an intersection. We keep medicines, poisons, weapons, and sharp instruments out of children's reach. We read the warning labels of over-the-counter and prescription drugs. We encourage good nutrition and physical fitness. We limit our intake of fat and salt. We protect the safety of our food and water, our housing, and our automobiles.

We make prevention happen in many ways and benefit from the results. Our children are not poisoned. We have fewer injuries. We do not experience overdoses. We avoid obesity and related illness.

We can do the same in terms of preventing alcohol, tobacco, and other drug problems and reap many benefits. Let's make prevention a priority. Let's keep our children in school, our workers employed, and our country on the leading edge in the global competition.

How Do I Get Additional Information?

Call or write:

National Clearinghouse for Alcohol and Drug Information
P.O. Box 2345
Rockville, MD 20852
1-800-729-6686

Free materials will be sent to you within 4 to 6 weeks.

Chapter 50

RADAR
(Regional Alcohol and Drug
Awareness Resource)
Network

The Center for Substance Abuse Prevention (CSAP) established the Regional Alcohol and Drug Awareness Resource (RADAR) Network to make current prevention information readily available to those who need it most—prevention practitioners at the State and community levels.

The RADAR Network responds to the need for prevention services closer to home, staffed by people who understand the unique assets and liabilities of local communities. The RADAR Network was formed in partnership with State governments and national constituency groups. The National Clearinghouse for Alcohol and Drug Information (NCADI) serves as the national center for information and services, but the satellite centers of the RADAR Network provide local support to prevention practitioners and other community members interested in addressing alcohol, tobacco, and other drug problems.

RADAR Network Centers

RADAR Network Centers are located in every State and U.S. Territory. Coordinated through NCADI, regular RADAR Network Centers services are available to all community members. Services include:

Excerpted from (SMA) 94-2060.

- Helping people find accurate and up-to-date information about prevention as well as effective materials and programs that can be adapted for their communities.

- Providing posters, booklets, and other materials with prevention and intervention messages for youth, parents, and other target audiences. Some of these products are offered in bulk for distribution to groups, while others are camera-ready for reproduction. Almost all materials are in the public domain and community members are encouraged to reproduce and distribute copies.

- Promoting and supporting outreach efforts to groups at high risk (e.g., children of alcoholics and other drug abusers, dropouts, pregnant teens, low-income families, juvenile delinquents, youths with disabilities, suicidal teens, and those with mental health problems).

- Responding to questions about prevention and intervention by mail or telephone and assisting visitors by providing hands-on assistance.

- Helping prevention practitioners design and implement programs tailored to meet the special needs of their communities. This includes assistance with services and materials that are culturally sensitive and age-appropriate.

RADAR Network Centers work closely with CSAP, NCADI, CSAP grantees, and each other through an electronic communications system (PREVline) that allows for the ready exchange of information and ideas, facilitating an unprecedented level of interstate cooperation on prevention issues. The system is available 24 hours a day, 7 days a week.

In addition to State RADAR Network Centers designated by State governments, the network includes Specialty RADAR Network Centers that operate at the national level, associate members that work at the community level, and international organizations.

Specialty RADAR Network Centers

Specialty RADAR Network Centers are national organizations and Federal agencies that focus on specific alcohol, tobacco, and other drug issues. For example, National Families in Action might help a caller track how the media is covering a specific alcohol, tobacco, and other drugs related issue.

Associate RADAR Network Members

Associate members are organizations that conduct information and referral services at the community level. In addition to serving the public, associate members assist and support the RADAR Network Centers in their activities.

International RADAR Network Members

Other countries are interested in information exchange with the United States. Some have established International RADAR Network Centers and have sent representatives to NCADI to learn how to set up similar clearinghouse activities.

Using the RADAR Network

Anyone may use the services offered by the RADAR Network. For the location of the nearest RADAR Network Center or for membership information, contact:

National Clearing House for Alcohol and Drug Information (NCADI)
P.O. Box 2345
Rockville, MD 20847-2345
1-800-729-6686
1-800-487-4889 TDD

445

Chapter 51

What Can You Do about Drug Use in America?

Americans have become concerned as never before about the dangers of alcohol and other drug use. Public opinion polls have repeatedly indicated a general intolerance for the use of alcohol by minors and the use of illegal drugs by anyone. Indicators show that most Americans are prepared to take a stand against such illegal alcohol and other drug use.

The abuse of alcohol and the use of illegal drugs have ravaged families, and have infiltrated our streets, neighborhoods, and schoolyards. These problems have also invaded the workplace and the highway. The American public has finally said, "We've had enough," and is joining forced against drug use.

What Early Education Information Do I Need?

Knowledge is a powerful weapon against drugs. Some excellent information available from private sources. The Federal Government has also compiled a great deal of information about the effects of alcohol abuse and other drug use and the successful strategies that can be used to combat these problems. Free materials may be obtained by writing to the National Clearinghouse for Alcohol and Drug Information, P.O. Box 2345, Rockville, Maryland 20852, or you may want to call the Clearinghouse's toll-free number: 1-800-729-6686.

Excerpted from DHHS Pub. No. (ADM) 91-1572.

How Can I Set an Example?

First and foremost, set an example by not using illegal drugs or misusing alcohol or prescription drugs. Period. No excuses or self-exceptions should be offered to yourself or to others. If alcohol is used it should be used only by persons of legal age and only in moderation. Prescription drugs should only be used when prescribed and closely monitored by a physician. And you should abstain from the use of any illegal drugs.

Don't keep illegal drugs in the house and don't allow their use in your home by others. Let your family and friends know that drugs are not acceptable in your home. And let others know that you do not tolerate illegal drugs at parties that you or your family attend. Talk to your neighbors about the fact that drug use should not be tolerated on your streets or anywhere else near you.

The best way to keep your family from abusing alcohol (any use of alcohol by youth is abuse) is by carefully looking at the example set in your home. Are your parties, entertainment, and celebrations centered around alcohol? Do you reach for a drink or another drug whenever you want to relax or to deal with any problem that comes up? Such behavior sends the wrong signal—that alcohol and other drugs are needed to have a good time or to cope with daily living.

How Can I Help My Younger Children to Say "No"?

First, talk to your child about alcohol and other drugs. Carefully explain the health consequences of alcohol and other drug use, and the dramatic effect they can have on a child's life and preparation for the future. Correct mistaken ideas perpetuated by peers and the media. And really listen carefully to your child talk about alcohol and other drugs. Children are more likely to communicate when they receive positive verbal and nonverbal cues that show parents are listening.

Second, help your child to develop a healthy self-image. Self-regard is enhanced when parents praise efforts as well as accomplishments. In turn, when being critical, criticize the actions and not the person.

Third, help your child develop a strong system of values. A strong value system can give children the criteria and courage to make decisions based on facts rather than pressure from friends.

Fourth, help your child deal with peer pressure. Explain that saying "No" can be an important statement about self worth. Help your child practice saying "No." Together, set out the reasons for saying "No" and discuss why it is beneficial to avoid alcohol and other drugs.

Fifth, make family policies that help your child to say "No." The strongest support your child can have in refusing to use alcohol and other drugs is to be found in the solid bonds created within the family unit. Always chaperon your children's parties. It is helpful when parents let other family members—and friends—know that drug use, and use of alcohol by minors, is a violation of the rules by which the family will operate, and that their use of alcohol and other drugs is simply unacceptable within the family. The consequences and punishment for such a violation must be clearly spelled out.

Sixth, encourage your child to join an anti-drug club. With over 10,000 clubs nationwide, chances are that your child's school has such a club. If not, it might be a good idea to contact the local principal about starting a club. These clubs help develop positive peer pressure, strengthen children's ability to say "No," and teach the harmful effects of alcohol and other drugs on children's bodies.

Finally, encourage healthy, creative activities that may help to prevent children from using alcohol and other drugs. Help your child live such a full life that there is no time or place for alcohol and other drugs. Meet the parents of your child's friends and classmates and encourage alcohol and other drug-free alternative activities. Learn about drugs and share a "no use" message of alcohol or other drugs for youth. Discuss guidelines and problem areas and agree to keep in touch. Consider forming parent-peer groups. There is strength in numbers. Making these contacts before there is a problem often prevents the problem from ever developing. When the entire peer group is on the right track, you stand a better chance of keeping your child drug free. [For more information on helping children avoid drug use, see Chapter 52 in this volume.]

Where Can I Go for Help

Sometimes the quickest way to find out what help is available in your local area is to join a group such as Al-Anon. Al-Anon is a group of family members and friends of problem drinkers who meet to share practical suggestions on day-to-day living with someone who has a drinking problem. These family members and friends of problem drinkers usually know where help is available in your community.

Listed below are some other sources of help and information:

Telephone services

1-800-729-6686—National Clearinghouse for Alcohol and Drug Information, Monday through Friday, 9:00 a.m.–7:00 p.m.

1-800-622-HELP—National Institute on Drug Abuse Information and Referral Line, Monday through Friday, 9:00 a.m.–3:00 a.m.

1-800-554-KIDS—The National Federation of Parents for Drug-Free Youth, Monday through Friday, 9:00 a.m.–5:00 p.m.

1-800-622-2255—National Council on Alcoholism, 7 days a week, 24 hours a day.

1-800-241-9746—Parent's Resource Institute for Drug Education (PRIDE), Monday through Friday, 8:30 a.m.–5:00 p.m. (Recorded service other times)

1-800-COCAINE—Cocaine Helpline, Monday through Friday, 9:00 a.m–3:00 a.m. Saturday and Sunday, 12:00 p.m.–3:00 a.m.

1-800-843-4971—The National Institute on Drug Abuse Workplace Helpline (For employers establishing workplace drug abuse programs), Monday through Friday, 9:00 a.m.–8:00 p.m.

For information on where to find treatment for alcohol and other drug problems, the best place to look is in the telephone book's Yellow Pages under "Alcoholism Information" or "Drug Abuse and Addiction Information." Usually there is a listing of the nearest Council on Alcoholism (or Council on Alcohol and Drug Abuse). These Councils provide information over the phone on the availability of the nearest alcohol treatment programs. Alcoholics Anonymous (AA) or Narcotics Anonymous (NA) may also be listed. Both offer immeasurable help in enabling people to cope with problems with alcohol and other drugs.

Private Organizations, Civic Groups, Religious Organizations

Adult Children of Alcoholics (ACoA)
P.O. Box 3216
Torrance, CA 90505
(213) 534-1815

450

Al-Anon Family Groups
P.O. Box 862
Midtown Station
New York, NY 10018
(212) 302-7240
(800) 344-2666

Alcoholics Anonymous (AA)
15 E. 26th Street Rm 1810
New York, NY 10010
(212) 683-3900

American Council for Drug Education
204 Monroe Street, Suite 110
Rockville, MD 20850
(301) 294-0600
(800) 488-DRUG

The Chemical People/WQED
1 Allegheny Square, Suite 720
Pittsburgh, PA 15212
(412) 391-0900

Cocaine Anonymous (CA)
3740 Overland Avenue, Suite G
Los Angeles, CA 90034
(213) 559-5833
(800) 347-8998

CoAnon Family Groups
P.O. Box 64742-66
Los Angeles, CA 90064
(213) 859-2206

Families Anonymous, Inc.
P.O. Box 528
Van Nuys, CA 91408
(818) 989-7841

Institute on Black Chemical Abuse
2616 Nicollet Avenue
Minneapolis, MN 55408
(612) 871-7878

Just Say No Foundation
1777 North California Blvd., Room 210
Walnut Creek, CA 94596
(415) 939-6666
(800) 258-2766

Mothers Against Drunk Driving
511 E. John Carpenter Freeway, Suite 700
Irving, TX 75062
(214) 744-6233

Nar-Anon Family Groups
P.O. Box 2562
Palos Verdes Peninsula, CA 90274
(213) 547-5800

Narcotics Anonymous (NA)
P.O. Box 9999
Van Nuys, CA 91409
(818) 780-3951

National Asian Pacific American Families Against Drug Abuse
6303 Friendship Court
Bethesda, MD 20817
(301) 530-0945

National Association for Children of Alcoholics (NACoA)
31582 Coast Highway, Suite B
South Laguna, CA 92677
(714) 499-3889

National Association of State Alcohol and Drug Abuse Directors
(NASADAD)
444 N. Capitol Street, NW, Suite 642
Washington, DC 20001
(202) 783-6868

National Black Alcoholism and Addictions Council (NBAC)
1629 K Street, NW, Suite 802
Washington, DC 20006
(202) 296-2696

National Coalition of Hispanic Health and Human Services
Organizations (COSSMHO)
1030 15th Street, NW, Suite 1053
Washington, DC 20005
(202) 371-2100

National Families in Action
2296 Henderson Mill Road, Suite 204
Atlanta, GA 30345
(404) 934-6364

National Federation of Parents for Drug-Free Youth
9551 Big Bend
St. Louis, MO 63122
(314) 968-1322

National Parents Resource Institute for Drug Education (PRIDE)
The Hurt Building
50 Hurt Plaza, Suite 210
Atlanta, GA 30303
(404) 577-4500

National Prevention Network
444 North Capitol Street, NW, Suite 642
Washington, DC 20001
(202) 783-6868

Quest International
537 Jones Road
P.O. Box 566
Granville, OH 43023
(614) 587-2800

Women for Sobriety
P.O. Box 618
Quakertown, PA 18951
(215) 536-8026

State Organizations

Alabama
Division of Mental Illness and Substance Abuse
Community Programs
Department of Mental Health
500 Interstate Park Drive, Room 527
P.O. Box 3710
Montgomery, AL 36109-0710
(205) 270-4650

Alaska
Office of Alcoholism and Drug Abuse
Department of Health & Social Services
P.O. Box H
Juneau, AK 99811-0607
(907) 586-6201

Arizona
Alcoholism and Drug Abuse
Office of Comm. Behav. Health
Dept. of Health Services
411 N. 24th Street
Phoenix, AZ 85008
(602) 220-6455

Arkansas
Office on Alcohol and Drug Abuse Prevention
Donaghey Plaza, North, Suite 400
P.O. Box 1437
Little Rock, AR 72203-1437
(501) 682-6650

California
Department of Alcohol and Drug Programs
1700 K Street
Sacramento, CA 95814
(916) 445-0834

Colorado
Alcohol and Drug Abuse Div.
Department of Health
4210 East 11th Avenue
Denver, CO 80220
(303) 331-8201

Connecticut
Connecticut Alcohol and Drug Abuse Commission
999 Asylum Avenue, 3rd Floor
Hartford, CT 06105
(203) 566-4145

Delaware
Delaware Division of Alcoholism, Drug Abuse and Mental Health
1901 N. DuPont Highway
Newcastle, DE 19720
(302) 421-6101

District of Columbia
Health Planning and Dev.
1660 L Street, NW, Suite 1117
Washington, DC 20036
(202) 673-7481

Florida
Alcohol and Drug Abuse Program
Department of Health and Rehabilitative Services
1317 Winewood Boulevard, Building 6, Room 182
Tallahassee, FL 32399-0700
(904) 488-0900

Georgia
Alcohol and Drug Services
878 Peachtree Street, NE, Suite 319
Atlanta, GA 30309
(404) 894-6352

Hawaii
Alcohol and Drug Abuse Div.
Department of Health
1270 Queen Emma Street, Suite 706
P.O. Box 3378
Honolulu, HI 96803
(808) 548-4280

Idaho
Dept. of Health and Welfare
450 West State Street, 3rd Floor
Boise, ID 83720
(208) 334-5935

Illinois
Department of Alcoholism and Substance Abuse
100 West Randolph Street, Suite 5-600
Chicago, IL 60601
(312) 814-3840

Indiana
Division of Addiction Services
Department of Mental Health
117 East Washington Street
Indianapolis, IN 46204
(317) 232-7816

Iowa
Department of Public Health Division of Substance Abuse and
Health Promotion
Lucas State Office Building 321
E. 12th Street, 3rd Floor
Des Moines, IA 50319-0075
(515) 281-3641

Kansas
Alcohol and Drug Abuse Services
300 SW Oakley
2nd Floor, Biddle Building
Topeka, KS 66606-1861
(913) 296-3925

Kentucky
Division of Substance Abuse
Department for Mental Health and Mental Retardation Services
275 East Main Street
Frankfort, KY 40621
(502) 564-2880

Louisiana
Office of Human Services
Div. of Alcohol and Drug Abuse
1201 Capitol Access Road
P.O. Box 3868
Baton Rouge, LA 70821-3868
(504) 342-9354

Maine
Office of Alcoholism and Drug Abuse Prevention
Bureau of Rehabilitation
35 Anthony Avenue
State House Station #11
Augusta, ME 04333
(207) 289-2781

Maryland
Maryland State Alcohol and Drug Abuse Administration
201 West Preston Street, 4th Floor
Baltimore, MD 21201
(301) 225-6910

Massachusetts
Div. of Substance Abuse Services
150 Tremont Street
Boston, MA 02111
(617) 727-8614

Michigan
Off. of Substance Abuse Services
Department of Public Health
2150 Apollo Drive
P.O. Box 30206
Lansing, MI 48909
(517) 335-8809

Minnesota
Chemical Dependency Program Division
Department of Human Services
444 Lafayette Road
St. Paul, MN 55155-3823
(612) 296-4610

Mississippi
Division of Alcohol and Drug Abuse
Department of Mental Health
Robert E. Lee State Office Building, 11th Floor
239 N. Lamar Street
Jackson, MS 39201
(601) 359-1288

Missouri
Div. of Alcohol and Drug Abuse
Department of Mental Health
1706 E. Elm Street
P.O. Box 687
Jefferson City, MO 65102
(314) 751-4942

Montana
Alcohol and Drug Abuse Div.
Department of Institutions
1539 11th Avenue
Helena, MT 59620
(406) 444-2827

Nebraska
Division of Alcoholism and Drug Abuse
Department of Public Inst.
P.O. Box 94728
Lincoln, NE 68509
(402) 471-2851, Ext. 5583

Nevada
Alcohol & Drug Abuse Bureau
Dept. Human Resources
505 East King Street, Room 50
Carson City, NV 89710
(702) 687-4790

New Hampshire
Office of Alcohol and Drug Abuse Prevention
State Office Park South
105 Pleasant Street
Concord, NH 03301
(603) 271-6100

New Jersey
Department of Health
CN 322
Trenton, NJ 08625-0362
(609) 292-3147

Division of Narcotic and Drug Abuse Control
CN 362
129 East Hanover Street
Trenton, NJ 08625-0362
(609) 292-5760

New Mexico
Substance Abuse Bureau
190 St. Francis Drive, Room 3200 North
Box 26110
Sante Fe, NM 87502
(505) 827-2589

New York
Division of Alcoholism and Alcohol Abuse
194 Washington Avenue
Albany, NY 12210
(518) 474-5417

Division of Substance Abuse Services
Executive Park South
Albany, NY 12203
(518) 457-7629

North Carolina
Alcohol and Drug Abuse Section
Division of Mental Health and Mental Retardation Services
325 North Salisbury Street
Raleigh, NC 27603
(919) 733-4670

North Dakota
Division of Alcoholism and Drug Abuse
Dept. of Human Services
State Capitol/Judicial
Wing 1839 East Capitol Street
Bismark, ND 58501
(701) 224-2769

Ohio
Bureau on Alcohol Abuse and Recovery
Ohio Department of Health
Two Nationwide Plaza
280 North High Street, 12th Floor
Columbus, OH 43215
(614) 466-3445

Bureau on Drug Abuse
Ohio Department of Health
Two Nationwide Plaza
280 North High Street, 12th Floor
Columbus, OH 43215
(614) 466-7893

Oklahoma
Oklahoma Department of Mental Health and Substance Abuse
Services
1200 NE 13th Street
P.O. Box 53277
Capitol Station
Oklahoma City, OK 73152-3277
(405) 271-7474

Oregon
Office of Alcohol and Drug Abuse Programs
1178 Chemeketa Street, NE, #102
Salem, OR 97310
(503) 378-2163

Pennsylvania
Drug and Alcohol Programs
Department of Health
P.O. Box 90
Harrisburg, PA 17108
(717) 787-9857

Rhode Island
Division of Substance Abuse
Department of Mental Health, Retardation and Hospitals
P.O. Box 20363
Cranston, RI 02920
(401) 464-2091

South Carolina
South Carolina Commission on Alcohol and Drug Abuse
3700 Forest Drive
Columbia, SC 29204
(803) 734-9520

South Dakota
Div. of Alcohol and Drug Abuse
Joe Foss Building
700 Governor's Drive
Pierre, SD 57501-2291
(605) 773-3123

Tennessee
Alcohol and Drug Abuse Services
Dept. of Mental Health and Mental Retardation
Doctor's Building
706 Church Street, 4th Floor
Nashville, TN 37243-0675
(615) 741-1921

Texas
Texas Commission on Alcohol and Drug Abuse
720 Brazos Street, Suite 403
Austin, TX 78701
(512) 463-5510

Utah
Division of Substance Abuse
Department of Social Services
120 N. 200 West, 4th Floor
P.O. Box 45500
Salt Lake City, UT 84103
(801) 538-3939

Vermont
Office of Alcohol and Drug Abuse Programs
103 South Maine Street
Waterbury, VT 05676
(802) 241-2170/241-2175

Virginia
Off. of Substance Abuse Services
Dept. of Mental Health, Mental Retardation and Substance Services
P.O. Box 1797
109 Governor Street
Richmond, VA 23214
(804) 786-3906

Washington
Bureau of Alcoholism and Substance Abuse
Washington Department of Social and Health Services
Mail Stop OB 21W
Olympia, WA 98504
(206) 753-5866

West Virginia
Div. of Alcohol and Drug Abuse
State Capitol
1900 Kanawha Blvd., East Building 3, Room 451
Charleston, WV 25305
(304) 348-2276

Wisconsin
Office of Alcohol and Other Drug Abuse
1 West Wilson Street, Room 434
P.O. Box 7851
Madison, WI 53707
(608) 266-3442

Wyoming
Alcohol and Drug Abuse Programs
Hathaway Building
Cheyenne, WY 82002
(307) 777-7115, Ext. 7118

Guam
Department of Mental Health and Substance Abuse
P.O. Box 9400
Tamuning, Guam 96911
(671) 646-9262-69

Puerto Rico
Departamento de Servicios Contra la Adicción
Box 21414
Rio Piedras Station
Rio Piedras, PR 00928-1414
(809) 764-3795

Virgin Islands
Div. of Mental Health
Alcoholism and Drug Dependency Services
P.O. Box 520
St. Croix, Virgin Islands 00820
(809) 773-1992

American Samoa
Social Services Division
Alcohol and Drug Program
Government of American Samoa
Pago Pago, AS 96799

Public Health Services
LBJ Tropical Medical Center
Pago Pago, AS 96799

For further information:

National Clearinghouse for Alcohol and Drug Information
P.O. Box 2345
Rockville, Maryland 20852
1-800-729-6686

Chapter 52

Growing Up Drug Free: A Parent's Guide to Prevention

What Parents Can Do

Introduction

Child rearing is one of the most important tasks anyone ever performs, and the one for which there is the least preparation. Most of us learn how to be parents through on-the-job training and by following the example that our parents set.

Today the widespread use of alcohol and other drugs subjects our children, families, and communities to pressures unheard of 30 or 40 years ago. Frankly, many of us need help to deal with this frightening threat to our children's health and well-being.

Recent surveys show that we are making progress in our national battle against some drugs. Casual use is declining, attitudes are changing, and we know more about what works to prevent drug use by our young people.

As parents, we can build on that progress in our own families by having strong, loving relationships with our children, by teaching standards of right and wrong, by setting and enforcing rules for behavior, by knowing the facts about alcohol and other drugs, and by really listening to our children.

Excerpted from *Growing Up Drug Free: A Parent's Guide to Prevention*, produced by the U.S. Department of Education, Washington, DC, nd.

465

Teaching Values

Every family has expectations of behavior that are determined by principles and standards. These add up to "values." Children who decide not to use alcohol or other drugs often make this decision because they have strong convictions against the use of these substances—convictions that are based in a value system. Social, family, and religious values give young people reasons to say no and help them stick to their decisions.

Here are some ways to help make your family's values clear:

- *Communicate values openly.* Talk about why values such as honesty, self-reliance, and responsibility are important, and how values help children make good decisions. Teach your child how each decision builds on previous decisions as one's character is formed, and how a good decision makes the next decision easier.

- Recognize how your actions affect the development of your child's values. Simply stated, children copy their parents' behavior. Children whose parents smoke, for example, are more likely to become smokers. Evaluate your own use of tobacco, alcohol, prescription medicines, and even over-the-counter drugs. Consider how your attitudes and actions may be shaping your child's choice about whether or not to use alcohol or other drugs.

This does not mean, however, that if you are in the habit of having wine with dinner or an occasional beer or cocktail you must stop. Children can understand and accept that there are differences between what adults may do legally and what is appropriate and legal for children. Keep that distinction sharp, however. Do not let your children be involved in your drinking by mixing a cocktail for you or bringing you a beer, and do not allow your child to have sips of your drink.

- *Look for conflicts between your words and your actions.* Remember that children are quick to sense when parents send signals by their actions that it's all right to duck unpleasant duties or to be dishonest. Telling your child to say that you are not at home because a phone call comes at an inconvenient time is, in effect, teaching your child that it is all right to be dishonest.

- *Make sure that your child understands your family values.* Parents assume, sometimes mistakenly, that children have "absorbed" values even though they may be rarely or never discussed. You can test your child's understanding by discussing some common situations at the dinner table; for example, "What would you do if the person ahead of you in line at the theater dropped a dollar bill?"

Setting and Enforcing Rules Against the Use of Alcohol and Other Drugs

As parents, we are responsible for setting rules for our children to follow. When it comes to alcohol and other drug use, strong rules need to be established to protect the well-being of a child. Setting rules is only half the job, however; we must be prepared to enforce the penalties when the rules are broken.

- *Be specific.* Explain the reasons for the rules. Tell your child what the rules are and what behavior is expected. Discuss the consequences of breaking the rules: what the punishment will be, how it will be carried out, how much time will be involved, and what the punishment is supposed to achieve.

- *Be consistent.* Make it clear to your child that a no-alcohol/ no-drug-use rule remains the same at all times—in your home, in a friend's home, anywhere the child is.

- *Be reasonable.* Don't add new consequences that have not been discussed before the rule was broken. Avoid unrealistic threats such as, "Your father will kill you when he gets home." Instead, react calmly and carry out the punishment that the child expects to receive for breaking the rule.

Getting the Facts

As parents, we need to know about alcohol and other drugs so that we can provide our children with current and correct information. If we have a working knowledge of common drugs—know their effects on the mind and body, and the symptoms of their use—we can discuss these subjects intelligently with our children. In addition, well-informed parents are better able to recognize if a child has symptoms of alcohol or drug-related problems.

At a minimum, you should:

- know the different types of drugs and alcohol most commonly used and the dangers associated with each;
- be able to identify paraphernalia associated with each drug;
- be familiar with the street names of drugs;
- know what drugs look like;
- know the signs of alcohol and other drug use and be alert for changes in your child's behavior or appearance;
- know how to get help promptly if you suspect your child may be using alcohol and other drugs.

[A list of resources for further help and information is included in Chapter 51 of this volume.]

Children and Alcohol. Parents who are clear about not wanting their children to use illicit drugs may find it harder to be tough about alcohol. After all, alcohol is legal for adults, many parents drink, and alcohol is a part of some religious observances. As a result, we may view alcohol as a less dangerous substance than other drugs. The facts say otherwise:

- 4.6 million teenagers have a drinking problem.
- 4 percent of high school seniors drink alcohol every day.
- Alcohol-related accidents are the leading cause of death among young people 15 to 24 years of age.
- About half of all youthful deaths in drowning, fires, suicide, and homicide are alcohol-related.
- Young people who use alcohol at an early age are more likely to use alcohol heavily and to have alcohol-related problems; they are also more likely to abuse other drugs and to get into trouble with the law.
- Young people whose body weight is lower than adults reach a higher blood alcohol concentration level than adults and show greater effects for longer periods of time.

Facts on Tobacco. We know that smokers are 10 times as likely as nonsmokers to develop lung cancer and 3 times as likely to die at early ages from heart attack. In fact, in 1985, smoking was the leading cause of early death among adults. Nicotine, the active ingredient in tobacco, is as addictive as heroin, and fewer than 20 percent of smokers are able to quit the first time they try. Despite these facts, many children use these products.

- 18 percent of high school seniors are smokers; 11 percent smoke 10 or more cigarettes per day.
- Young people who use cigarettes are also at risk for all other drug use.
- 70 percent of all children try cigarettes, 40 percent of them before they have reached high school.
- Cigarettes contain more than 4,000 harmful substances, several of which cause cancer.
- 12 percent of boys and 1 percent of girls have chewed tobacco or used snuff. Smokeless tobacco is just as addictive and harmful as tobacco that is smoked.

A Quiz for Parents

1. What is the most commonly used drug in the United States? (a) heroin; (b) cocaine; (c) alcohol; (d) marijuana

2. Name the three drugs most commonly used by children.

3. Which drug is associated with the most teenage deaths?

4. Which of the following contains the most alcohol? (a) a 12-ounce can of beer; (b) a cocktail; (c) a 12-ounce wine cooler; (d) a 5-ounce glass of wine; (e) all contain equal amounts of alcohol

5. Crack is a particularly dangerous drug because it is: (a) cheap; (b) readily available; (c) highly addictive; (d) all of the above

6. Fumes from which of the following can be inhaled to produce a high: (a) spray paint; (b) model glue; (c) nail polish remover; (d) whipped cream canisters; (e) all of the above

7. People who have not used alcohol and other drugs before their 20th birthday: (a) have no risk of becoming chemically dependent; (b) are less likely to develop a drinking problem or use illicit drugs; (c) have an increased risk of becoming chemically dependent

8. A speedball is a combination of which two drugs? (a) cocaine and heroin; (b) PCP and LSD; (c) valium and alcohol; (d) amphetamines and barbiturates

9. Anabolic steroids are dangerous because they may result in: (a) development of female characteristics in males; (b) development of male characteristics in females; (c) stunted growth; (d) damage to the liver and cardiovascular system; (e) over-aggressive behavior; (f) all of the above

10. How much alcohol can a pregnant woman safely consume? (a) a 6-ounce glass of wine with dinner; (b) two 12-ounce beers each day; (c) five 4-ounce shots of whiskey a month; (d) none

Answers

1. (c) Because it is legal for adults and widely accepted in our culture, alcohol is the drug most often used in the United States.

2. Alcohol, tobacco, and marijuana. These are the "gateway" drugs, drugs that children are first exposed to and whose use often precedes use of other drugs.

3. Alcohol. More than 10,000 teenagers died in alcohol-related traffic accidents in 1986; 40,000 more were injured.

4. (e) All four contain approximately 1.5 ounces of alcohol.

5. (d) Small quantities of crack can be bought for as little as $5.00. The low price makes it easily affordable to young people. In addition, crack is thought to be one of the most addictive drugs.

6. (e) Virtually anything that emits fumes or comes in aerosol form can be inhaled to obtain a high.

7. (b) Early use of alcohol and other drugs—often by age 15 or less—is strongly associated with drug-related problems such as addiction.

8. (a) Combining cocaine and heroin is increasingly popular as a way of trying to lessen or control bad side effects.

9. (f) Steroid users subject themselves to more than 70 side effects. The liver and cardiovascular and reproductive systems are most seriously affected by steroid use. In females, irreversible masculine traits can develop. Psychological effects in both sexes can cause very aggressive behavior and depression.

10. (d) Medical researchers have not established any safe limits for alcohol intake during pregnancy.

Talking with and Listening to Your Child

Many parents hesitate to discuss alcohol and other drug use with their child. Some of us believe that our children couldn't become involved with illegal substances. Others delay because we don't know what to say or how to say it, or we are afraid of putting ideas into our children's heads.

Don't wait until you think your child has a problem. Many young people in treatment programs say that they had used alcohol and other drugs for at least two years before their parents knew about it. Begin early to talk about alcohol and other drugs, and keep the lines of communication open.

Don't be afraid to admit that you don't have all the answers. Let your child know that you are concerned, and that you can work together to find answers. [A list of reading material is provided at the end of this chapter; in addition, Chapter 51 lists sources for more information.]

Here are some basic hints for improving your ability to talk with your child about alcohol and other drugs:

- *Be a good listener.* Make sure your child feels comfortable bringing problems or questions to you. Listen closely to what your child says. Don't allow anger at what you hear to end the discussion. If necessary, take a 5-minute break to calm down before continuing. Take note of what your child is not saying, too. If the child does not tell you about problems, take the initiative and ask questions about what is going on at school or in other activities.

- *Be available to discuss even sensitive subjects.* Young people need to know that they can rely on their parents for accurate information about subjects that are important to them. If your child wants to discuss something at a time when you can't give it full attention, explain why you can't talk, set a time to talk later, and then carry through on it!

- *Give lots of praise.* Emphasize the things your youngster is doing right instead of always focusing on things that are wrong. When parents are quicker to praise than to criticize, children learn to feel good about themselves, and they develop the self-confidence to trust their own judgment.

- *Give clear messages.* When talking about the use of alcohol and other drugs, be sure you give your child a dear no-use message, so that the child will know exactly what is expected. For example, "In our family we don't allow the use of illegal drugs, and children are not allowed to drink."

- *Model good behavior.* Children learn by example as well as teaching. Make sure that your own actions reflect the standards of honesty, integrity, and fair play that you expect of your child.

Communication Tips

Effective communication between parents and children is not always easy to achieve. Children and adults have different communication styles and different ways of responding in a conversation. In addition, timing and atmosphere may determine how successful communication will be. Parents should make time to talk with their children in a quiet, unhurried manner. The following tips are designed to make communication more successful.

Listening

- Pay attention.
- Don't interrupt.
- Don't prepare what you will say while your child is speaking.
- Reserve judgment until your child has finished and has asked you for a response.

Looking

- Be aware of your child's facial expression and body language. Is your child nervous or uncomfortable—frowning, drumming fingers, tapping a foot, looking at the clock? Or does your child seem relaxed—smiling, looking you in the eyes? Reading these signs will help parents know how the child is feeling.

- During the conversation, acknowledge what your child is saying—move your body forward if you are sitting, touch a shoulder if you are walking, or nod your head and make eye contact.

Responding

- "I am very concerned about...." or "I understand that it is sometimes difficult ...." are better ways to respond to your child than beginning sentences with "You should," or "If I were you," or "When I was your age we didn't ..." Speaking for oneself sounds thoughtful and is less likely to be considered a lecture or an automatic response.

- If your child tells you something you don't want to hear, don't ignore the statement.

- Don't offer advice in response to every statement your child makes. It is better to listen carefully to what is being said and try to understand the real feelings behind the words.

- Make sure you understand what your child means. Repeat things to your child for confirmation.

Applying the Principles

The preceding sections have outlined some general guidelines for talking with children about alcohol and other drugs. We can make these messages more effective by taking into account the knowledge youngsters already have and their readiness to learn new information at different ages.

Preschoolers

Drug education may seem unnecessary for preschoolers, but the attitudes and habits learned early can have an important bearing on the decisions children make later.

Three- and four-year-olds are not yet ready to learn complex facts about alcohol and other drugs, but they can learn the decision-making and problem-solving skills that they will need to refuse alcohol and other drugs later. Remember that children in this age group are not able to listen quietly for very long; they are more interested in doing things for themselves.

It's tempting for busy parents to do things for young children because it's quicker and easier. With a little planning, however, you can use the learn-by-doing approach to teach your preschooler how to make decisions. Let your child pick from a range of options that are acceptable to you. When the choice is made, make sure your child sticks with it.

Suggested Activities

- Set aside regular times when you can give your child your full attention. Playing together, reading a book, and taking a walk are special times that help to build strong bonds of trust and affection between you and your child.

- Point out to your child poisonous and harmful substances that can be found in your home. Household products such as bleach, lye, and furniture polish all have warning labels that you can read to your child. Keep all household products that could harm a small child away from the place you store foods and out of your child's reach.

- Explain how medicine can be harmful if used incorrectly. Teach your child not to take anything from a medicine bottle unless you give it to the child yourself or specify someone else who can give it, such as a babysitter or grandparent.

- Explain why children need good food and should put only good things into their bodies. Have your child name several good foods that he or she eats regularly, and explain how those foods will make your child strong and healthy.

- Provide guidelines that teach your child what kind of behavior you expect. Teach your child the basic rules of how to get along with other children: Play fair. Share toys. Tell the truth. Treat others the way you want them to treat you.

- Encourage your child to follow instructions. For example, invite your child to help you cook; following a recipe—measuring ingredients, cracking eggs, kneading dough—can help children have fun while learning about step-by-step procedures. Playing simple board games with your child can give practice in following instructions and rules.

- Take advantage of opportunities to use play as a way to help your child handle frustrating situations and solve simple problems. A tower of blocks that continuously collapses can drive a child to tears. You can offer a few suggestions to keep the tower up, but at the same time you should ask your child what he or she thinks is the best way to do it. Turning a bad situation into a success reinforces a child's self-confidence.

- To help your child learn decision making in a practical way, lay out some clothing from which the child can select what he or she wishes to wear. Don't worry if the choices don't quite match. Let your child know that you think he or she is able to make good decisions.

Kindergarten–Grade 3

Five- to nine-year-olds usually feel good about themselves. They like growing up, and they generally like school and all the new opportunities it provides. They still think and learn primarily by experience, and they don't have a good understanding of things that will happen in the future. Fact and fantasy mingle easily; the world is seen as the child wishes it to be, and not as it actually is. Children of this age need rules to guide their behavior and information to make good choices and decisions.

Discussions about alcohol and other drugs must be in the here and now, and related to people and events the child knows about. Most children are very interested in how their bodies work, so discussions should focus on maintaining good health and avoiding things that might harm the body.

Adults are very important both as teachers and as role models. Children are generally trusting, and they believe that the decisions adults make for them are right. Helping your child know whom to trust is important. They need to understand that just because someone tells them to do something, it is not always right to do it.

By the end of the third grade, your child should understand:

- what an illicit drug is, why it is illegal, what it looks like, and what harm it can do;
- how foods, poisons, medicines, and illicit drugs differ;
- how medicines may help during illness, when prescribed by a doctor and administered by a responsible adult, but also how medicines are drugs that can be harmful if misused;
- why it is important to avoid unknown and possibly dangerous objects, containers, and substances;
- which adults, both at school and outside, you want your child to rely on for answers to questions or help in an emergency;
- which foods are nutritious and why exercise is important;
- what the school and home rules are about alcohol and other drug use; and
- how using alcohol and other drugs is illegal for all children.

Suggested Activities

- Children in this age group need to understand the family's rules. You can explain the need for rules by talking about traffic safety rules and school rules with which your child is already familiar.

- Emphasize the importance of good health by talking about things people do to stay healthy, such as brushing teeth after each meal, washing hands, eating good foods, getting plenty of rest and sleep. You can use this discussion to contrast the harmful things that people do, such as taking drugs, smoking, or drinking to excess.

- Discuss how TV advertisers try to persuade children to buy their products, including high-sugar/additives-loaded cereals, candy bars, and toys named after characters in cartoon shows that children find appealing.

- Discuss illnesses with which your child is familiar and for which prescription drugs are often necessary. Many children have had strep throat, ear infections, flu, and colds. Discussing such illnesses can help your child understand the difference between medicine and illicit drugs.

- Practice ways to say no with your child. Describe situations that may make your child feel uncomfortable: being invited to ride a bike where you do not allow your child to go, for example, or being offered medicine or other unfamiliar substances. Give your child some responses to use in these situations.

- Develop a "helpers" file of people your child can rely on. Put together a phone list of relatives, family friends, neighbors, teachers, religious leaders, and the police and fire departments. Illustrate the list with photos. Talk with your child about the kind of help each person on the list could provide in case of various unexpected situations, such as being approached by strangers or losing a house key.

Grades 4-6

This is a period of slowed physical growth when typically a lot of energy goes into learning. Children 10 to 12 years old love to learn facts, especially strange ones, and they want to know how things work and what sources of information are available to them.

Friends—a single best friend or a group of friends—become very important. What children this age are interested in or will be committed to often is determined by what the group thinks. Children's self-image is determined in part by the extent to which they are accepted by peers, especially popular peers. As a result, a lot of "followers" are unable to make independent decisions and choices.

This age is perhaps the most important time for parents to focus on increased efforts at drug prevention. These late elementary school years are crucial to decisions about the use of alcohol and other drugs. The greatest risk for starting to smoke comes in the sixth and seventh grades. Research shows that the earlier youngsters begin to use alcohol and other drugs, the more likely they are to have real trouble.

Your child will need a clear no-use message, factual information, and strong motivation to resist pressures to try alcohol and other drugs and to reinforce the determination to remain drug free. Appropriate new information could include:

477

- ways to identify specific drugs, including alcohol, tobacco, marijuana, inhalants, and cocaine in their various forms;
- the long- and short-term effects and consequences of use;
- the effects of drugs on different parts of the body, and the reasons why drugs are especially dangerous for growing bodies; and
- the consequences of alcohol and other illegal drug use to the family, society, and the user.

Teaching Your Child to Say No

Here are some steps that you can practice with your child to make it easier for the child to refuse an offer of alcohol and other drugs. Tell your child to:

- *Ask questions.* If unknown substances are offered, ask, "What is it?" and "Where did you get it?" If a party or other gathering is proposed, ask, "Who else is coming?" "Where will it be?" "Will parents be there?"

- *Say no.* Don't argue, don't discuss. Say no and show that you mean it.

- *Give reasons.* "I'm doing something else that night" or "The coach says drugs will hurt my game" are examples of some reasons that youngsters can use. Also, don't forget the oldest reason: "My parents will kill me."

- *Suggest other things to do.* If a friend is offering alcohol or other drugs, saying no is tougher. Suggesting something else to do—going to a movie, playing a game, or working together on a project—shows that drugs are being rejected, not the friend.

- *Leave.* When all these steps have been tried, get out of the situation immediately. Go home, go to class; join a group of friends, or talk to someone else.

Suggested Activities

- Create special times when you are available to talk to your child. Try to give your child undivided attention. A walk together, dinner in a quiet place, or a visit to the ice cream parlor after a movie are some ways to make talking together a little easier.

- Encourage your child to participate in wholesome activities that will allow the child to form new friendships and have fun. Sports, Scouts, religious-sponsored youth programs, and community-sponsored youth organizations are excellent ways for children to meet others of their own age.

- Teach your child to be aware of how drugs and alcohol are promoted. Discuss how children are bombarded with messages—from TV, song lyrics, billboards, and advertisements—that using alcohol and other drugs is very glamorous. Clearly separate the myths from the realities of alcohol and other drug use.

- Continue to practice ways to say no with your child, emphasizing ways to refuse alcohol and other drugs. It is not uncommon for sixth graders to be offered beer and cigarettes and to know other children who smoke and drink alcohol.

- Encourage your child to join a local anti-drug club or peer assistance group that encourages drug-free activities.

- Ask your child to scan the morning newspaper and to circle any article that has to do with alcohol and other drug use. No doubt there will be articles about drug-related murders, strife in other countries due to drug trafficking, and alcohol-related auto accidents. Talk with your child about the tremendous loss of lives and resources because of the use of alcohol and other drugs.

- Make friends with the parents of your child's friends so that you can reinforce one another's efforts in teaching good personal and social habits. A neighborhood social gathering, sporting event, or school assembly are good places to meet.

- Join with other parents in providing supervised activities for young people to limit "free time," which often leads to experimentation with alcohol and other drugs.

Grades 7-9

During the early teens "fitting in" with friends is a controlling influence. In some ways, the onset of puberty is like a "rebirth." Children want and need to let go of the past and to find their own unique identity. This often means letting go of old friendships and ties with teachers and other adults, as well as old ways of doing things. The decision-making and problem-solving methods that they learned as young children are still helpful, but young teens will be making new decisions based on new information and new goals.

Young people this age can begin to deal with abstractions and the future. They understand that their actions have consequences, and they know how their behavior affects others. They sometimes have a shaky self-image: they are not sure whether they are growing and changing adequately, they are often in conflict with adults, they are not sure where they are headed, and they tend to see themselves as not "okay." Strong emotional support and a good model of adult behavior are particularly important now.

Young people who use alcohol, tobacco, and other drugs typically begin before leaving the ninth grade. Be sure that family discussions about drugs emphasize the immediate, unpleasant effects of alcohol and other drug use. Telling junior high school students who are smoking that they will get lung cancer or heart disease in several decades is less likely to make an impression than talking about bad breath, stained teeth and fingers, and burned clothing.

Many young people use drugs because their friends use drugs. A large portion of your prevention efforts during these years should be spent reinforcing your child's motivation to avoid alcohol and other drugs. Here are some important steps:

- *Counteract peer influence with parent influence.* Reinforce your no-alcohol/no-drug-use rules and expectations so that your child clearly understands that drinking and using drugs are unacceptable and illegal. Children may argue that "everyone is doing it" and not experiencing any harmful effects. Inform your child that alcohol and other drug use is illegal for children and that "everyone is not doing it." Emphasize how unpredictable the effects of alcohol and other drugs can be, so that although many drug users may appear to function properly, drug use is extremely risky, and all it takes is one bad experience to change a life.

- *Get to know your child's friends and their parents.* Meet your child's friends. Invite them to your home frequently. Share your expectations about behavior with other parents. Work together to develop a set of rules about curfews, unchaperoned parties, and other social activities.

480

- *Monitor your child's whereabouts.* If your child is at "a friend's house," be sure that you know the friend and the parents. If your child is at the movies, be sure you know what film is playing and at which theater. Last-minute changes in plans, such as visiting a different friend or going to a different movie, should not be permitted unless the child checks with Mom, Dad, or another designated adult.

By the end of ninth grade your child should know:

- the characteristics and chemical nature of specific drugs and drug interactions;
- the physiology of drug effects on the circulatory, respiratory, nervous, and reproductive systems;
- the stages of chemical dependency and their unpredictability from person to person;
- the ways that drug use affects activities requiring motor coordination, such as driving a car or participating in sports; and
- family history, particularly if alcoholism or other drug addiction has been a problem.

Suggested Activities

- Continue to practice ways to say no with your child. Teach your child to recognize problem situations, such as being at a house where no adults are present and young people are smoking or drinking beer. Make up situations in which your child may be asked to try alcohol and other drugs and let the child practice saying no using the steps outlined. Try many variations until you are confident that your child knows how to say no.

- Children this age are very concerned about how others see them. You can help your child develop a positive self-image by making sure that the child looks good and feels healthy. In addition to providing well-balanced meals, keep your refrigerator and pantry stocked with appealing alternatives to junk food.

- Continue to spend private time with your child to discuss what your child feels is important in his or her life right now. Your child's fears about emerging sexuality, appearing different from friends, and going on to high school are real problems and deserve your concern and attention.

- Periodically review and update, with your child's participation, your house rules and your child's responsibilities regarding chores, homework, time limit on TV watching, and the curfew on school and weekend nights. Discuss these questions with your child: Are the rules fair and the consequences appropriate? Is it time to switch to some new chores? Should there be fewer or different chores because of added homework assignments or after-school activities? Should the curfew be adjusted?

- Talk with your child about friendship. Make the point that true friends do not ask each other to do things they know are wrong and risk harm to themselves, their friends, or their families.

- Plan supervised parties or other activities for your child in your home which reflect a no-alcohol/no-drug-use rule. For example, have your child invite friends to share a pizza and watch TV.

Grades 10-12

High school students are future-oriented and can engage in abstract thinking. They have an increasingly realistic understanding of adults. Young people therefore want adults to discuss their concerns and the ways they solve problems and make decisions. You may have a tremendous new opportunity to help your children at this age. At the same time, the teenagers continue to be group-orientated, and belonging to the group motivates much of their behavior and actions. During these years, young people often develop a broader outlook and become more interested in the welfare of others.

By the end of high school, your child should understand:

- both the immediate and long-term physical effects of specific drugs;
- the possibly fatal effects of combining drugs;
- the relationship of drug use to other diseases and disabilities;
- the effects of alcohol and other drugs on the fetus during pregnancy;
- the fact that drug use is not a victimless crime;
- the effects and possible consequences of operating equipment while using alcohol and other drugs;
- the impact that drug use has on society; and
- the extent of community intervention resources.

You may want to focus on the potential long-term effects of alcohol and other drugs during these years: drugs can ruin your teen's chances of getting into college, being accepted by the military, or being hired for certain jobs. Your teen may also be impressed by the importance of serving as a good role model for a younger brother or sister.

Although young people long for independence, it is particularly important to keep them involved in the family and family activities. They should join the rest of the family for dinner regularly, be part of family vacations, and remain part of family routines.

Suggested Activities

- Continue to talk with your teenager about alcohol and other drug use. Chances are your teen has friends who use alcohol and other drugs or knows people who do. Talk about how alcohol and other drug use threatens lives and may limit opportunities for the future.

- Plan strategies to limit your teen's unsupervised hours at home, while you are at work. Researchers have found that lunchtime and 3:00-6:00 p.m. are periods teenagers are likely to experiment with alcohol and other drugs.

- Encourage your teenager to work on behalf of a drug prevention program by being trained as a volunteer to answer hot-line calls or as a peer counselor.

- Talk with your teenager about joining a sports club, drama club, arts and crafts center, or dance studio or about volunteering to work for a church group or community organization. The busier your teenager is, the less likely he or she is to be bored and to seek an outlet in alcohol or other drugs. Volunteer with your teenager, if you have time.

- Plan alcohol- and drug-free activities with other families during school vacations and major holidays, which can be high-risk idle times for teens.

- Make sure your teen has access to up-to-date information on alcohol and other drugs and their effects. Make an effort to be informed about any new drugs that are popular, and know their effects. [For suggested reading, see the resources section at the end of this chapter. You may also wish to contact some of the organizations listed in Chapter 51.]

- Cooperate with other parents to make sure that the parties and social events your teenager attends are alcohol- and drug-free. Some families choose to draw up a contract holding adults responsible for parties given in their homes; the contract specifies that all parties will be supervised and that there is to be no use of alcohol or other drugs.

- Help plan community-sponsored drug-free activities such as alcohol- and drug-free dances and other recreational activities such as "midnight basketball."

- Talk with your teenager about the future. Discuss your expectations and your teenager's ambitions. Collect college or vocational catalogs for your teenager, and discuss different educational and career options. Plan a family outing to local colleges and universities.

What to Do If Your Child Is Using Drugs

Young people use drugs for many reasons that have to do with how they feel about themselves, how they get along with others, and how they live. No one factor determines who will use drugs and who will not, but here are some predictors:

- low grades or poor school performance;
- aggressive, rebellious behavior;
- excessive influence by peers;
- lack of parental support and guidance; and
- behavior problems at an early age.

Being alert to the signs of alcohol and other drug use requires a keen eye. It is sometimes hard to know the difference between normal teenage behavior and behavior caused by drugs. Changes that are extreme or that last for more than a few days may signal drug use.

Consider the following questions:

- Does your child seem withdrawn, depressed, tired, and careless about personal grooming?
- Has your child become hostile and uncooperative?
- Have your child's relationships with other family members deteriorated?
- Has your child dropped his old friends?
- Is your child no longer doing well in school—grades slipping, attendance irregular?
- Has your child lost interest in hobbies, sports, and other favorite activities?
- Have your child's eating or sleeping patterns changed?

Positive answers to any of these questions can indicate alcohol or other drug use. However, these signs may also apply to a child who is not using drugs but who may be having other problems at school or in the family. If you are in doubt, get help. Have your family doctor or local clinic examine your child to rule out illness or other physical problems.

Watch for signs of drugs and drug paraphernalia as well. Possession of common items such as pipes, rolling papers, small medicine bottles, eye drops, or butane lighters may signal that your child is using drugs.

Even when the signs are clearer, usually after the child has been using drugs for a time, parents sometimes do not want to admit that their child could have a problem. Anger, resentment, guilt, and a sense of failure as parents are common reactions.

If your child is using drugs, it is important to avoid blaming yourself for the problem and to get whatever help is needed to stop it. The earlier a drug problem is detected and faced, the more likely it is that your child can be helped.

First, do not confront a child who is under the influence of alcohol or other drugs, but wait until the child is sober. Then discuss your suspicions with your child calmly and objectively. Bring in other members of the family to help, if necessary.

Second, impose whatever discipline your family has decided on for violating the rules and stick to it. Don't relent because the youngster promises never to do it again.

Many young people lie about their alcohol and drug use. If you think your child is not being truthful and the evidence is pretty strong, you may wish to have your child evaluated by a health professional experienced in diagnosing adolescents with alcohol- and drug-related problems.

If your child has developed a pattern of drug use or has engaged in heavy use, you will probably need help to intervene. If you do not know about drug treatment programs in your area, call your doctor, local hospital, or county mental health society for a referral. Your school district should have a substance abuse coordinator or a counselor who can refer you to treatment programs, too. Parents whose children have been through treatment programs can also provide information.

Getting Involved

The most promising drug prevention programs are those in which parents, students, schools, and communities join together to send a firm, clear message that the use of alcohol and other drugs will not be tolerated.

School-Parent Cooperation

The development of strong policies that spell out rules governing use, possession, and sale of alcohol and other drugs is a key part of any school-based prevention program. Learn what your school's policies are and actively support them. If your school has no policy, work with teachers, administrators, and community members to develop one. Good school policies typically specify what constitutes an alcohol or other drug offense, spell out the consequences for violating the policy, describe procedures for handling violations, and build community support for the policy.

Visit your child's school and learn how drug education is being taught. Are the faculty members trained to teach about alcohol and other drug use? Is drug education a regular part of the curriculum or limited to a special week? Is it taught through the health class, or do all teachers incorporate drug education into their subject area? Do children in every grade receive drug education, or is it limited to selected grades? Is there a component for parents?

If your school has an active program to prevent drug use, ask to see the materials that are being used. Do they contain a clear message that alcohol and other drug use is wrong and harmful? Is the information accurate and up-to-date? Does the school have referral sources for students who need special help?

Let other parents know about the school's policies through meetings of the parent-teacher organization. At least one meeting each year should be devoted to issues of alcohol and other drug use. Knowledgeable local physicians and pharmacists can be invited to discuss how drugs affect the growth and development of children, police officers can outline the scope and severity of the drug problem in your community, and substance abuse counselors can discuss symptoms of alcohol and other drug use and treatment options.

Parent-Community Activities

Help your child to grow up alcohol and drug free by supporting community efforts to give young people healthy alternatives. Alcohol- and drug-free proms and other school-based celebrations are growing in popularity around the country. You can help to organize such events, solicit contributions, and serve as a chaperon.

Local businesses are also an excellent source of support for alternative activities such as athletic teams and part-time jobs. Shops and restaurants in one community in Texas, for example, now offer discounts to young people who test negative for drugs in a voluntary urinalysis.

Parent Support Groups

Other parents can be valuable allies in your effort to keep your child drug free. Get to know the parents of your child's friends. Share expectations about behavior and develop a set of mutually agreed upon rules about such things as curfews, unchaperoned parties, and places that are off-limits. Helping youngsters stay out of trouble is easier when rules of conduct are clearly known and widely shared.

Build a network of other adults with whom you can talk. Join a parent organization in your community, or talk informally with your friends about common concerns in rearing children. Sharing experiences can provide insights that help you deal with your child's behavior. It also helps to know that other parents have faced similar situations.

Despite the grim stories that fill our newspapers and dominate the evening news, most young people do not use illicit drugs, they do not approve of drug use by their friends, and they share their parents' concern about the dangers posed by drugs.

Successful prevention efforts, whether in a family, school, or community setting, have many elements in common: a concern for the welfare and well-being of young people, dedicated adults who are willing to devote their time and energy, and an unwavering commitment to being drug free.

That commitment led a small group of parents in Bowling Green, Kentucky, to form Bowling Green Parents for Drug-Free Youth. The organization has worked closely with the local schools and community to provide training and education for all members of the community, and it has raised more than $35,000 to help finance its efforts. Questionnaires administered to students in grades 7-12 for 6 consecutive years have shown a steady decline in the use of alcohol and other drugs.

Gail Amato, president of the Bowling Green Parents for Drug-Free Youth, speaks persuasively about why parents must be involved in helping to prevent alcohol and other drug use:

People often ask me why I think parents are the answer, and I think it's because we have the most to lose. Schools can help, churches can help, law enforcement can help, but no one can replace the family. Being involved with drug and alcohol prevention lets our children know that we care. It strengthens the family and helps us to be the kind of parents our children need us to be.

A similar commitment leads parents of students in Commodore Stockton Skills School in Stockton, California, to donate more than 400 volunteer hours each month helping in the classrooms. Last year a family picnic held during Red Ribbon Week, a national drug awareness week, drew 500 participants for a day of games and activities focused on prevention of drug use.

In addition to helping in the classroom, Stockton parents work to maintain discipline, to reinforce students' respect for other people, and to foster personal responsibility at home.

As a result, behavioral problems in the school are infrequent, attendance is high, and area police report juvenile drug arrests from every school in the city *except* Commodore Stockton.

Successful efforts to rid a neighborhood of drugs are often joint efforts. Two years ago in New Haven, Connecticut, the residents of six housing projects joined forces to solve a neighborhood problem—drugs. The residents were afraid for the safety of their children and sick of the murders and other nightly violence related to drug deals.

Representing more than 1,400 families from the six projects, the group drafted an action plan to rid the neighborhood of drugs. The residents asked the local police to conduct "sting" operations periodically. Members of the New Haven news media have been invited to the project, where residents speak openly about the problems they encounter. The residents have invited local community groups and the Greater New Haven Labor Council to join in the fight. In addition, the mayor has become directly involved in their struggle.

One member, speaking on behalf of the residents, stated its main objective: "We are banding together to stop this madness so that we can have a peaceful and livable neighborhood and community." Today, drug sales have decreased, and members of the community feel safer and more hopeful about the future.

Resources

General Reading List for Parents

Drug-Free Kids: A Parents' Guide, 1986. Scott Newman Center, 6255 Sunset Blvd., Suite 1906, Los Angeles, CA 90028. Available in English and in Spanish. $6.50 plus tax for the English-language version.

Kids and Drugs: A Handbook for Parents and Professionals, by Joyce Tobias, 1987. PANDAA Press, 4111 Watkins Trail, Annandale, VA 22003. $6.90

Peer Pressure Reversal, by Sharon Scott, 1985, reprinted 1988. Human Resource Development Press, 22 Amherst Road, Amherst, MA 01002. $9.95.

Pot Safari, by Peggy Mann, 1982, reprinted 1987. Woodmere Press, Cathedral Finance Station, P.O. Box 20190, New York, NY 10125. $6.95.

Preparing for the Drug-Free Years: A Family Activity Book, by J. David Hawkins, et al., 1988. Developmental Research and Programs, Box 85746, Seattle, WA 98145. $10.95.

Team Up for Drug Prevention with America's Young Athletes, Drug Enforcement Administration, Demand Reduction Section, 1405 I Street, N.W., Washington, DC 20537. Free.

Ten Steps To Help Your Child Say "No": A Parent's Guide, 1986. National Clearinghouse for Alcohol and Drug Information, P.O. Box 2345, Rockville, MD 20852. Free.

The Fact Is...Hispanic Parents Can Help Their Children Avoid Alcohol and Other Drug Problems, 1989. National Clearinghouse for Alcohol and Drug Information, P.O. Box 2345, Rockville, MD 20852. Free.

The Fact Is...You Can Prevent Alcohol and Other Drug Problems Among Elementary School Children, 1988. National Clearinghouse for Alcohol and Drug Information, P.O. Box 2345, Rockville, MD 20852. Free.

The Fact Is...You Can Help Prevent Alcohol and Other Drug Use Among Secondary School Students, 1989. National Clearinghouse for Alcohol and Drug Information, P.O. Box 2345, Rockville, MD 20252. Free.

Young Children and Drugs: What Parents Can Do, 1987. The Wisconsin Clearinghouse, 1954 E. Washington Avenue, Madison, WI 53704. $6.00 per 100 brochures.

What Works: Schools Without Drugs, U.S. Department of Education, 1986, revised in 1989. National Clearinghouse for Alcohol and Drug Information, Box 2345, Rockville, MD 20852. Free.

General Reading List for Elementary School Children

A Little More About Alcohol, 1984. Alcohol Research Information Service, 1120 East Oakland Avenue, Lansing, MI 48906. $0.75. A cartoon character explains facts about alcohol and its effects on the body.

Alcohol: What It Is, What It Does, by Judith S. Seixas, 1977. Greenwillow Books, 105 Madison Avenue, New York, NY 10016. $5.95. An easy-to read illustrated primer on the use and abuse of alcohol.

An Elephant in the Living Room: The Children's Book, by Marion H. Hyppo and Jill M. Hastings, 1984. CompCare Publications, Box 27777, Minneapolis, MN 55427. $6.00. An illustrated workbook designed to help children from alcoholic homes understand that alcoholism is a disease and that they are not alone in coping with its effects.

490

Buzzy's Rebound, by William Cosby and Jim Willoughby, 1986. National Clearinghouse for Alcohol and Drug Information, P.O. Box 2345, Rockville, MD 20852. Free. An 18-page "Fat Albert" comic book that describes the pressure on a new kid in town to drink.

Kids and Alcohol: Get High On Life, by Jamie Rattray et al., 1984. Health Communications, Inc. 1721 Blount Road, Suite 1, Pompano Beach, FL 33069. $5.95. A workbook designed to help children (ages 11-14) make important decisions in their lives and feel good about themselves.

Kootch Talks About Alcoholism, by Mary Kay Schwandt, 1984. Serenity Work, 1455 North University Drive, Fargo, ND 58102. $3.00. A 40-page coloring book in which Kootch the worm helps young children understand alcoholism and alcoholics.

The Sad Story of Mary Wanna or How Marijuana Harms You, by Peggy Mann, illustrated by Naomi Lind, 1988. Woodmere Press, P.O. Box 20190, Cathedral Finance Station, New York, NY 10025. $2.95. A 40-page activity book for children in grades 1-4 that contains pictures of the damage that marijuana does to the body.

Whiskers Says No to Drugs, 1987. Weekly Reader Skills Books, Field Publications, 245 Long Hill Road, Middletown, CT 06457. $1.50. This book contains stories and follow-up activities for students in grades 2 and 3 to provide information and form attitudes before they face peer pressure to experiment.

General Reading List for Secondary School Children

Chew or Snuff Is Real Bad Stuff. National Cancer Institute, U.S. Department of Health and Human Services Building 31, Room 10A24, Bethesda, MD 20892. Free. This 8-page pamphlet describes the hazards of using smokeless tobacco.

Christy's Chance, 1987. Network Publications, P.O. Box 1830, Santa Cruz, CA 95061-1830. $3.95. A story geared to younger teens that allows the reader to make a nonuse decision about marijuana.

Different Like Me: A Book for Teens Who Worry About Their Parents' Use of Alcohol / Drugs, 1987. Johnson Institute, 7151 Metro Boulevard, Minneapolis, MN 55435. $6.95. This 110-page book provides support and information for teens who are concerned, confused, scared, and angry because their parents abuse alcohol and other drugs.

Don't Lose a Friend to Drugs, 1986. National Crime Prevention Council, 1700 K Street, N.W., 2d Floor, Washington, DC 20006. Free. This brochure offers practical advice to teenagers on how to say "no" to drugs, how to help a friend who uses drugs, and how to initiate community efforts to prevent drug use.

Videos

A Gift for Life: Helping Your Children Stay Alcohol and Drug Free, 1989. American Council on Drug Education, 204 Monroe Street, Suite 110, Rockville, MD 20850. $29.95.

Drug-Free Kids: A Parent's Guide, 1986. Scott Newman Center, 6255 Sunset Blvd., Suite 1906, Los Angeles, CA 90028. $32.50

Say NO! to Drugs: A Parent's Guide to Teaching Your Kids How To Grow Up Without Drugs and Alcohol, 1986. PRIDE, The Hurt Building, 50 Hurt Plaza, Suite 210, Atlanta, GA 30303. Order No. F008S, $25.95.

Part Six

Intervention, Treatment, and Recovery

Chapter 53

If Someone Close to You Has a Problem with Alcohol or Other Drugs

The person who has someone close who drinks too much or who uses other drugs has plenty of company. People experiencing alcohol and other drug problems often feel they hurt only themselves. That isn't true. They also hurt their families, friends, coworkers, employers, and others.

There are millions of people with alcohol and other drug problems in this country. A recent study reported that 28 million people age 12 and older used illicit drugs during the past year. By current estimates, more than 76 million people have been exposed to alcoholism in the family. Experience shows that for every person with an alcohol or other drug problem, at least four others are affected by their behavior.

However, looking at it another way—as we should—millions of Americans have a personal stake in helping "someone close" find the way to overcome alcohol and other drug problems.

How Can I Tell If Someone I Know Is Using Alcohol or Other Drugs?

Certain warning signs may indicate that a family member or friend is drinking too much alcohol or using other drugs. Although these warning signs are not foolproof, each by itself or many signs combined over time should be cause for concern.

This chapter contains excerpted text from DHHS Pub. No. (ADM) 92-1916 and DHHS Pub. No. (ADM) 91-1572; subheads added.

These are some of the signs to look for which involve drinking:

- Does the person pour a drink as an immediate reaction when faced with any problem?
- Does the person drink until intoxicated?
- Is there a record of missed work because of drinking or an ill-disguised odor of alcohol on the breath during work hours even though attendance may be regular?
- Does the person drive a car while intoxicated?
- Has his or her home life become intolerable because of drinking or arguments resulting from drinking?
- Does he or she handle all social celebrations and stress with alcohol?

The above are signs of an adult problem drinker. It is important to note, however, that any use of alcohol by youth is abuse and cause for concern. When these signs are present, it means that a person's drinking pattern, if not already out of control, is heading that way. A person does not have to be an alcoholic to have problems with alcohol.

There are numerous signs of illegal drug use. For example, when a person is carrying drugs or has them hidden around the house, there is a strong possibility of use. Obviously, possession of drug paraphernalia also is a likely sign of use.

Indications of prescription drug misuse vary according to the type of drug in question. Drug misuse may lead to dependence and withdrawal symptoms can be severe if drug use is stopped suddenly.

Certain additional behavioral characteristics also seem to accompany the use of alcohol and other drugs. The clues can be found in all people who abuse alcohol or use other drugs, regardless of age. Examples of these clues include:

- An abrupt change in mood or attitudes.
- Sudden and continuing decline in attendance or performance at work or in school.
- Sudden and continuing resistance to discipline at home or in school.
- Impaired relationships with family members or friends.
- Unusual flares of temper.
- Increased amount and frequency of borrowing money from family and friends.
- Stealing from the home, at school, or in the workplace.
- Heightened secrecy about actions and possessions.

- Associating with a new group of friends, especially with those who use drugs.

Helping and Caring

The person who sets out to help someone with an alcohol or other drug problem may at first feel quite alone, possibly embarrassed, not knowing where to turn for help. We have preserved so many wrong ideas and attitudes about problem drinking and other drug abuse, too often thinking of them as moral weakness or lack of willpower.

You may have learned to better understand alcohol and other drug problems and already made contact with nearby sources of services. This does not mean that "someone close" will cooperate at once by going for treatment. Those with alcohol and other drug problems may deny they have a problem. They may find it difficult to ask for or accept help.

If there is one thing true about alcohol and other drug abusers, it is that, as with all people, each one is different—different in human needs and responses, as well as in their reasons for drinking and taking other drugs, their reactions to these drugs, and their readiness for treatment.

You are in a good position to help your relative or friend, because you know a good deal about their unique qualities and their way of life. And having made the effort to gain some understanding of the signs and effects of problem drinking or other drug abuse, you should be in a better position to consider a strategy for helping.

Be active, get involved. Don't be afraid to talk about the problem honestly and openly. It is easy to be too polite, or to duck the issue by saying, "After all, it's their private affair." But it isn't polite or considerate to let someone destroy their family and life. You may need to be persistent to break through any denial they have. You also may need to let them know how much courage it takes to ask for help, or to accept it. You will find that most people with drinking- or other drug-related troubles really want to talk it out if they find out you are concerned about them.

Rejecting Myths

To begin, you may need to reject certain myths that in the past have done great harm to alcoholics and other drug abusers and hampered those who would help them. These untruths come from ingrained public attitudes that see alcoholism and other drug problems as personal misconduct, moral weakness, or even sin. They are expressed in such declarations as, "Nothing can be done unless the alcohol or drug abuser wants to stop," or "They must hit bottom," that is, lose health, job, home, family, before they will want to get well." These stubborn myths are not true, and have been destructive. One may as well say that you cannot treat cancer or tuberculosis until the gross signs of disease are visible to all.

The truth is that with alcohol and other drug problems, as with other kinds of acute and chronic illness, early recognition and treatment intervention is essential—and rewarding.

Be compassionate, be patient—but be willing to act. Experience proves that preaching does not work. A nudge or a push at the right time can help. It also shows that you care. Push may even come to shove when the person with alcohol or other drug troubles must choose between losing family or job, or going to treatment. Thousands of alcohol and other drug abusers have been helped when a spouse, employer, or court official made treatment a condition of continuing family relationships, job, or probation.

You cannot cure the illness, but when the crucial moment comes you can guide the person to competent help.

How Can I Help a Family Member or a Friend?

If someone confides in you that he or she has a problem with alcohol or other drugs, some ways of dealing with this situation clearly work better than others. You should try to be:

- Understanding—listen to reasons why he or she uses/abuses alcohol or other drugs;
- Firm—explain why you feel that use of alcohol or other drugs can be harmful, causing problems which require counseling and treatment;
- Supportive—assist the user in finding help and provide moral support through the tough times ahead;
- Self-examining—ask yourself whether you have provided a good role model.

Actions that you should avoid include being:

- Sarcastic,
- Accusatory,

- Stigmatizing,
- Sympathy seeking for yourself, or
- Self-blaming.

You should also refuse to ride with anyone who's been drinking heavily or using other drugs.

Intervening in the case of a family member or friend who has a problem can be very difficult and hurtful. The person with the problem will most likely deny the problem and try to put you on the defensive—"I thought you were my friend; are you calling me a drunk?" Or "You've used drugs; where do you get off calling me an addict?" In a case such as this, what you don't do is as important as what you should do:

- Avoid emotional appeals, which may only increase feelings of guilt and the compulsion to drink or use drugs.
- Don't cover up or make excuses for the person
- Don't take over his or her responsibilities, which will leave the person with no sense of importance or dignity.
- Don't argue with the person when he or she is under the influence of alcohol or other drugs.
- Don't hide or dump bottles nor shelter your loved one from situations where alcohol is present.
- Above all, don't accept responsibility for the person's actions nor guilt for his or her drinking.

Treatment

Treatment attempts to disover the relationship between a person's problematic drinking and other drug use to their real needs—an understanding of what they would really strive for if they were not disabled by their problems. One goal is building up their capacity for control which becomes possible in periods of sobriety.

Persons with drinking and other drug problems have the same needs as all other people—food, clothing, shelter, health care, job, social contact and acceptance and, particularly, the need for self-confidence and feelings of competence, self-worth, and dignity. This is where "support" comes in.

What may be needed most is warm, human concern. The kinds of support given depend, of course, on finding out from the person what they feel they need. Strained family and friend relationships, money troubles, worry about job or business, sometimes matters that may seem trivial to us, all confuse their life situation and may contribute to their drinking and other drug problems.

What to Do to Support Your Friend or Family Member

- Let the person with the problem know that you are reading and learning about alcohol and other drug abuse, attending Al-Anon, Nar-Anon, Alateen, and other support groups.

- Discuss the situation with someone you trust—someone from the clergy, a social worker, a counselor, a friend, or some individual who has experienced alcohol or other drug abuse personally or as a family member.

- Establish and maintain a healthy atmosphere in the home, and try to include the alcohol/drug abuser in family life.

- Explain the nature of alcoholism and other drug addiction as an illness to the children in the family.

- Encourage new interests and participate in leisure time activities that the person enjoys. Encourage them to see old friends.

- Be patient and live one day at a time. Alcoholism and other drug addiction generally take a long time to develop, and recovery does not occur over night. Try to accept setbacks and relapses with calmness and understanding.

Moral support in starting and staying with treatment, reassurances from employer or business associates, willing participation by spouse or children in group therapy sessions—are examples of realistic support.

The long range goal is healthy living for the person and their family—physical health, social health, emotional health—an objective we all share.

Rehabilitation

Three out of four alcohol and drug abusing men and women are married; living at home; holding onto a job, business, or profession;

and are reasonably well accepted members of their communities. For those in this group who seek treatment, the outlook is good. Regardless of life situation, the earlier treatment starts after troubles are recognized, the better the chances for success.

Many therapists now use rehabilitation as a measurement of outcome—success is considered achieved when the patient maintains or reestablishes a good family life and work record, and a respectable position in the community. Relapses may occur but do not mean that the person or the treatment effort has failed.

A successful outcome, on this basis, can be expected for 50 to 75 percent depending upon the personal characteristics of the patient; early treatment intervention; competence of the therapists; availability of hospital and outpatient facilities; and the strong support of family, friends, employer, and community.

"It is doubtful that any specific percentage figure has much meaning by itself," says one authority. "What does have a great deal of meaning is the fact that tens of thousands of such cases have shown striking improvement over many years."

National Clearinghouse for Alcohol and Drug Information

The Office for Substance Abuse Prevention offers information on all aspects of the prevention of alcohol and other drug problems. It also maintains a State-by-State listing of most public and private alcohol and other drug information, counseling, and treatment facilities. Call or write:

OSAP's National Clearinghouse for Alcohol and Drug Information
P.O. Box 2345
Rockville, MD 20847-2345
(800) 729-6686

Information and referral to community services can be obtained from such national organizations as:

Alcoholics Anonymous (AA)
15 E. 26th Street, Room 1817
New York, NY 10010
(212) 683-3900

Narcotics Anonymous (NA)
P.O. Box 9999
Van Nuys, CA 91409
(818) 780-3951

Al-Anon Family Groups
P.O. Box 862
Midtown Station
New York, NY 10018
(800) 344-2666

Nar-Anon Family Groups
P.O. Box 2562
Palos Verdes Peninsula, CA 90274
(213) 547-5800

Local Alcoholics Anonymous Chapters and Al-Anon Family Groups are listed in most telephone directories.

National Council on Alcoholism and Drug Dependence

National Council on Alcoholism and Drug Dependence (NCADD)
12 West 21st Street, 8th Floor
New York, NY 10010
(212) 206-6770

The NCADD offers a list of organizations in more than 100 cities that will refer clients to physicians, and public and private agencies providing treatment for alcoholism and other drug dependence. Some of these local NCADD organizations also offer counseling and treatment services:

National Association for Children of Alcoholics
11426 Rockville Pike, Suite 100
Rockville, MD 20852
(301) 468-0985

National Black Alcoholism Council, Inc.
1629 K Street, NW, Suite 802
Washington, DC 20006
(202) 296-2696

National Association for Native American Children of Alcoholics
P.O. Box 18736
Seattle, WA 98118
(206) 322-5601

Latino Council on Alcohol and Tobacco
1875 Connecticut Avenue, NW, Suite 300
Washington, DC 20009
(202) 332-9110 or (908) 463-5041

Chapter 54

Drug Abuse Information and Treatment Referral Line

1-800-662-HELP

Introduction

The National Drug Information and Treatment Hotline, 1-800-662-HELP is a toll-free number that can be dialed from any State in the country, Puerto Rico and the Virgin Islands. Its purpose is to provide drug related information to the general public, to help drug users find and use local treatment programs and to acquaint those affected by the drug use of a friend or family member (i.e., significant other) with much needed support groups and/or services.

The Hotline is staffed from 9:00 a.m.–3:00 a.m., Monday through Friday and 12 noon–3:00 a.m. Saturday and Sunday. Information Specialists trained to provide counseling, information, and referrals spend an average of 10-15 minutes with each caller. All Hotline staff are caring individuals who have been carefully chosen for their sensitivity, insight, and understanding of the issues involved in drug use and then trained to skillfully provide information about drug abuse and treatment.

Background

The Hotline has been operated by the National Institute on Drug Abuse (NIDA) since its inception in mid-April, 1986. It was initially

National Institute on Drug Abuse (NIDA), *Capsules*, C-86-10, April 1989.

publicized through public service announcements during phase one of NIDA's "Cocaine: The Big Lie" campaign. Subsequent media attention continues to promote public awareness of the Hotline number.

Services

The Hotline provides confidential discussion and/or referrals. Callers who request treatment are referred to drug treatment programs, including profit/nonprofit, Federal/State, inpatient/outpatient or residential facilities. The main source of referrals is the National Directory of Drug Abuse and Alcoholism Treatment and Prevention Programs.

Because many callers have few resources due to their drug use, frequent referrals are made to public or nonprofit programs. Callers receive the name, address and phone number of facilities close to them along with information about the range of services at the facility. As a backup, callers are given the number of their State Substance Abuse Agency.

Referrals are also made to State and local crisis or information Hotlines and support groups such as Cocaine Anonymous, Narcotics Anonymous and Alcoholics Anonymous. Support group referrals that focus on concerns of significant others of drug users, such as National Federation of Parents, CO-ANON, NAR-ANON and Families Anonymous are also made. Free NIDA pamphlets and brochures are sent to those seeking written information.

Statistics/Number of Calls

During the first year of operation nearly 50,000 calls were answered. Now after three years, Hotline staff has handled nearly 180,000 calls. While calls originate from all over the country, the greatest number have come from California, New York and Florida. Of course this may reflect frequency in the airing of cocaine-related campaign materials as much as the extent of drug use in those States.

Findings from a preliminary sampling of calls conducted by NIDA revealed that:

- 75% of the calls were received between 8 a.m. and 8 p.m. EST.

- 50% of callers were seeking help for themselves, usually during the crash/depression period. The majority in this group were males. Of the remaining 50%, the majority called with concerns about the drug use of others. These callers were typically female. Other callers sought general drug information, including literature or contacts for prevention and education efforts.

- The majority of users were over 18 years of age.

Spanish-Speaking Callers—(800) 66-AYUDA

Since August 1988, bilingual Hotline staff have been responding to Spanish-speaking callers on a separate dedicated line: 1-800-66-AYUDA. The Spanish Hotline number will be included on all Spanish-language print materials and radio PSA's.

Drug Abuse and AIDS

NIDA has begun a major AIDS and intravenous (IV) drug use public education campaign. It is designed to educate and inform IV drug users of their risks and encourage them to get treatment. Since January 1987, Hotline staff have been trained to talk about AIDS to callers if they are intravenous drug users. The 1-800-662-HELP number will be printed on all NIDA-produced materials on AIDS and IV drug use. Calls from IV drug users who are in need of treatment as well as calls from sexual partners and others close to drug users are expected to increase.

Chapter 55

Methadone Treatment

Repeated studies over the years show that methadone maintenance is both cost-effective and safe as a treatment for people addicted to heroin.

Methadone maintenance involves giving patients an oral dose of methadone each day to treat chronic dependence on heroin and other opiates. Methadone has been used for more than 25 years, in combination with medical, rehabilitative, and counseling services. Treatment experts say methadone maintenance is a way to manage opiate addiction, but it is not a cure. Typically, maintenance treatment may last more than 6 months to many years.

A graphic report on the costs of three types of opiate treatments—methadone maintenance, residential drug-free, and outpatient drug-free—compared with no treatment or incarceration was presented at the National Methadone Conference held in Washington, D.C., last spring. The report, *Drug Abuse Treatment: An Economical Approach to Addressing the Drug Problem in America*, compiled figures from several studies. The report, which was prepared by the former Alcohol, Drug Abuse, and Mental Health Administration, showed that the costs to society over a 6-month period were $21,500 for an untreated drug abuser, $20,000 for an imprisoned drug abuser, and $1,750 for someone undergoing methadone maintenance treatment.

The cost-effectiveness figures were applauded by drug treatment practitioners attending the methadone conference. Several of these

---

"Research Demonstrates Long-Term Benefits of Methadone Treatment," *NIDA Notes*, November/December 1994.

clinicians said the figures provide dramatic documentation that they can use in their communities to answer criticisms of methadone maintenance treatment. There is "a large body of evidence" to answer the critics on cost savings and other issues, said Dr. Frank Vocci, deputy director of NIDA's Medications Development Division.

For example, NIDA-funded studies completed as far back as the early 1980s show that 65 percent to 85 percent of people undergoing methadone maintenance stay in treatment for a year or more, according to *Drug Abuse and Drug Abuse Research: The Second Triennial Report to Congress From the Secretary, Health and Human Services,* which was prepared by NIDA. In addition, these patients show a dramatic decrease in criminal behavior and an increase in gainful employment during their time in treatment. In 1990, an Institute of Medicine report, *Treating Drug Problems* found similar results.

Time spent in methadone treatment has other benefits as well. Dr. John Ball, formerly of NIDA's intramural research program at the Addiction Research Center in Baltimore, demonstrated that when methadone treatment is continuous and serves as a focal point for HIV risk reduction and patient education, it can have a significant impact or the rate of HIV infection among patients. "Methadone treatment definitely reduces the risk of AIDS infection" and, as a result, it lowers the costs to society of providing health care to AIDS patients, said Dr. Vocci.

Studies also show that methadone can be used safely to treat heroin addicts, even after 15 or more years of treatment. In a study funded in part by NIDA, Dr. Mary Jeanne Kreek and her colleagues at Rockefeller University in New York City assessed 111 male patients who had been in methadone maintenance treatment for 11 to 18 years. The scientists found "that prolonged methadone maintenance treatment is safe and is not associated with unexpected adverse effects." Ten years earlier, Dr. Kreek and others had found that "the most important medical consequence of chronic methadone maintenance treatment" is a marked improvement in the patients' general health and nutrition.

In fact, methadone treatment helps keep patients alive, said Dr. Vocci. Studies show that death rates for patients undergoing methadone maintenance treatment are as much as one-tenth of those not receiving treatment, he said. However, the figures were compiled before prevalence rates for AIDS and tuberculosis increased to current levels, indicating differences in death rates may now be even greater, he added.

Methadone therapy is more effective when accompanied by appropriate counseling and social services, according to a NIDA-funded study by Dr. A. Thomas McLellan and his colleagues at the Philadelphia Veterans Affairs Medical Center. The study showed that 69 percent of patients randomly assigned to receive 65 milligrams a day of methadone but no counseling or other social services continued regular use of opiates or cocaine and had medical or psychiatric emergencies. Patients who received the same dose of methadone as well as weekly counseling showed a 50 percent reduction in opiate and cocaine use. A third group of randomly assigned patients who received the same dose of methadone and counseling plus on-site medical and psychiatric care showed an 81 percent reduction in opiate and cocaine use. "Methadone alone, even in substantial doses, may only be effective for a minority of eligible patients," the study concluded.

For methadone maintenance to be effective, a doctor must determine the daily dosage level for each patient. Otherwise, the clinic may dispense inadequate doses that result in patient discomfort and treatment dropout, said Dr. J. Thomas Payte of Drug Dependence Associates in San Antonio, Texas. Treatment practitioners must also resist misguided pressures to keep doses "as low as possible," Dr. Payte said during a presentation at the National Methadone Conference. To develop individualized methadone doses that are adequate to treat each patient, doctors should rely on clinical and laboratory data because absorption, metabolism, and excretion of the medication can vary from person to person, he noted.

In a NIDA-funded study, Dr. Gerald H. Friedland and others at Montefiore Medical Center in the Bronx examined possible interactions between methadone and the AIDS treatment medication zidovudine (AZT). The study showed that blood levels of methadone are not affected by AZT, which is used to treat individuals infected with HIV, which causes AIDS. However, methadone may affect blood levels of AZT. In some patients, methadone may cause an increase in the blood level of AZT that is potentially toxic, according to the study. Similar studies are examining interactions between methadone and antibiotics, such as rifampin and isoniazid, which are used in the treatment of tuberculosis.

Despite these findings, the researchers caution physicians against making immediate changes in the dosage of AZT that they prescribe for HIV-positive patients who are taking methadone. Instead, doctors should carefully monitor these patients for signs of dose-related AZT toxicity, the researchers suggest.

A number of methadone maintenance patients attended last spring's methadone conference. Some of these patients are supporters of a methadone patient advocacy movement that seeks to give those in therapy a greater voice in the treatment process.

"I believe methadone saved my life," said Diane Fleury-Seaman of Sacramento, California, who told listeners that she has a 25-year history of addiction and has been a methadone patient for more than 9 years. As a methadone patient advocate, she now tries to provide other patients with the help and support that were not available to her, she said.

Advocacy groups also are trying to reduce the stigmatization of methadone patients, make treatment more affordable and available, and persuade clinics to grant patients greater dignity and respect. Fleury-Seaman said her patient advocacy group of 300 members encourages patients to register to vote, many of them for the first time in their lives, and produces a newsletter for patients and providers.

The Sacramento group is part of a growing national network of methadone patient advocacy organizations. The National Alliance of Methadone Advocates, based in New York City, now has more than 7,000 members in the 50 States, Puerto Rico, and 9 foreign countries.

References

Alcohol, Drug Abuse, and Mental Health Administration. *Drug Abuse Treatment: An Economical Approach to Addressing the Drug Problem in America.* DHHS Pub. No. (ADM) 911834. Rockville, Md.: ADAMHA, 1991.

Ball, J. *The Effectiveness of Methadone Maintenance Treatment.* New York: Springer-Verlag, 1991.

Gerstein, D.R., and Harwood, H.J., eds. *Treating Drug Problems, Vol. 1: A Study of the Evolution, Effectiveness, and Financing of Public and Private Drug Treatment Systems.* Washington, DC: National Academy Press, 1990.

Kreek, M.J. Health consequences associated with the use of methadone. In: Cooper, J.R.; Altman, F.; Brown, B.S.; and Czechowicz, D., eds. *Research on the Treatment of Narcotic Addiction: State of the Art.* NIDA Treatment Research Monograph Series. DHHS Pub. No. (ADM) 83-1291. Washington, DC: Supt. of Docs., U.S. Govt. Print. Off., 1983. pp. 456-494.

Kreek, M.J.; Novick, D.M.; Richman, B.L.; Friedman, J.M.; Friedman, J.E.; Fried, C.; Wilson, J.P.; and Townley, A. The medical status of methadone maintenance patients in treatment for 11-18 years. *Drug and Alcohol Dependency* 33(3):235-45, 1993.

McLellan, A.T.; Arndt, I.O.; Metzger, D.S.; Woody, G.E.; and O'Brien, C.P. The effects of psychosocial services in substance abuse treatment. *JAMA* 269(15):1953-1959, 1993.

Schwartz, E.L.; Brechbuhl, A.B.; Kahl, P.; Miller, M.A.; Selwyn, P.A.; and Friedland, G.H. Pharmacokinetic interactions of zidovudine and methadone in intravenous drug-using patients with HIV infection. *Journal of Acquired Immunodeficiency Syndrome* 5(6):619-26, 1992.

—by Neil Swan, NIDA Notes *Contributing Writer*

For Further Information

American Methadone Treatment Association, Inc.
253-255 Third Ave.
New York, NY 10010

Chapter 56

LAAM
(Levo-Alpha-Acetyl-Methadol)

A new approach to bringing drugs to market won high marks last year when the Food and Drug Administration approved levo-alpha-acetyl-methadol (Orlaam, also known as LAAM) in record time. LAAM is only the second synthetic narcotic medication approved to treat heroin and other opioid addiction through outpatient narcotic maintenance treatment programs. The other medication is methadone, approved almost 25 years ago.

Chronic and relapsing, heroin addiction controls its victims. It wastes lives and addicts newborns along with their mothers. It spreads infection with HIV, the virus that causes AIDS, and other infectious diseases through the sharing of dirty needles. It is connected with violent crime and casts a heavy economic burden upon society.

More than 586,000 Americans use heroin at least weekly, the Office of National Drug Control Policy reports.

LAAM was approved July 20, 1993, only 18 days after FDA received the new drug application.

The "new approach" that made this speedy approval possible involved cooperation among FDA drug review and compliance staffs, a new division of the National Institutes of Health's National Institute on Drug Abuse (NIDA), the Drug Enforcement Administration, and industry—in this case, Biometric Research Institute Inc., of Arlington, Va.

"New Drug Approval Approach Boosts Fight Against Heroin Addiction," *FDA Consumer*, November 1994.

The cooperative clinical tests underpinning the approval took just 18 months from protocol development to patient enrollment, completion of the first phase of the study, and report to the agency.

NIDA's Medications Development Division (MDD) was established in 1990 to encourage development of anti-addiction medications. Although LAAM had been studied for many years, it was sitting on a "back burner" at NIDA.

About the same time MDD was created, FDA set up its Pilot Drug Evaluation Staff to streamline drug approval. The agency assigned review of anti-addiction medications to the new staff, and hired experts in drug abuse issues, including senior scientist Michael Klein, Ph.D.

"In 1990, we advised NIDA," Klein says, "to reassemble the data on LAAM submitted in the 1980s in two rejected new drug applications, and give them back to us as an investigational new drug application. The IND gave us a way to get involved in development from step 1, and make recommendations for the eventual submission of the NDA."

Klein and others reviewed the IND and parceled out certain older studies for review by FDA's Drug Abuse Advisory Committee.

"We also wanted studies of the new population of patients," Klein says. "Many people abusing heroin today also use other drugs, such as crack cocaine, which wasn't around in the early 1980s."

MDD conferred with FDA to develop directions for using LAAM. Researchers were to follow the directions, spot problems, and try to correct them. To eliminate bias, FDA specified using only clinics that had never studied LAAM.

MDD contracted for the FDA-guided trials with 26 Department of Veterans Affairs (VA) medical centers and university clinics. According to MDD health scientist administrator Paul Coulis, Ph.D., "We worked with FDA all along, sharing our findings as they developed."

Klein says, "We got a very nice picture of the adequacy of the labeling and potential problems today, which we could couple with the old studies, some of which did show efficacy."

Maintenance Medications, Close Up

Methadone and LAAM are oral narcotics that work in the body much like morphine does. When taken for short periods by non-addicts, they kill pain, sedate the central nervous system, and relax smooth muscle tissues.

516

Both medications can themselves produce dependence. But when taken as part of a maintenance treatment program, they do not cause euphoria. They in fact block the "highs" of other opioid narcotics, such as heroin, and suppress the symptoms of withdrawal. These symptoms include increased blood pressure and temperature, rapid heartbeat, "goose-flesh" (piloerection), runny nose (rhinorrhea), watery eyes (lacrimation), tremors, insomnia, vomiting, abdominal cramps, restlessness, weakness, headache, hot or cold flashes, and drug craving. Withdrawal from methadone or LAAM causes similar symptoms, but starts more slowly, is less severe, and continues for a longer time.

LAAM's advantage is that it works for 48 to 72 hours after a dose is taken, compared to 24 hours for methadone. With fewer required visits, patients have the chance to lead a more normal existence and clinics have the option to treat more patients.

Methadone must be given every day, and take-home doses are permitted in selected cases.

LAAM is not approved for daily treatment because daily use of the usual doses will lead to serious overdose. Evaluated only as an in-clinic medication, LAAM is not allowed in take-home doses. In extreme situations, however, certain LAAM patients may be temporarily switched to methadone for a take-home dose when they know in advance they can't come to the clinic for a scheduled LAAM dose. Also, in-clinic dosing reduces the likelihood of patients' diverting the medication to street sales.

Methadone and LAAM can interact adversely with tranquilizers, tricyclic antidepressants, alcohol, and other drugs. They can worsen low blood pressure and asthma. They can cause breathing difficulty and impaired circulation. Less serious methadone side effects include dizziness, vomiting, and sweating; LAAM can cause flu-like symptoms, diarrhea, and muscle aches.

Maintenance Works

"If your goal is to reduce drug abuse," says Nicholas Reuter, a consumer safety officer in FDA's Office of Health Affairs, "a properly administered maintenance program appears to be the most effective treatment." Reuter is executive secretary of the federal interagency review board that coordinates regulation of the programs. Last year, the board reviewed U.S. and international research on methadone—which has been studied extensively—following media reports that questioned the safety of methadone treatment.

According to MDD's Coulis, effectiveness of maintenance treatment can be measured by these outcomes: reduced heroin use, staying in treatment, and perceptions by both patient and doctor of improved well-being.

Reuter adds that patients receiving maintenance treatment have a death rate 10 times lower than untreated addicts and an incidence of needle-sharing of 14 percent, compared to 47 percent before treatment. In a recent Swiss study of people with HIV infection, he says, 24 percent of maintenance program cases progressed to AIDS, compared to 41 percent of untreated heroin abusers.

"Retention in treatment is crucial," Reuter says. "In a direct line with the time patients spend in treatment, their general health and social productivity improve, and their drug abuse and criminal activities diminish." He says some studies show that patients stay in maintenance programs at a rate two-and-a-half times that of patients in self-help residential programs, and five times that of patients in drug-free outpatient programs. Of those who stop treatment, more than 80 percent relapse within a year.

"While maintenance treatment can't guarantee relapse prevention even during treatment," Reuter says, "it is consistent with medical management of chronic diseases such as diabetes, heart disease, and arthritis."

Suspicion

Despite more than two decades of documented success of maintenance therapy, the idea of treating addiction with addictive medications is often viewed by the public with suspicion.

One source of this uneasiness is a misunderstanding of heroin addiction, says Robert Lubran, chief of the Quality Assurance and Evaluation Branch, Division of State Programs, in the Substance Abuse and Mental Health Services Administration's (SAMHSA) Center for Substance Abuse Treatment.

"Many people," Lubran says, "don't realize that heroin addicts must fight their addiction all their lives. Others equate patients in maintenance programs with street addicts. In fact, the patients are at some level of recovery, which benefits society as well as the patient."

Another source of suspicion is the ineffectiveness of some programs, which Lubran attributes to poor medical or clinical practices, such as inappropriate medication dosing to control withdrawal, failure to properly screen and assess patients' needs for counseling and support services, and lack of qualified counseling staff. "Research indicates that a few patients may do all right with minimum services," he says. "Most do not."

Strong Medicines, Strong Rules

Narcotic maintenance treatment is regulated by FDA, the Drug Enforcement Administration, and state authorities. FDA approves only programs previously approved at the state level and registered with DEA. Currently approved are 791 maintenance programs and 282 hospital programs (see Figure 56.1), serving some 115,000 patients. Of these programs, 46 are approved to use LAAM. Maintenance medications are unique in drug regulation, and this type of regulation is unique in medical practice, says FDA Associate Commissioner for Health Affairs Stuart Nightingale, M.D., who chairs the programs' interagency review board.

"For no other class of drugs do we write and enforce rules that directly affect how they're used in treatment," Nightingale says. "With these medications, we specify rules for clinical practice, such as requiring physicians to prepare and sign a treatment plan for each patient and document all changes in dosing regimens."

Because of the implications for medical practice and other broad societal concerns, Nightingale says, "the interagency committee has been critical to the success of the federal coordination." The committee includes representatives from FDA, NIDA, SAMHSA, DEA, VA, the Office of the Secretary of Health and Human Services, the Office of the Assistant Secretary for Health, and the Office of National Drug Control Policy.

Treatment clinics must register with DEA and meet security rules because methadone and LAAM are controlled substances (drugs regulated by the Federal Controlled Substances Acts). DEA requires additional registration by the physicians who treat narcotic addiction with narcotics.

In light of the addictive potential and potential for overdose, both FDA and state authorities require safety measures and medication control rules in programs using methadone or LAAM. The Department of Health and Human Services, FDA's parent agency, must by law provide treatment standards for narcotics used to treat narcotic dependence. These are minimum standards, currently in the form of regulations. Individual states can, and some do, develop stricter rules.

Under FDA rules, programs may admit only current addicts with at least a one-year history of addiction, although previously addicted pregnant women at risk of returning to addiction may also be admitted.

519

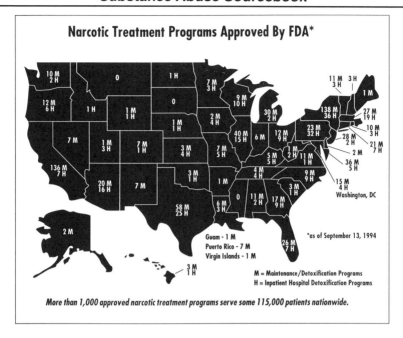

Figure 56.1. Approved maintenance programs.

Methadone maintenance, but not LAAM, is approved for patients under 18 who have twice failed detoxification or other drug-free treatment. A parent, guardian, or other designated responsible adult must sign the consent form.

Enrollment is voluntary. Patients must report to the same program, except in an emergency.

Among other agency requirements, comprehensive programs must provide:

- medical services, counseling, vocational rehabilitation, and treatment plans
- tuberculosis skin testing during the initial medical evaluation
- HIV counseling
- information to women about drug risks to the fetus
- pregnancy tests for women of childbearing potential before admission to LAAM maintenance, and monthly tests thereafter
- individualized dosage to control withdrawal symptoms without causing sedation or other effects of intoxication, with the lowest effective doses for pregnant women
- regular physician review of dosage levels

- observed dosing at the clinic (With methadone, visits are six days a week to start but, with successful treatment, may be reduced with use of take-home doses. With LAAM, visits are every other day to start but eventually may be every third day.)
- complete patient records, which physicians must sign and date to document dosage changes and reasons for reducing visits
- frequent random urine tests for drugs of abuse—including an initial screening test for prospective patients.

Publicly funded treatment accounts for the vast majority of patients in treatment, says FDA's Nightingale. These programs may be free or have sliding scale fees. The cost of private programs varies.

In addition, FDA and SAMHSA in 1993 issued interim narcotic maintenance program standards for heroin addicts who can't get into a nearby comprehensive program within two weeks. The ADAMHA Reorganization Act of 1992 required the standards to reduce the AIDS threat posed by injection of illegal drugs—the major source of new AIDS infection in the general population, according to NIDA. States would guarantee patients' transfer to comprehensive treatment no later than 120 days. Although no clinics have applied to enroll patients in interim programs, any programs adopted would be restricted to public, nonprofit clinics with federal- and state-approved comprehensive programs.

Managing Compliance Problems

FDA field staff inspect programs every two or three years, reporting problems to the agency's regulatory management branch. Follow-up visits are on a case-by-case basis. "If there are serious violations and we send a warning letter," says compliance officer Gerald Hajarian, "three to six months after the program responds with its correction plan, the district inspects again to make sure the violations no longer exist." (The facility must submit its correction plan to FDA within 15 days of receiving the warning letter.)

DEA inspects programs on a routine cycle or more frequently if a program has a history of violations or pending allegations of impropriety. DES requires that programs follow all security and record-keeping regulations. Violations may result in actions such as an Investigative Warning or Letter of Admonition for less serious violations, or an Administrative Hearing, Order to Show Cause, or civil or criminal actions for serious violations.

States inspect also.

There is continuing concern about some patients selling their take-home methadone doses on the street. In July 1990, FDA, DEA and NIDA warned program sponsors and medical directors that federal and state investigations confirmed increasing diversion of take-home medications, pointing out that diversion was one reason FDA requires frequent urine tests. (A negative test would indicate the patient hadn't taken the take-home medication.) They warned that, if necessary, they would revoke DEA registration or FDA approval.

Indeed, FDA and DEA in 1991 allowed two New York programs to stay open only after they presented evidence showing how they intended to remedy their problems. FDA, DEA, and Texas authorities in 1992 did close two Texas programs, with a third one closing voluntarily. Last February, FDA closed a New Mexico program.

Improving the Programs

Included among the Center for Substance Abuse Treatment's series of Treatment Improvement Protocols (or "TIPS") are several that cover narcotic maintenance treatment. These are developed by non-federal treatment experts.

"We take the scientific research and expertise of leading clinicians," the center's Lubran says, "and translate that into practical guidance that can help states, maintenance programs, and others improve the quality of services."

Several TIPS—some of which are still under development—provide recommendations about the most effective maintenance treatment practices for such groups as pregnant women and infants exposed to methadone, methadone patients who abuse stimulants (especially cocaine), and patients on LAAM treatment.

Technical assistance, training, and financial support to states and communities are also available. For example, when the state of Texas asked for assistance after media criticism of maintenance programs in the state, the center arranged for state and program representatives, treatment experts, and FDA and DEA officials to meet in Texas. The conferees identified system-wide problems and solutions and recommended improvement activities.

The center helped the state of Arkansas open its first program last December in Little Rock, which Lubran says reached three-fourths of the target population within three months. "We enabled them to gain invaluable exposure to quality treatment programs around the country to see how they work, and provided guidance with their state regulations," he says.

Another project educates judges and court administrators on how the programs can serve as alternative sentencing for people convicted of crimes related to heroin use or other drug abuse.

Incentives

As an incentive to firms to develop anti-addiction medications, FDA permits this class of drugs fast-track review and eligibility for orphan drug status, which confers tax credits and research grants. Orphan drugs receive seven years of marketing exclusivity. LAAM is a designated orphan drug.

MDD encourages development of maintenance medications by assisting firms with research. MDD deputy director Frank Vocci, Ph.D., says his division is analyzing data from a study in 736 patients evaluating the safety and effectiveness of an oral sublingual (administered under the tongue) form of buprenorphine (Buprenex) in blocking heroin's euphoria. The drug is approved as an injectable narcotic analgesic.

A buprenorphine-naloxone formulation also is being developed. Although oral buprenorphine may block heroin's effects, the injected form can produce euphoria. However, injected naloxone (Narcan), approved to treat overdose, blocks the euphoria, inducing withdrawal.

"The idea," Vocci says, "is if the drug is taken as prescribed, the naloxone won't kick in. But if patients abuse it by injecting it, the naloxone effect will predominate."

In another study, MDD tested a sustained-release naltrexone formulation that blocked heroin euphoria up to 30 days. Dosage in future trials will be based on the results of this study, Vocci says. Naltrexone (Trexan) is approved for use with maintenance medication, but not as a maintenance medication itself.

These efforts, along with the new approach that brought LAAM to market, offer hope for more safe and effective maintenance medications, possibly to treat other addictions as well.

While there is no cure for heroin addiction, there is hope for recovery through narcotic maintenance treatment programs. Using legal oral synthetic narcotics, maintenance programs wean addicts off heroin, the first step to stable, productive lives.

For More Information

The Center for Substance Abuse Treatment National Drug Hotline
1-800-662-HELP

The National Clearinghouse for Alcohol and Drug Information
P.O. Box 2345
Rockville, MD 20847-2345
1-800-729-6686
1-800-487-4889 TDD

American Methadone Treatment Association, Inc.
253-255 Third Ave.
New York, NY 10010

—by Dixie Farley

Dixie Farley is a staff writer for *FDA Consumer*.

Chapter 57

Ibogaine

On August 25, 1993, the Drug Abuse Advisory Committee of the U.S. Food and Drug Administration (FDA) voted to permit an individual academic investigator to conduct a limited human investigation of ibogaine. Ibogaine is believed by some to interrupt the addiction of some heroin and cocaine dependent persons. Ibogaine comes from the root of the iboga plant found primarily in certain West African nations and is used in certain African rituals. Ibogaine is also reported to be an hallucinogenic drug.

As part of its Medications Development Program, the National Institute on Drug Abuse (NDA) sponsored much of the preclinical scientific research on ibogaine that has assisted the FDA and its Drug Abuse Advisory Committee in the review of the compound for clinical safety trials.

The National Institute on Drug Abuse made a decision to evaluate ibogaine as a potential treatment medication in April 1991, after NDA International, Inc. met with NIDA with compelling anecdotes from about 25 heroin addicts who reported losing their craving for heroin after taking ibogaine. In May 1991, NIDA formed a project team to evaluate ibogaine in the same manner as it would any other potential medication: by following the medication development process of studies involving chemistry, dosage form development, pharmacokinetics, pharmacology, animal safety, and possibly human clinical trials, if warranted. The preclinical portion of the project is

National Institute on Drug Abuse (NIDA), *Capsules*, C-93-04, September 1993.

currently proceeding and is focused on addressing three major issues: the toxicology of ibogaine, the development of an assay for ibogaine and its metabolites in biological fluids, and the development of a suitable dosage form of ibogaine.

Prior to conducting any studies on ibogaine, it was necessary for NIDA to take several actions. First, NIDA had to arrange to acquire ibogaine, controlled under the Controlled Substances Act as a Schedule I drug, the most restricted classification as having no medical utility. NIDA awarded contracts and worked with the U.S. Drug Enforcement Administration (DEA) to secure registration for its grantees and contractors to legally acquire and study this Schedule I compound. These steps were accomplished in about 16 months. Next, NDA prepared to analyze ibogaine by conducting chemistry, pharmacokinetics, and pharmacology/toxicology studies, as there was little existing preclinical or clinical data, which would meet FDA Good Laboratory Practices and Good Clinical Practices guidelines.

Shortly after obtaining ibogaine in August 1992, NIDA began its first study with it. Since then, NIDA has sponsored 18 animal studies to evaluate the pharmacology and toxicology of ibogaine. NIDA is continuing to work toward developing the necessary preclinical safety data to assess the possibility of additional clinical trials (human testing), if warranted.

During this testing, a NIDA contractor discovered a specific dose-related neurotoxicity in rats. This finding does not preclude evaluation of ibogaine at this point as there may be species differences and an effective dose at which this neurotoxicity does not occur. NIDA will, however, be conducting more studies on other species to further evaluate and define ibogaine's toxicological profile.

NIDA will also be following and evaluating the results of any other testing performed by non-NDA funded sources, to the extent they become available.

Chapter 58

Buprenorphine

Buprenorphine is a partial μ-opioid agonist and κ-antagonist marketed in the United States as an injectable analgesic by Reckitt & Colman Pharmaceutical Division. Recent studies performed in large part by the National Institute on Drug Abuse (NIDA) Addiction Research Center and by NIDA grantees indicate that buprenorphine possesses an interesting and unique mixed partial μ-agonist-antagonist profile, which should make it useful therapeutically for detoxification and maintenance treatment of heroin- and methadone-dependent persons. Thus, buprenorphine combines the characteristics of methadone and naltrexone, having both agonist and antagonist actions depending on the circumstances of its use. Buprenorphine potentially has important clinical significance because it offers the possibility of being acceptable to opiate-abusing patients seeking treatment; it decreases their heroin use, has a better safety profile than pure agonists (e.g., methadone), and does not produce a clinically significant level of physical dependence; thus, discontinuation from buprenorphine is easier than detoxification from methadone.

Buprenorphine from the scientific viewpoint illustrates the potential promise offered by various novel opioid compounds that were developed following recent advances in understanding the neuropharmacology of opioids. In humans, buprenorphine has less intrinsic agonist activity than morphine and should have a low abuse potential compared with other opioid agonists. In the initial and limited clinical

Excerpted from DHHS Pub. No. (ADM) 92-1912 *Buprenorphine: An Alternative Treatment for Opiod Dependence.*

studies, buprenorphine treatment by the sublingual route appears to be acceptable to narcotic addicts. These clinical studies demonstrate that buprenorphine can be substituted for reasonable doses of heroin or methadone in dependent persons and can be subsequently withdrawn without undue discomfort and with excellent safety. Therefore, buprenorphine appears to be a promising alternative to the currently available treatments for opioid dependence. More recently, scientists have also been exploring its potential for the treatment of cocaine addiction.

One of the major advantages of using buprenorphine as a treatment drug is that addicts are willing to take it. Buprenorphine is somewhat reinforcing but does not produce the "rush" effect so familiar to opiate addicts. A daily sublingual dose of 8 mg has been shown to be effective in suppressing heroin self-administration and does not produce clinically significant physical dependence based on the mild nature of abstinence symptoms noted after abrupt discontinuation of the medication. Buprenorphine appears to be a safe drug; the potential for lethal overdose is remote even at 10 times the therapeutic dose. That it may be administered sublingually removes association with injection apparatus, which in itself may be reinforcing to some intravenous drug users. Finally, buprenorphine may even have an effect on cocaine as well as heroin self-administration. This is especially important since many serious heroin addicts use both heroin and cocaine when available.

However, there are problems yet to be solved. One of these is the formulation of the drug for a practical treatment regimen. Buprenorphine has low bioavailability when administered orally. The preferred route of administration is sublingual, but this presents problems for take-home medication programs because the sublingual formulation would be vulnerable to diversion and abuse by injection. However, if the product is not available for home dosing its usefulness for long-term maintenance is limited. Some creative solutions have been proposed for the problem such as incorporating naloxone or naltrexone, both of which have low bioavailability sublingually but would antagonize the effect of the agonist if the capsule were dissolved and injected. Combination formulations would not discourage use by nondependent opiate users or subjects maintained on buprenorphine but would contain sufficient antagonist to precipitate the abstinence syndrome in an opiate-dependent individual if the buprenorphine-antagonist combination product were injected. [Researchers believe] combination products could be made less attractive to nondependent users if sufficient naltrexone were present to attenuate the agonist effects of buprenorphine.

The abuse potential of any treatment drug must be balanced against its safety and efficacy relative to other pharmacotherapies currently available. Considering all the data currently available, it would appear that buprenorphine is a promising treatment drug for opiate addiction and may even be useful when that addiction is combined with occasional-to-frequent cocaine use. Buprenorphine appears to be as effective as methadone for detoxification of heroin addicts but does not induce significant physical dependence in humans and can be discontinued without severe withdrawal symptoms.

Although some preliminary studies seem to indicate that buprenorphine has a modulating, therapeutic effect on cocaine usage, contradictory data have also been reported recently. NIDA must evaluate, in larger, well-controlled clinical trials, how buprenorphine affects the practice of speedballing (intravenous use of heroin combined with cocaine), methadone plus cocaine usage, and solo cocaine usage in various forms and with varying frequencies. Although buprenorphine appears to be a bright new tool in the treatment of heroin addiction, it is important to refrain from viewing it as a chemical panacea. Drug addiction has multiple causes and is a complicated disorder. NIDA anticipates that buprenorphine and its successor pharmacotherapies will attenuate drug addiction, but it is unlikely that any single drug will eliminate it.

—*by Jack D. Blaine, M.D.*
Chief,
Treatment Research Branch
Division of Clinical Research
National Institute on Drug Abuse
Parklawn Building, Room 10A-30
5600 Fishers Lane
Rockville, MD 20857

Chapter 59

Aftercare

What Is Aftercare?

Aftercare suggests different things to different people, and even treatment specialists are often unclear as to what the term means. In one sense, it simply refers to whatever follows a given form of treatment. But it can also be understood with reference to the process of recovery itself. This text examines the latter view and then relates it to conventional treatment efforts.

The Recovering Addict as Immigrant

A recovering heroin addict who played an important role in the development of [an aftercare] project once compared recovering drug addicts to immigrants. That was a valuable insight. Addiction is not only a disease; for most drug addicts, it is also a way of life within a distinct subculture. Recovery is not just the cessation and deactivation of drug use; usually, it also demands adjustment to a new way of life within the culture of the larger community. As do immigrants everywhere, recovering addicts need hope and determination in the face of change. But—proceeding with the analogy—to make a truly new way of life and not just relocate the old one, people need much

Excerpts from NIH Pub. No. 93-3521, *Recovery Training and Self-Help; Relapse Prevention and After Care for Addicts*. A complete copy of this manual may be purchased from the U.S. Government Printing Office: 1994 300-988/ 80034.

more than grit. People must have guidance, acquire new skills, and make new contacts so that they can cease being immigrants.

While more research about addiction and recovery is needed, important truths are already known. For a person who is clean and sincere about staying clean, the main challenges to recovery can be identified.

First, there is drug craving, which can remain strong for months following cessation of drug use and which may seem to renew itself upon one's discharge from a drug-free environment such as a residential facility (even if a person has spent years in it). Craving appears to be largely the result of drug conditioning and is stimulated by a host of settings and internal events that a recovering person must gradually learn to handle or avoid altogether.

Next, there is need for a new social network, since the old one is almost always too dangerous. This challenge usually demands significant social risks and, at the same time, socializing regularly in unfamiliar ways. Moreover, a recovering person often greatly fears being known as an recovering addict. So telling about oneself, usually a principal way of becoming known to new friends, is itself charged with anxieties. Like extended families and ethnic enclaves for immigrants, recovery groups and the recovering community (e.g., participants in Hong Kong's Alumni Associations and in American 12-Step fellowships) can help new arrivals from the world of addiction by providing them with a way station on the journey to conventional life.

People must adjust to drug-free activities and satisfactions. These adjustments constitute a learning process, and the failure of recovering addicts (and their friends and supporters) to recognize the learning process can lead to needless doubt and despair. Simply enjoying a movie without being high requires a new kind of attentiveness. Going to a party without using drugs requires developing a whole set of social skills before it can be fun. Therefore, even as old forms of fun must be discarded, new ones will take some getting used to.

While learning or relearning conventional recreational skills and pleasures, recovering opiate addicts must also learn how to respond safely to pain and stress. Lacking substantial experience, modeling, and reassurance regarding normal discomforts, newly drug-free persons could easily feel that their pain is abnormal, become discouraged, and turn again to pain- or stress-relieving drugs.

The desire for interpersonal intimacy—rather than dependence— frequently grows quickly in recovery; but initiating and learning to sustain healthy relationships can come much more slowly. Many relationships from the past are deeply damaged; other people who were once close may still be available but may be hard to approach. Intimacy can be vital but especially problematic for a person whose self-esteem is fragile. Old associations between drugs and sex must be unlearned and new attitudes developed. Early in recovery, intimate relationships can be distracting even when they are relatively trouble free. An unsuccessful effort may be so painful that it becomes more than the newly recovering person can manage. Timing and maturity are therefore critical if intimacy is to contribute to, rather than undermine, a promising recovery.

Finally, the risks of relapse are great because alcohol and drugs and various pressures to indulge are so common in our society. Drugs of abuse are widely available, whether from party hosts, coworkers, or physicians. A recovering addict must learn to say no. And if a relapse occurs, how one responds, and with what help and resources, critically affects whether a full-blown reactivation of addiction will ensue.

All these challenges must be managed as the person begins to assume, and often catch up with, the essential conventional tasks of adult life—employment, education, parenting, paying bills, homemaking, and so on. While these activities are keys to structuring time, supporting oneself materially, and assuming a legitimate social identity, they also impose major stresses and require rapid skill development of many sorts. These adaptations are both challenging and inescapable for someone who really wants to make it as a clean, recovering person.

An earnest desire to stay clean—in fact, just staying clean—is often not enough to keep recovery going very long. For so many recovering addicts, stress and dissatisfaction will slowly but surely erode their resolve, and temptations will exceed their controls. Especially painful are the relapses of people who have made sincere and sustained efforts; their return to drugs can deeply hurt and confuse the family, counselors, and friends who have stood by them and encouraged them so long.

What Drug Programs Try to Do

Recovering people who first hear the above issues articulated often respond with a delighted shock of recognition—"Yes! Yes! Exactly!"—as if they had never before heard their major concerns so well identified. But in spite of how common and predictable those issues are, drug treatment programs rarely deal with them systematically as a related set of problems. Why is this so?

At this point, it is worth reviewing briefly the content of conventional efforts of drug rehabilitation. Drug rehabilitation is a large term, comprising many theories, techniques, and modalities. It is useful to subdivide this diverse field into four general categories and rethink the focal efforts of each to distinguish them from the program described in this text:

- Cessation/detoxification/stabilization
- Primary treatment
- Twelve-Step fellowships
- Aftercare and followup counseling

Cessation/Detoxification/Stabilization

Cessation refers to interventions designed to help an active addict stop using drugs and to sustain abstinence during the first few days after use ceases. Although hospitalization or residential confinement have been essential features of cessation programs historically, cessation involves more than just physical confinement. Counseling, psychiatric and social assessment, encouragement, drug education, and emotional support are common features of nonmedical cessation programming. Recently, outpatient drug-free cessation programs have begun to appear.

Detoxification is part of cessation treatment for drugs that produce unpleasant and potentially life-threatening withdrawal symptoms. Usually supervised by medical professionals, detoxification may include pharmacotherapy designed to reduce health risks and minimize the physiological and psychological discomforts of withdrawal that are powerful relapse triggers. Stabilization, as on methadone, presumably allows a person to function well enough without using illicit drugs to make other gains. For some clients, stabilization is a step toward detoxification.

Primary Treatment

Most rehabilitation efforts, be they through individual, group, or family therapy, residential or outpatient, over weeks or even years, try to assist clients in eliminating or reducing the initial causes of or immediate contributors to the compulsion to use drugs. Physiological, psychological, and social factors are addressed, with some variations in emphasis depending upon the treatment modality. Primary treatment must address any resistance to change and denial of addiction or denial that an addict lifestyle perpetuates one's problems. Clients may need help ending an intimate relationship with an active user or even moving out of their home where drugs are being used, and they usually need help in letting go of long-held ideas, attitudes, or habits. For many addicts, particularly for those who live amidst overwhelming addictive forces and whose personal styles are deeply entrenched, nothing short of residential programs, such as a therapeutic community, or the powerful support of chemicals, such as naltrexone or methadone, may be needed. In this text, therefore, primary treatment refers to whatever interventions help addicted persons to accomplish the following:

- Eliminate or reduce the most pressing contributors to recent use such as physiological and psychological distress, physical pain, or social attitudes and influences.

- Acknowledge their addiction, its implications, and the particular impact of drug use in their life.

- Commit themselves fully to doing whatever sustained recovery requires.

These are profound and interrelated achievements. To sustain them, most people will need continuing inspiration, encouragement, and stark reminders of the price of drug use.

Twelve-Step Fellowships

Alcoholics Anonymous (AA) and the analogous organizations, Narcotics Anonymous and Cocaine Anonymous, are successful mutual help programs to support abstinence. For participants who have already achieved primary treatment goals, the testimony of others can be powerful reinforcements. Many people, in fact, seem to have a vital need for recalling the pain and damage of the past, acknowledging their growth and sources of strength—their own "Higher Power," the program's creed, and mutual help—and recommitting themselves openly to continued abstinence. For participants who are not abstinent, the meetings can provide real help in that direction, in effect, serving the purposes of primary treatment or pretreatment.

AA and NA focus upon the experience of addiction and how, in each member's life, it has unfolded and can be managed through abstinence. The shared experiences usually support and express a program philosophy, frequently with strong spiritual and ethical elements. Friendships often develop out of the program fellowship, but most of all, members are encouraged to see themselves as belonging to a community that is unified through a shared, lifelong, recovery experience. AA and NA can be uniquely powerful. No other settings seem better able to infuse recovering addicts with hope and to honor the virtues of abstinence.

When we formed our first New England groups in 1980, we could not take advantage of the many benefits that a well-developed 12-Step fellowship movement provides. AA was not attracting many nonalcoholic addicts, and NA had barely taken root in New England. Even as our staff became increasingly convinced of the unique power of 12-Step fellowships, we found ourselves, somewhat by default, trying to do much of what those programs could do so much better. That is, along with attempting to offer training in the relapse prevention and lifestyle adaptations that lie at the heart of Recovery Training, we had become for many clients their prime support for sustaining commitment and bolstering spiritual and attitudinal growth.

An important finding in our subsequent efforts and those reported to us has been the compatibility between RTSH [Recovery Training and Self Help] and AA/NA. Although some programs report the value of RTSH for clients who are uncomfortable with AA/NA, more notable has been a therapeutic synergy. As we began to recognize how effective this combination was, a goal of early recovery in the RTSH model became socialization into the broader recovering community, including 12-Step fellowships and their support systems. McAuliffe's [researcher W. E. McAuliffe] cocaine project attracted some clients who were initially put off by the size and spiritual orientation of 12-Step fellowship meetings, but through individual counseling and participation in our small recovery groups, whose members and recovering leaders were highly active in fellowships, most of these individuals gradually found CA and NA valuable.

Aftercare and Followup Counseling

If the goals of primary treatment appear to have been largely met, programs may offer clients continued group or individual counseling. Typically, the sessions address crises, recall past experiences and insights, support positive gains, summon inspiration to avoid the old ways, and confront backsliding. Increasingly, aftercare services feature program alumni groups whose main purpose is to maintain support among local graduates and encourage ongoing 12-Step fellowship participation. In addition, some programs have begun to offer relapse prevention as part of aftercare counseling. A client may also be referred to adjunctive services, such as vocational counseling and training.

While traditional drug treatment services address aftercare needs in varying degrees, experts in the field have long noted that aftercare resources are poorly developed overall. Studies of the outcomes of drug abuse treatment have found that graduates from all primary treatment modalities are at risk of relapse. Most treatment program administrators recognize the need for aftercare and would like to do more if they had additional resources. Even the research on drug treatment—limited as it is—has largely studied detoxification, methadone maintenance, or the dynamics of primary treatment, rather than the later issues of recovery. To date, only a few well-organized efforts have been made to improve aftercare services.

The Need for More Effective Aftercare

A key problem is simply that many programs see too few people who really do well. It is an unfortunate irony that as people achieve greater success in disengaging from old lifestyles and problems, they often become less available to others who most need to learn how they did it. So the people who are moving out of the recovering addict community become lost to programs—lost as role models, inspiration, and sources of wisdom.

A related problem is that most treatment programs have too few graduates at any given time to keep up a specialized aftercare service. Moreover, most clients who do complete primary treatment have been given little education about what difficulties lie ahead and are in a hurry to be done with the program. Staff may hesitate to demand more than minimal counseling on a followup basis, lest clients terminate treatment prematurely.

When primary treatment programs make aftercare available, clients sometimes avoid dealing with real problems. They may fear the consequences of honesty, or they may feel ashamed because other clients seem to be doing so much better, or they may think the others are avoiding the truth, so why should they be open? "Problems" frequently is interpreted as drug use that the program opposes. Other issues of aftercare are sometimes not even recognized as problems, even though they may be serious.

On the other side, staff can subtly collude in ignoring aftercare issues if they become overly invested in the success of the program graduates and really do not want to acknowledge new challenges to recovery. This occurs mostly when the aftercare counselor was also a client's primary treatment counselor and wants very much to believe the main problems were resolved. Related counseling difficulties can arise if staff view a client's relapse as a sign of treatment failure. This viewpoint can lead an anxious counselor to underrespond by ignoring or denying the signs of a relapse, or overrespond by trying to rush a person back to primary treatment. In either case, the significance of a relapse as a common but telling event in recovery is lost; clients are sent messages saying, "Relapse doesn't belong in aftercare—and if you relapse, neither do you!"

Program staff often interpret posttreatment problems in terms of primary treatment issues—that is, principally in terms of the psychological resistance and denial forces that characterize the active drug user. Those interpretations can become self-fulfilling because, as clients fail to progress for lack of appropriate assistance, their attitudes may well suffer. Then, indeed, maladaptive attitudes become central concerns, and the real issues are missed.

Make no mistake: Recovering people may often need counseling or psychotherapy as they make major life changes throughout the course of recovery. Many people also find that as drug problems per se recede, old unresolved issues come to the fore. What one should understand is that many problems of the aftercare experience are not primarily psychological, even though significant stress and psychological turmoil may result if those problems are not effectively addressed. Clinicians should therefore consider these various distinctions and help clients be clear about them too. Then, together, they can focus on the specific issues that are most amenable to therapy.

And what about NA and CA? By focusing on the continuing issue of attitude and commitment, are they addressing real aftercare needs? Yes—because maintaining commitment is the most common and lasting need of everyone in recovery. But the style and substance of these two organizations is largely defined by their spiritual program, the Twelve Steps, and the Twelve Traditions.

Many self-help organizations have another need—a comprehensive resource that can supplement the insights and guidance of the people who are on hand at any given meeting. This does not mean that peer wisdom should take a back seat to professional or impersonal advice, but simply that peer groups often need a resource that can offer, in an organized way, the best thinking of many people, including peers.

An Effective Program Devoted Exclusively to Aftercare Issues

This text [describes important issues in aftercare. It is excerpted from a manual describing a model aftercare program designed and tested to address the problems of aftercare. The complete manual, which may be obtained from the U.S. Government Printing Office or through the National Institute on Drug Abuse,] tells how to run groups for people who are already clean, where the focus is on lifestyle change and dealing with the aftermath of addiction; where issues like making new friends, learning new pleasures, and coping with drug craving are primary; where people are able to learn systematically how others have done these things and where group members are actively helping each other to do them. But the model cannot be all things to all recovering addicts, and throughout these pages the special value of NA, AA, CA, individual therapy, and other resources is acknowledged.

After concentrating its energies for years on developing aftercare capabilities, the research team found that its program does indeed appeal to the people for whom it was designed and believes it represents a good, workable response to the largely neglected needs of aftercare.

The Program Structure

Taken together, the components are a form of drug-free outpatient addiction treatment in which the therapeutic actions are extinction of drug conditioning and socialization into a drug-free lifestyle that will be naturally self-sustaining.

This schema represents the essential program structure:

Fellowship Meetings

Peer led, members

- personal sharing
- problem solving

- group planning
- social support for motivation and facilitation of continued behavior change
- leadership legitimacy based on personal experience
- help self by helping others

Recovery Training Sessions

Professionally led, members and guests

- systematic program of discussion/planning/learning that addresses aftercare issues

- based on research and clinical observations

Group Social Recreation

Members and friends

- Opportunities for learning new social and recreational styles and developing networks

Network of Senior Recovering Addicts

Offering a base of experience and guidance

- Concrete models of success

Two Kinds of Meetings

Recovery Training and Self-Help [RTSH] uses two kinds of formal weekly meetings: the Recovery Training session and the Fellowship meeting. Lasting 90 minutes each, they are best held on different days.

Recovery Training sessions are professionally led workshops, each one focusing on a specific topic. In all, the manual has 24 different topic formats as part of its systematic and comprehensive approach to aftercare needs. The complete set of topics or units constitutes the Recovery Training curriculum.

Recovery Training (hereafter referred to as RT) is open to outside guests. The sessions stimulate careful group consideration of recovery experiences and help participants prepare to face the most common and predictable aftercare problems. Neither psychotherapy sessions nor lectures, the sessions are exercises in group learning and behavior change that facilitate good planning, practical approaches, specific skills, and effective social support. A full cycle of weekly RT sessions spans approximately 6 months. Although the units complement each other, most can stand alone without reference to any other. First-time guests find the discussions clear and valuable, and new members can begin attending at any point in the curriculum.

The Fellowship meetings are for members only. These meetings are more like conventional support-group get-togethers. They should be led by the recovering-group leader. Whereas the RT sessions systematically identify the common challenges of recovery and elaborate strategies for overcoming them, the Fellowship sessions motivate and fine tune their application. The Fellowship meeting is a forum in which RT material can be further explored and adjusted to personal situations. Using a simple, flexible format, the meetings can also address a wide range of personal and group issues that are not part of the RT curriculum. The Fellowship meetings are a primary context for building active peer support and strong friendships; they allow for planning drug-free social activities of all sorts. Again, the emphasis is always on identifying and supporting practical steps.

The Membership

The program should be understood with reference to the membership's select nature. Membership is open to recovering addicts who have achieved the goals of primary treatment, whether with recent program help or not, and who demonstrate commitment and personal initiative in remaining drug-free and pursuing fuller recovery. To assess applicants, the groups have defined screening policies that require new people first to attend several consecutive RT sessions and then to be interviewed by leaders and other members at a Fellowship meeting.

New members agree to attend all Fellowship meetings, RT sessions, and group-sponsored social/recreational activities for at least 6 months. They agree to abide by group rules, to share problems of recovery openly with the other members, and to work hard on achieving all that a full recovery demands. By their own word, they must have been drug-free for at least a month prior to acceptance as a member, and they must be living freely in the community—that is, not in residential treatment or prison.

These high standards help keep the attrition low and mutual trust high. They also give newcomers meaningful goals so that admission confers esteem and the expectation of achievement. Most of all, these standards allow the group to concentrate on aftercare rather than primary treatment issues and to offer each member an unusually strong support network to prevent relapse and build healthier lifestyles.

Social and Community Activities

Many recovering addicts are comfortable at drug-free meetings but not at drug-free parties. So the group organizes parties, as well as dinners, outings, and get-togethers of all sorts. Offering members peer support along with steady exposure to mainstream recreation is a priority. Special attention is given to ensure social recreation during weekends and holidays when members face dangerous idle times and high-stress periods. Friends, families, group graduates, and senior recovery persons often participate in group events, thus helping social networks to grow.

The Senior Network

The program has had significant help from an informal group of recovering addicts who have been clean for years and have healthy and productive lifestyles. These seniors have constituted an invaluable pool of wisdom, energy, and good fellowship and individually personify real recoveries. The seniors come from diverse backgrounds and have pursued diverse life directions since their addictions. Their recovery stories—personal accounts of adjustments to abstinence (rather than recollections of addiction)—supplement RT sessions. Through participation in group events, seniors extend their friendships to members and constitute a social network into which group graduates may enter.

A Counselor's Advice about Craving to a Recovering Addict

"To understand craving better, let's first consider a basic mental operation: automatically associating one thing with another. Think about how different things can get linked up by events and how we suddenly think of one thing when the other occurs. For example, a certain song may instantly bring to mind someone from the past, or seeing a string tied around our finger will help to remind us of something we need to remember. These mental associations happen all the time. Sometimes associations occur at a much deeper level, as with drug use.

"One of the critical events of drug use is that as patterns of behavior develop with it—such as doing certain things to get the drugs, and getting the drugs at certain times, from certain people, in certain places, while in certain moods, and on and on—many powerful associations also develop. These associations leave a person with more than just memories of drug use that come up now and then. The associations, such as seeing an old drug partner who is high, can trigger a powerful craving to use drugs. Craving occurs because the central nervous system was powerfully stimulated by drugs so often when these associations were being formed. Oftentimes, a person does not even realize when triggers are at work, because associations do not require the conscious part of the mind. The important thing to know is that after years of drug use a person will have many situations that trigger strong drug craving, even after the drug user gets fully clean and decides to remain clean. Craving is an indicator of the strength of one's addiction. The more a person's whole life revolved around drug use, the more associations with drugs, and, consequently, the more craving that person can expect to have during recovery.

"Craving can be made to fade away almost totally. This process takes time, however, because triggers lose their power slowly. Strong craving early in recovery is to be expected, and a person has to develop effective coping strategies. Reduction of craving happens not simply through determination or the passage of time, but rather as a person builds enough support and grows enough to consistently refuse to give in to craving each time it is experienced. *Triggers lose their power to produce craving little by little each time a person responds to them by doing something other than taking drugs.*

"If people are never exposed to sources of temptation, they cannot reduce craving fully. This fact is one important reason why people often get high when they leave a residential treatment program or prison, or after a 'geographical' cure, and return to an environment or situation that has many triggers from them. The person may have a positive attitude but be unprepared for the sudden desire to get high and will feel confused, weak, and guilty.

"To extinguish addiction and the craving that goes with it, you must progress carefully, patiently, and use good support and planning so that powerful triggers or the combination of several all at once do not overpower you and result in relapse. This gradual process is called deactivation of addiction. (This is not the same thing as detoxification. That is just getting drugs out of the body.) For most people, deactivation of addiction will probably take at least several months to a year. Even after more than a year of deactivation, craving may occur when triggers are especially strong.

"One of the most significant aspects of deactivation of craving is how easily it can be defeated if you give in to temptation and use drugs. Each time you do this, you bring back more craving and tend to make all your triggers more powerful.

"Try thinking of it this way: imagine that a stray cat has come to your door each day because you leave food out for it to eat. Finally you decide to stop doing this. For a while the cat still comes by and cries out for food. Eventually, though, the cat will stop coming by. But if you put food out again, even once, the cat—who is still stalking the neighborhood looking for a meal—will start coming back more often, loud and strong, because he quickly relearned what a generous and easy household you have and that persistence will pay off at least some of the time.

"Your addiction is like that cat that can whine and gnaw at your door. The surest and quickest way you can be free of it is to stop feeding it once and for all. Any use of drugs will bring it back a little more. If you substitute other drugs or alcohol in order to avoid the ones you were addicted to, rather than reducing your craving, you may just be keeping it going, just as feeding the cat scraps tends to keep it lurking around your door waiting for a full meal. So the cleaner you stay, the quicker you will probably achieve significant deaddiction.

"A person who was once addicted will never be totally free of craving; there may always be a slight tendency to feel tempted once in a while, particularly in the presence of one's strongest triggers. But eventually the desire to get high can become so diminished that it is almost unnoticeable—no more than a fleeting thought or memory of what it was like to be high. And that is when it is so important not to decide the addiction is over and it is safe to use drugs again. *The cat inside your nervous system never totally leaves, and if you give him reason to return to your doorstep, even a few times, he can soon begin to howl again as loud or even louder than before.*

"In order to avoid temptation, a person needs strength. But this strength—an ability to resist what is negative and to exert effort for what is positive—is not just willpower. It grows and develops over time. You can help it along by learning how to handle certain situations, recognizing your needs, and absorbing strength from the strong support of others who assist, encourage, and show the way. Strength also comes from constant practice in situations that you can handle. Resistance to temptation grows step by step. You should consider having reliable people with you the first few times you are in predictably difficult situations, such as going to a party drug-free, or getting your pay check after a tough day. You should avoid unhealthy situations as much as possible—for example, take routes around rather than through old drug neighborhoods, and avoid old drug-using friends and associates.

"Achieving deactivation of addiction also means you do not test yourself. Life itself will offer you all the tests you need. Do not add new ones. Recovery is not a game.

"At the same time that people learn to say 'no' to old triggers, they need to say 'yes' to new forms of satisfaction and coping and build a new lifestyle that makes drugs less tempting. These are the keys to strength. They are basic facts for all growth and development. They are the principles, too, of a person's healthy recovery from addiction."

Some Principles of Deactivation of Craving

- Drug craving is a natural product of drug use, and it usually continues on and off well after drug use stops and any physical withdrawal from drugs is complete. The principle is basically the same regardless of whether the drug being used is heroin, cocaine, marijuana, or alcohol.

- Craving can be stimulated or triggered automatically if a recovering person experiences certain situations that were strongly associated with patterns of former drug use. Triggers can include internal states, such as depression, or external cues, such as people, places, and things.

- For a recovering addict, any drug use—even with prescription medication—tends to keep the craving triggers strong. This is why attempts at controlled use—such as "I'll just do it now and then"—do not work; the craving gets too strong.

- Gradually being exposed to craving situations and not getting high, with the help of strong support and good planning, can work to weaken or extinguish the craving triggers. The process of extinguishing the many craving triggers in a recovering person's life is called the deactivation of craving.

- Complete abstinence—which means not getting high at all—is the surest and quickest way to reduce craving.

- Certain old triggers that have not been properly dealt with—such as the old neighborhood you return to for the first time in years—can remain strong even after years of abstinence. Especially powerful, but infrequent triggers, such as loss of a loved one, can evoke old habits in an otherwise solid recovery. Be careful.

- Determination and willpower are poor defenses against craving. Changing your lifestyle—to gain friends and support, to learn new ways to relax and have fun, and to be a productive and growing person—can reduce craving and its dangers to your recovery. Real strength grows with time, work, guidance, and support.

- You *might* relapse. If that happens, get back on the recovery road *immediately*. You should have a plan to follow if you relapse. A relapse does not mean that you have failed or have totally wasted your efforts. It means rather that you must learn from it and need to plan better, go more slowly, and get more support.

- Even though craving is a natural aftereffect of the disease of addiction, remember that you have the power of choice. You can take steps now to reduce it and conquer it, or you can remain its slave.

The Ten Most Common Dangers

1. Being in the presence of drugs, drug users, or places where you used to cop or get high.

2. Negative feelings, particularly anger; also sadness, loneliness, guilt, fear, and anxiety.

3. Positive feelings that make you want to celebrate.

4. Boredom.

5. Getting high on any drug, including alcohol.

6. Physical pain.

7. Listening to war stories and just dwelling on getting high.

8. Suddenly having a lot of cash.

9. Using prescription drugs that can get you high even if you use them properly.

10. Believing that you are finally cured—that is, that you are no longer stimulated to crave drugs by any of the above situations or by anything else—and that therefore it is safe for you to get high occasionally.

For More Information

For more information about relapse prevention and aftercare programs call or write:

The National Clearinghouse for Alcohol and Drug Information
P.O. Box 2345
Rockville, MD 20847-2345
(800) 729-6686
(301) 468-2600
(301) 468-6433 fax

Chapter 60

Mutual Self-Help Groups

Mutual self-help groups are based on the premise that sharing with others who have similar problems can be emotionally healing for people with alcohol, tobacco, and other drug problems, including family members and friends. Also, people who have experienced similar problems can be among the best sources for referrals, advice, and moral support. The following are some of the major self-help groups, many of which are available in most communities:

Adult Children of Alcoholics (ACOA)

ACOA groups are for adults whose parents and/or grandparents had or currently have alcohol problems. Contact Adult Children of Alcoholics (ACA) World Services, P.O. Box 3216, Torrance, CA 90505, (310) 534-1815. For a printed ACA meeting guide, send a legal size self-addressed stamped envelope. Information is also available through Al-Anon Family Groups (see below). Children of alcoholics may also be interested in the activities of the National Association for Children of Alcoholics (NACoA). NACoA is a national nonprofit organization that is a resource for children of alcoholics of all ages. NACoA may be contacted at 11426 Rockville Pike, Suite 100, Rockville, MD 20852, (301) 468-0985.

Excerpted from (SMA) 94-2060.

Al-Anon Family Groups

Al-Anon Family Groups include Al-Anon for adult family members and friends of alcoholics, Al-Anon Adult Children Groups for adult children of alcoholics, and Alateen for youthful family members of alcoholics. Local groups are listed in most telephone directories. The headquarters of Al-Anon is at P.O. Box 862, Mid-town Station, New York, NY 10018-0862, (212) 302-7240 and 1-800-356-9996.

Alcoholics Anonymous (AA)

AA is for alcoholics who want to stop drinking and regain sobriety. AA has more than one million members in 114 countries. Through AA's 12 Steps of recovery and participation in a group, members uphold that (1) they are willing to accept help, (2) self-examination is critical, (3) the admission of personal shortcomings to another individual is necessary, and (4) helping peers through this process helps their personal growth and recovery. Local groups are listed in most telephone directories under "alcohol" or "alcoholism" in the yellow pages. The world headquarters may be contacted at P.O. Box 459, Grand Central Station, New York, NY 10163, (212) 686-1100.

COCANON Family Groups

People whose lives have been affected by a friend or family member's cocaine habit may benefit from COCANON. These groups are organized into local chapters, which are often listed in the telephone book. They exist to help families of drug users rather than users themselves. In the groups, members share experiences and common concerns and work to increase their understanding of how the drug problem affects them. The address of COCANON Family Groups is P.O. Box 64742-66, Los Angeles, CA 90064, or call (213) 859-2206.

Families Anonymous, Inc. (FA)

FA is for families facing alcohol and other drug problems. FA is a group of concerned relatives and friends "who have faced up to the reality that the problems of someone close to us are seriously affecting our lives and our ability to function normally." Based on the 12 Steps of Alcoholics Anonymous, the organization was formed primarily for persons concerned about alcohol and other drug problems of a family member, especially children. Over the years, it has expanded to include concern about related behavioral problems, including hostility, truancy, and running away. FA may be contacted at P.O. Box 528, Van Nuys, CA 91408, (818) 989-7841.

Nar-Anon Family Groups

This group is a companion, but separate, program to Narcotics Anonymous. It is for family members of those with drug problems. They learn to view addiction as a disease, reduce family tension, and encourage the drug user to seek help. Contact Nar-Anon World Service Office at P.O. Box 2562, Palos Verdes Peninsula, CA 90274, (213) 547-5800.

Narcotics Anonymous (NA)

NA is a mutual self-help program based on the 12 Steps of Alcoholics Anonymous. NA members are "men and women for whom drugs had become a major problem." It is a program of complete abstinence from all mind-altering drugs. If a local group is not listed in your telephone directory, the World Service Office can provide information by writing to P.O. Box 9999, Van Nuys, CA 91409, or calling (818) 780-3951.

Rational Recovery

Rational Recovery is a mutual self-help group for alcohol and other drug problems that uses a mental health approach based on rational emotive therapy. Most people attend meetings for a year and, unlike AA, don't identify themselves as powerless over alcohol. Following the principles described in *The Small Book* by Jack Trimpey, members learn mental health tools to change their thinking. Nationwide, groups are now available in about 500 cities. Groups are also available in Canada, Australia, Japan, Panama, and the U.S. Virgin Islands. For additional information write to Rational Recovery, P.O. Box 800, Lotus, CA 95651-0800 or call (916) 621-4374 to obtain a local contact.

Women for Sobriety, Inc. (WFS)

WFS is a national organization with local units that address the specific needs of women with alcohol-related problems. The program can be used in combination with other alcohol treatment programs or as an alternative to other mutual-help groups. Consult the telephone listings for a local unit, or contact Women for Sobriety, Inc. at P.O. Box 618, Quakertown, PA 18951, (215) 536-8026.

Mutual self-help groups have a long history of helping people experiencing problems related to their own or others alcohol and other drug use. Often they are included as part of formal treatment programs, but participation in formal treatment services is not required. Many participate in mutual self-help groups to support lifelong recovery from alcohol and other drug problems. Groups are located in most communities, and are usually free of charge, relying on donations alone to offset expenses, such as meeting room space.

References

If Someone Close Has a Problem with Alcohol or Other Drugs (1992) PH317.

Moving Forward: Leaving Alcohol and Other Drugs Behind (1993) PHD626.

Index

Index

Note: Page numbers in *italics* refer to illustrations.

B

babies *see* infants
barbiturate abstinence syndrome 381
barbiturates 381
  in alcohol withdrawal 371
  in cocaine withdrawal 380
  withdrawal from 381-382
beer, adolescent consumption of 203-5, *205*
benzodiazepines
  in alcohol withdrawal 182-83
  control systems for 269
Berkson's fallacy 176
binge drinking 135-36
  by adolescents 135-36, 206
blood alcohol concentration 132, 147-49
  measurement of 148
bone disease is alcohol abuse 154
brain
  alcohol effects on 11, 108, 109, 143-46, 154, 177
  cocaine effects on 9-10
  depressant drug effects on 11
  designer drug effects on 11-12
  drug effects on 3-19
  hallucinogen effects on 10-11
  inhalant effects on 246
  marijuana effects on 10-11
  MDMA effects on 12
  in narcotic-exposed baby 361-62
  opiate effects on 8-9
  PCP effects on 11
  structures of 4-5
brain stem 4
Brazelton Neonatal Behavior Assessment Scale 402
breast cancer, alcohol and 121-22, 159
breastfeeding of drug-exposed infants 404-5
bromocriptine in cocaine withdrawal 380
bulimia in alcohol abuse 178
buprenorphine treatment 527-29
butane abuse 251

C

CAGE questionnaire 138
cancer
  alcohol-related 121-22, 132, 157-62
  initiation of 157-58
  oncogenes in 159
  snuff dipping and 231-32
Cannabis sativa see marijuana
cardiomyopathy, alcoholic 177
cardiovascular risks
  of anabolic steroid abuse 471
  of barbiturate abstinence syndrome 381
  of methamphetamine abuse 332-333
  neonatal complication of maternal cocaine use 401, 403
  of nicotine abuse 216, 218-19, 436
  see also heart attacks
casual drug use 33-36, *35, 36*
"cat" *see* methcathinone abuse
central nervous system
  alcohol withdrawal syndrome and 181-82, 184
  cocaine and 313
  cranial sonograms 403
  fetal alcohol syndrome and 372, 393
  inhalant abuse and 251
  maternal complications of cocaine abuse 401
  neonatal abstinence syndrome and 396
  neonatal complications of cocaine exposure 402
  nicotine and 216-17
  role in craving 543, 544
central nervous system lymphoma 308
cerebral cortex 4
cessation
  drug use 534
  cigarette smoking 220, 221-226
chemical neurotransmission 7-8
chemical toxicity in alcoholic liver disease 167
chewing tobacco *see* spit tobacco

D

E

F

G

H

I

J

K

L

M

O

P

Q

R

Z